THE GREATEST
STORIES
EVER TOLD

VOLS. I — III

GREG LAURIE

GREATEST STORIES EVER TOLD, VOL. I–III

Copyright © 2009 by Greg Laurie. All Rights Reserved.

Unless otherwise indicated, all Scripture quotations are taken from:
The Holy Bible, New King James Version © 1984 by Thomas Nelson, Inc.

Scripture quotations marked (NIV) are from *The Holy Bible*, New International Version®,
NIV®. © 1973, 1978, 1984 by International Bible Society. Used by permission of
Zondervan Publishing House.

Scripture quotations marked (TLB) are taken from The Living Bible,
© 1971 by Tyndale House Publishers, Wheaton, Illinois.

Scripture quotations marked (NLT) are taken from The New Living Translation,
© 1996, 2004 by Tyndale Charitable Trust. Used by permission of Tyndale House
Publishers. All rights reserved.

Scripture quotations marked (THE MESSAGE) are taken from The Message,
by Eugene Peterson. © 1993, 1994, 1995, 1996, 2000, 2001, 2002. Used by permission
of NavPress Publishing Group. All rights reserved.

Scripture quotations marked (PHILLIPS) are from The New Testament
in Modern English, Revised Edition © 1958, 1960, 1972 by J. B. Phillips.

ISBN: 0–9801831–9–7
Published by: Allen David Publishers—Dana Point, California
Coordination: FM Management, Ltd.
Cover design by Highgate Cross + Cathey
Designed by Highgate Cross + Cathey
Printed in Canada

Contents

VOLUME ONE

Contents

VOLUME TWO

Contents

VOLUME THREE

THE GREATEST
STORIES
EVER TOLD

VOLUME ONE
GREAT ENCOUNTERS WITH GOD

Chapter One

ENCOUNTER IN PARADISE:
RESISTING THE TEMPTER

I n the immortal words of Julie Andrews, *"Let's start at the very beginning, a very good place to start…."*

When it comes to *The Greatest Stories Ever Told*, no book ever written holds a candle to the Bible. And within the pages of Scripture, no stories are more foundational, more sweeping in scope, and more bursting with insights than those found within the book of Genesis. Six of the eleven dramatic encounters with God described in this book are drawn from the first book of the Bible.

Genesis is the book of beginnings. Just think of all the origin accounts woven through its fifty chapters…

Genesis records the origin of the universe. The first book of the Bible stands alone in accounting for the actual creation of the space-mass-time continuum which constitutes our physical universe.

Genesis declares the origin of the solar system. The Earth, as well as the sun, the moon, the planets, and all the stars of heaven, were likewise brought into existence by the Creator.

Genesis describes the origin of man. The widely believed theory of evolution is a complete illusion. The true record of man's beginnings is given only in Genesis, detailing man's creation, purpose, and uniqueness.

Genesis details the origin of marriage. God's unique and special plan for the man and woman is given. We also have the origin of the family—the basic infrastructure for any successful culture and society.

Genesis chronicles the origin of language—language in general, and also the various national languages in particular.

Genesis speaks to the origin of government. The development of organized systems of human government is described in Genesis, with man being responsible not only for his own actions, but also for the maintenance of orderly social structures through systems of laws and punishments.

Finally, *in Genesis, we have the origin of evil.*

Many believe and teach that man is basically good, and when he does bad things, it's the result of his environment or outward circumstances. If you believe this, you must have a hard time making sense of this wicked world. The Bible teaches that man is basically sinful, and does bad things as a reflection of his true nature. We're not sinners because we sin, but rather we sin because we are sinners. It comes naturally.

And the third chapter of Genesis tells the story of how it all started. It is truly a great story. Although the account is unspeakably sad, it also reveals a God who is determined to seek and save His lost and finest creation: humankind.

ADVENTURES IN PARADISE

I heard the story of a pastor who had just moved into a new town and wanted to get to know some of the people in his congregation. So one Saturday he went out to visit, paying pastoral calls on many people from his new church.

All was going well until he came to a house where he could clearly see someone was home—but they wouldn't answer the door. He knocked and knocked again, but no one came to answer it. So, with a little smile, he took out one of his business cards and wrote *Revelation 3:20* on the back, and stuck it in the door. You know the verse: "Behold, I stand at the door and knock. If anyone hears My voice and opens the door, I will come in to him and dine with him, and he with Me."

The next day at the morning church service, after the offering was counted, an usher found the pastor's card that he left on that person's door with another biblical reference below his.

It was Genesis 3:10.

"And he said, 'I heard thy voice in the garden, and I was afraid, because I was naked: so I hid myself.'"

Adam and Eve had been placed in a veritable paradise. Adam's job description was to tend and keep the garden, discovering and marveling in all God had done, and walking in fellowship with Him.

Talk about having it made in the shade! This first couple was told they could eat of any tree in the garden—excepting only the Tree of the Knowledge of Good and Evil.

And yet there was Eve, hanging out by that very tree.

FATAL ATTRACTION

Why is it that we are always attracted to that which can harm us? You tell a child to not touch a certain thing or go to a certain place and that's exactly where they will be when given a chance. It's human nature!

In our warped minds we think that God is keeping something good from us. Scripture, however, tells us: "No good thing will He withhold from those who walk uprightly."[1]

God gave them a warning label and they ignored it.

Warning labels exist because someone at some point did something stupid with a given product, injured themselves, sued the company, and quite possibly won.

These labels have become wackier and wackier through the years. Following are just a few real life examples I've collected.

A label on a baby stroller warns: *"Remove child before folding."*

A brass fishing lure with a three-pronged hook on the end warns: *"Harmful if swallowed."*

A flushable toilet brush warns: *"Do not use for personal hygiene."*

The label on a bottle of drain cleaner warns: *"If you do not understand, or cannot read, all directions, cautions and warnings, do not use this product."*

A cartridge for a laser printer warns, *"Do not EAT toner."*

A thirteen-inch wheel on a wheelbarrow warns: *"Not intended for highway use."*

A can of self-defense pepper spray alerts users, *"May irritate eyes."*

A snow blower cautions: *"Do not use snow blower on roof."*

A popular manufactured fireplace log warns: *"Caution—risk of fire."*

A dishwasher carries this warning: *"Do not allow children to play in the dishwasher."*

A household iron warns users: *"Never iron clothes while they are being worn."*

Or how about the one that just came out this year? This wins my "Wacky Warning Label of the Year" award. On a heat gun/paint remover that reaches a temperature of one thousand degrees: *"Do not use this tool as a hair dryer."*

Second place in this contest is a label the manufacturer placed on a kitchen knife, *"Never try to catch a falling knife."*

The following passage records how our first parents, Adam and Eve, ignored the one warning label in the whole world, were fatally injured, and had no one to blame but themselves.

Now the serpent was more cunning than any beast of the field which the Lord God had made. And he said to the woman, "Has God indeed said, 'You shall not eat of every tree of the garden'?"

And the woman said to the serpent, "We may eat the fruit of the trees of the garden; but of the fruit of the tree which is in the midst of the garden, God has said, 'You shall not eat it, nor shall you touch it, lest you die.'"

Then the serpent said to the woman, "You will not surely die. For God knows that in the day you eat of it your eyes will be opened, and you will be like God, knowing good and evil."

So when the woman saw that the tree was good for food, that it was pleasant to the eyes, and a tree desirable to make one wise, she took of its fruit and ate. She also gave to her husband with her, and he ate. Then the eyes of both of them were opened, and they knew that they were naked; and they sewed fig leaves together and made themselves coverings.

And they heard the sound of the Lord God walking in the garden in the cool of the day, and Adam and his wife hid themselves from the presence of the Lord God among the trees of the garden.

Then the Lord God called to Adam and said to him, "Where are you?" So he said, "I heard Your voice in the garden, and I was afraid because I was naked; and I hid myself."

And He said, "Who told you that you were naked? Have you eaten from the tree of which I commanded you that you should not eat?"

Then the man said, "The woman whom You gave to be with me, she gave me of the tree, and I ate."

And the Lord God said to the woman, "What is this you have done?" The woman said, "The serpent deceived me, and I ate." (Genesis 3:1-13)

This account of Satan's first temptation of the human race provides us with a wealth of information concerning his tactics.

TACTICS OF THE ENEMY

Here are three ploys Satan used to bring Eve to her fall:

1. He Questioned GOD's Word

Satan didn't deny that God had spoken. He simply questioned whether God had really said what Eve *thought* He had said. He wanted her to think that perhaps she had misunderstood God's command. He wanted to "interpret" God's words for Eve. It's the same in our world today. Satan still twists the truth to try to alienate people from God.

2. He Questioned GOD's Love

Satan wanted to make Eve think that God was holding something back. In reality, God Himself had placed this lone restriction in Adam and Eve's life to keep them from sinning. In the same way, the barriers God places in our lives are there because He loves us.

3. He Substituted His Own Lie

Satan led Eve to believe that if she ate of the tree she would become like God. At that point Eve had a choice: She could take God at His word, or believe Satan's lie.

Satan knows that our minds are "command central." This is where we reason, fantasize, and imagine. He will attempt to make you second-guess what God has said in His Word, or try to get you to dwell on the "what if's" in life.

Our counterattack is found in 2 Corinthians 10:4-5: "I use God's mighty weapons, not those made by men, to knock down the Devil's strongholds. These weapons can break down every proud argument against God and every wall that can be built to keep men from finding him." (NLT).

We see from this an important principle of satanic attack. Satan works from without to within, which is the very opposite of God's method. God begins His work in man's heart, with changes radiating outward that begin to effect his whole lifestyle. (If this isn't happening, it's questionable a true work of God has even begun).

Having eaten now of the "forbidden fruit," something unusual happens to Adam and Eve: "The eyes of both of them were opened" (v. 7).

The Day Everything Changed

Sometimes "ignorance is bliss," and what Adam and Eve didn't know certainly didn't hurt them. Now their eyes are opened to the wickedness of sin, the deceitfulness of Satan, the weakness of their own nature, and the corruption that had wormed its way into God's perfect paradise.

It's sad to see a child lose his or her innocence—to be exposed to something corrupt, wicked, or depraved at an early age. In that sense, their eyes are opened. Far too often we know more about this wicked world than we need to know—and far less from the Word than we need to grow.

Paul wrote to the Romans: "I would have you well versed and wise as to what is good and innocent and guileless as to what is evil" (Romans 16:19, AMP). Now Adam and Eve had opened a "Pandora's box" that could never be closed again. Their eyes were opened to earth, but closed to heaven.

> And they heard the sound of the LORD God walking in the garden in the cool of the day. (Genesis 3:3)

This was normally a welcome event—the crowning moment of the whole day. But now they dreaded it because of their sin. When you are walking with God, you *love* fellowship with God and His people. His Word is attractive, and you find a strong desire to worship the Lord with other believers. But when you are in sin, you begin to dread the very things you used to love.

Note that it says, that the Lord came to them "in the cool of the day." What a beautiful picture that is, my favorite time of the day. The day has ended, but night has not yet fallen. The air begins to cool as the sun slips over the western horizon, bathing the world in a warm, golden light. Was this a special time that the Lord and Adam spent together each day? Perhaps the Lord even took some kind of human form to do this. If so, Adam must have greatly looked forward to it. (I would have!)

When something came up in the course of a day, Adam might have thought, "I must talk to the Lord about that this evening, in our time together." Perhaps some new discovery in the Garden he was commanded to tend had captured his imagination, and he could hardly wait to share his excitement with the Creator.

But now instead of looking forward to this daily event with joy, Adam deeply dreaded it.

GOD COMES CALLING

It's interesting to note *when* God came to visit Adam and Eve. Not in the heat of the day—say, twelve noon, so Adam would think God was coming in the heat of passion. Not in the early morning, lest Adam think God couldn't wait to nail him for his sin. No, God came in the cool of the day. Loving, patient, grieved, yet demanding confession.

Adam had plenty of time to think about what he had done. The initial thrill of sin was gone. Now the guilt was kicking in, the remorse, the regret, that dead empty feeling that sin brings.

When God didn't find Adam waiting in their usual meeting place, He called out to him, "Adam, where are you?"

Why did God call out to Adam? Among other things, it was meant to reveal the deadly consequences of his sin. Often He needs to do that with us as well, because we have rationalized our sin in such a way that we don't even admit we've done it.

"Adam, Where are you?"

What tone of voice do you think God used?

"Adam! (You miserable failure!) Where are you?"

"Adam? (as in I can't find you) Where are you?"

I don't think it was either of the above. Rather, I believe there was hurt in that voice, but love as well, as a Father called out to His wayward son.

And there was Adam, the crown of God's creation, cowering behind a bush in fear. I can imagine God saying, "Well Adam, where has your sin taken you?"

What did God intend by asking Adam and Eve a series of questions in that terrible moment?

"Where are you?"

"Who told you that you were naked?"

"Have you eaten from the tree of which I commanded you that you should not eat?"

"What is this you have done?"

Obviously, God already knew the answers to those questions—in a deeper way than the man and woman could ever know them. It wasn't because God didn't know what was right and wrong, it was because He wanted to be sure that *they* knew it was wrong. He was looking for an admission of wrong-doing, an admission of sin. He desired nothing short of a full-blown confession.

God and His spokesmen in Scripture frequently asked questions to help people think through what they have just done.

Remember God with Elijah? *"What are you doing here?"*

Elisha with Gehazi: *"Where have you been?"*

Jesus to Judas *"Why have you come?"*

Instead of acknowledging his sin, however, Adam offers the mother of all excuses—in fact, it was the first recorded excuse in all of human history. "The woman who you gave to be with me…."

This shows the absolute wickedness of sin. Eve had been deceived—Scripture is clear on that.[2] But Adam, to his discredit and destruction, willfully and knowingly sinned. If that wasn't bad enough, he had the audacity to actually blame God for it! He was in essence saying, "*You* Lord, have sinned! This is *Your* doing. It's the woman *You* gave me! You're the one who brought Eve along!"

How easily God could have struck Adam down right where he stood. Like a spoiled little brat, he dared to suggest that it was God and not him who had failed. *God*, who had literally put him in paradise—with every possible comfort, surrounded by breath-taking beauty, such as has never been seen since. And yet in spite of all this, Adam lashed out at the very God who had provided so much for him. Jeremiah wrote, "Through the LORD's mercies we are not consumed, because His compassions fail not" (Lamentations 3:22).

That's what sin does. It blinds you to reality. And that's why we need God's provision for our forgiveness, so we can be restored into fellowship with Him.

God desires to walk with you in the cool of the day, just as He had enjoyed the company and fellowship of the first human beings. He wants to draw near to you, comfort you, instruct you, guide you, and lead you into a life of abundance and joy.

Could He be calling out to you right now, just as He called out to Adam? *Where are you?*

Even as you begin this book—just a few pages in—you have the opportunity to respond to Him in a fresh way, to evaluate your life before His searching gaze.

Maybe it's time to ask yourself, *"Where am I? What am I doing here? How did I get to this place? Do I want to change?"* If so, you need to come to Jesus, asking His help to do that.

In the pages that follow, we'll be exploring some of the greatest true stories ever told on this world of ours. But *your* greatest story hinges on your relationship to your Creator and Savior, and allowing His life to flow through your life.

The cool of the day would be a good time to start.

But right now works, too.

Chapter Two

ENCOUNTER EAST OF EDEN: OVERCOMING SIN

D id you hear about the parrot in England that exposed a girl's sin? This was a real news story, datelined, London, England.

A computer programmer found out his girlfriend was having an affair when his pet parrot kept repeating her lover's name, British media reported.

The African grey parrot kept squawking, "I love you, Gary" as his owner, Chris Taylor sat with girlfriend Suzy Collins on the sofa of their shared flat in Leeds, Northern England. When Taylor saw Collins' embarrassed reaction, he realized she had been having an affair, meeting her lover in the flat while Ziggy looked on.

Taylor said he had been forced to part with Ziggy after the bird continued to call out Gary's name, and refused to stop squawking the phrases in his ex-girlfriend's voice, media reports said.

"I wasn't sorry to see my old girlfriend Suzy go, after what she did, but it really broke my heart to let Ziggy go" he said. "I love him to bits and I really miss having him around, but it was torture hearing him repeat that name over and over again. I still can't believe he's gone, I know I'll get over Suzy, but I don't think Ill ever get over Ziggy."

You have to watch out for those parrots! In fact, the Bible warns all of us, *"You may be sure that your sin will find you out"* (Numbers 32:23, NLT). How will it happen? I can't tell you. It might even be through a parrot who becomes a stool pigeon!

We've all heard it said that man is basically good. In all of us, it is said, there's a desire to do the right thing, and it's only our upbringing, environment, or conditioning that makes us go bad.

I think it takes more faith to believe *that* than anything else I can think of. For if history tells us anything, it is that man is not good at all, but just the opposite. In fact, history as we know it is the story of the wars, intrigues, betrayals, injustice, destruction, and bloodshed of mankind.

But why? Why is this? Why has humanity throughout its entire history wrestled unendingly with this terrible problem of human hatred and bloodshed? Why are we at war with terrorists? Why the endless bloodshed in Iraq? Why the increasing tensions with North Korea and Iran?

If you want shallow, superficial answers to questions like these, you can find them in abundance. But Scripture teaches that the key to our Twenty-first century dilemma lies in a story of two brothers at the dawn of history.

THE FIRST FAMILY'S TRAGEDY

Now Adam knew Eve his wife, and she conceived and bore Cain, and said, "I have acquired a man from the LORD." Then she bore again, this time his brother Abel. Now Abel was a keeper of sheep, but Cain was a tiller of the ground. And in the process of time it came to pass that Cain brought an offering of the fruit of the ground to the LORD. Abel also brought of the firstborn of his flock and of their fat. And the LORD respected Abel and his offering, but He did not respect Cain and his offering. And Cain was very angry, and his countenance fell.

So the Lord said to Cain, "Why are you angry? And why has your countenance fallen? If you do well, will you not be accepted? And if you do not do well, sin lies at the door. And its desire is for you, but you should rule over it." (Genesis 4:1-7)

The story of the first family began happily enough. Adam and Eve conceived their first child. Neither the man nor woman had ever seen a human pregnancy before, much less a birth, so this was all new to them.

I was talking to a pastor friend of mine who was performing the wedding for his daughter. He wanted to say something really profound and moving as he was recounting her life. He began by saying to her and all the assembled guests, "I was there at your conception."

That was certainly assuring to hear! What he had meant to say was that he had been there at her *birth*.

Adam and Eve were present for both. One can only guess at Adam's amazement as he watched the changes in Eve.

"Eve, you seem to be putting on a lot of weight lately! What's with all these little socks you keep knitting? You want…what? Pickles and ice cream?"

After Adam had sinned with Eve in the Garden, God gave the very first messianic prediction.

"And I will put enmity
Between you and the woman,
And between your seed and her Seed;
He shall bruise your head,
And you shall bruise His heel."
(Genesis 3:15)

Isn't that just like our God? Even before He declared the consequences of their sin, He gave them a promise of ultimate deliverance and victory. You see that over and over in the prophetic portions of Scripture. There are plenty of warnings and pronouncements of judgment, but woven in and through these dark tidings are golden threads of hope and promise.

Adam and Eve, then, knew one was coming who would bruise Satan's head.

Eve probably wondered, could this child in her womb be the one?

Finally the day came, and their firstborn arrived. They named him Cain, which means, *acquired*. In light of the promise of a Deliverer, the name might have meant, *"Here he is, I've gotten him."*

But tragically, Cain was not to be the Deliverer they hoped for…but a murderer instead. With the birth of the second child, a new and ominous element begins to enter the story.

Playing Favorites

Adam and Eve named their second son, Abel, which means "frail". This suggests that the physical effects of sin were already becoming apparent in the race. Regardless of whether this was physically true or not, it would certainly suggest a difference in the attitude of these parents toward their two boys. Cain was the strong one, the first born. Abel, weaker and more frail, was not as strong as Cain.

The names tell the story.

Son #1: Look, here comes….Here he is!

Son #2: The weakling.

It would be very natural for them to favor Cain as the firstborn and the stronger of the two. "After all," they might have reasoned, "he may be the Deliverer God told us about." This strong hint of favoritism, found here at the beginning, may offer an insight into what was to follow.

If we follow this scenario, then the seeds of arrogance and pride had already been planted in Cain by his unsuspecting parents. We have to be so very careful as we raise our children to avoid favoritism at all costs. Later in Genesis, we see this same pattern in the way Isaac favored Esau, and Rebecca his wife favored Jacob. The favoritism drove a wedge between the two boys, setting into motion a conflict that followed them well into their adult years… and for many generations to come.

But did Jacob learn from those circumstances of his youth, bringing wisdom into his own parenting? Not a chance! Jacob so obviously favored his son Joseph that the young man became an object of hatred among his jealous brothers.

We must recognize that each child, though different, is a precious gift from God that we never, ever want to take for granted. They're not there for us to form into "our image," but rather for us to point them to God and help them to discover their God-given talents and abilities.

I read an article about this some time ago. It spoke of how parents, in their quest to raise happy, safe, and successful kids, go overboard in the praise department. They're called "helicopter parents," hovering over their kids and micromanaging their lives. They've bought into the myth that a child's self-esteem depends on never experiencing even the slightest adversity, upset, failure, or setback.

But this "no more tears" approach to raising kids is doing more harm than parents and teachers realize. "Of course we love our kids like crazy," says Betsy Hart, a Chicago-area mother of four and author of *It Takes a Parent.* "But when we idolize and idealize them, we're not doing them any favors. In fact, the result of these good intentions is often just the opposite. There's strong scientific evidence that undeserved praise can do long-term harm, especially when doled out to malleable teenagers. What's more, kids with a solution-minded parent constantly lurking don't develop the mettle to solve life's inevitable problems. So, by giving undeserved praise you can hurt a child's development."[3]

But then there's the problem of under-praising a child as well. A child who is never complimented or encouraged by his parents is bound for trouble! Did you know that by the time the average child enters kindergarten he has heard the word "No" over 40,000 times? If he is only told what is wrong with him and never right, he will soon lose hope and become convinced he's incapable of doing anything right. This false self-impression can carry through even into his adult years, and be passed on to his own children.

A child needs approval and encouragement in things that are good, every bit as much as he needs correction in things that are not.

I read about a young man named Antoine Fisher. A movie has been made about his life and how he rose from the worst of conditions. He was born in prison and sent to be raised in foster care. His father was killed by a girlfriend two months before Antoine was born. As the little boy grew, his foster mother tormented him with this singsong.....*You ain't nothing. You're never gonna be nothing, because you come from nothing.*

What a wicked thing to say to a child. Antoine eventually proved her wrong, but this certainly made his journey that much harder. Make sure you let your kids know you love and value them today. It seems Adam and Eve over-favored Cain and under-favored Abel.

But even if Abel wasn't favored by his parents, he was favored by God! Those who are not favored by their parents often become the beloved of the Lord. With a gaping hole in their soul where the love of mom and dad should be, they turn to God with great desperation and desire.

And that's a good thing.

This was certainly the case with young David. You remember the story. When David's father Jesse understood that Samuel wanted to meet each of his sons, he paraded seven of his boys before the prophet. When Samuel said, "Is this all?", Jesse reluctantly called David in from the sheep pasture. And to the astonishment of everyone, the young shepherd was anointed as the next king of Israel.

It was so obvious—Jesse had little regard for his youngest son, and I can't imagine that the old sheep rancher spent much time with the boy. Perhaps because David's dad wasn't there for him when he needed a dad (we know little of his mother), the young man turned to God as a father.

In later years he wrote:

Even if my father and mother abandon me,
the LORD will hold me close.
(Psalm 27:10, NLT)

Do those words strike a chord in your heart? Perhaps that was your situation. You weren't favored by your parents. Maybe they divorced or never had time for you. But God is there as a heavenly Father for you, just as He willingly embraced David. He always has time for you, longs for your best, is more than willing to share His great wisdom and love, and will never fail or forsake you.

A TALE OF TWO OFFERINGS

The Bible tells us that a day came when Cain and Abel brought their offerings to God. "Here He Is" and "Weakling" brought the fruit of their labor before their Creator as a sacrifice. God accepted Abel's offering, but rejected Cain's.

Why?

Cain wasn't rejected because of his offering, but his offering was rejected because of Cain! The text makes it clear that Abel made his offering in the right way, and Cain did not.

Consider this: Cain and Abel were both raised in a godly home. Both heard the word of God from their youth, both of them were no doubt taught to pray and walk with God. But one of the boys grew up to be a true worshipper, offering an acceptable act of worship, while the other became a false worshipper, offering an unacceptable act of worship. One was accepted, the other rejected.

This reminds us that there is a right and wrong way to approach God. It all came down to the "why," or the motive. Because as far as God is concerned, motive is everything. The reason God accepted Abel's offering over Cain's is found in Hebrew 11:4.

By faith Abel offered to God a more excellent sacrifice than Cain, through which he obtained witness that he was righteous, God testifying of his gifts; and through it he being dead still speaks.

"By faith Abel. ..." Adam and Eve's second-born exercised faith in his worship, Cain did not. Scripture reminds us "without faith it is impossible to please God." We must remember that worship is really a form of prayer. And the sad but amazing truth is that we can sing worship songs to God without a single thought of God while we're doing it!

Jesus once declared: "These people draw near to Me with their mouth, and honor Me with their lips, but their heart is far from Me. And in vain they worship Me, teaching as doctrines the commandments of men" (Matthew 15:8-9).

So there we are in a worship service, going through the motions. We sing the song. Maybe we lift our hands. But honoring God is really the farthest thing from our minds. As we drone on, we're really thinking, *I don't like this song...Look at the outfit that lady is wearing!...I'm kinda hungry. I wonder what I should have for lunch?...It's too cold in here...It's too hot in here... When is this service over?*

On any given Sunday, in any given worship service, we can look to our left and notice a man standing there with arms outstretched toward heaven, tears rolling down his cheeks, singing God's praises with a loud, clear, beautiful voice. *Look at that*, we say to ourselves. *Now that guy is really worshipping.*

Next to him might be a lady who has only raised her hands shoulder high, singing quietly (and not very well). And we find ourselves drawing a contrast, thinking, *She's not worshipping much at all.*

But what is worship? A lot of it comes down to what's happening within our hearts. There can be a place for outstretched arms as well as quiet voices. And as to the quality of the singing? Heaven couldn't care less!

Jesus told the story of a Pharisee and a tax collector who went to pray (or worship) at the temple.

> "The Pharisee stood and prayed thus with himself, 'God, I thank You that I am not like other men—extortioners, unjust, adulterers, or even as this tax collector. I fast twice a week; I give tithes of all that I possess.' And the tax collector, standing afar off, would not so much as raise his eyes to heaven, but beat his breast, saying, 'God, be merciful to me a sinner!' I tell you, this man went down to his house justified rather than the other; for everyone who exalts himself will be humbled, and he who humbles himself will be exalted." (Luke 18:11-14)

Those listening to the story were no doubt shocked by the way Jesus ended it. They were probably thinking Jesus would commend the Pharisee. But instead, He threw them a real curve ball. "I tell you, this sinner, not the Pharisee, returned home forgiven!" (TLB)

Why did Jesus say such a thing? Because even though that religious leader may have lived an outwardly pure and devout life, inwardly his heart was full of pride.

And you cannot come into God's present with pride.

The apostle James tells us: "Humble yourselves in the sight of the Lord, and He shall lift you up" (James 4:10). Generations before those words were penned, the prophet Micah wrote:

> He has shown you, O man, what is good;
> And what does the LORD require of you
> But to do justly,
> To love mercy,
> And to walk humbly with your God?
> (Micah 6:8)

When we think of terrible sins against God, transgressions like adultery, stealing, and lying come to mind. And those sins certainly grieve His heart.

But so does pride.

In fact, the book of Proverbs underlines pride by listing it as one of the seven things God hates. By contrast, the distraught tax collector in the Lord's story saw himself for who he really was, praying, "God, be merciful to me a sinner."

A QUESTION AND A WARNING

When Cain saw that God had accepted his brother's sacrifice and not his, he was angry. The Living Bible says "this made Cain both dejected and very angry, and his face grew dark with fury." Cain was hot. Seeing where this was headed, God lovingly reached out to the firstborn of humanity with a question.

The Lord said to Cain, "Why are you angry?"

With his over-the-top reaction to Abel's success, Cain began to show his true colors. Knowing Cain's heart, God was seeking to nip this murderous anger in the bud. Years before, as we read in the previous chapter, God had asked Cain's father an important question: "Adam, where are you?"

Instead of acknowledging what he had done, Adam replied, "I heard Your voice in the garden, and I was afraid because I was naked; and I hid myself" (Genesis 3:10).

Again, the Lord sought an admission of sin with a question.

"Who told you that you were naked?" (v. 11)

And once again, instead of owning up to what he had done, Adam turned around and pointed a finger at Eve. "It's the woman you gave me!"

When God asked Cain, "Why are you angry?", what would the right answer have been? A humble admission of wrong. "Lord, I'm angry because I'm petty, sick with jealousy, and way off track. Please forgive me."

But Cain didn't respond to God at all. Just as his parents had done, he tried to cover up his sin instead of admitting his guilt. As they say, the apple doesn't fall far from the tree. Like father, like son. God wanted confession, because that is the way to forgiveness. There is no other way!

The Bible says, "If we confess our sins, He is faithful and just to forgive us our sins and to cleanse us from all unrighteousness. If we say that we have not sinned, we make Him a liar, and His word is not in us" (1 John 1:9-10).

God knew very well where this sin could lead, and He gave Cain a stern warning: "If you do well, will you not be accepted? And if you do not do well, sin lies at the door. And its desire is for you, but you should rule over it" (Genesis 4:7).

Sin lies at your door! In the original language the verse reads literally: *Sin is crouching at your door.* God could see it, like a crouching beast ready to tear Cain and his family apart. But Cain couldn't see it in that moment—or didn't want to see it.

Clearly Cain had not been doing well up to this point. But God, "who is not willing that any should perish," placed a stop sign—a red light—right in front of him. The Lord was saying, "If you don't heed this warning, you're flirting with disaster."

A LION AT THE DOOR

It's no different today. Sin crouches at the door of every home, every office, every school, and even every church. It waits to attack and destroy the unwary. It is ever on the prowl, searching for the one it can take down.

A big game hunter named Peter H. Capstick wrote a chilling book called, *Death in the Long Grass*. The author tells one incredible story after another—not just on hunting lions, but on being hunted *by* lions.

After developing a taste for human blood, the huge cats would sneak into camp very late in the evening. Stepping over several men without waking them, the lions would choose their prey, and then drag them into the night. One large lion stalked and killed over a hundred men.

Charging lions can cover over 100 yards in just 3 seconds. The author wrote of keeping his ears open even as he slept in the camp, knowing that the lion would come swiftly and with deadly force.

It sounds like the picture of Satan that Peter used, doesn't it?

> Be self-controlled and alert. Your enemy the Devil prowls around like a roaring lion looking for someone to devour. (1 Peter 5:8, NIV)

This is why we don't want to give the Devil any kind of foothold in our lives. And we don't want to let down our guard, either. Listen to this warning in Ephesians 4:26-27: "Don't sin by letting anger gain control over you. Don't let the sun go down while you are still angry, for anger gives a mighty foothold to the Devil" (NLT).

Sin is crouching at our doors, too! For some of us, it's already across the threshold. What that vulnerability might be will vary from person to person. But know this, just like that lion, the Devil is sizing up his prey, readying himself to strike!

But what can we do? How can we protect our homes from the power of Satan and his demon forces?

First of all, know this: *We cannot do it ourselves.*

Jesus drove that point home with this story: "When an evil spirit leaves a person, it goes into the desert, seeking rest but finding none. Then it says, 'I will return to the person I came from.' So it returns and finds its former home empty, swept, and clean. Then the spirit finds seven other spirits more evil than itself, and they all enter the person and live there. And so that person is worse off than before" (Matthew 12:43-45, NLT).

You might say this person was "repossessed."

The truth is, the victim went from bad to worse.

So what do we do when sin crouches at our door…when it seems to be creeping over the threshold and threatening our lives and our families? The only defense is Jesus Christ! When Satan knocks at my door I like to say, "Lord, would You mind getting that?"

Before a word is mentioned about what armor we are to wear into the spiritual battle, Ephesians 6 reminds us we are to "be strong in the Lord and in the power of His might" (v. 10).

If we are to master sin, we must first be mastered by Him who masters it! Tragically, Cain did not allow himself to be mastered by God, and so he became enslaved by the Devil.

MY BROTHER'S KEEPER?

The Bible doesn't tell us what caused Cain to go so far as to murder his own brother. But I think it would be safe to say there was some jealousy and envy there, as he saw Abel's sacrifice accepted and his rejected.

Shakespeare called envy the "green-eyed monster." I heard the story of a crab fisherman who said he never needed a top for his crab basket. What kept them in their trap? He explained that if one of the crabs started to climb up the sides of the basket, the other crabs would reach up and pull it back down!

We can be a lot like those crabs, can't we? Though we would probably never admit it out loud, sometimes it bothers us to see others applauded, recognized, or rewarded. Cain allowed his jealousy and bitterness to get the best of him, and when he was overpowered, he struck out at his brother.

> Now Cain talked with Abel his brother; and it came to pass, when they were in the field, that Cain rose up against Abel his brother and killed him.

> Then the LORD said to Cain, "Where is Abel your brother?" He said, "I do not know. Am I my brother's keeper?" And He said, "What have you done? The voice of your brother's blood cries out to Me from the ground." (Genesis 4:8-10)

God had a couple more questions for Cain—very, very sad questions. "*Where is your brother?*" Cain bitterly responded, "How am I supposed to know? Am I my brother's keeper?"

What an evil reply. This is the first blatant lie. Cain knew perfectly well where his brother was…lying dead in the field. But sin had so completely mastered Cain that he not only lied, he lied to God. (No doubt thinking that he could get away with it.)

Whoever said sin made sense? How greatly sin had worked in just one generation. It was true that Adam and Eve, Cain's parents, tried to shift the blame when God confronted them with their sin. But they didn't lie. They told the truth even though they were desperately ashamed and trying to escape from under it.

But now, one generation later, Cain outright lies to God. And then he sets himself up to question God. *"Am I my brother's keeper?"*

This is even worse than the lie. He suggests that this brother, whom he just happened to kill, is not his responsibility. Cain is saying, "If something has happened to Abel, it's his own fault! Who knows…maybe he even deserved it."

God had given him fair warning, now Cain had to face the music.

> "So now you are cursed from the earth, which has opened its mouth to receive your brother's blood from your hand. When you till the ground, it shall no longer yield its strength to you. A fugitive and a vagabond you shall be on the earth."

> And Cain said to the LORD, "My punishment is greater than I can bear! Surely You have driven me out this day from the face of the ground; I shall be hidden from Your face; I shall be a fugitive and a vagabond on the earth, and it will happen that anyone who finds me will kill me."

> And the LORD said to him, "Therefore, whoever kills Cain, vengeance shall be taken on him sevenfold." And the LORD set a mark on Cain, lest anyone finding him should kill him. Then Cain went out from the presence of the LORD and dwelt in the land of Nod on the east of Eden. (vv. 11-15)

Cain protested his punishment, but it's worth noting that he never repented of his sins. His words reveal remorse and regret…but no repentance.

We often confuse remorse and repentance. Remorse is being sorry for the *consequences* of your sin. Repentance is being sorry enough to stop doing it. Scripture says that "godly sorrow produces repentance." Cain was not repentant, he was simply sorry for the repercussions and results of sin in his life.

This is typical of the unrepentant person. Here they are, essentially reaping what they have sown, and they're angry with God for it! One of the clearest marks of sin is our almost innate desire to excuse ourselves and complain if we are judged in any way.

In our old nature, we don't like to admit our sin any more than Cain did.

VOICES FROM THE GRAVE

Hebrews 11 tells us that Abel, being dead, still speaks. From him, we learn a lesson of faith and presenting acceptable offerings to the living God. But Cain's life speaks, too. The Bible warns us that even today there is "the way of Cain."

> Woe to them! For they have gone in the way of Cain…. (Jude 11)

What is this "way of Cain" Scripture warns of?

First, it is worshipping with impure motives. It doesn't matter how sacrificial your gift may be or how loudly you sing, if your heart is in the wrong place, it goes nowhere. The heart of the matter is the matter of the heart.

Second, the "way of Cain" is to allow your heart and life to become gripped by jealousy, envy, and hatred. There will always be people who will do better than you. They will have nicer things, larger ministries, closer families, better looks, and better health.

So what?

Hasn't God been good to you? Hasn't He done above and beyond what you could ask or think? Praise God if He has blessed or used someone besides yourself in a powerful way. Jealousy and envy are sins. And if left undealt with, they can become deadly. Remember the lion at the door!

Third, the way of Cain is to lie to God about what you have done, excusing your actions. *"Am I my brother's keeper?"* Do you think anything escapes the knowledge of our all-knowing Father?

In the book of Jeremiah, God asks a couple more very thought-provoking questions.

> "Can anyone hide himself in secret places,
> So I shall not see him?" says the Lord;
> "Do I not fill heaven and earth?" says the Lord.
> (Jeremiah 23:24)

There's no hiding from Almighty God. He calls on us to come out of our hiding places and come clean. He convicts us of our sin and even warns us of "sin crouching at our door." He speaks to us in many ways: through our personal devotions or a preacher or friend. We brush it off, rationalize it, and try all kinds of mental gymnastics to justify it. But deep down, we know the truth.

The shepherd has two primary tools he uses with sheep. David wrote: "Thy rod and thy staff, they comfort me" (Psalm 23:4, KJV).

The Lord will try to get your attention, using that staff. To switch metaphors, He will "fire one over the bow." Why does God do this? Hebrews 12 tells us...

> For the Lord disciplines those he loves, and he punishes those he accepts as his children. As you endure this divine discipline, remember that God is treating you as his own children. Whoever heard of a child who was never disciplined? If God doesn't discipline you as he does all of his children, it means that you are illegitimate and are not really his children after all.

> For our earthly fathers disciplined us for a few years, doing the best they knew how. But God's discipline is always right and good for us

because it means we will share in his holiness. No discipline is enjoyable while it is happening—it is painful! But afterward there will be a quiet harvest of right living for those who are trained in this way. (Hebrews 12:6-8, 10-11, NLT).

God warned Cain. But he just wouldn't listen. And the "way of Cain" led to a very unhappy end.

Don't walk that way! Don't follow Cain down the highway by letting jealousy and envy control and ruin your life. Don't let impure motives hinder your worship of God. Don't let sin master you!

Walk instead in the "way of Abel."

"It was by faith that Abel obeyed God and brought an offering that pleased God more than Cain's offering did. God accepted Abel and proved it by accepting his gift; and though Abel is long dead, we can still learn lessons from him about trusting God" (Hebrews 11:4, TLB).

Abel's way is the way of faith. It is the way of trust, the way of obedience, and the way of the cross.

In other words, it is the *only* way to life.

Chapter Three

ENCOUNTER IN CANAAN:
MAKING RIGHT CHOICES

E veryday of our lives, we are faced with literally hundreds of choices. Walk into the door of your local supermarket. The very word "super" in front of "market" says it all. You can have a Super K-Mart on one corner, and a Wal-Mart Super Store on the other.

And talk about choices! In most such stores these days you'll find 24 different mixtures of bagged salads (organic or otherwise), a 107 varieties of cheese, 30 kinds of muffins, and 40 flavors of coffee. Stroll down the breakfast aisle and you'll encounter 80 brands of cereal—in the first ten feet!

Then you want to purchase a book? Go to Amazon.com for literally millions of titles—new or used. Break out the Ipod and you can play 20,000 songs, view 25,000 images, or watch 150 hours of video.

Slide into a booth at many restaurants and you'll find yourself confronted with a menu that's more like a small book. There are way too many choices!

Now what I eat or drink or what I wear probably won't have many long-lasting implications (except for having to let my clothes out because of the food I ate). But there are those significant, transforming choices we make in life. Like who we will marry. Or what career path we'll follow. Then there's the most important choice of all...the choice to follow Christ.

The pages of the Bible are filled with the stories of men and women who made choices that impacted the entire course of their lives.

- Moses chose to help his fellow Jews over the riches and power of Egypt.

- Joseph chose obedience to God over yielding to strong temptation.

- Daniel chose to eat kosher meals of vegetables over the unclean meat on the king of Babylon's banquet table.

Each one of these choices became major crossroads in the lives of these individuals. What happened in those moments of decision would set the course for the rest of their lives.

Moses, Joseph, and Daniel came to a dividing of the trails and took the right paths. But what about those who made bad choices at the parting of the ways? The Bible doesn't shy away from describing the consequences.

Adam's choice cost him Paradise.

Esau's choice cost him his birthright.

Saul's choice cost him his kingdom.

Judas's choice cost him his apostleship, his life, and his eternal soul.

Pilate, Agrippa, and Felix all chose wrong and missed eternity with Christ.

As difficult as this idea may be to process, the choices we make in time are binding in eternity. We make our decisions…and then our decisions make us.

Yes, choices are incredibly important, as we will see in the story before us.

Excess Baggage

God cares deeply about the choices we make in the course of our lives. As human beings created in His image, we have a free will, and both the ability and the responsibility to choose our own destiny.

Because He loves us, God wants us to make decisions that will lead us toward success and joy and fruitfulness in our lives on earth, and then into His presence for eternity after we pass from this life.

The Lord's heart for man and his choices can be summarized in Moses' heartfelt plea as the children of Israel stood on the brink of the Promised Land. Can you hear the heart of God ringing in these words?

> "Today I have given you the choice between life and death, between blessings and curses. I call on heaven and earth to witness the choice you make. Oh, that you would choose life, that you and your descendants might live! Choose to love the Lord your God and to obey him and commit yourself to him, for he is your life." (Deuteronomy 30:19-20, nlt)

In order to help and encourage us to choose life, the Bible gives us striking examples of those who chose well as well as those whose choices destroyed them. One such story details the choices of Abraham, and his nephew, Lot. Abraham made mostly right choices in life, while Lot made a series of wrong choices that he would live to bitterly regret.

Even though God will clearly show you the right choice to make, it's still up to *you* to decide. And you can't get around those moments of decision. Even when you have to make a choice and don't make it, that is in itself a choice!

God came one day to Abraham, then known as Abram, and told him to follow Him. He told him to make a clean break with his pagan family and follow.

Abram obeyed, but only partially. He had a very difficult time with this decision, and really "drug his feet." He also allowed his nephew Lot to tag along on the journey, something that the Lord really did not want him to do, and a decision that Abram no doubt regretted.

Choose Your Companions With Care

The Lord had said to Abram:

"Get out of your country,
From your family

And from your father's house,
To a land that I will show you."
(Genesis 12:1)

God was asking Abram to make a difficult separation in his life. And He asks us to do the same. Why? Because we all know people who both build us up or tear us down spiritually. There are certain people who, after you've spent a few hours with them, have actually diminished your spiritual appetite and drawn you in the wrong direction. Sometimes these can even be professing Christians who really don't have a heart for spiritual growth. They're more interested in worldly things, gossiping, complaining, or putting other people down.

The bottom line is they drag you down.

But then there are people who actually kindle a fire in your heart for God. The more time you spend with them, the more your spiritual appetite grows. They build you up in the faith and make you want to be more like Jesus!

Paul told his young friend Timothy to "run from anything that stimulates youthful lust. Follow anything that makes you want to do right. Pursue faith and love and peace, and enjoy the companionship of those who call on the Lord with pure hearts" (2 Timothy 2:22, NLT).

This is not to say that we should avoid relationships with nonbelievers. Not at all. Jesus wants us to seek to be a witness to them. Paul told the church at Corinth:

When I wrote to you before, I told you not to associate with people who indulge in sexual sin. But I wasn't talking about unbelievers who indulge in sexual sin, or who are greedy or are swindlers or idol worshipers. You would have to leave this world to avoid people like that. What I meant was that you are not to associate with anyone who claims to be a Christian yet indulges in sexual sin, or is greedy, or worships idols, or is abusive, or a drunkard, or a swindler. Don't even eat with such people. (1 Corinthians 5:9-11, NLT)

There's a difference between relationship and fellowship. I have relationships with people I come into contact with daily—neighbors, co-workers, extended family, and others. You can get to know the mailman who comes every day—and even have an extended conversation with him if you happen to bump into him in the mall. But that doesn't mean he's part of your inner circle of friends.

It's when you choose to spend time with someone that influence comes into play; you influence them and they influence you. And this is where we want to choose godly people to be our companions.

As we will see, Lot was not the kind of person God wanted Abe to hang with. They had different hearts, different priorities, different values. That's why He told Abram to separate from him.

Who was Lot? He was the son of Abram's brother, Haran, who remained back in the land of the Chaldeans when Abram went to Canaan. In the absence of his father, Lot may have looked to Abram to be that father figure in his life. There was something in Uncle Abraham that Lot so admired that he was willing to leave his country and immediate family to follow this man of God into the unknown.

That whole departure from their hometown of Ur is amazing when you think about it. Hebrews 11 tells us that "it was by faith that Abraham obeyed when God called him to leave home and go to another land that God would give him as his inheritance. *He went without knowing where he was going*" (vv. 8-9).

Can't you just hear their conversation?

"Where are you going, Uncle Abe?"

"I don't know, Lot. God hasn't told me yet."

"You don't know? You're pulling up stakes and leaving everything behind and you don't know where your even going?"

"That's right. That's the way it is."

"Oh…. Uncle Abe?

"Yes?"

"Can I come with you?"

Lot also chose to leave his community and all that was familiar. It wasn't because *he* had heard the voice of God, but simply because he admired and trusted his uncle.

Even so, it wouldn't be too long before a conflict developed…which led to a parting of the ways.

A PARTING OF THE WAYS

Then Abram went up from Egypt, he and his wife and all that he had, and Lot with him, to the South. Abram was very rich in livestock, in silver, and in gold. And he went on his journey from the South as far as Bethel, to the place where his tent had been at the beginning, between Bethel and Ai, to the place of the altar which he had made there at first. And there Abram called on the name of the LORD.

Lot also, who went with Abram, had flocks and herds and tents. Now the land was not able to support them, that they might dwell together, for their possessions were so great that they could not dwell together. And there was strife between the herdsmen of Abram's livestock and the herdsmen of Lot's livestock. The Canaanites and the Perizzites then dwelt in the land.

So Abram said to Lot, "Please let there be no strife between you and me, and between my herdsmen and your herdsmen; for we are brethren. Is not the whole land before you? Please separate from me. If you take the left, then I will go to the right; or, if you go to the right, then I will go to the left."

And Lot lifted his eyes and saw all the plain of Jordan, that it was well watered everywhere (before the LORD destroyed Sodom and Gomorrah) like the garden of the LORD, like the land of Egypt as you go toward Zoar. Then Lot chose for himself all the plain of Jordan, and Lot journeyed east. And they separated from each other. Abram dwelt in the land of Canaan, and Lot dwelt in the cities of the plain and pitched his tent even as far as Sodom. But the men of Sodom were exceedingly wicked and sinful against the LORD. (Genesis 13:1-13)

During their journey through Canaan, Abraham and Lot had each acquired great wealth. By this time, Lot was feeling pretty good about his decision to latch onto his uncle. Abraham's prosperity seemed to have an overflow into his nephew's pockets.

Prosperity, of course, isn't necessarily bad or good. It all depends on how it affects a person. Over the course of time, a conflict developed between those that kept the flocks for Abraham and Lot. In reality, however, the problem between Abraham and Lot wasn't caused by the land, the famine, their wealth, or even their herdsmen.

The heart of every problem is the problem in the heart.

Lot's heart was centered on wealth and worldly achievement, while Abraham wanted only to please the Lord. Abraham acquired wealth along the way, but it never became important to him. For Lot, however, the wealth and the prestige it brought became his reason for living. These two men had walked together for a time, but eventually a friction developed because of the spiritual direction each had chosen to go in life.

The Bible asks, "Can two walk together, except they be agreed?" (Amos 3:3). Abraham was a man who wanted to walk closely with God and enjoy fellowship with Him. In contrast, Lot wanted a friendship with God like his uncle had—but he also wanted friendship with the world.

The Bible clearly warns against this sort of divided allegiance. The apostle James wrote: "You adulterers! Don't you realize that friendship with this world makes you an enemy of God? I say it again, that if your aim is to enjoy this world, you can't be a friend of God" (James 4:4).

But Lot wanted to have it both ways. He had a knowledge of God and knew what was right, but he was weak. He didn't want to make a stand, and tended to lean on Abraham for strength.

Abraham walked with God...and Lot walked with Abraham! There are many like Lot today: They know what is right and deep-down want to know God. But there is a weakness in their faith and character. They need other believers to constantly prop them up, or they will fall. At the same time, they have a fascination with this world, and flirt on the edges on sin.

Interestingly enough, these are often people who have been raised in church. For those who have already tried what this world offers, that attraction isn't nearly so strong. *Been there, done that, bought the T-shirt.* In Luke 7:47, Jesus said, "A person who is forgiven little shows only little love." But when you've never "been there or done that" you can take your spiritual heritage for granted.

This is what Lot was doing, hoping he could ride along on his uncle's spiritual coattails. But it didn't work. In fact, it never works. We can't live off of someone else's faith. God has no grandchildren. The thing that kept Abraham from sin was his friendship with God—walking with God, talking with God, enjoying His presence. It was that love for the Lord that kept everything else in perspective. When you know and love God and see Him for who He is, you will also see this world for what it is.

Leaving The Results To God

The day finally came for Lot and Abraham to separate. Friction between the herdsmen was the surface reason—but it really went much deeper than that, to a basic difference in focus and purpose. Lot was at war with Abraham because he was at war with himself. And he was at war with himself because he was at war with God.

Abraham, however, was determined to be a peacemaker, and generously gave Lot his choice of territory. By not choosing for himself, Abraham was making a profound choice. He had decided to put God first and simply trust Him to take care of him and his family.

"Is not the whole land before you? Please separate from me. If you take the left, then I will go to the right; or, if you go to the right, then I will go to the left" (Genesis 13:9).

By not choosing for himself, Abraham chose to leave the outcome up to God. "You go ahead, Lot," he says. "I'll be fine whichever way it goes." Abraham felt that if he had to give up anything in the process, it really didn't matter. What mattered was obedience to God and His word.

Do you find yourself in a similar situation right now?

Maybe you're afraid that if you are honest and forthright in business, that lying cheat of a competitor will take advantage of you and steal away your customers. And that's exactly what might happen. You very well might lose some ground. But what's more important, the fast buck or the smile of God?

Maybe you're apprehensive that if you're are upfront with some of your friends about your faith in Christ and the convictions you hold as a result of that faith, they'll walk away from you. They may. But what's more important, friendship with God or friendship with this world?

Maybe you're living with your boyfriend or girlfriend outside of marriage. You can't separate, you say, because it would be so much more expensive. You couldn't afford to do it. The truth is, you can't afford *not* to do it. At the end of the day, the will of God is all that matters.

We, like Abraham, must face tough choices. Will we opt for the easy way and make the choice that pleases ourselves, or will we take the more difficult path of obedience, and leave the results up to God?

Lot made the wrong choice, opting for what looked to be the better land—not realizing the hidden costs that would be assessed against his family.

As it turned out, it was much, much more than he could afford.

DOWNWARD STEPS

Lot took a long look at the fertile plains of the Jordan Valley in the direction of Zoar. The whole area was well watered everywhere, like the garden of the LORD or the beautiful land of Egypt. (This was before the LORD had destroyed Sodom and Gomorrah.) Lot chose that land for himself—the Jordan Valley to the east of them. He went there with his flocks and servants and parted company with his uncle Abram. (Genesis 13:10-11, NLT)

There were a series of steps that led to the situation in which Lot ultimately found himself. Whenever we end up in sin, it's always the cumulative product of small indulgences and seemingly minuscule compromises. The immediate consequences of those actions, at the time, seem almost indiscernible.

So what did Lot do wrong?

First Step Down:
He Looked The Wrong Way

And Lot lifted his eyes and saw all the plain of Jordan, that it was well watered everywhere…like the land of Egypt. (v. 10)

Lot's point of reference was Egypt. He liked Sodom because it reminded him of Egypt. What is your point of reference?

My wife tells me that I always compare every place I go to Hawaii. I lived there in my childhood, and have visited many times since. The Hawaiian Islands have always held a special place in my heart.

So whenever we are visiting someplace that has a tropical feel to it, I might say, "Well, this is nice. But not as nice as Hawaii!" Or maybe, "This reminds of a place in Hawaii."

Lot's point of reference was Egypt.

He looked around at the land, caught sight of Sodom and Gomorrah, and made his first step down. The wording in the original language reveals that Lot "looked with longing" on that well-watered plain.

This reminds us of what happened to Eve. "So when the woman saw that the tree was good for food, that it was pleasant to the eyes, and a tree desirable to make one wise, she took of its fruit and ate" (Genesis 3:6).

The apostle John made a strong statement about that long look in the wrong direction:

For all that is in the world—the lust of the flesh, the lust of the eyes, and the pride of life—is not of the Father but is of the world. And the world is passing away, and the lust of it; but he who does the will of God abides forever. (1 John 2:16-17)

Instead of lifting up his eyes to heaven, Lot lifted up his eyes to the plain of Jordan and stopped there. The eyes see what the heart loves. Abraham had taken Lot out of Egypt, but he could not take Egypt out of Lot.

Our outlook helps to determine our outcome. Abraham walked by faith, and Lot walked by sight.

Second Step Down:
He Separated Himself From Abraham

Separation may have been a good thing for Abraham, who had his own walk with the living God. But it was disastrous for Lot, who didn't have that kind of heart-tie to the Lord. A sure sign of spiritual decline is when we find ourselves wanting to get away from godly people, preferring the company of friends and the activities that "remind us of Egypt." For instance, we attach a token prayer to the beginning or the end of an otherwise completely godless evening, and imagine we have spiritually "sanitized" everything.

Third Step Down:
He Pitched His Tent Toward Sodom (Genesis 13:12)

What was it that so fascinated Lot about the two evil cities on the plain? The music? The bright lights? The urban sophistication? The flashy chariots? The freewheeling lifestyle? The Bible doesn't tell us what became such a drawing card for Abraham's nephew. We only know that he edged closer and closer, imagining that he could still keep his faith and character, and that he could "handle" any temptations that came his way.

If you had asked Lot why, at this time of his life, he settled near Sodom but didn't actually go and live in the city, he might have explained to you that Sodom was a very wicked place. At the same time, however, there were certain advantages to living nearby.

I've spoken to many people like this through the years. They don't want to plunge whole-hog into a pagan lifestyle...but they don't completely walk away from it, either. They want to be close enough to the world to still "keep an eye on it," but not actually participate in it.

At heart, Lot was still a righteous man, as Peter tells us in the New Testament. He writes that Lot "was oppressed by the filthy conduct of the wicked," and that it "tormented his righteous soul from day to day by seeing and hearing their lawless deeds" (2 Peter 2:7, 8). So before the man and his family became completely swallowed by the evil of that place, God sent a strong warning.

In an interesting turn, Lot was captured by an alliance of kings who had made war on Sodom and its allies and defeated them. Raiding the city of Sodom, the invaders took Lot as a hostage and marched away. Surely this was a warning to Lot from God that he was moving in the wrong direction!

Have you ever had a "wake-up call" from heaven, where you distinctly sensed God warning you about something? Lot probably cried out to God, "O Lord, if You get me out of this, I'll serve You! I'll be Your friend like Uncle Abraham. I'll stay away from Sodom!"

God doesn't want us to fall or fail. And He will send us warnings about our direction, beginning with our conscience. That little "warning buzzer" goes off when you start to cross the line…and what do you do with it? Ignore it? Shut it out with lots of noise and activities? Do you try to disable it, like pulling the battery out of a smoke alarm?

Besides the voice of our conscience, God will set obstacles to our path. For Balaam, it was an angel in the middle of the road—and a talking donkey. For Jonah, it was a great fish with an appetite for runaway prophets. For Peter, it was a servant girl who identified him while he stood by the enemy's fire. But even in the face of such obstacles we may persist in our stubborn way.

Maybe God is warning you right now. That relationship with that co-worker of the opposite sex is getting a little too close. Those lunches together, those e-mails, instant messages, and phone calls. That habit you have of "stretching the truth" when asked about some of your actions. And then you have to tell another lie to cover up the one you previously told. Deep down, you know you're flirting with disaster. Stop! Before it's too late. You don't want to end up like Lot!

Uncle Abraham bravely led an attack and saved his compromising nephew. And how did Lot show his gratitude to God? He pulled up stakes and moved right into Sodom!

Fourth Step Down:
He Sat In The Gateway Of Sodom (Genesis 19:1)

Sitting in the gateway means he had actually become one of the leaders in this wicked and perverse city. I wonder what kind of compromises he had to make to pull this off? Graham Scroggie once said of compromise: "It prompts us to be silent when we ought to speak for fear of offending. It prompts us to praise when it is not deserved to keep people our friends. It prompts us to tolerate sin and not to speak out because to do so might give us enemies."

How important it is for us to realize that compromise reaches no one. If it causes us to lower our standards in order to extend our reach, we have defeated our very purpose. In Lot's case, it led him to the leadership of a city he should have been calling into account. Like a moth attracted to a flame, Lot had been unable to keep his distance—and now he was in the very place God was about to destroy. By this time, Lot had become so spiritually dull he didn't even realize how bad things had become. Sin had worn him down.

Jesus told us that as Christians in this world, we are to be both salt and light. Some are salt but not light (they live it but they don't share it). Others are light but not salt (they share it but they don't live it). It appears that Lot was neither.

But in all fairness, Lot is not a prototype of a non-believer pretending to be one. Rather, he is a picture of a believer living a compromised life.

Remember the word about this unhappy man in 2 Peter? Lot was "a good man who was sick of all the immorality and wickedness around him" (2:7, NLT).

Poor Lot. He was so worn down spiritually he didn't seem to know which way was up. So what did Uncle Abraham do? Did he "pile on" and condemn Lot? No, he prayed. And that's exactly what God would have us do for those who have compromised their faith and fallen onto hard times. They need to see this for themselves, and God can bring that about through the conviction of His Holy Spirit.

Out of regard for Abraham—and mercy for Lot—God sent two angels to literally take Lot and his family by the hand and pull them out of that perverse place before the judgment of God fell. I see two powerful realities at work in that rescue: the incomparable mercy of God and the mighty power of prayer.

ABRAHAM'S CHOICE

Let's go back to that destiny-making moment when Abraham and Lot stood on that high ridge overlooking the plain of the Jordan. Abraham seemingly left the choice up to Lot, as to which direction the younger man would go—but he actually left the matter with God.

After Lot went off toward what would become a bitter future in the lush fields surrounding Sodom and Gomorrah, the word of the Lord came to Abraham with a stunning promise.

> And the Lord said to Abram, after Lot had separated from him: "Lift your eyes now and look from the place where you are — northward, southward, eastward, and westward; for all the land which you see I give to you and your descendants forever. And I will make your descendants as the dust of the earth; so that if a man could number the dust of the earth, then your descendants also could be numbered. Arise, walk in the land through its length and its width, for I give it to you."

> Then Abram moved his tent, and went and dwelt by the terebinth trees of Mamre, which are in Hebron, and built an altar there to the LORD. (Genesis 13:14-18)

You don't lose when you choose God. You might not look like a winner in world's eyes, and your life may have its share of hardships and sorrows. But God knows how to reward His own, and He is a generous Father. We hear the phrase "treasure in heaven" and picture something in earthly terms, like a big chest of gold or diamonds. But we really don't have a clue how majestic and awesome and incredibly joyous God's rewards will be for His faithful children.

When I think about these things, I remember how Peter reminded the Lord of the sacrifice he and his fellow disciples had made.

"We have left everything to follow you! What then will there be for us?"

Jesus said to them... "Everyone who has left houses or brothers or sisters or father or mother or children or fields for my sake will receive a hundred times as much and will inherit eternal life." (Matthew 19:27, 29, NIV)

This saying is vividly illustrated here in Abraham's life. He had now given up everything to follow God—not only his own country and people but now some prime real estate in Canaan, giving Lot first choice in the matter. Not only that, but he had lost Lot, too, for whom he had some real affection.

Lot had lifted up his eyes and seen what the world had to offer. So God said to Abraham, "Lift up your eyes and see all I have given you." Had Abraham lost the best land? Well, in its place God was giving him the entire land of Canaan. He was to have it all. Had Abraham lost family for the sake of obedience? Now God would give to him offspring like the dust of the earth.

We all choose what path our life will take. God always gives His very best to those who leave the choice with Him.

This reminds me of the tragic pioneer story of the Donner Party. It took place in high Sierra Nevadas in the winter of 1846. George and Jacob Donner, James Frazier Reed, and their families packed up everything to head for the "Promised Land" in California, some 2,000 miles away. Their caravan had state of the art covered wagons laden with more than enough supplies. By the time they set out, their party had swelled to 87 men, women, and children.

Their journey ended in tragedy, however, when forced to camp for the winter at a small lake about 13 miles northwest of Lake Tahoe. There they suffered heavy snows—and the deaths of forty of their company. Some of the others, desperate to survive, turned to cannibalism. That aspect of the story of the Donner party is well known. What is not so well known is how they ended up in this miserable place.

A man named Lansord Hastings had told them he knew of a shortcut to California. Though it was untried, the Donner party took it. And it cost them everything. One wrong foolish, impetuous decision resulted in disaster.

Perhaps you, like the Donner Party, find yourself at a crossroads in your life. You know the right way to go, but then...there's that shortcut that looks so tempting. Abraham made the right choices, and lived the right way. Lot made the wrong choice, and to a large degree, lived the wrong way.

As Elijah said to the faithless people of Israel up on Mount Carmel: "How long are you going to waver between two opinions? ...If the Lord is God, *follow* him! But if Baal is God, then follow *him!*" (1 Kings 18:21, TLB).

You know what is right. Don't take the shortcut of Lot. Walk in the right way like Abraham.

Having lived 54 years now, I have the perspective of viewing several generations: my grandparents' generation, my parents' generation, my generation that is still unfolding, my children's generation, and my grandchildren's generation, that is just beginning. It's sobering to see how choices made by one generation can have a ripple effect for decades to come...bringing either life, peace, and prosperity, or sorrow and brokenness.

As I said, the choices of time are binding in eternity. Contrast two men from the Nineteenth Century: Max Jukes and Jonathan Edwards.

Max Jukes lived in New York. He did not believe in Christ or in raising his children in the way of the Lord. He refused to take his children to church, even when they asked to go. Since he walked this planet, Max Jukes has had 1,026 descendants. Of this number, 300 were sent to prison for an average term of thirteen years; 190 were public prostitutes; 680 were admitted alcoholics. The descendants of this man made no contribution whatsoever to society.

Jonathan Edwards lived in the same state, at the same time as Jukes. Edwards, however, loved the Lord and saw that his children were in church every Sunday, as he served the Lord to the best of his ability. He has had 929 descendants, and of these 430 were ministers, 86 became university professors, 13 became university presidents, 75 authored good books, 7 were elected to the United States Congress, and one was Vice President of the United States.

Choices! We all make them. Hundreds every day. To whom do you relate most in this message: Abraham or Lot? Are you a "friend of God" or a "friend of this world"?

Chapter Four

ENCOUNTER IN HARAN:
KNOWING THE WILL OF GOD

Does God still speak to man today? Is He interested in what happens to us as individuals?

Does He truly have a master plan for our lives?

If so, how do I discover it? How do I hear His voice? How can I know the will of God?

These are all important questions, and the answer to the first one sets us an exciting journey of discovery. *Yes.* God does speak to man today—and especially to His own sons and daughters. We as Christians are not simply victims of chance in a random world, hoping against hope our luck won't run out on us. Just as God led men and women in the pages of Scripture, so He wants to lead us. There are, however, no foolproof formulas or easy 1-2-3 steps we can follow that will instantaneously reveal God's will to us at our every whim.

But let there be no doubt: God guides His own. The gospel of John tells us that Jesus "calls his own sheep by name and leads them out. And when he brings out his own sheep, he goes before them; and the sheep follow him, for they know his voice" (John 10:3-4).

God speaks to us and shows us His will—in terms both general and specific—and in the next few pages we will examine some of the foundational principles of His guidance in our daily lives.

The good news is that God does not play hide and seek with us. *He wants to lead you even more than you want to be led.* God is more concerned about keeping us in His will than we are to be kept in it!

HIS WILL IS BEST

Far too often, we can make knowing God's will into something misty, mystical, and other-worldly. And yet through my years of walking with God, I have found that there are concrete, practical steps we as believers can take to more easily grasp and understand His will.

God's way becomes plain when we start walking in it. But sometimes we fear or don't like His plan, and don't want to follow it. The following is a reported transcript of a conversation between the captain of a US Navy ship with Canadian authorities off the coast of Newfoundland.

Canadians: Please divert your course 15 degrees to the south to avoid a collision.

Americans: Recommend you divert your course 15 degrees to the north to avoid a collision.

Canadians: Negative. You will have to divert your course 15 degrees to the south to avoid a collision.

Americans: This is the captain of a US Navy ship. I say again, divert your course!

Canadians: No. I say again, you divert your course.

Americans: This is the aircraft carrier USS Lincoln, the second largest ship in the United States Atlantic fleet. We are accompanied by 3 destroyers, 3 cruisers and numerous support vessels. I demand that you change your course 15 degrees north. I say again, that's one five degrees north, or counter measures will be undertaken to ensure the safety of this ship.

Canadians: This is a lighthouse. Your call!

Often we're just like that Navy captain when it comes to the will of God. We want Him to divert His course, when we're in desperate need of diverting our own. Above all else, however, we should keep one important fact in mind: In the long run, God's will is *always* better than our will.

In the long run?

The reality is, at certain times in our lives we may not understand or even like God's will. If you were to interview young Joseph, deep in the bowels of an Egyptian prison on a trumped up rape charge (Genesis 39-40), he may have not been all that excited about the will of God for his life. But if you were to talk to him just a short time later, after he came into power as the second in command of Egypt, he might have preached a sermon to you about the value of waiting for God's will.

Keep this in mind. God is always looking out for your spiritual and eternal welfare. We tend to look out for our physical and immediate welfare. But what is good *now* may not be for eternity. And what is difficult now may be the best thing for the endless ages to come.

Paul wrote these encouraging words to the church in Corinth:

For our present troubles are quite small and won't last very long. Yet they produce for us an immeasurably great glory that will last forever! So we don't look at the troubles we can see right now; rather, we look forward to what we have not yet seen. For the troubles we see will soon be over, but the joys to come will last forever. (2 Corinthians 4:17-18, NLT)

The story before us in this chapter uncovers several essential principles for knowing the will of God in our life. It also happens to be a beautiful love story—on two levels. First, it's the story of a man and woman who come together against almost impossible odds, all because of the providence of God. Second, it's a picture or type of God's love for each of us, how He sought us out and graciously brought us to Himself.

MATCHMAKER, MATCHMAKER

When the patriarch Abraham was an old man, at this point pushing 140 years, his miracle son Isaac was about 40. Sarah, Isaac's mother, had died, and Isaac was lonely and heartsick.

Abraham may have been old, but there was nothing wrong with his intellectual powers.

It didn't take him long to figure out what his son needed.

Isaac needed a wife.

Hard as it might be to imagine, there weren't any Internet matchmaking sites in those days, so Abraham called his most trusted servant, and gave him some specific instructions.

> Abraham said to the oldest servant of his house, who ruled over all that he had, "Please, put your hand under my thigh, and I will make you swear by the LORD, the God of heaven and the God of the earth, that you will not take a wife for my son from the daughters of the Canaanites, among whom I dwell; but you shall go to my country and to my family, and take a wife for my son Isaac."

> And the servant said to him, "Perhaps the woman will not be willing to follow me to this land. Must I take your son back to the land from which you came?"

> But Abraham said to him, "Beware that you do not take my son back there. The LORD God of heaven, who took me from my father's house and from the land of my family, and who spoke to me and swore to me, saying, 'To your descendants I give this land,' He will send His angel before you, and you shall take a wife for my son from there. And if the woman is not willing to follow you, then you will be released from this oath; only do not take my son back there." So the servant put his hand under the thigh of Abraham his master, and swore to him concerning this matter.

> Then the servant took ten of his master's camels and departed, for all his master's goods were in his hand. And he arose and went to Mesopotamia, to the city of Nahor. (Genesis 24:2-10)

As the servant, Eliezer, arrived at his destination, he shot a quick prayer heavenward and asked God for direction and success in his mission: This is the privilege of a man or woman who enjoys a moment-by-moment walk with God. Scripture tells us to "pray without ceasing" (1 Thessalonians 5:17). That doesn't mean we're to be on our knees 24/7, but it does mean staying tuned into heaven's frequency every waking hour of our day. Then, when the road forks in front of us, when a sudden need arises in our lives, we can launch a swift "arrow" prayer toward heaven, confident that God is watching and that He will hear us.

That's what Eliezer did. When he saw some young women approaching the well where he stood with his mini-caravan, he prayed that the one whom God had chosen for Isaac would not only offer him a drink of water (a common courtesy), but also offer to water his camels (a great inconvenience).

Before he had finished his prayer, a gorgeous young woman named Rebekah approached the well. (*Lord, let her be the one! Let her be the one!*) As she was drawing water, Eliezer asked her for a drink. She graciously complied, and then offered to get water for his camels until their considerable thirst was completely satisfied.

Don't minimize that act of courtesy. Watering these animals was no small feat when you consider the fact that an average camel drinks more than 20 gallons of water—especially after a long day's journey through the desert. And Eliezer had 10 camels with him. You do the math…that's a lot of water to be hauled up from a well with a bucket.

In fact, if Rebekah's pitcher held a gallon, that meant she would have had to make 200 trips from the spring to the watering trough. At the least, it would have involved several hours of labor. And remember, at that point Rebekah had no idea who this stranger was. She had no clue about a wealthy and godly eligible bachelor named Isaac waiting many miles away. She simply saw a stranger in need and took it upon herself to help him.

Eliezer was overjoyed, and immediately pulled out a ring and some bracelets from his bag, asking the surprised Rebekah who her family was and if he could meet them. When Rebekah arrived at the family tent, bedecked with beautiful jewelry, followed by a distinguished stranger, and with ten camels in tow, she definitely had her brother Laban's attention.

When the young woman told Laban the story, he was all smiles. Opening his arms in welcome, he declared, "Come in, O blessed of the LORD! Why do you stand outside? For I have prepared the house, and a place for the camels" (Genesis 24:31). Laban must have been expecting company!

Eliezer, however, wasted no time in declaring his mission. At the request of Abraham, he had come seeking a bride for his master Isaac. Then he related the story of his prayer at the well, and what Rebekah had done. Rebekah's family couldn't deny the evident hand of God in these developments, and they agreed to her going back with Eliezer to be the bride of Isaac. Realizing they would probably never see her again, they asked if she could wait awhile, allowing them to say a long goodbye. But Eliezer knew he was on God's business, and said no, she must leave immediately.

So they said, "We will call the young woman and ask her personally."

Then they called Rebekah and said to her, "Will you go with this man?"

And she said, "I will go." (Genesis 24:58)

1. Search The Scriptures For God's General Will

The first principle of laying hold of God's will is that you must look for it. And the best and primary place to being your search is in the pages of Scripture. When this story unfolded, nothing approaching Scripture as we have it today existed. But the principles of biblical truth already existed, being passed on orally from generation to generation. In this situation, God's word came through the lips of Abraham.

> "The Lord God of heaven, who took me from my father's house and from the land of my family, and who spoke to me and swore to me, saying, 'To your descendants I give this land,' He will send His angel before you, and you shall take a wife for my son from there." (Genesis 24:7)

Abraham also added that this wife for Isaac was not to come from the pagan Canaanites. She was to be of his extended family, which was the equivalent of being a believer at this time.

Today, God speaks to us through His Word. That is the bedrock of truth by which we measure all other truth, the clear revelation by which we measure all other so-called revelations. It is the rock of stability by which we measure our fickle human emotions. The way we know something is true or right is by comparing it to what Scripture teaches.

Everything you need to know about God is found in the pages of Scripture. Paul told his young disciple Timothy that "All Scripture is inspired by God and is useful to teach us what is true and to make us realize what is wrong in our lives. It straightens us out and teaches us to do what is right. It is God's way of preparing us in every way, fully equipped for every good thing God wants us to do" (2 Timothy 3:16, NLT).

From this verse—and others like it—we know that God would never lead us contrary to the plain teachings of Scripture. This truth seems obvious (and it is), but it's amazing how many seem to miss it. They're busy seeking some mystical word from God when He has plainly spoken to them in the Bible sitting on their nightstand.

It would be like wanting desperately to hear from someone that you deeply loved. Then one day you looked in your mailbox and found a letter from them. (Or an e-mail on your computer.) But instead of opening that piece of correspondence, you simply continued to whine about how this person never communicates with you.

Don't be ridiculous…open the letter!

In the same way we must open The Book! Jesus said, "Behold, I have come—in the volume of the book it is written of Me—to do Your will, O God" (Hebrews 10:7).

Whenever you begin to imagine that the will of God is mysterious, mystical, or out-of-reach, remember that Scripture plainly states God's specific will for you—again and again. Are you looking for God's will but don't know where to begin? Start with what God has already told you. If you're not ready to obey His clearly written instructions, what makes you think you will follow special revelation out of the blue?

> *For this is the will of God,* your sanctification: that
> you should abstain from sexual immorality.
> (1 Thessalonians 4:3)

> Rejoice always, pray without ceasing, in everything give thanks;
> *for this is the will of God in Christ Jesus for you.*
> (1 Thessalonians 5:16-18)

Therefore do not be unwise, *but understand what the will of the Lord is.* And do not be drunk with wine, in which is dissipation; but be filled with the Spirit, speaking to one another in psalms and hymns and spiritual songs, singing and making melody in your heart to the Lord, giving thanks always for all things to God the Father in the name of our Lord Jesus Christ, submitting to one another in the fear of God. (Ephesians 5:17-21)

2. Ask For God's Specific Will

When I was a young man, I never found any specific passage in Scripture that told me I must marry a girl named Cathe. What do I do, then? I take God's principles, keeping them in the forefront of my mind and heart, and then ask Him for His specific will in my life. From the Scripture, I understand that it's not good for a man to be alone, that an excellent wife is the crown of her husband, and that he who finds a wife finds a good thing, and obtains favor from the Lord. Not to mention the verse that says it's better to marry than to burn with passion![4]

Having understood God's general will for my life through the Scriptures, I seek His specific will for individual situations as they arise.

This is what Eliezir did.

> Then he said, "O LORD God of my master Abraham, please give me success this day, and show kindness to my master Abraham." (Genesis 24:12)

Nothing is too insignificant, too minute, to take to the Lord in prayer. There's an old Jewish proverb that says, "It is better to ask the way ten times than to take the wrong road once." The apostle James reminds us, "If you need wisdom—if you want to know what God wants you to do—ask him, and he will gladly tell you. He will not resent your asking" (James 1:5, NLT).

3. Wait For His Timing

The timing of God is just as important as the will of God. And it is clear that God has both His perfect will and time to do what He wants. Ecclesiastes 3:11 tells us that "He has made everything beautiful in its time."

Eliezir waited for the right moment to act. He saw the beautiful Rebekah, and hoped she might be the one.

> And the man, wondering at her, remained silent so as to know whether the Lord had made his journey prosperous or not. (Genesis 24:21)

The problem with so many of us is that having found God's will, we want to act quickly. Eliezir waited to see if this was indeed the one. The Lord answered his prayer, Rebekah responded, and Eliezir knew it was time to move.

We're so prone to rush things, aren't we? In our culture of instant gratification it's hard for us to "be still, and know that He is God."[5] But if God says no—or even slow down—it's for your own good.

If the request is wrong, God says, "No."

If the timing is wrong, God says, "Slow."

If *you* are wrong, God says, "Grow."

But if the request is right, the timing is right, and you are right, God says, "Go!"

4. Act On GOD's Will

> But he said to them, "Do not detain me, now that the LORD has granted success to my journey. Send me on my way so I may go to my master." (v. 56, NIV)

Obedience to revealed truth guarantees guidance in matters unrevealed. The wind of God is always blowing...but you must hoist your sail! In the book of Acts, when God spoke to the apostle Philip with orders to go to the desert, he went—even though it made no logical sense at the time.[6] We must do the same. God won't necessarily give you a detailed blueprint. He will reveal to you as much as you need to know, nothing more, nothing less.

God leads us step by step, from event to event. It will only be afterwards, when we look back with the luxury of hindsight, that we will discover how God led us more than we ever realized or dreamed. God used important moments of our lives, even times of crisis, or situations we may have balked at or complained about at the time, to lead us in His will through life.

5. GOD Confirms His Will

How did Isaac deal with being a forty-year-old single guy? Here's a little snapshot from the Bible.

He went out to the field one evening to meditate, and as he looked up, he saw camels approaching. Rebekah also looked up and saw Isaac. She got down from her camel and asked the servant, "Who is that man in the field coming to meet us?"

"He is my master," the servant answered. So she took her veil and covered herself.

Then the servant told Isaac all he had done. Isaac brought her into the tent of his mother Sarah, and he married Rebekah. So she became his wife, and he loved her; and Isaac was comforted after his mother's death. (vv. 63-67)

So many singles I have known work themselves up into a mad rush to find that right person. And there's certainly nothing wrong with wondering and praying about such a deep, God-given desire. In Genesis 2:18, God said of Adam, literally, "Not good is the aloneness of man." It was God Himself who brought Eve to Adam's side. And if He sees that aloneness is ultimately "not good" for you, He will bring your mate to you, in His perfect timing. But there's nothing wrong with bringing your desire before Him in prayer. You can start praying for that future husband or wife right now.

While you're still single, however, you need to take advantage of your mobility and availability. Paul had these things in mind when he penned these words to the single men and women in the church at Corinth:

In everything you do, I want you to be free from the concerns of this life An unmarried man can spend his time doing the Lord's work and thinking how to please him. But a married man can't do that so well. He has to think about his earthly responsibilities and how to please his wife. His interests are divided. In the same way, a woman who is no longer married or has never been married can be more devoted to the Lord in body and in spirit, while the married woman must be concerned about her earthly responsibilities and how to please her husband.

I am saying this for your benefit, not to place restrictions on you. I want you to do whatever will help you serve the Lord best, with as few distractions as possible. (1 Corinthians 7:32-35)

Sometimes we think of singles as second class citizens. ("What? You're not married *yet*?") But many of the great movers and shakers of scripture were unmarried. Elijah had no wife, and he shook a nation. The apostle Paul turned his world upside down. Jesus never had a wife. And the list goes on.

The bottom line? While you're single serve the Lord with all your heart. But at the same time, don't feel guilt over your desire for companionship. Wait on the Lord. Jesus said, "Your heavenly Father already knows all your needs, and he will give you all you need from day to day if you live for him and make the Kingdom of God your primary concern" (Matthew 6:32-33, NLT).

Isaac wasn't running around like a chicken with its head cut off, he was meditating in the field. And then...in the very place of meditation and prayer, the beautiful Rebekah appeared on the horizon.

Seeing him, Rebekah said, "Who is this man walking in the field to meet us?" Or as it says in the Greg Translation, "Who is that *fox* out there in the field?" Eliezer replied, "That's my master."

Rebekah wrapped a veil around her face. Could it have concealed a big smile? *Yes, Lord!*

God's plans for you are always better than your plans for yourself. God provided Abraham's son with a beautiful bride, who also had a beautiful heart. And Isaac loved her.

It's a charming love story, but it's much more than that. It's also a picture of God's love for us and His call upon our lives. He will reveal His general will to us in the Bible, He will give us wisdom on specific matters as we wait on Him, and once we feel we have the sense of His direction, He will confirm that in our lives in multiple ways.

He may cause a verse from Scripture to leap out at you from the page, speaking exactly to your situation. He may move obstacles and shift circumstances in such a way that you can recognize His hand clearing the way for you. He may speak to you through a trusted Christian friend, family member, or pastor. God's creativity is endless, and He knows how to move you into the main current of His will if you're ready to wade out into the water with a humble, obedient heart. This story is a beautiful picture of God's love for you, and how He sought you and brought you to Himself.

CHOSEN AND TREASURED

Rebekah was thought of before she even knew it.

Abraham had told his servant:

"But you shall go to my country and to my family, and take a wife for my son Isaac." (v. 24)

In the same way, God thought of us and chose us, the Bride of Christ before we were ever aware of it. Paul reminds us of this in his letter to the church of Ephesus.

For he chose us in him before the creation of the world to be holy and blameless in his sight. (Ephesians 1:4, NIV)

Jesus said "You have not chosen Me, but I have chosen you...." Before you were even aware of His presence, He was thinking of you, loving you, getting ready in His timing to reveal His unique and wonderful plan for your life.

PROCLAIMING THE MESSAGE

Abraham didn't just sit back and wait for Rebekah to come to his son, he sent his servant to seek her out. The one objective of the servant was to announce Abraham's purpose, which was to find a bride for his son.

It's the same with the Lord. He has not only chosen us, but He also sought us out. Make no mistake about it, the Bible clearly teaches predestination. *And it also teaches the free will of man.* It teaches that God has chosen me, but it also teaches that I must choose Him.

> "Choose for yourselves this day whom you will serve...." (Joshua 24:15)

> "I have set before you life and death, blessing and cursing; therefore choose life, that both you and your descendants may live." (Deuteronomy 30:19)

> "Whoever believes in Him should not perish..." (John 3:16)

How then do I reconcile those two contradictory ideas? I don't.

You don't have to reconcile friends. I just concentrate on what He has told me to do, and leave the "choosing part" up to Him. He has told me to know Him and make Him known, to believe and then to proclaim. He has asked me to simply trust Him and obey Him—not try to unravel the mysteries of the universe. What a relief!

The Bible says: "We are therefore Christ's ambassadors, as though God were making his appeal through us. We implore you on Christ's behalf: Be reconciled to God. God made him who had no sin to be sin for us, so that in him we might become the righteousness of God" (2 Corinthians 5:20, 21, NIV).

Notice the words here: God makes His appeal through us. Christ implores non-believers through us. In other words, the Almighty God of the universe pleads with fallen man through you and me. If this doesn't inspire us, I don't know what will.

THE POWER OF THE MESSAGE

There was power in the message Eliezir brought. As a servant, his objective was to simply declare the facts. He was not to add to them or take away from them, just proclaim what was true.

The same is true of each of us. We are to proclaim the Gospel. Paul wrote: "For Christ didn't send me to baptize, but to preach the Good News—and not with clever speeches and high-sounding ideas, for fear that the cross of Christ would lose its power" (1 Corinthians 1:17, NLT).

He is reminding us that there is a distinct power in the simple message of the life, words, death, and resurrection of Jesus Christ from the dead. We often underestimate the raw power the Gospel message has in reaching even the most hardened heart.

Don't underestimate its appeal.

Don't be ashamed of its simplicity.

Don't add to it or take away from it.

Just proclaim it and stand back and watch what God will do.

I have been amazed time and time again how God so powerfully uses this simple yet incredibly profound message to radically change lives. From outright Satanists to moral, yet lost people. From broken families and people addicted to drugs to those deceived by the cults. From the hardened atheist to the deceived cultist. The words of the Gospel, driven home to hearts by the Holy Spirit, is the most powerful message in all the world.

THE DOWN PAYMENT

Upon accepting the offer of marriage, Rebekah received the down payment of things to come.

> Then the servant brought out jewelry of silver, jewelry of gold, and clothing, and gave them to Rebekah. He also gave precious things to her brother and to her mother. (Genesis 24:53)

In the same way, God sent His Holy Spirit into our lives as a down payment of things to come.

> And you also were included in Christ when you heard the word of truth, the gospel of your salvation. Having believed, you were marked in him with a seal, the promised Holy Spirit, who is a deposit guaranteeing our inheritance until the redemption of those who are God's possession—to the praise of his glory. (Ephesians 1:13-14, NIV)

We have received a down payment on heaven—and it is the most amazing deposit that could ever be made. The Holy Spirit, God Himself, the Third Person of the Trinity takes up residence in our own inner being.

But what does that part about "marked in him with a seal" mean? Back in the first century, when goods were shipped from place to another they would be stamped with a wax seal, imprinted with a signet ring bearing a unique mark of ownership. It was the same with important documents. If a king sent an important letter to one of his officials, it would be sealed with wax, and imprinted with the royal seal.

If anybody messed with that seal, they would be messing with the king himself. And that was big, big trouble. No one would dare break that seal unless they were the person it was addressed to. In the same way, God has put His royal seal of ownership on us. He has made the down payment, and we will follow through with our full inheritance in Christ.

MAKING THE BREAK

Rebekah had to make a break with all that would slow her down or hinder her progress.

Then they had supper, and the servant and the men with him stayed there overnight. But early the next morning, [Eliezer] said, "Send me back to my master."

"But we want Rebekah to stay at least ten days," her brother and mother said. "Then she can go."

But he said, "Don't hinder my return. The LORD has made my mission successful, and I want to report back to my master."

"Well," they said, "we'll call Rebekah and ask her what she thinks." So they called Rebekah. "Are you willing to go with this man?" they asked her.

And she replied, "Yes, I will go."
(vv. 54-58, NLT)

When the work of the Holy Spirit has begun in our lives, Satan tries to stop us. Even close friends and family can be a real snare. Jesus said "If anyone comes to Me and does not hate his father and mother, wife and children, brothers and sisters, yes, and his own life also, he cannot be My disciple" (Luke 14:26-27).

In response to a man who wanted to wait until mother and father died before he followed the Lord, Jesus said, "Let the dead bury their own dead, but you go and preach the kingdom of God" (Luke 9:60).

Rebekah's family took her aside and said, "Will you go with this man?" (Translation: *Are you SURE, honey?*)

And she said, "I will go."

If you deal with one excuse to keep you from completely following Christ, another will invariably take its place. And though God will do what is necessary to bring an awareness of our need for Him, He will not force the issue. He will convict us, speak to us, and most importantly love us, but the ultimate decision lies with us.

Eliezir used no high pressure appeals. He presented the simple facts of the case. But Rebekah said, "I will go!"

She had made up her mind to leave everything she had ever known behind, and travel to a far country to meet astranger. And the first step of that journey was probably the hardest of all.

But it was probably all forgotten when she looked up one evening and saw her bridegroom walking toward her through the field.

She was home.

Chapter Five

ENCOUNTER AT PENIEL:
WRESTLING WITH GOD

We've all had those moments in life when we look up to heaven with a perplexed or heavy heart and say, *"Why?"*

Have you ever prayed and prayed for something and no answer came? Maybe it was for a wayward prodigal or an unsaved mate. Perhaps you've asked God again and again for His healing touch on a nagging health problem, or for an understanding of His will in your life. It could be you've been asking God for years to find you a mate, open a door of ministry, or rescue you from a difficult personal circumstance.

In other words, you've desired with all your heart for God to do what *you* want Him to do. And there's not a single thing wrong with that. The Lord wants us to bring our requests to Him. Scripture reminds us that, "You do not have because you do not ask."[7] Clearly, Jesus told us to "keep on asking, and you will be given what you ask for. Keep on looking, and you will find. Keep on knocking, and the door will be opened."[8]

From where you stand, it seems you've been asking for good and worthy things…but for whatever reason, God hasn't budged. *And sometimes it feels like you're wrestling with Him.*

It could be that you've felt God's leading to do a certain thing or pursue a specific direction, and you've refused. You really don't want to grant Him full access to that particular area of your life, and you've actually found yourself fighting and resisting Him. Once again, you feel like you're in a wrestling match with Someone bigger and stronger than you.

Is wrestling with God a bad thing, then?

Not necessarily.

A TURNING POINT

Years ago, it happened with a man named Jacob. His wrestling match with the Almighty began with resisting and ended with resting. At first, he tried to move God his way, but in the end Jacob moved God's way. Clinging to the Lord, he said, "I will not let You go until You bless me" (Genesis 32:26).

The book of Hosea gives this brief account of that wrestling match: "Before Jacob was born, he struggled with his brother; when he became a man, he even fought with God. Yes, he wrestled with the angel and won. He wept and pleaded for a blessing from him. There at Bethel he met God face to face, and God spoke to him" (Hosea 12:3-4, NLT).

Maybe that's where you find yourself today. Fighting with God. Trying to run from Him or turn away from His work in your life. Deep in your heart, you know the Lord is pointing you in a certain direction, but you're dragging your feet. You don't want to go. You want your will, not His.

Here's what you need to know about that situation.

It won't work.

You can't win it.

Any wrestling match you have with the Lord will end in failure. *Your arms are too short to box with God.* But don't let that discourage you. The fact is, God's plan for you is infinitely better than your plan for yourself.

Perhaps you find yourself trying to do what you want to do in life, and you keep facing crisis after crisis. One step forward and three steps back. Maybe something fairly traumatic has happened in your life recently that has really gotten your attention. God has given you a wake up call beyond anything you've experienced for a long time.

If you had a little perspective on where you are right now, if you could somehow get above time and space and look down on your life, you might conclude that you're approaching a watershed moment, a turning point, an epiphany. The Bible might call it a revelation.

Let's think together in the pages of this chapter what He may be seeking to say to you.

JACOB'S BACK TRAIL

Isaac and Rebekah's fraternal twin boys, Jacob and Esau, were as different as they could be—not "identical" in any sense of the word.

Jacob, the second born, was given his name at birth when he emerged from the womb clutching his brother's heel. His parents must have believed this to be something significant, because the name Jacob means "Heel-catcher." The name might also be rendered Contender, Supplanter, or Grabber. A strange name for a baby boy, you might say. Yet it truly became prophetic of his life.

At first glance, you might conclude that Jacob's brother Esau was the more admirable of the two. Hairy as a bear, he was a man's man who loved hunting and the open fields. And Jacob? Well, he liked to hang around the family tent and help Mom in the kitchen.

But as we all know, first appearances can so often be deceptive. Time would show that Jacob—in spite of serious flaws—was a righteous man, and Esau—in spite of his apparent qualities—was an ungodly man.

Things aren't always as they initially appear. It isn't difficult to think of men and women who began the Christian life with such great promise, only to later crash and burn at the end.

Esau may have looked like he had it all together, but Scripture says he was a profane and godless man who in the end lost all that really mattered. Jacob's life was no walk in the park, either. Not many people have had more starts and stops than he had through his long life. But in the end, this son of Isaac finished well, literally limping across the finish line in the race of life.

From before his birth, God had clearly promised the birthright to Jacob[9]. Yet instead of waiting on God's provision and timing, Jacob took matters into his own hands, catching his brother at a vulnerable moment and persuading him to sell the birthright—for a bowl of stew! Make sure that no one is immoral or godless like Esau. He traded his birthright as the oldest son for a single meal. And afterward, when he wanted his father's blessing, he was rejected. It was too late for repentance, even though he wept bitter tears. (Hebrews 12:16-17, NLT)

Then to add insult to injury, Jacob conspired with Rebekah to steal the blessing of the blessing of Isaac intended for his Esau.

Jacob's basic issue was that he kept resisting doing God's work in God's way. He was always conniving, plotting, and scheming, and the repercussions of those actions would haunt him for the rest of his life. As a result of what Jacob did to his brother, Esau was ready to kill him. Realizing this, Rebekah dispatched her second-born to visit her brother Laban in faraway Paddan-aram.

And Jacob would never see his mother again.

STAIRWAY TO HEAVEN

On his way to the land of the north, Jacob had an unusual encounter with God. As he slept one night out in the open country, God gave him a stunning vision he would never forget.

Meanwhile, Jacob left Beersheba and traveled toward Haran. At sundown he arrived at a good place to set up camp and stopped there for the night. Jacob found a stone for a pillow and lay down to sleep. As he slept, he dreamed of a stairway that reached from earth to heaven. And he saw the angels of God going up and down on it.

At the top of the stairway stood the LORD, and he said, "I am the LORD, the God of your grandfather Abraham and the God of your father, Isaac. The ground you are lying on belongs to you. I will give it to you and your descendants. Your descendants will be as numerous as the dust of the earth! They will cover the land from east to west and from north to south. All the families of the earth will be blessed through you and your descendants. What's more, I will be with you, and I will protect you wherever you go. I will someday bring you safely back to this land. I will be with you constantly until I have finished giving you everything I have promised." (Genesis 28:10-15, NLT)

God was essentially saying to his wayward servant, "Jacob, please, I can do it Myself. Believe it or not, I can do this work without even you!"

So often, we get the idea that God needs us. As a result, we will try to step into the role of the Holy Spirit, and "help Him out" a little.

Listen, God doesn't need your help. He doesn't need my help. He doesn't need *anyone's* help—He's the Almighty! In the Psalms He says of Himself:

> I know all the birds of the mountains,
> And the wild beasts of the field are Mine.
> If I were hungry, I would not tell you;
> For the world is Mine, and all its fullness.
> (Psalm 50:11-12)

Jacob seemed deeply moved by the vision. He knew this was no ordinary dream, and the experience awed him.

> Then Jacob woke up and said, "Surely the Lord is in this place, and I wasn't even aware of it." He was afraid and said, "What an awesome place this is! It is none other than the house of God —the gateway to heaven!" The next morning he got up very early. He took the stone he had used as a pillow and set it upright as a memorial pillar. Then he poured olive oil over it. He named the place Bethel—"house of God."
> (Genesis 28:16-19, NLT)

You would think such a dramatic encounter with God would have changed Jacob forever, wouldn't you? Think of it! A vision of heaven, with awesome heavenly beings strolling up and down a stairway to the stars—and God Himself standing at the top of the stairs! That ought to make an impression on anyone. We can easily imagine a shaken Jacob saying, "All right, Lord. I'm a changed man. No more deception, no more trickery, no more trying to help You out."

Initially, that night at Bethel did seem to have a profound effect on him. Afterwards, a literal translation of Scripture says that "he lifted up his feet." His heart was full of joy, and he moved into a new chapter of his life with fresh confidence.

But even an experience with God doesn't guarantee we won't fall back into our old ways or our old habits. So it was with Jacob. All too soon, he slipped back into his old identity as Heel-Grabber.

REAPING WHAT WE'VE SOWN

Finally arriving at his destination, Jacob saw the beautiful Rachel and sent the other men off to water the sheep to assure he would be alone with her. Deciding he wanted to marry her (not one for waiting), he went to her father Laban.

In Laban, Jacob finally met his match—and got a strong dose of his own medicine. The con-artist met the master con-artist (they deserved each other). Laban demanded seven years labor for Rachel, *which seemed as but a few days for the love he had.*

On the wedding night, however, Laban pulled a classic bait-and-switch.

Jacob thought he was honeymooning with his beloved Rachel, but Laban had secretly substituted Leah, the older sister. It was the custom (he explained later) that the firstborn was entitled to be married first.

What was that about the rights of the firstborn?

Jacob had to learn a principle he himself had violated, and the lesson didn't go down very easy. The deceiver had been deceived, and had to work for the woman he loved for another seven years.

After being with Laban twenty years, Jacob demanded his wages that he might return home. Through a complicated sting operation, Jacob managed to coral many more sheep than the miserly Laban had planned to give him.

Jacob wanted to go home, and God gave him the green light.

Then the LORD said to Jacob, "Return to the land of your fathers and to your family, and I will be with you." (Genesis 31:3)

How could the message have been any more straightforward? *Return… and I will be with you."* It was a crystal clear word from God. Wouldn't you imagine that with an iron-clad promise like that, Jacob could have said his goodbyes with a smile and set off for Canaan at an easy pace?

Of course, that is *not* what happened. Instead of leaving well with hand-shakes all around, Jacob and his family "got out of Dodge" while Laban and sons were shearing sheep in a distant field. Instead of counting on God's blessing and protection, Jacob pretty much slipped away like a fugitive from justice.

Why the secrecy? Because he was afraid. "If I let Laban know I'm about to leave, he'll strip me of everything I own" (again, not trusting God). What Jacob did not know, however, was that his beloved Rachel had stolen the household gods. It's not clear if Rachel did this as an act of spite because of her anger over the way Laban had treated her husband, Jacob, or if she still believed in the idols herself. Maybe she felt in taking them she was essentially covering all her bases.

Laban found out, however, and didn't spare the horses chasing Jacob's tribe down on the road to Canaan. Once again, Jacob found himself reaping the hard consequences of his conniving ways.

How many lessons does it take? How many times did he have to be broken? (It's a question we might ask ourselves, isn't it?) You would think he would be saying, "Okay Lord—I get it! Let me up from the mat, You've pinned me!"

OUT OF THE FRYING PAN…

Jacob was able to work out his differences with his father-in-law, but there was still some more reaping to do. It was time to deal face-to-face with his brother he had betrayed, Esau. Jacob could not retreat. He couldn't run. He had nowhere to go but forward. And forward was where his brother Esau was. The brother he had cheated out of his birthright and blessing some twenty years earlier.

In a sense, he'd been running from Esau for twenty years, hiding out in Haran. This just reminds us that we will reap what we sow.

Scripture is clear on this subject. It might be a verse we wish would go away sometimes, but it will be there forever, so we might as well face up to it.

Don't be misled; remember that you can't ignore God and get away with it: a man will always reap just the kind of crop he sows! If he sows to please his own wrong desires, he will be planting seeds of evil and he will surely reap a harvest of spiritual decay and death; but if he plants the good things of the Spirit, he will reap the everlasting life that the Holy Spirit gives him. (Galatians 6:7-9, TLB)

If you sow a crop of righteousness and integrity you will reap that. If you sow a crop of deceitfulness, manipulation, and self-effort, you will reap that, too. Jacob had done more of the latter, and there was no escaping it. But he had received a word from God who told him it was time to return.

It was time for Jacob to own up to his past—to come face to face with the wrongs he had done. And Jacob was about to find out the hard way the truth of Proverbs 18:19: "A brother offended is harder to win than a strong city, and contentions are like the bars of a castle."

That's not to say we shouldn't try, for that's what the Lord would have us do. The Bible tells us, "If it is possible, as much as depends on you, live peaceably with all men."[10]

As he approached the dreaded moment of meeting Esau, Jacob was about to encounter the Lord in a way beyond anything he'd ever experienced. It was time for a turning point in his life. This show that God will meet us at whatever level He finds us in order to lift us to where He wants us to be.

Do you need God to come to you right now? What problem are you facing? He will be more than sufficient.

A friend of mine recently had his father die. Then a few days later, his son died in a tragic accident. One Monday he buried his father, the next Monday, his son. What could be harder than this to face? I offered what words of comfort I could find, but frankly, I didn't really know exactly what to say. He wrote me a note in response, and spoke of how Jesus had been enough. Then he added *"more than enough!"*

That's what Jesus said to Paul regarding the troubling thorn in his flesh. *"My grace is sufficient for you."* God will give you what you need when you need it. He will come to you in just the right way, as He did for Jacob. The Bible says, "Let us therefore come boldly to the throne of grace, that we may obtain mercy and find grace to help in time of need" (Hebrews 4:16).

To Abraham, the pilgrim, God came as a traveler. You remember the three mysterious visitors that came to Abraham's tent before the destruction of Sodom and Gomorrah. The Lord was one of them.[11] To Joshua, the general, Jesus came as the commander of the Lord's army, with sword drawn.[12] And to Jacob? Well, here was a man who had, figuratively speaking, wrestling with people most of his life...his father, his brother, his father-in-law, and even his two wives. So how did the Lord appear to Jacob?

As a wrestler.

It was as if He was saying to Jacob, you want to wrestle? Do you want some of this? I'll show you wrestling!

In the psalms, David spoke of how the Lord reveals Himself in different ways to different people.

> With the merciful You will show Yourself merciful;
> With a blameless man You will show Yourself blameless;
> With the pure You will show Yourself pure;
> And with the devious You will show Yourself shrewd.
> (Psalm 18:25-26)

THE ALL-NIGHT WRESTLING MATCH

And he arose that night and took his two wives, his two female servants, and his eleven sons, and crossed over the ford of Jabbok. He took them, sent them over the brook, and sent over what he had. Then Jacob was left alone; and a Man wrestled with him until the breaking of day. Now when He saw that He did not prevail against him, He touched the socket of his hip; and the socket of Jacob's hip was out of joint as He wrestled with him. And He said, "Let Me go, for the day breaks."

But he said, "I will not let You go unless You bless me!"

So He said to him, "What is your name?"

He said, "Jacob."

And He said, "Your name shall no longer be called Jacob, but Israel; for you have struggled with God and with men, and have prevailed."

Then Jacob asked, saying, "Tell me Your name, I pray."

And He said, "Why is it that you ask about My name?" And He blessed him there.

So Jacob called the name of the place Peniel: "For I have seen God face to face, and my life is preserved." (Genesis 32:22-30)

With whom did Jacob wrestle that night? It was no mere angel! This was a preincarnate appearance of God's Son. Jacob was wrestling with Jesus Christ! He called the place Peniel, which means "I have seen God face to face."

When Jacob finally got alone with God, things began to happen.

Bible commentator C. H. Macintosh wrote, "To be let alone with God is the only true way of arriving at a just knowledge of ourselves and our ways. No matter what we may think about ourselves, or what others may think of us, the great question is what does God think of us?"

When we get away from all the distractions, alone with God, we can get a correct assessment of ourselves. Some are afraid to do this! So they clutter their lives with activities. Remember Martha? She could have been sitting at the feet of Jesus, like her sister Mary, but instead she distracted herself banging around pots and pans in the kitchen.

Have you been alone with God lately? In our "connected society" do we even have a moment to think? We are barraged with information on demand, e-mail, instant messaging, cell phones, Blackberries, and on and on. The use of Blackberries is so rampant they have been described as "crack-berries"! We are all communicating with each other—constantly! People walk around with little devices clipped on their ears. You see them walking down the street by themselves, talking loudly and gesturing with their arms. They look like they're talking to you...or to themselves.

It's crazy. Are all these conversations necessary? Are we afraid to be alone with our thoughts? Or, more to the point, are we afraid to be alone with God? Where can God get a word in edgewise?

So here is the conniving plotting, scheming, Jacob all alone with God. The Lord shows up, and Jacob starts wrestling with Him! This would be like a three year old going up against Hulk Hogan. If you score a point or two, it's only because he *let you*. I suspect that God would gain a little advantage, and then allow Jacob to feel that he was gaining.

This went on and on all night long. But it was necessary. Jacob needed to reach the point where he had no more strength. The Lord continued on and on until Jacob was just about spent. Then God touched him, knocking his hip out of joint.

It was a life-changing moment for the old heel-grabber. In that instant, a change took place. Now, instead of fighting with God, Jacob clung to Him! He had a death-grip on the Lord, and would not let go.

With the night almost over, and dawn on the eastern horizon, the Lord said, "Let Me go, the day is breaking." Jacob responded, "I will not let You go unless You bless me!"

In surrender to God's plan, Jacob would find what he'd always wanted.

This is the proper kind of wrestling with God—where you are desperately calling out to Him and not giving up because you believe what you ask for is His very will. Paul mentioned it when he saw this level of get-after-it prayer in one of his co-workers in ministry. "Epaphras...is always wrestling in prayer for you" (Colossians 4:12, NIV).

Again Paul alludes to this kind of persistence and struggle in prayer in Romans 15: "Dear brothers and sisters, I urge you in the name of our Lord Jesus Christ to join me in my struggle by praying to God for me. Do this because of your love for me, given to you by the Holy Spirit" (v. 30, NLT).

Yes, prayer can sometimes be a struggle. In that light, we start to see wrestling matches all over scripture.

We see Abraham, praying with persistent intensity for Sodom.[13]

We find Moses spending forty days and nights fasting and pleading mercy for Israel.[14]

We find Elijah, pressed to the ground with his face between his knees, praying seven times for God to send rain.[15]

We see this persistent intensity of prayer again and again with David, when he calls out, "Hear my prayer, O LORD, and give ear to my cry; do not be silent at my tears."[16]

So don't give up! Keep praying for that work of God in your life, where you will be more like Jesus. Keep praying for that healing for you or someone else, unless God directs otherwise. Keep praying for the salvation of that loved one. Keep praying for that spiritual awakening our country needs to experience.

After Jacob had lost this match, the Lord asked him an unusual question. *"What is your name?"* (Genesis 32:7).

Why did the Lord ask this of Jacob? Had he suddenly been afflicted with short term memory loss so that he couldn't remember his own name?

No, it wasn't that. God asked because for Jacob to state it was an *admission*—and one he didn't really want to make. As we have said, the name Jacob meant "heel-catcher, supplanter, grabber." In essence, the Lord was asking Jacob, "Are you going to continue living up to your name, continually deceiving others? Or will you admit what you are and let Me change you?"

This was a question only Jacob could answer. And it's a question God asks each of us as well.

"Do You Want To Be Made Whole?"

The apostle John tells the story of a man who had suffered from a severe disability for thirty-eight very long years. For much of that time, he had waited by a little pool of water in Jerusalem called Bethesda. The local story about that place said that an angel would periodically appear and stir up the water—and whoever scrambled into the water first would be healed.

So the disabled man sat there day after day, night after night, just waiting and hoping.

Then Jesus walked by.

The Lord saw him lying there, and knew he already had been in that condition a long time. He said to him, "Do you want to be made whole?"

Why would Jesus ask such a question. Wasn't it obvious a man in this state would want to change?

Not necessarily.

As strange as it may seem, there are many people today who don't want help. They like the lifestyle they've chosen. They find a certain comfort there. They feel security in the darkness. It's home to them just like a pigsty is home to a pig. It's comfortable, and they really don't want to come to the light or make changes in their lives. This pattern continues on until eventually these people become so hardened in their sin that they prefer the dark ways of eternal death.

Scripture says, "A man who remains stiff-necked after many rebukes will suddenly be destroyed—without remedy" (Proverbs 29:1, NIV). Along that same theme, Oswald Chambers wrote: "Sin enough and you will soon be unconscious of sin."

That was the case with Jacob. When God asked him, "What is your name?", He was essentially saying, "Do you want to be a Heel-Grabber forever? Do you really want to live this way—conniving, scheming, lying, manipulating—or would you like to let Me take control and change your life?"

God will not force His will or His way in our lives. He asks us, "Are you finally willing to give *Me* control? Jesus said, "Take My yoke upon you and learn of me...." A yoke is a steering device. Jesus was saying, "Let Me steer and guide your life! Are you willing?"

I can't help wondering what Jacob must have thought when that all-night wrestling match began. Was it a bandit? Was it one of Laban's angry sons? Was it an assassin sent by Esau—or maybe Esau himself? The more he wrestled however, the more he came to understand that this was no ordinary mugger in the dark. Something big was in the works!

Jacob wasn't wrestling with God to get something from Him, rather God was wrestling with Jacob to get something. What was it? *Surrender.* It was to reduce Jacob to a sense of his nothingness, to cause him to see what a poor, helpless, and weak person he really was.

Before Jacob ever walked the planet, God brought a man named Job to the same place. After his own long wrestling match with the Almighty, he surrendered with the words: "I am nothing—how could I ever find the answers? I will put my hand over my mouth in silence. I have said too much already. I have nothing more to say" (Job 40:4-5, NLT).

Perhaps the main reason God challenged Job to a wrestling match was for you and me. In Jacob, we learn the all important lesson that our true strength lies in admitting our weakness.

Why? For the same reason He sent most of Gideon's army home, or told the great Namaan to strip off all his clothes and dunk seven times in the muddy Jordan. Or repeatedly went out of His way to find obscure instruments to work through like Jeremiah, David, or Peter. Because, as He says in 2 Corinthians 12:9, "My grace is sufficient for you, for My strength is made perfect in weakness." A more literal reading of the verse tells us: *"My grace is enough for you, for power is moment by moment coming to its full energy and complete operation in the sphere of weakness."*

Again, by losing you win.

Through defeat you find victory.

Have you ever had God wrestle with you when you wanted your way or were persisting in some course that you knew displeased Him? Maybe that's even happening to you right now. I'll give you a hint of what the outcome will be. You're going to lose, and lose big!

But don't let that frighten you. Again, God's plan and pur-pose for your life is far better than any you may have thought up for yourself.

Jacob had finally surrendered. Instead of fighting with the Lord he asked for His blessing. God had brought him from cunning to clinging, from resisting to resting. Jacob had now been brought to the end of his resources, and having surrendered, he was given a new name...*Israel*.

Scholars differ on the meaning of the name. It has been variously translated as "One who God commands," "Let God rule," "One who fights victoriously with God," or "A prince with God." Still another renders it, "God's fighter."

Whatever the precise meaning of Israel, it's clear that a complete surrender took place in Jacob's relationship with God. God was saying "You are no longer the heel-catcher, the supplanter. Now you are a Prince with God, God's fighter!"

And now in the long-dreaded encounter with Esau—and beyond—God Himself would be his advocate. And from that time on, the countless descendants of Jacob would be known by his new name, Israel.

Jacob may have lost the wrestling match, but by doing so, he scored the biggest victory of his life. At last, Jacob had surrendered himself. He won by losing and now was able to go on in new strength as he walked in God's power, will, and timing.

This is precisely what Jesus meant when He said, "He who finds his life will lose it, and he who loses his life for My sake will find it."[17]

In his second letter to the church at Corinth, Paul spoke about a wonderful-if-mysterious aspect of the Christian life. He wrote:

> And we, who with unveiled faces all reflect the Lord's glory, are being transformed into his likeness with ever-increasing glory, which comes from the Lord, who is the Spirit. (2 Corinthians 3:18, niv)

At a lonely place called Peniel, Jacob saw God's face, and his life changed forever. Paul is saying that we too are changed when we gaze into His face. The face of God always changes Jacobs to Israels, grabbers to receivers, supplanters to princes and princesses.

No doubt about it, we all have our Esaus. We all have those situations in life that cause us great fear and stress. But when we have spent time alone with God, seeing His face, it can transform and prepare us for whatever lies ahead.

Surrender to God and discover His plan for your life. If you've felt like you can't win for losing, try losing to the God who loves you and experience the biggest win of your life.

Chapter Six

ENCOUNTER IN EGYPT:
STANDING STRONG IN LIFE'S STORMS

We all know the story of Cinderella. A poor, unloved girl grows up in a house with her cruel stepmother and jealous step-sisters. Through a set of stunning circumstances, she is given the opportunity to attend the royal ball at the palace. But what will she wear? Her clothing is little more than rags.

Depending on which version you've heard, she is aided by a bunch of mice and a fairy godmother, who pitch in to create a stunning evening gown. Cinderella goes to the ball looking like a princess, meets the handsome prince, loses her glass slipper, becomes the object of a kingdom-wide woman hunt, and ends up in the forest with seven dwarves.

Or…something like that.

Now that's called a fairy tale, and you might tell yourself that it's beyond belief and really just for fun. It's an enjoyable bedtime story and makes a great Disney cartoon, but that's about as far as it goes.

But I know a story that's far more extraordinary than any Cinderella tale—whatever the version. And what makes this story all the more remarkable is that it's true.

This is a story that has the earmarks of a great novel—a page turner. The author weaves all of the elements of an enthralling plot through its pages: jealousy, betrayal, sex, intrigue, an international crisis—and dreams come true! Throw attempted murder, a seductress, and accusations of rape into the mix, and you've got a real summer sizzler.

But it's so much more than that. It's also an historical account of real people working through situations that remind us of trials in our own lives. And if those things weren't enough, it's a story that reveals the Lord at work in the daily experience of His own. The hand of God shows up in every scene, ruling and overruling the decisions people make. And in the end, God builds a hero, saves a family, and creates a nation that will bring blessing to the whole world.

Cinderella is pablum, truly kids' stuff, compared to the real-life drama springing out of the first book in the Bible. The story of Joseph is the classic rags to riches tale, as he rose from complete obscurity and unbelievable adversity to the second most powerful position in all of Egypt—the superpower of his day. Here was a young man who clung to his faith in the living God, even in the face of gross injustice and crushing disappointments. As a result, God's blessings on his life were mighty.

THE RISE OF A HERO

Joseph's life initially showed little promise. A simple shepherd boy, twelfth of thirteen children—he was a young man apparently given to visions of grandeur. As any other teenager, Joseph enjoyed sleeping. But there was a difference. When Joseph experienced a couple of strange dreams, he firmly believed they were from God Himself.

And they were.

To his older brothers, it appeared this kid had his "head in the clouds," always trying to dodge a hard day's work. Yet young Joseph was on his way to becoming God's man. Daring to be a dreamer, he was transformed from a favored (perhaps pampered), immature, naïve teenager into a great world leader.

If anyone could have ever had an excuse for turning out bad, it was Joseph. He grew up in the midst of a family dominated by lying, deceit, immorality, manipulation, and even murder. He could have turned out rotten to the core—and blamed his step-mom, dad, brothers, and like many others, even God Himself.

For seventeen years he put up with these challenges, and surprisingly turned out to be a godly young man with a sterling character. Joseph's life is a strong illustration of Psalm 76:10:

> Human opposition only enhances your glory,
> for you use it as a sword of judgment. (NLT)

Do you live in an ungodly, messed up, dysfunctional home that might qualify for an appearance on the Jerry Springer show? Take heart. It can't be any worse than Joseph's home! God preserved and blessed him, and He can do the same for you.

As I look back on my own upbringing, being raised in a home of seven divorces and alcoholism, I can see how God preserved me. Even when I was a little boy, He was working in my life, setting me into an earnest "search-mode," as I sought to understand the meaning of life.

As with Joseph, the age of seventeen was a turning point in my life. For that was the age I was when I gave my life to Jesus Christ after hearing the Gospel on my high school campus.

Looking back now, I really don't blame anyone for anything. In fact, God has been able to use my past as I've pursued my ministry. I can better understand the skepticism that so many have toward the Gospel, for I once had it myself.

SOLD DOWN THE RIVER

> Now Jacob dwelt in the land where his father was a stranger, in the land of Canaan. This is the history of Jacob. Joseph, being seventeen years old, was feeding the flock with his brothers....Now Israel loved Joseph more than all his children, because he was the son of his old age. Also he made him a tunic of many colors. (Genesis 37:1,2,3)

You would have thought that Jacob's own painful personal experience with favoritism in his growing up years would have convinced him to never repeat that destructive pattern. What a mess that had been! Isaac had openly favored Esau, Jacob's twin brother, while mother Rebekah clearly loved Jacob the most. And it ended up tearing the family apart.

It could happen to any of us. If we're not careful, if we're not drawing our wisdom and strength from the Lord, we can fall back into the same old negative parenting techniques that we hated so much growing up. Jacob favored Joseph because he was the son of the only woman he ever really loved—his beautiful, long-departed Rachel. He doted on the boy, indulging him and spoiling him to the point that his older eleven brothers were thoroughly disgusted.

Adding salt to that wound, Jacob presented Joseph with a multi-colored tunic—or "coat of many colors," as it says in the King James Version. Yet another translation calls it "a richly ornamented robe."

This was more than a case of young Joseph getting the nicest school clothes in the family. Basically, this was a long-sleeved garment that extended to the angles. Obviously you can't do to much manual labor in a fancy coat like that. In Joseph's day, the working garb was a short, sleeveless tunic, leaving the arms and legs free. When Joseph wore that fancy coat around, it would be like going to work in a tuxedo. In fact, we read in another place in scripture that this kind of garment was worn by royalty.

It was a clear statement that Jacob planned on giving "firstborn" status to Joseph, the youngest. By giving a coat of this sort to Joseph, Jacob was essentially saying, "You don't have to work like your brothers."

No wonder his siblings became bitter! No doubt their resentment grew deeper with every passing day. But matters went from bad to worse when Joseph took upon himself the role of family informant. That *really* enraged them.

> Joseph…was feeding the flock with his brothers. And the lad was with the sons of Bilhah and the sons of Zilpah, his father's wives; and Joseph brought a bad report of them to his father. (v. 2)

As a young Christian, I could be very hard on people. Several people took me aside in those days, pointing out how I was always correcting others. Do I do that today? I hope not! I'm banking on the assumption that as you grow in knowledge, you also grow in grace as well. It's not a matter of lowering your standards, it's more an issue of finding balance. Paul tells us to "let your conversation be gracious and effective so that you will have the right answer for everyone" (Colossians 4:6, NLT).

In the eyes of Joseph's brothers, however, he was nothing less than a snitch. But the fact of the matter is, Joseph was a godly man. Scripture says "Everyone who does evil hates the light, and will not come into the light for fear that his deeds will be exposed."[18] If you have taken an unpopular stand for righteousness as a Christian, you already know what it's like to be ostracized, rejected, mocked, or even hated.

However honest and godly Joseph may have been, you would think he might have used a little more tact! Showing up in his fancy Dad-loves-me-best coat to check on the brothers he had already reported on probably wasn't the best idea. The story of Joseph's betrayal might have been different if he had left the cloak hanging up in a closet at home on that trip.

These brothers were so filled with anger and venom they couldn't say a kind word to him. Was he oblivious to this? And what about reporting the dreams that had his brothers bowing down to him, paying him homage? Couldn't he have kept those things to himself? Was he actually flaunting his favored position in the family, standing there in his multi-colored tunic, speaking of ruling over everyone—a mere seventeen-year-old boy?

Then to make matters worse he related yet another dream, this time to his dad. In this second dream, Joseph saw all his brothers and even his father and stepmother bowing before him. In reality, that was a prophetic dream from the Lord, because that is exactly what happened years later, when he became the vice-Pharaoh.

But sometimes it's not wise to talk freely about the all the dreams, visions, or things that God has revealed to you. Sometimes the wiser course is to be like Mary, the mother of Jesus, when she was confronted with the supernatural. Scripture says she "quietly treasured these things in her heart and thought about them often."[19]

When Joseph finally found his brothers in that remote place, their thoughts immediately turned to murder.

> Then his brothers went to feed their father's flock in Shechem. And Israel said to Joseph, "Are not your brothers feeding the flock in Shechem? Come, I will send you to them."
>
> So he said to him, "Here I am."
>
> Then he said to him, "Please go and see if it is well with your brothers and well with the flocks, and bring back word to me." So he sent him out of the Valley of Hebron, and he went to Shechem.
>
> ...So Joseph went after his brothers and found them in Dothan. (Genesis 37:12-17)

The brothers went off to tend to the sheep in Shechem. Genesis 34 tells us that this was a place of dark memories. It was the very area where their sister Diana had been raped—and where Simeon and Levi committed mass murder in retaliation. As you might imagine, there was still "bad blood" between the sons of Jacob and the dwellers in that area. Jacob, probably concerned about their safety, sent Joseph to check up on them and bring word back.

Big mistake.

Now when they saw him afar off, even before he came near them, they conspired against him to kill him. Then they said to one another, "Look, this dreamer is coming! Come therefore, let us now kill him and cast him into some pit; and we shall say, 'Some wild beast has devoured him.' We shall see what will become of his dreams!" (vv. 12-14, 17-20)

"Here comes the dreamer!" they mocked. They had almost decided to kill him, but instead threw him into a pit. Providentially, a caravan of slave traders were passing by, and so they sold their brother for 20 pieces of silver. Taking Joseph's beautiful coat, the brothers soaked it in goat blood, and sent it to Jacob, saying a wild animal had killed him.

Jacob was devastated. He went into deep mourning and would not be comforted. It crushed him to the very core.

And Joseph? He found himself on his way to Egypt, in chains. He had been abandoned by man—even by his own brothers. *But not by God.* In fact, God would begin to show Himself strong on Joseph's behalf through the many trials that were to come. One day, the young man would come to learn the truth about God expressed by Corrie Ten Boom: "There is no pit so deep that He is not deeper still."

STRANGER IN A STRANGE LAND

Now Joseph had been taken down to Egypt. And Potiphar, an officer of Pharaoh, captain of the guard, an Egyptian, bought him from the Ishmaelites who had taken him down there. The LORD was with Joseph, and he was a successful man; and he was in the house of his master the Egyptian. And his master saw that the LORD was with him and that the LORD made all he did to prosper in his hand. So Joseph found favor in his sight, and served him. Then he made him overseer of his house, and all that he had he put under his authority. So it was, from the time that he had made him overseer of his house and all that he had, that the LORD blessed the Egyptian's house for Joseph's sake; and the blessing of the LORD was on all that he had in the house and in the field. Thus he left all that he had in Joseph's hand, and he did not know what he had except for the bread which he ate. (Genesis 39:1-6)

Sold into slavery by his own brothers, Joseph soon found himself in a county and culture he didn't know, surrounded by a language he didn't understand. He had truly gone from feasting to famine. His world came crashing down overnight! Think about it. One night Joseph was safe and secure, tucked in his own bed, the next night possibly shackled and shivering as he was carted off like an animal to be sold on the open slave market. The bottom had dropped out for Joseph in a mere matter of hours. But that wasn't the end of the story. Not by a long shot. He was soon to experience success beyond anything he had ever known.

His dreams were going to come true.

Egypt was a completely pagan country filled with religious superstition. The people recognized at least 2,000 gods and goddesses, including the Pharaoh himself. The Egyptians were great builders, and the rulers conscripted both slaves and their own citizens for vast building projects. Into this teeming city of wickedness and idolatry came Joseph, a wide-eyed country boy far from home.

As providence would have it, Joseph was purchased by a man named Potiphar, a captain of the guard and high-ranking Egyptian official. He most likely served as head of the military police assigned as the royal bodyguard—the secret service of his day.

Clearly, Potiphar was not a man to be trifled with. Yet Scripture tells us, "The LORD was with Joseph, and he was a successful man; and he was in the house of his master the Egyptian" (Genesis 39:2).

Do you remember reading about the blessed man in Psalm 1?

> He shall be like a tree
> Planted by the rivers of water,
> That brings forth its fruit in its season,
> Whose leaf also shall not wither;
> And whatever he does shall prosper.
> (v. 3)

That was Joseph. Whatever he did, prospered. Success followed him like his shadow. He had the "Midas touch" because he kept his priorities straight. Though he had been stripped of his coat, he had not been stripped of his character. And he clearly did *not* hide his faith from his powerful, intimidating master. Scripture gives us these incredible words:

> And his master saw that the LORD was with him and that the LORD made all he did to prosper in his hand. (Genesis 39:3)

Potiphar, a hardened, pagan military officer, recognized and acknowledged the hand of the living God on this teenager's life. The Lord was with him. Joseph was really a model of how a Christian should function in the workplace. Faithful and hard-working, he was a young man who did his very best.

Augustine wrote: "Preach the Gospel, and when necessary use words." Because of his hard work and integrity, Joseph was promoted and given a great platform for his faith. Perhaps Solomon had Joseph in mind when he wrote: "Do you see a man who excels in his work? He will stand before kings; he will not stand before unknown men."[20]

Joseph's behavior and performance were so outstanding and above reproach he became Potiphar's executive assistant! But all of this hard work was not only a blessing to the household, but to Joseph as well. Had he stayed home with his pampering father, Joseph might not have developed the kind of character that comes from hard work and obeying orders. This was a time of testing in his life, for if he was going to learn to be a leader, he must first learn how to be a servant.

Maybe you find yourself in such a time right now—laboring somewhere in obscurity, keeping long hours and doing hard work without much recognition. You wonder at times, *Will my day ever come? Does anyone even notice what I'm doing here? Will God ever use me?* Know this...Your Father, who sees you in secret, will one day reward you openly.

Needless to say, Satan wasn't one bit happy about this turn of events in Joseph's life. Perhaps sensing God's significant plans for this young man, Satan had set out to utterly destroy Joseph—first by casting him in a pit, then by selling him as a slave. But everything Satan threw at Joseph seemed to boomerang, and work out for good. Now the son of Jacob found himself in good standing in the household of a powerful Egyptian official.

But the Evil One wasn't through yet. He was about to strike another devastating blow.

WHEN TEMPTATION COMES

We never really know when we're about to be hit with a serious test. You can wake up on an ordinary morning, have your usual bowl of cereal, take your every-day route to school or the office, and begin your walk through what would seem to be a day like a hundred other days before it.

Yet by the afternoon, you could find yourself in the biggest crisis of your life. That's the way it must have been with Joseph, as he went about his normal duties as an overseer in Potiphar's household.

What he was about to face was in many ways a more difficult trial than being sold into slavery by his own brothers. As a robust, healthy, twenty-something young man, with hormones running at their peak, he was about to be blindsided by sexual temptation. How would he handle it? How would he handle this new position of prestige and power?

When we are struggling to get ahead in life or find ourselves facing some kind of crisis, we often turn to God in complete dependence and weakness. We realize just how frail, vulnerable, and susceptible we really are, and we cling to Him. But when success comes, when the health is good, when the bills are paid and the skies are blue, we sometimes tend to forget the very God who brought us to that point.

Greater success leads to greater times of vulnerability. Prosperity, acclaim, and success can put us directly in the cross-hairs of hell. All of us should walk very,

very carefully in life, but men and women who have reached new levels of success and prominence in the business world or in ministry need to be especially alert.

Our human tendency is to begin to take such things for granted, to let down our guard a little, to ease back. Before long, we get lazy, sloppy, slothful. And that is when the enemy springs a surprise attack, firing his flaming arrows at our faith, commitment, and integrity.

Think for a moment about the life of David. When did temptation hit him between the eyes? It wasn't when he was a lonely shepherd boy, watching over the flock out in the wilderness (and wrestling the occasional lion or bear). It wasn't when he was running for his life from the paranoid King Saul, hiding in desolate canyons and gloomy limestone caves. No, David got hit when he was at the *top* of his game. He was king. He was rich. He was famous. He was powerful. He was well loved. He had a powerful ministry leading his nation to the throne of God in praise and worship.

But one fateful spring day, after sending Joab out to lead the army (instead of leading it himself), David decided to kick back and take it easy for awhile. Feeling a little restless that evening, he took a walk on his rooftop terrace....

As it turned out, David was a much safer man dealing with adversity than with prosperity. And so it is for many of us. Our enemy knows very well that "pride goes before destruction, and a haughty spirit before a fall."[21]

The Proposition

And it came to pass after these things that his master's wife cast longing eyes on Joseph, and she said, "Lie with me."

But he refused and said to his master's wife, "Look, my master does not know what is with me in the house, and he has committed all that he has to my hand. There is no one greater in this house than I, nor has he kept back anything from me but you, because you are his wife. How then can I do this great wickedness, and sin against God?" So it was, as she spoke to Joseph day by day, that he did not heed her, to lie with her or to be with her.

But it happened about this time, when Joseph went into the house to do his work, and none of the men of the house was inside, that she caught him by his garment, saying, "Lie with me." But he left his garment in her hand, and fled and ran outside. And so it was, when she saw that he had left his garment in her hand and fled outside, that she called to the men of her house and spoke to them, saying, "See, he has brought in to us a Hebrew to mock us. He came in to me to lie with me, and I cried out with a loud voice. And it happened, when he heard that I lifted my voice and cried out, that he left his garment with me, and fled and went outside." (Genesis 39:7-15).

Joseph was certainly a good looking young guy. Verse 6 says that "Joseph was handsome in form and appearance." Another translation says, "Joseph was a very handsome and well-built young man."[22]

Joseph may have been both shocked and flattered by this offer from Pot's wife. Those advances had to be a tremendous ego boost. Imagine how a slave would feel being approached by a beautiful, powerful woman. No doubt, Mrs. Potiphar wife was attractive and alluring.

Keep in mind that for about ten years now, he's been saturated with Egyptian values. Those old values he had learned from his parents must have seemed a little rusty or archaic by this time. At the very least, they would have seemed quite distant. Besides that, *no one would ever know*. They were completely alone. He could have easily rationalized, "When in Egypt, *walk like an Egyptian*."

But deep in Joseph's heart was the conviction that even if no one else might find out about their little fling, *God* would know.

"How then can I do this great wickedness, and sin against God?"

Joseph knew very well that God was watching. And God was and is watching each and every one of us as well.

Verse 8 tells us that "he refused." Now that may seem impossible to do to in a moment of intense temptation...but it isn't. Joseph had evidently made that determination a long time before the lustful Mrs. Potiphar cornered him in the bedroom. Joseph recognized that temptation is not a sin; it's a call to battle.

What made this particular temptation so difficult was that it went on and on. The Bible says, "She kept putting pressure on him day after day, but he refused to sleep with her, and he kept out of her way as much as possible" (Genesis 39:10, NLT).

Maybe after he had resisted that first time, he breathed a sigh of relief. But the woman was relentless. And you can bet she knew how to dress and how to present herself in a way that would make it as difficult as possible on the young man.

But if she propositioned Joseph again and again, he resisted again and again. Temptation—any temptation—can be effectively resisted! As scripture says "Submit yourselves, then, to God. Resist the Devil, and he will flee from you."[23]

The reason it seems like we "can't resist" at times is because we have set ourselves up for a fall. We have filled our minds with lustful things, and we're like rags doused in gas waiting for the match. For temptation to properly work its evil there must be a desire on our part. The apostle James writes: "But each one is tempted when he is drawn away by his own desires and enticed. Then, when desire has conceived, it gives birth to sin; and sin, when it is full-grown, brings forth death" (James 1:14-15).

For Satan to succeed, we must listen, yield, and most importantly *desire* what he offers. Satan will use different types of bait to tempt us, but remember, it's not the bait that constitutes sin, it's the bite! Potiphar's wife dropped the bait day after day in front of Joseph, but he kept saying "no." How? I see four points in Joseph's successful battle with temptation.

1. Everyone Will Be Tempted

We may think that if we're really spiritual or mature in the Lord, we won't be tempted any more. But the very opposite is true. If you are truly spiritual you *will* be tempted. Why? Because you are a direct threat to Satan and his agenda.

At the very beginning of His ministry, Jesus was led into the wilderness to be tempted by the Devil. At the end of His ministry, on the cross, Satan tempted Him through the thief and the soldiers who challenged Him to come down from the cross if He was really the Son of God.

If Jesus faced temptation from the beginning to the end, so will we. An old minister was asked by a young man, "Preacher, when will I cease to be tempted by sins of the flesh?"

The wise old man said, "Son, I wouldn't trust myself until I'd been dead three days!"

2. Sin Has Consequences

"Look," he told her, "my master trusts me with everything in his entire household. No one here has more authority than I do! He has held back nothing from me except you, because you are his wife." (Genesis 39:8-9, NLT)

Joseph was loyal to the man who had trusted him and been so good to him. He thought about how this sin would affect others. When he could have easily thought only of himself ("I want this...I deserve this"), Joseph rather said, "I can't do this, because it would hurt Potiphar."

In the same way, when you're tempted to have that affair, or have sex before marriage, it might be a good idea for you to stop and think about somebody besides yourself. Your spouse, your family, your parents, the other person, their family. *Everyone* is affected by unfaithfulness and sexual immorality.

And how about thinking about that person's spouse, or spouse to be? And what about their children?

Listen, you have no right take something that belongs to them. And most importantly, think of the damage this can do to the cause of Christ. What a terrible witness it is when a believer falls in this way. In fact, it's just the same as giving ammunition to our enemies. As the prophet Nathan told David, "You have given the enemies of the Lord great opportunity to despise and blaspheme him."[24]

And just for the record, if you begin a relationship with an act of betrayal and immorality—no matter who this person may be—it will not work out. One researcher has stated that of those who break up their marriage to marry someone else, 80 percent are sorry later. Of those who do marry their lover—which happens only about 10 percent of the time—nearly 70 percent will end up divorcing their new spouse. Of that 25 to 30 percent who stay married, only half of them are happy.[25]

Committing adultery throws open the door to a storm of pain and tragedy, with the effects rolling on for the rest of your life, and the lives of your children as well.

3. God's Standards Are Absolute

The years, decades, and centuries may come and go, but God's standards don't change. It didn't matter that Joseph had been mistreated and had a rough childhood. It didn't matter that he was far from home. It didn't matter that he was lonely. It didn't matter that the Egyptian culture was completely immoral. And it didn't matter that Joseph's life was completely taken from him and that he was forced to be a slave.

Wrong is wrong.

Given enough time and enough motivation, every one of us is capable of rationalizing almost anything. If we want something bad enough, if we entertain the desire long enough, we can talk ourselves into lies that would have shocked and repelled us at an earlier point in our lives.

I'm lonely. I need this.

He/she has a selfish, unresponsive spouse.

God wants me to be happy.

I can always ask for forgiveness later.

If he had been so inclined, Joseph could have come up with a list of justifications for adultery as long as your arm. But he refused to indulge such thoughts, and denied them room to take root in his soul.

4. All Sin Is Against God

"How then can I do this great wickedness, and sin against God?"

This—not fear of the consequences—should be our strongest deterrent against sin. Yes, dreading what God might do or allow to happen to us if we turn against Him is certainly a factor. *But the greatest deterrent against sin is a consuming love for God.* Our response to temptation is an accurate barometer of that love.

The psalmist wrote: "Let those who love the LORD hate evil, for he guards the lives of his faithful ones."[26]

Our Father hates sin, and so should we as His children. The Bible tells us to "Abhor what is evil. Cling to what is good" (Romans 12:9). We may try to justify certain sins—jealousy, anger, revenge, and so on—against "certain people," because we feel they deserve it. But as David said, "Against you, and you alone, have I sinned; I have done what is evil in your sight."[27]

Besides that, Potiphar was not a believer, and Joseph knew that. And to violate God's will in this matter would irreparably damage his witness. Though God will forgive us, others may not—at least not so quickly—and a tarnished reputation is very difficult to repair.

Joseph could have played around the edges with adultery, dabbling in it, like Samson who thought he could "always handle it." He, like Lot, was "worn down by sin" and was soon so hooked he failed to notice how Delilah was no longer even subtle. *"Please tell me what makes you so strong and what it would take to tie you up securely."*[28] Delilah must have been one enticing lady to keep Samson coming around the way he did.

Joseph wasn't afflicted with brash self-confidence, either—like Simon Peter. *"Even if all fall away on account of you, I never will.... Even if I have to die with you, I will never disown you."* (Then what was he doing just a few hours later by that charcoal fire?) Scripture says, "Let him who thinks he stands take heed lest he fall."[29] Joseph, however, knew very well that he was vulnerable—so he fled!

There's an old Chinese proverb that says: "He who would not enter the room of sin must not sit at the door of temptation." This is basically a no-brainer. It would be like walking across a field and coming upon a coiled rattlesnake, looking at you through those glazed, beady eyes, ready to strike. What do you do? Try to negotiate with the rattler? Reach some sort of a compromise perhaps? Do you just stand there, or maybe even approach it to show how strong you are? If so, I hope your will is in order! No, if you have half a brain you back off and run as fast as you can.

Flee temptation—and don't leave a forwarding address. Every temptation is an opportunity to flee to God.

> And so it was, when she saw that he had left his garment in her hand and fled outside, that she called to the men of her house.... (v. 13)

Joseph preferred to leave his jacket behind rather than lose his hide. And this young man's "No" to her was a "Yes" to God.

Are you being tempted right now in some area of your life? Does it seem like too much to handle, too strong to resist? That's not true! God promises us that He will *not* give you more than you can handle (see 1 Corinthians 10:13).

As we, like Joseph, resist each temptation, we will grow stronger with every passing day. Not in our own strength but in God's. Recognizing our vulnerability, we will distance ourselves from anyone or anything that could potentially pull us down.

You'll be glad you did in the long run. It's far better to shun the bait than to struggle on the hook.

THE LESSON OF JOSEPH'S BROTHERS

What happened to Joseph's brothers, back in Egypt? As you zero in on the end of the story in Genesis 42-50, it's obvious that they were never able to put their treacherous act behind them. Through the long years, the knowledge of what they had done gnawed away at their souls like acid. I'm guessing they could never look their dad straight in the eye from that day forward. Whenever Joseph's name came up, it must have been like a knife twisting in their hearts. Even on the best days of harvest or feasting or gatherings of the family, there would always be that shadow of guilt and regret.

We sold our own brother as a slave.

We've deceived our father for years.

He's surely dead now, and it's our fault.

I think there are at least two lessons to be learned in the latter chapters of Joseph's story.

1. Never Let Envy And Jealousy Get A Foothold In Your Life

These are among the more subtle but deadly sins in the satanic arsenal. They're like time bombs ticking away, waiting to explode. Left unchecked, these sins can lead to far worse. The apostle James wrote: "For wherever there is jealousy and selfish ambition, there you will find disorder and every kind of evil."[30]

As we saw in Chapter Two, envy is what filled Cain's heart resulting ultimately in murder. Envy is what drove the Pharisees to crucify Jesus. Pilate accurately diagnosed the situation: "He knew for envy they had delivered Him" (Matthew 27:18).

What a wicked thing jealousy is. Shakespeare called it "The green eyed monster that mocked." William Penn said, "The jealous are troublesome to others; a torment to themselves."

The sad truth is, our old nature doesn't like to see others succeed sometimes. Paul warned some of the people in Corinth: "You are still controlled by your own sinful desires. You are jealous of one another and quarrel with each other. Doesn't that prove you are controlled by your own desires? You are acting like people who don't belong to the Lord."[31]

An ancient Greek story tells of a statue erected in honor of a famous athlete. A rival athlete was so enflamed with envy he vowed to destroy the monument. So every night in the dark, he chiseled at its base to weaken its foundation. But when it finally fell, it fell on him, crushing him.

So nip envy in the bud before it crushes you! F. B. Meyer has the best advice: "At the first consciousness of sin, seek instant cleansing in the precious blood of Christ...."

2. God Will Work All Things Together For Good

"Do not be afraid, for am I in the place of God? But as for you, you meant evil against me; but God meant it for good, in order to bring it about as it is this day, to save many people alive." (Genesis 50:19-20)

It's easy for us to see (now) how God worked all the events of Joseph's life for good, because most of us know the end of the story. But *he* didn't! All he knew was that he was a boy who had been sheltered by his doting father from many of the harsh realities of life, and now he had lost it all—probably forever. He was a common slave in a faraway country, and all his dreams had turned to ashes.

In every way, however, Joseph's life illustrates the truth of Romans 8:28:

And we know that all things work together for good to those who love God, to those who are the called according to His purpose.

"We know...."

Those things that happen to us in life have nothing to do with fate, random chance, or dumb luck. Doris Day's old hit song expresses the attitude of many: *"Que sera, sera, whatever will be, will be. The future's not ours to see. Que sera, sera...."*

While it's true that we can't see over the horizon and know the future, we can know that there is a master plan for every believer, custom-designed by the Creator Himself. *I may not know what the future holds, but I know who holds the future.*

God works "all things" in life for our good—not just the "good things" or happy things. The psalmist wrote: "for all things serve you."[32]

This doesn't mean that all things are good things, for there are many circumstances and occurrences in our lives that, in themselves, aren't good at all! They are painful and bitter. Yet ultimately their place in the whole pattern of God's divine purpose will cause them to be resolved ultimately into good—on our behalf.

The phrase "work together" in Romans 8:28 could better be translated "are working together." In other words, there are no breaks or lapses in God's good plan for your life. It's not as though it's operational today, but goes off-line tomorrow. God is always paying careful attention to even the smallest detail of your life, and is in complete control of all circumstances that surround you.

Our God never sleeps. As it says in the psalms, "Behold, He who keeps Israel shall neither slumber nor sleep" (Psalm 121:4).

Aren't you glad God doesn't take a sabbatical and put you on voice mail when you pray? You know...push #1 if you need forgiveness...push #2 if you need healing...push #3 if you need direction...push #4 if you have another problem.

Our God is always on duty. David could readily say, "God is our refuge and strength, a very present help in time of trouble."

Corrie Ten Boom used to show the reverse side of an embroidered bookmark which seemed to be nothing but a senseless mass of tangled threads.

Then she would turn the bookmark over, where the threads spelled out in a beautiful design, "God is love."

That was Joseph's experience. Tangled years. Impossible knots. A jumble of seemingly meaningless and random trials. But at the end of it all…the Master Craftsman revealed the beauty, worth, purpose, and healing of His design.

And so it will be with you, as you place your whole life—past, present, and future—into His skillful hands.

Chapter Seven

ENCOUNTER AT PHARAOH'S COURT: REJECTING A COMPROMISED LIFE

There is no soft, politically correct way to say it: Prior to coming to know Jesus Christ, you were under the power and control of the Devil. He had been jerking your chain for quite a long time...

...promising pleasure, he brought you misery...

...promising fun, he brought you guilt...

...promising life, he brought you death....

And the most clever strategy of all was causing you to think he didn't even exist! You thought you were in control all this time.

Then one day it hit you like a lightning bolt from heaven, and your eyes were opened. You not only realized there was a Devil, but more importantly, a God he was trying to keep you from. A God who loved you enough to send His own Son to die on the cross.

You realized you could find meaning and purpose in this life, and the absolute hope of heaven in the next. You carefully thought about it. You counted the cost. And finally, you took the plunge and made a stand for Jesus.

I hope you weren't expecting a standing ovation in hell.

THE EVIL EMPIRE STRIKES BACK

The Devil is not happy with your decision to follow Christ. In fact, it enrages him. He's lost one of his own! But he's not going to take it lying down. He will hit back—hard. Someone has said, "Conversion has made our hearts a battlefield." The genuine believer may be known by his inward warfare as well as his inward peace. In fact, if you are *not* experiencing this spiritual tug of war, that in itself is cause for concern.

What we are facing here is a spiritual battle with a very real adversary. So if you are feeling beat up, if you've been experiencing what seems like more than your share of temptations and attacks, cheer up! It's a strong indicator that you are doing the right thing and heading in the right direction.

Satan knows all too well he cannot overpower God. His strategy, then—really from the beginning of time—has been to draw men and women out from under God's protection and covering. If he can persuade you to live in the realm of your will, your plans, your perspective, and your own strength, then he has you where he wants you...and you are in grave danger.

Know this: the Devil may be evil, but he is no fool. He's not about to tip his hand and show you what he's really up to in your life. He didn't want you to believe in Jesus in the first place, but once you give your heart to Christ, he has to concede that battle. But that doesn't mean the war is over. Now his purpose in your life is to persuade you to compromise, and in the process, spiritually neutralize you.

So he will try to take you one bite at a time, through the subtle yet extremely effective medium of compromise. This technique is well illustrated in the story before us in this chapter.

One-On-One With Pharaoh

This is the story of Moses and his confrontation with the Pharaoh over the deliverance of the Israelites from Egypt.

The Lord had told Moses to go back to Pharaoh's court, back to the very place where he had grown up, for a face-to-face encounter with the king who may have been the most powerful man in the world at that time.

God had made it very clear to Moses that he was to take the Jews a good three days journey from the land of the bondage. And He warned him that this battle of wills with Pharaoh wasn't going to be a walk in the park.

> "You must go straight to the king of Egypt and tell him, 'The LORD, the God of the Hebrews, has met with us.
>
> Let us go on a three-day journey into the wilderness to offer sacrifices to the LORD our God.'
>
> "But I know that the king of Egypt will not let you go except under heavy pressure. So I will reach out and strike at the heart of Egypt with all kinds of miracles. Then at last he will let you go. (Exodus 3:18-20, NLT)

The Lord was warning Moses that Pharaoh would harden his heart, *and would not let them go.*

In this we have a picture of the Devil and his unwillingness to let his captives go. Let's consider the passage together.

> Afterward Moses and Aaron went in and told Pharaoh, "Thus says the LORD God of Israel: 'Let My people go, that they may hold a feast to Me in the wilderness.'"
>
> And Pharaoh said, "Who is the LORD, that I should obey His voice to let Israel go? I do not know the LORD, nor will I let Israel go."
>
> So they said, "The God of the Hebrews has met with us. Please, let us go three days' journey into the desert and sacrifice to the LORD our God, lest He fall upon us with pestilence or with the sword." (Exodus 5:1-3)

So...the big moment had finally come.

Moses may have thought he could just stroll into Pharaoh's court, demand the release of God's people, and that would be that. Pharaoh would comply, and the Israelites would be on their way to the land of milk and honey.

But not so fast.

Pharaoh wasn't about to let go easily. And Moses was about to run into a brick wall. It's often the same for us. Sometimes we think the will of God should always be smooth sailing. After all, if Almighty *God* is involved in this thing, then He'll just steamroll all the obstacles out of the path.

But sometimes He doesn't...for His own good reasons.

Not only did Pharaoh flatly refuse to release the Jews, he actually increased their workload!

Ever have one of those bad days when nothing seems to be going your way? Or have you ever been certain that something is the will of God, but instead of the doors opening as you expect, they seem to slam shut in rapid succession?

That's surely how Moses must have felt that day. There he was, doing the hard thing, obeying God and boldly walking into the inner sanctum of this world superpower, and demanding the release of the Israelites. Now Moses knew this wasn't going to be a one-two-three game of hopscotch. But he certainly hadn't anticipated a complete disaster! And that's what he got.

By the end of Exodus 4, Moses and his brother Aaron had already met with the leaders of Israel, and told them of their God-given mission. Moses even did miracles to show he had indeed been sent by God. The miracles had the desired effect, and they agreed together and prayed. Moses and Aaron went before Pharaoh with the blessing of the people and the leading of God.

> So Moses and Aaron went in to Pharaoh, and they did so, just as the LORD commanded. And Aaron cast down his rod before Pharaoh and before his servants, and it became a serpent.
>
> But Pharaoh also called the wise men and the sorcerers; so the magicians of Egypt, they also did in like manner with their enchantments. For every man threw down his rod, and they became serpents. But Aaron's rod swallowed up their rods. And Pharaoh's heart grew hard, and he did not heed them, as the Lord had said. (Exodus 7:10-13)

In verse 3, the Lord says, "I will harden Pharaoh's heart." What does that mean? Does it mean Pharaoh really had no choice in the matter—that he was little more than a robot, and just did what God made him do? The word "harden" could also be translated, *strengthen*, or *stiffen*. So what was God really doing? He was strengthening Pharaoh in the decision the Egyptian king had *already made*.

A HEART OF CEMENT

As we will see, Pharaoh began to harden his heart when Moses and Aaron performed this first of many miraculous signs. He hardened his heart further when the magicians counterfeited the signs. He even hardened it when his magicians could not counterfeit the signs. It just got harder and harder—like quick-dry cement.

The Lord had given him more than enough evidence to convince him that the "gods of Egypt" were false, and the God of Israel was the true and living God. God was giving Pharaoh a chance to cooperate. He was dealing in love and longsuffering with Pharaoh. Scripture records the true heart of God:

> As surely as I live, says the Sovereign LORD, I take no pleasure in the death of wicked people. I only want them to turn from their wicked ways so they can live. Turn! Turn from your wickedness, O people of Israel! Why should you die? (Ezekiel 33:11-12, NLT)

God was leaving the door open for Pharaoh to change his mind, *but he would have none of it.* To turn from the truth is to become more thoroughly entrenched in darkness. Pharaoh saw miracles and heard the Word of God, and that brings responsibility. He had to *do* something with what he had seen and heard. He had to consider the evidence right before his eyes and make a decision. But one rejection led to another and another. And with every rejection, his heart turned further away from the Lord...until he came to that point where the door was shut and locked, and he had no inclination to change—ever.

The writer of the Hebrews issues this warning: "You must warn each other every day, as long as it is called 'today,' so that none of you will be deceived by sin and hardened against God" (Hebrews 3:13, NLT).

We often think the worst thing that can happen to a person is if they become entangled in some sinful lifestyle with drugs, illicit sex, alcohol, partying, and so on. But appearances can be deceiving. If that individual still retains a soft heart and a tender conscience, there is hope that he or she may hit bottom, and in desperation reach out to God. But once a person becomes hard—deliberately steeling their heart and turning away from the truth—the hope of reaching them with the Good News grows fainter and fainter.

And how do we become hardened? *By continued exposure to the truth of God and a refusal to obey and respond to it.*

In other words...you know it's true, yet you don't accept it. You accept it intellectually, yet you don't respond. You become hardened by the very truth that should have softened you. As with Pharaoh, you become judged by the very message that should set you free.

God had sent a series of ten plagues or judgments to bring Pharaoh to his senses, each one gaining in intensity as Pharaoh allowed his heart to cure like concrete in the afternoon sun. What makes this drama even more interesting is that there was a specific strategy behind these judgments. Each was leveled at a specific "god" of Egypt.

The nation of Egypt claimed millions of gods, worshiped in thousands of temples across the land. God leveled these judgments to show the emptiness and futility of any god when compared with the true and living One.

The account tells us that Moses' rod became a serpent. The serpent was one of the special creatures in Egyptian religion—particularly the cobra, which was a symbol of immortality.

But note how Satan countered this miracle.

But Pharaoh also called the wise men and the sorcerers; so the magicians of Egypt, they also did in like manner with their enchantments. For every man threw down his rod, and they became serpents. (Exodus 7:11-12)

Here is something we need to understand about Satan: He is an *imitator*.

KNOCK-OFFS FROM HELL

Our adversary will try to stop a work of God altogether, but if that doesn't work, he will *imitate* it. In this way, he not only deceives people, he minimizes the power and glory of God. The purpose is to neutralize the impact of our life and testimony—and to divert us from the truth.

Do you desire a relationship with God? You need to be careful...and discerning. Satan offers a plethora of false religions laden with rituals and symbols—with just enough truth to keep you from *real* truth.

Jesus told a story about a farmer who had an enemy. Late one night after the farmer had sown his fields with wheat, the enemy slipped in under the cover of darkness and sowed tares—or darnel seeds—throughout the same fields. As the tares begin to sprout, they look just like wheat—you can't tell the difference. But in the end, the tares actually uproot the wheat, and destroy the crop.

That's one of Satan's strategies. He has flooded the market with cheap substitutes of truth, each with enough accuracy to make it appealing, but enough poison to make it deadly. Cyanide with a dark chocolate coating.

One of the sobering things this passage in the book of Exodus teaches is that Satan can do miracles, too, imitating the signs and wonders Moses and Aaron had performed in the presence of Pharaoh. These miracles were completely within his power.

This is why I am always suspicious of so-called "miracle ministries." Satan is in the miracle business, too! None of the apostles had "miracle ministries"... they had a simple call to proclaim Jesus. The signs would follow their ministries, but they were never the primary focus. You never read in the book of Acts where the apostles would announce a "healing service" ahead of time. Rather, God healed where and when He chose to—often as a direct confirmation of the message of the Word of God.

Scripture tells us that in the last days, the Antichrist will have a "miracle ministry."

This evil man will come to do the work of Satan with counterfeit power and signs and miracles. He will use every kind of wicked deception to fool those who are on their way to destruction because they refuse to believe the truth that would save them. So God will send great deception upon them, and they will believe all these lies. (2 Thessalonians 2:9-11)

The second satanic beast in the book of Revelation was also given power to perform "great and miraculous signs, even causing fire to come down from heaven to earth in full view of men" and "because of the signs he was given power to do...he deceived the inhabitants of the earth" (Revelation 13:13, 14, NIV).

In view of these powerful counterfeits, the apostle John warns us, "Do not believe every spirit, but test the spirits , whether they are of God; because many false prophets have gone out into the world" (1 John 4:1). God's Word is our measuring stick.

Let's look now at the various plagues God sent to Egypt.

THE TEN PLAGUES

Plague 1: The Nile River Turns To Blood

God directed Moses to stand on the bank of the Nile and wait for Pharaoh to join him there. Moses was instructed to tell Pharaoh that he had been sent by God to deliver the Israelites. Then he described the impending judgment:

"Thus says the Lord: 'By this you shall know that I am the Lord. Behold, I will strike the waters which are in the river with the rod that is in my hand, and they shall be turned to blood. And the fish that are in the river shall die, the river shall stink, and the Egyptians will loathe to drink the water of the river.'"

Then the Lord spoke to Moses, "Say to Aaron, 'Take your rod and stretch out your hand over the waters of Egypt, over their streams, over their rivers, over their ponds, and over all their pools of water, that they may become blood....'"

But not sooner had the judgment been leveled against Egypt than Pharaoh's court magicians duplicated it.

Then the magicians of Egypt did so with their enchantments; and Pharaoh's heart grew hard, and he did not heed them, as the Lord had said. And Pharaoh turned and went into his house. Neither was his heart moved by this. (Exodus 7:16-19, 22-23)

How did they do it? How did these pagan magicians duplicate the miracle of turning water into blood? Slight of hand? Smoke and mirrors? Demonic power? It would have been a bit more impressive if they had been able to turn the bloody Nile water back into clean water, rather than simply duplicating God's judgment. (Whoever said sin made sense?)

But the enchanters did accomplish one thing. It was all the excuse Pharaoh needed to once again harden his heart to God's word.

The ancient Egyptians revered the Nile River as a god. Not only that, the river was basic to life itself. Well-water in that day was often contaminated, so the Egyptian depended on the Nile for all his water needs—bathing, cooking, cleaning, laundry, and of course drinking.

To strike the Nile was to strike at the very heart of Egypt. And it also showed that their so-called "god" had no power to help them.

Plague 2: An Invasion Of Frogs

God told Moses to go back to Pharaoh and demand the release of the Israelites or all of Egypt would be covered in *wall-to-wall frogs*.

Once again Pharaoh refused to budge. Believe it or not, even the frog was a god to the Egyptians. (For that matter, so was the dung beetle.) The frog deity (no, it wasn't Kermit) was called "Heqet." This goddess of the resurrection, fertility, and childbirth had the head of a frog. In this judgment, God was essentially saying, "You want gods? I've got gods for you." And the invasion was on.

> "I will send vast hordes of frogs across your land from one border to the other. The Nile River will swarm with them, and they will come out into your houses, even into your bedrooms and right into your beds! Every home in Egypt will be filled with them. They will fill your ovens and your kneading bowls; you and your people will be immersed in them!" (Exodus 8:2-4, TLB)

Immersed in frogs! Can you imagine?

When I lived in Hawaii as a young boy, we used to have lots of frogs. It was always an adventure having one in the house and stepping on it in your bare feet. But the Egyptians couldn't walk anywhere without stepping on countless, slimy, croaking frogs. They were in their ovens, their dishes, even their beds. You try to sleep at night and you've got frogs crawling across your face.

Pharaoh's magicians, however, copied this miracle, too. They couldn't get rid of the frogs; but they could evidently summon more of them. (Just what everyone needed.)

This time, however, God at least had Pharaoh's attention. He asked Moses to entreat God to *get rid of those frogs,* and then they could discuss releasing all the Jews from captivity. So Moses and Aaron cried out to the Lord, and the frogs all croaked, *en masse.* They gathered the dead frogs together in great heaps and the Bible says *the land stank.*

But when Pharaoh saw that there was relief, he hardened his heart yet again, and refused to heed the word of the Lord.

This is so typical of many non-believers. They will call on God to get them out of some crisis, resulting from their own sinful choices. They will make great and lofty promises of what they will do in return—after God rescues them. Then, when God comes through, they shrug their shoulders, chalk it up to coincidence, and go back to their old ways.

I heard about a hospital chaplain who kept a record of some 2,000 patients with whom he had visited, all apparently in grave condition, who had responded to gospel and showed signs of repentance. But among those who rallied and returned to health, only *two* followed through on their commitment to follow the Lord.

Pharaoh somehow convinced himself that the water-turned-to-blood and the invasion of frogs were some freak anomalies of nature, and his heart went back into lock-down.

And then came the gnats.

Plague 3: "Gnats All, Folks"

Then the Lord said to Moses, "Tell Aaron, 'Stretch out your staff and strike the dust of the ground,' and throughout the land of Egypt the dust will become gnats." They did this, and when Aaron stretched out his hand with the staff and struck the dust of the ground, gnats came upon men and animals. All the dust throughout the land of Egypt became gnats. But when the magicians tried to produce gnats by their secret arts, they could not. And the gnats were on men and animals. (Exodus 8:16-18, NIV)

This third plague came with no warning at all. Oftentimes in His grace and mercy God will warn us of what is coming if we continue in sin, giving us time to repent. But if He sees an ongoing, willful pattern of outright disobedience, He just might spring a surprise attack.

These gnats (or lice, in some translations) were apparently biting, stinging insects that penetrated the nostrils and ears of their victims—and every square inch of skin that happened to be exposed. This was especially hard for the Egyptians, who were fanatical about cleanliness. The priests would frequently wash and shave their bodies in order to be acceptable to their gods. And now they were crawling with bugs!

Note also that these plagues were getting progressively worse. The plague on the Nile was a blow to everyone, but people adapted and got by. The frogs were a gross nuisance. People were sickened by them, but no one was hurt.

But these gnats...this was becoming unbearable.

Interestingly, Pharaoh's magicians could not duplicate this plague. They told their boss, "This is the finger of God."[33]

With that strong pronouncement from his own inner circle, would Pharaoh begin to think about repenting? Would he still harden his heart?

In fact, he would. A man or woman's heart can grow so hard to God that only the most radical measures will get their attention.

Plague 4: Enter...The Swarm

And the Lord said to Moses, "Rise early in the morning and stand before Pharaoh as he comes out to the water. Then say to him, 'Thus says the Lord: "Let My people go, that they may serve Me. Or else, if you will not let My people go, behold, I will send swarms of flies on you and your servants, on your people and into your houses. The houses of the Egyptians shall be full of swarms of flies, and also the ground on which they stand...." And the Lord did so. Thick swarms of flies came into the house of Pharaoh, into his servants' houses, and into all the land of Egypt. The land was corrupted because of the swarms of flies. (Exodus 8:20-21, 24)

If you're reading from the New King James Bible, you will note that when Scripture says "swarms of flies," the words *of flies* are in italics, meaning, they weren't in the original. In other words, the Lord brought *swarms* into the house of Pharaoh and into all the land.

The Hebrew words for swarm means "mixture," speaking of a massive jumble of creepy, crawly, multi-legged, tentacled insects. This would include spiders, fleas, ticks, and flying beetles. (The first instance, perhaps, of "Beatlemania.")

But something very interesting happened with this plague. God intervened in an astounding way for His people. Within the Lord's message to Pharaoh were these pointed words: "And in that day I will set apart the land of Goshen, in which My people dwell, that no swarms of flies shall be there, in order that you may know that I am the Lord in the midst of the land. I will make a difference between My people and your people. Tomorrow this sign shall be" (Exodus 8:22-23).

This swarm of creepy crawlers swept every corner of Egypt except Goshen. Goshen was bug free.

Once again, Pharaoh had to admit he was outgunned—or outplagued. But rather than waving the white flag and surrendering to God, he simply changed his tactics, offering a series of compromises. In this, we see a picture of the Devil's strategy to bring us down...a little here, and a little there.

Then Pharaoh called for Moses and Aaron, and said, "Go, sacrifice to your God in the land."

And Moses said, "It is not right to do so, for we would be sacrificing the abomination of the Egyptians to the Lord our God. If we sacrifice the abomination of the Egyptians before their eyes, then will they not stone us? We will go three days' journey into the wilderness and sacrifice to the Lord our God as He will command us."

So Pharaoh said, "I will let you go, that you may sacrifice to the LORD your God in the wilderness; only you shall not go very far away. Intercede for me" (Exodus 8:25-28)

What had God specifically commanded Moses and the Israelites? "We will go three day's journey into the wilderness and sacrifice to the LORD our God as He will command us."

But Pharaoh, like the proverbial used car salesman, tried to work the angles.

"Sure, go sacrifice. *But do it in the land.*"

"Fine. Go ahead and follow your God. *But don't go very far.*"

Wasn't he being fair-minded and reasonable? Not at all, because any compromise of obedience to God's commands is *disobedience*.

God had specifically commanded a three-days journey into the wilderness—the whole nation, young and old, along with their livestock and children. God wanted ample room between the people and their Egyptian overlords.

But Pharaoh wanted to play "Let's Make a Deal," and tried to draw Moses in with a few concessions. They could worship their own God if they wanted to. They could go a little ways away. Wasn't that reasonable?

No. It was a trap. You don't make deals with the Devil. If God calls for a complete break, *He means a complete break.*

Do you see how subtle the enemy's tactics can be? If he can't get us to go completely his way, he will seek to draw us just a little bit in his direction. It's not a complete denial of what we know is right and true...it's just a compromise. We push back from our old habits, our old lifestyle, or our old unbelieving crowd, but we don't make a clean break. The Devil says to us, "Fine, believe in God if you must. Do your little religious thing if it makes you feel better. But be practical about it! Don't be a fanatic. You can have your cake and eat it too."

The Bible, however, warns us against such compromises. In the book of Ephesians, Paul says, "Do not give the Devil a foothold."[34]

That's all he's looking for, you know. A foothold. A toehold. A chink in your armor. Give him an inch, and he'll take a mile. Give him a minute, and he'll take an hour...or a day...or a decade. You cannot make deals with Satan. You will always lose if you do. The Bible says, "You cannot drink from the cup of the Lord and from the cup of demons, too. You cannot eat at the Lord's Table and at the table of demons, too" (1 Corinthians 10:21, NLT).

How we need to guard our hearts on this issue! The apostle Paul reminds us that Satan seeks to outwit us with his schemes.[35] For instance...let's say you're sharing the gospel with someone who is dragging you down spiritually. It might be a romantic relationship (a mistake). At some point, you wisely decide to break it off, only to have the man or woman respond, "But I'm getting closer to coming to Christ! Don't cut me off—pray for me."

In Exodus 8:28, Pharaoh wrapped up his little compromise offer with the words, "Intercede for me." *Pray for me, Moses.*

If Moses hadn't been on his guard, he might have thought, "Well...Pharaoh is softening. He wants me to pray for him. Maybe this little compromise wouldn't be so bad." But that's not what happened. Moses certainly agreed to intercede for the king. He said: "As soon as I leave you, I will pray to the LORD" (8:29, NIV). But he wasn't fooled—and he wasn't willing to walk a single inch away from the Lord's clear commands.

What are we saying here? We should never shy away from trying to influence and win people to Christ. But if we yoke ourselves to them, if we compromise our faith or our convictions to please them, it is *we* who will be pulled down, they won't get pulled up.

Paul stated this clearly in his letter to the believers in Corinth:

> Don't team up with those who are unbelievers. How can goodness be
> a partner with wickedness? How can light live with darkness? What
> harmony can there be between Christ and the Devil? How can a be-
> liever be a partner with an unbeliever? And what union can there be
> between God's temple and idols? For we are the temple of the living
> God. As God said:

> "I will live in them and walk among them. I will be their God, and they
> will be my people. Therefore, come out from them and separate your-
> selves from them," says the Lord. (2 Corinthians 6:14-17, NLT)

If Pharaoh couldn't keep them *in* Egypt, he would at least try to keep them *near* it. Why? So they would still be under Egypt's influence...and because it would be easier to reel them back in again. The fact is, if you're not willing to "go far away," then you'd better not go at all.

Plagues 5, 6, And 7: Pestilence, Boils, And Hail

Pestilence on the livestock and boils on everyone was followed by a severe hailstorm. How severe? This storm would have made prime time on the Weather Channel for weeks on end.

> The Lord sent thunder and hail, and lightning flashed down to the
> ground. So the Lord rained hail on the land of Egypt; hail fell and light-
> ning flashed back and forth. It was the worst storm in all the land of
> Egypt since it had become a nation. Throughout Egypt hail struck ev-
> erything in the fields—both men and animals; it beat down everything
> growing in the fields and stripped every tree. (Exodus 9:22-25, NIV)

Where were Pharaoh's ace magicians in all this? They were out of the picture because they, too, had issues with the head-to-toe boils.

And the magicians could not stand before Moses because of the boils, for the boils were on the magicians and on all the Egyptians. (Exodus 9:10)

The boils-and-hail one-two punch was just too much for Pharaoh. He finally showed signs of cracking.

So Moses and Aaron were brought again to Pharaoh, and he said to them, "Go, serve the LORD your God. Who are the ones that are going?"

And Moses said, "We will go with our young and our old; with our sons and our daughters, with our flocks and our herds we will go, for we must hold a feast to the LORD."

Then he said to them, "The LORD had better be with you when I let you and your little ones go! Beware, for evil is ahead of you. Not so! Go now, you who are men, and serve the LORD, for that is what you desired." And they were driven out from Pharaoh's presence. (Exodus 10:8-11)

Pharaoh was willing to let them go, but...not with the kids. He knew that if they went to the wilderness while the children remained in Egypt, they'd come right back again. He would have them on a short leash.

Once again, however, God's man stood firm. Moses refused this compromise as well.

Plagues 8 And 9: Locusts And Darkness

By the time the ninth plague rolled around, Pharaoh was ready for one final, desperate grasp at accommodation.

Then Pharaoh called to Moses and said, "Go, serve the LORD; only let your flocks and your herds be kept back. Let your little ones also go with you." (Exodus 10:24)

One more time, Pharaoh attempted to sound magnanimous. "Okay, go to the wilderness. Sacrifice to your God. And take your kids, since you insist on it. Just leave the animals behind."

Again, this is a picture of how our adversary, the Devil, will fight us tooth and nail for every inch of kingdom territory. He does not yield ground easily.

Why would Pharaoh care about their animals? Think of the progression here: First, he tried to keep the near the land. Next, he tried to get them to leave part of themselves in the land. And finally, he attempted to send them out without any sacrifices to offer to the Lord.

But Moses would have none of it. I love his response in verse 26: *"Not a hoof shall be left behind!"*

That's what we need to say to our adversary: Satan, you get nothing. Nada. Zip. Zero. You've ripped me off long enough, and I'm not going to give you so much as the time of day. *Get behind me!*

Are you trying to live the Christian life but toy with the dark side? Are you trying to keep one foot in both worlds?

Stop. Now. Before it's too late.

If Moses had compromised, he would have found himself outside the protection and power of God...and Pharaoh would have eaten him alive. And remember how Scripture describes our enemy: "Be careful! Watch out for attacks from the Devil, your great enemy. He prowls around like a roaring lion, looking for some victim to devour."

And the solution?

Take a firm stand against him, and be strong in your faith. Remember that your Christian brothers and sisters all over the world are going through the same kind of suffering you are. (1 Peter 5:8-9, NLT)

This is the only way to live a fruitful and successful life as a Christian. Otherwise, you will place yourself in a self-imposed wilderness of wandering, a miserable state of compromise...where you have "too much of the Lord to be happy with the world...and too much of the world to be happy with the Lord." You won't be able to enjoy fellowship with the Lord and His people, and you won't feel comfortable on the dark side, with Satan's people.

Standing on the barren top of Mount Carmel, silhouetted against the sky, the prophet Elijah challenged Israel, "Choose you this day whom you will serve."

We should respond like Joshua, who confronted his nation's compromises and said, "As for me and my house, we shall serve the LORD."

Chapter Eight

ENCOUNTER AT SINAI, PART 1: PUTTING GOD FIRST

T hank God for absolutes. In His wisdom and mercy, God has given us bedrock truths on which to build our lives, regardless of the shifting winds of modern culture. Those absolutes, standing strong and tall through the millennia, are the Ten Commandments.

It is my conviction that one of the reasons for the unprecedented blessings and great success of the United States of America over our 200 plus year history can be found in our origins, in the fact that our founding fathers built this country on a belief in Scripture and in the Ten Commandments.

James Madison, the man most responsible for the U.S. Constitution, wrote: "We have staked the whole future of American civilization, not upon the power of the government, far from it. We have staked the future of all our political constitutions upon the capacity of each and all of us to govern ourselves according to the Ten Commandments of God."

Abraham Lincoln said, "But for the Ten Commandments, we wouldn't know right from wrong."

That is certainly a far cry from where we are today. It seems like every time you turn around there's a new attempt to ban the commandments from public view, or remove every evidence of them from courtrooms, classrooms, and public squares.

It's ironic, because we desperately need to know and follow these commandments—not only for our personal survival, but for the survival of our nation. The fact is, we can either accept their truths, or fight against them and reap the inevitable results.

A LIGHTHOUSE IN THE FOG

Vance Havner said, "You cannot break the laws of God. You break yourself against them." Unfortunately, that is not the opinion of many today. Many of us don't like to be told what to do.

Consider the words Ted Turner, founder of CNN: "We're living with outmoded rules. The rules we're living under is the Ten Commandments, and I bet nobody here even pays much attention to 'em because they are too old. When Moses went up on the mountain, there were no nuclear weapons, there was no poverty. Today, the commandments wouldn't go over. Nobody around likes to be commanded. Commandments are out."

So what do we have in the place of the Ten Commandments? *Moral relativism*. It is the outright denial of any moral absolutes. In other words there is no right or wrong. It teaches that we are all products of the evolutionary process. There is no God, no plan, nor purpose for our lives. And Satan? Well, he's nothing more than a medieval myth.

Moral relativism teaches that we make our own luck or fate. We are all basically good inside, and if we go bad, it's because we are products of our environment. When it comes to truth, well, each of us has our own truth. The result is a life (or so they would like to think) of complete freedom from all restraint. And if you happen to disagree with this philosophy, holding on to a belief in right and wrong, you are an insensitive, intolerant, narrow-minded bigot! If you dare to quote the Bible, then you are imposing your puritanical value system. ("Cramming it down their throat"...have you heard that one before?)

Many of our young people are being raised with only the flimsiest of value systems. A recent article in the *Boston Globe* chronicled a phenomenon called "moral illiteracy" on America's college campuses. It started when William Kilpatrick, a professor of education at Boston College, began noticing what he would come to call signs of moral illiteracy among his students.

In one of his classes, they were discussing the Ten Commandments, and Professor Kilpatrick wanted to list them on the board. "It wasn't that individuals couldn't think of them all," he related later. "The whole class working together to come up with the complete list couldn't do it."

No wonder 67 percent of Americans say there is no such thing as right and wrong. A Barna report showed Generation X leading the way toward moral relativism. Born between 1965 and 1983, this generation rejected absolute truth by a staggering 78 percent.

I'm a chaplain with the police department, and recently attended a briefing on gang activity in our city. Here you have an entire sub-culture with their own values, rules, and beliefs.

I asked what the solution was.

The officer in charge said, "It has to happen in the home."

The cure for crime is not in the electric chair but in the high chair, laying a godly foundation for our children and their children. It's time to get back to God's unchanging absolutes. It's time to go back to the Ten Commandments. They are straight forward, concise, to the point—a clear grid to live by. In a culture where morality has been lost in the fog, the Ten Commandments are like the bright beam from a lighthouse, showing us right from wrong, good from evil, true from false, up from down—and warning lost and disoriented lives away from the rocks.

After wasting his life and unimaginable potential, Solomon wrote these words at the close of the book of Ecclesiastes: "Now all has been heard; here is the conclusion of the matter: Fear God and keep his commandments, for this is the whole duty of man."[36]

The whole duty of man. That's another way of saying that if a man or woman keeps God's commandments, he or she will be a whole person. Solomon himself had violated many of these commands and knew what he spoke of.

For instance, when he said, "Nothing my eyes desired did I keep from them," it was a direct violation of the tenth commandment: *"You shall not covet."* When he stated, "I had concubines," he was living in opposition to the seventh commandment: *"You shall not commit adultery."* As an old man looking back on his failures and tragic decisions, Solomon is saying, "If you violate these—if you turn your back on God's commandments—your life will be out of balance. And you will be the great loser."

MEANWHILE, BACK AT MOUNT SINAI...

When we last left Moses he was demanding the release of the Israelites from a persistently hard-hearted Pharaoh. Finally—and with great reluctance—the Pharaoh agreed...only to change his mind again and set off in hot pursuit.

When they stood at the brink of the Red Sea, God opened up a path through its midst for Israel to cross on dry land—but closed it back on the pursuing Egyptian armies. As they advanced through the wilderness, the Lord led His people with a cloud by day and a pillar of fire by night. Each and every day He had manna waiting for them to sustain them on their journey.

Now they have come to Mount Sinai, and God instructs Moses to ascend, while the people remain behind, and wait for God's Word. Up in that awesome, frightening cloud at the top of the mountain, God began to deliver His Ten Commandments to His servant.

And God spoke all these words, saying:

"I am the LORD your God, who brought you out of the land of Egypt, out of the house of bondage.

"You shall have no other gods before Me.

"You shall not make for yourself a carved image—any likeness of anything that is in heaven above, or that is in the earth beneath, or that is in the water under the earth; you shall not bow down to them nor serve them. For I, the LORD your God, am a jealous God, visiting the iniquity of the fathers upon the children to the third and fourth generations of those who hate Me, but showing mercy to thousands, to those who love Me and keep My commandments.

"You shall not take the name of the LORD your God in vain, for the LORD will not hold him guiltless who takes His name in vain.

"Remember the Sabbath day, to keep it holy. Six days you shall labor and do all your work, but the seventh day is the Sabbath of the LORD your God. In it you shall do no work: you, nor your son, nor your daughter, nor your male servant, nor your female servant, nor your cattle, nor your stranger who is within your gates. For in six days the LORD made the heavens and the earth, the sea, and all that is in them, and rested the seventh day. Therefore the LORD blessed the Sabbath day and hallowed it.

"Honor your father and your mother, that your days may be long upon the land which the LORD your God is giving you.

"You shall not murder.

"You shall not commit adultery.

"You shall not steal.

"You shall not bear false witness against your neighbor.

"You shall not covet your neighbor's house; you shall not covet your neighbor's wife, nor his male servant, nor his female servant, nor his ox, nor his donkey, nor anything that is your neighbor's." (Exodus 20:1-7)

If you and I set out to reorganize the Ten Commandments, we might list them differently, moving murder or adultery to the top of the list. Surely, "Having another God before Him" is not as serious as *those* sins.

But for God, breaking commandment Number One is the Number One offense. In the eyes of heaven, there is nothing worse than putting another god before the true and living One.

One day a man came to Jesus and asked Him, "What is the greatest commandment?"

Jesus answered him, "The first of all the commandments is: 'Hear, O Israel, the Lord our God, the Lord is one. And you shall love the Lord your God with all your heart, with all your soul, with all your mind, and with all your strength.' This is the first commandment. And the second, like it, is this: 'You shall love your neighbor as yourself.' There is no other commandment greater than these." (Mark 12:29-31)

With that statement Jesus really sums up the Ten Commandments. "Have no other gods before Me" is *the first of all.* It's also the one most of us don't think we ever break. A survey revealed that 76 percent of all Americans consider themselves completely faithful to the first commandment.

Is that true? Have most Americans avoided placing another "god" in the place of the God of the Bible?

I doubt that. But let's check it out…let's take a closer look at the implications of that primary command.

DEALING WITH NUMERO UNO

It all starts with the place of God in your life.

Why? *Because you will serve who or what you worship.* Jesus said, "You shall worship the Lord your God, Him only shall you serve." If God is Who He says He is, then He deserves our undivided attention. If the Lord is Number One in your life, everything and everyone else will find its proper balance. But if He's not in first place, everything else will be in chaos. Note the wording that the Lord uses here in Exodus 20:2:

"I am the LORD your God, who brought you out of the land of Egypt, out of the house of bondage."

It's amazing how much can be revealed by a simple little word such as "I." This little pronoun, only one letter long, conveys a profound and fundamental truth about who God is. As James Kennedy points out, when He said, "I am the Lord," He is refuting all other belief systems—including pantheism, polytheism, deism, and New Age thinking.[37]

When Moses stood before the burning bush out in the desert, God declared the essence of His identity: "I AM WHO I AM…Thus you shall say to the children of Israel, 'I AM has sent me to you.'"[38]

When God said "I Am," He revealed that He is a person. He was in essence saying, "I am, I feel, I act." God is not, as pantheism teaches, an impersonal force.

Pantheism alleges that All is God, the universe is God, everything is God. Plants. Trees. Rocks. Bugs. You name it. But the Lord says, "I am the LORD, and there is no other; there is no God besides Me" (Isaiah 45:5).

Polytheism—such as practiced by Hindus—believes in many gods. But God didn't say "We are the Lord, your gods." He said, "I am the Lord, your God." As Paul said so clearly to Timothy, "For there is one God and one Mediator between God and men, the Man Christ Jesus, who gave Himself a ransom for all."[39]

Deism proposes that God created the world, wound it up like a clock, then went off and forgot all about it. Deists would say that God has no interest in the affairs of men. But the Bible clearly reveals a God who sees, hears, and cares. And this same God, *Yahweh*—who led, protected, and blessed His people—still wants to do that today for us.

New Age thinking claims that the answer is inside of you. You are God. New Age thinking is nothing but the original lie of Satan recycled for our times in hip, politically correct terminology. In the Garden, remember, the Evil One said to Eve, "You shall be as gods….." Malcolm Muggeridge has aptly noted that "all new news is old news happening to new people."

Today, we have substituted religion for faith, and "spirituality" for godliness. *Spirituality.* That's clearly the buzzword of the day. "I'm not into organized religion," people will tell you, "I'm simply a spiritual person."

As a culture, we want to have our cake and eat it, too. We want a belief system, but one that doesn't get in our way or place boundaries on our lives. As you might imagine, there all sorts of leaders and proponents willing to step forward for this "new and improved spirituality."

In contrast to all of that, we have God's bedrock truth in these commandments—inscribed by His very finger.

In the preamble to the Ten Commandments, God reminds the Israelites of what He had already done for them. How He had so graciously answered their prayers and demonstrated His love. How He brought them from a miserable life of slavery and delivered them.

This is the God who gives them basic rules for living. He doesn't start by threatening or scaring them. He starts by reminding them of what kind of God He is: A loving, caring God who rescued them from captivity and a hopeless future.

Well, that's great for *them*, you might say. But I've never been a slave in Egypt. True...yet you were a slave to sin on your way to Hell. But God loved you so much He sent His son Jesus to die on the cross in your place. Now if we really appreciate what He has done, if we know anything of His all-encompassing forgiveness, it should be our privilege and pleasure to live a life pleasing to Him. Not because we have to but because we want to! *We love Him because He first loved us.*

COMMANDMENTS 1 AND 2: "NO OTHER GODS, NO IDOLS"

What does it mean to have another god before Him?

In many places in the world, you can still see grotesque idols carved from wood or stone, and people bowing down to them and worshiping them. But in America? That's not something we see very often—even in Southern California, where I live.

The truth is, "other gods" covers a lot more territory than that.

An idol is anything or anyone that takes the place of God in our lives. And know this, *everybody has a God.* Even atheists have a god. They might call it "knowledge" or "human reason" or "science," but it is their god, nonetheless, and one whom they worship and serve.

The question is: who or what is your God? What gets you excited? What gets you out of bed in the morning? What do you think about most? What do you dream about, plan for, perhaps scheme for. What are you really passionate about?

That is your God.

Now most people reading this book would say, "The Lord is my God." Maybe He is. Then again, maybe He isn't. Our God isn't just One we might name, He is One whom we serve.

What is the focus of your life? Is it your career, your family? That, for all practical purposes, becomes your God.

Once again, the Second Commandment says: "You shall not make for yourself a carved image...you shall not bow down to them nor serve them."

You wonder, how could this happen? How did Israel end up throwing God over so quickly and worshiping the Golden Calf? It happens easier than you may think.

There were two phases to the Israelites' idolatry in Exodus 32: the first more subtle and less obvious, the second blatantly radical. And the first phase will always grow out of the other. The root of their open idolatry was the previous departure of their hearts from the Lord, leaning too much on the man who was God's chosen instrument and spokesman. *Moses.*

"Let's Lower The Bar A Little..."

Moses was their first idol, the Golden Calf their second. After Moses disappeared into the cloud on top of Mount Sinai for weeks on end, they started getting restless. Their "idol" was out of sight, so what were they to do?

> When Moses failed to come back down the mountain right away, the people went to Aaron. "Look," they said, "make us some gods who can lead us. This man Moses, who brought us here from Egypt, has disappeared. We don't know what has happened to him." (Exodus 32:1, NLT)

They were essentially saying, "We don't know about Moses anymore. Anyway, his standards were awfully high. We still want 'spirituality,' but let's just lower the bar a little. Let's create something we can see and touch, something which appeals to the senses. We don't want to feel guilty if we don't do what God says. So let's just make up our own version.

What's wrong with that? How would you like it if an airline pilot said something similar? "I'm sick of all these charts and buttons and lights, constantly worrying if we have enough fuel. Let's just go with the flow, man!" Or what if a surgeon picked up that line of reasoning? "Who cares about all these extra arteries all over the place! They're just in the way! Just give me a scalpel and I'll figure it out as I go!"

What if one individual decided that traffic laws didn't really apply to him? "Hey man, that's your truth, and that's good for you. I've got my own truth." So he decides that a red light means go, and a green light means stop, and the sign that says "yield" really means "go for it."

Is it any more ridiculous when people try to give God a twenty-first century makeover? You can say, "The Bible says God is a jealous God. But I don't want Him to be jealous. I want Him to be mellow and laid back. I want Him to be tolerant and adaptable. So that's the God I'm going to worship." Or maybe, "I know the Bible says Jesus is the only way to God, but I don't believe in judgment. I believe in a God who accepts everybody no matter what."

Statements like those go directly against the first and foremost of the Ten Commandments. By creating your own version of God, you are placing another god before the true God.

The Israelites rationalized it, of course. They called partying before the Golden Calf "a festival to the Lord." In a similar way, you may be out all night breaking the commands of God, but say grace before a meal. As if that will somehow satisfy God or make what you are doing acceptable. Or you pray "ten Hail Mary's" and five "Our Fathers," and everything is ok with God.

What the Israelites were doing would be like saying, "Lord, bless this night as we get drunk and commit fornication." God doesn't want us bowing before images *period*.

With idolatry all around them in Egypt, it may have been difficult for the Israelites to get used to the idea of worshiping an invisible God. And it may not be easy for us sometimes, either. Even so, Jesus said, "God is Spirit, and those who worship Him must worship in spirit and truth."[40]

Why, then, do we have people bowing before statues of saints, or an image of Jesus on the cross? Well, they might reply, it helps them to relate to God because it's something they can actually see.

Listen! A person who really knows God, who's experienced the new birth and is living in fellowship with Him, doesn't *need* an image or representation to help him pray. God becomes very real to the individual who is filled with the Holy Spirit and walking daily with Jesus Christ. You don't need a physical reminder.

This is not to say that a painting or representation of Jesus is necessarily wrong. It's most likely inaccurate, but it's not bad in and of itself. But it is wrong—terribly wrong—when bit by bit the image begins to take the place of God. It is violating the Second Commandment.

The crucifix is a good example. It's meant as a reminder of the fact that Jesus suffered and died on the cross. But some people carry them as good luck charms, thinking that the little cross will somehow fend off evil. It becomes a holy object to them. The same is true of a statue of Jesus. You bow before it, saying it represents the Lord to you. But doesn't that look a lot like bowing before a graven image?

If it walks like a duck, and quacks like a duck, I think it is one.

Imagine I'm returning from a long ministry trip, and my wife Cathe meets me at the airport. Now, I usually try to carry a photo of my wife in my wallet. But how would Cathe feel if when I saw her, I stopped short, pulled out that photo and began kissing it—instead of her! Someone would probably call the guys in the white coats to take me away.

Why kiss a picture when the real deal is right in front of me? And why bow before an image, picture, or symbol when the real God is there for you?

The same thing can even happen with a Bible. Some people won't set another book on top of the Bible. Others are shocked when they see people writing notes on its pages. Not me! I like to see a Bible all beat up, with dog-eared pages and a worn cover. That shows it's been used. A Bible that's falling apart probably belongs to someone who isn't.

We cannot create anything that will ever be a true representation of the living God. Why? Because it will give us a false concept of what God is really like. If the image is false, the thought of God is false, and that produces character which is false.

Speaking of idols, the psalmist wrote:

> They have mouths, but they do not speak;
> Eyes they have, but they do not see;
> They have ears, but they do not hear;
> Noses they have, but they do not smell;
> They have hands, but they do not handle;
> Feet they have, but they do not walk;
> Nor do they mutter through their throat.
> Those who make them are like them;
> So is everyone who trusts in them.
> (Psalm 115:5-8)

A man becomes like the thing he worships. If he puts any-thing in the place of God, he ultimately becomes like it. After all, what does it mean to be a Christian? It is to become like Jesus.

"Dear children," the elderly apostle John wrote, *"keep away from anything that might take God's place in your hearts"* (1 John 5:21, TLB). Is the Lord Number One in your life today? Are you allowing other gods to crowd Him out?

Remember, Jesus brought all the commandments into context when He said, "'You shall love the LORD your God with all your heart, with all your soul, with all your mind, and with all your strength.' This is the first commandment. And the second, like it, is this: 'You shall love your neighbor as yourself.' There is no other commandment greater than these."

With that statement Jesus really sums up the Ten Commandments. The first four relate to my relationship with God; the second six relate to my relationship to others.

Numbers 1 through 4 teach love for God.

Numbers 5 through 10 teach love for others.

Numbers 1 through 4 are vertical.

Numbers 5 through 10 are horizontal.

If I truly love God, I will not have other gods before Him, bow before graven images, or take His name in vain. If I truly love my neighbor as myself, I won't steal from him, lie to him, covet what is his, or kill him.

But going back to the First Commandment, we all need to be very careful to make sure that God truly is Number One in our hearts and lives. It is deceptively easy to *say* you worship the Lord, yet allow your heart to be captured by other "gods."

SOME WORSHIP MONEY OR POSSESSIONS

Their mantra is "born to shop," or "he who dies with the most toys wins." Of course the great difficulty here is that once you get what you want, you soon tire of it and want more!

> Hell and Destruction are never full;
> So the eyes of man are never satisfied.
> (Proverbs 27:20)

When John D. Rockefeller was the richest man in the world, someone asked him, "How much money is enough."

He replied, "Just a little bit more".

The Bible warns us saying, "The love of money is a root of all kinds of evil. Some people, eager for money, have wandered from the faith and pierced themselves with many griefs."[41]

Those people "eager for money" in the above passage may squander the little cash they have gambling, buying lotto tickets. They tell themselves that if they could only win "Who Wants To Be A Millionaire," they would finally find a little happiness. If we learn nothing else from those who have been successful in Hollywood, surely we have seen the emptiness of merely possessing things. How many of these people are on drugs, in rehab, miserable, and empty?

Jesus said, "What will it profit a man if he gains the whole world, and loses his own soul? Or what will a man give in exchange for his soul?" (Mark 8:36-38).

This was the case with the rich young ruler. He had it all: he was wealthy, young, even moral…but still empty inside. Jesus told him to sell all he had and give it to the poor, and he went away sorrowful. His God was the *stuff* that kept him from the living Savior who loved him.

SOME WORSHIP THEIR OWN BODIES

They worship at the First Church of the Perfect Physique. There is never quite enough exercise, weight lifting, running, or whatever. It can become addicting. Doesn't it drive you crazy when someone who looks like they're in perfect shape say, "Oh, I can't eat that, I'm getting so fat."

Have you seen how more and more people seem to be turning to cosmetic surgeons. People are getting just a little carried away. I saw a piece on TV not long ago about two girls who wanted to look exactly like Barbie. Another woman wanted to look like a *cat!*

SOME WORSHIP PLEASURE

I say it again now with tears in my eyes, there are many who walk along the Christian road who are really enemies of the cross of Christ. Their future is eternal loss, for their god is their appetite: they are proud of what they should be ashamed of; and all they think about is this life here on earth. (Philippians 3:18-9, TLB)

You know people like this. They live for that buzz, that experience, that thrill. The Bible says, "In the last days perilous times will come: For men will be...lovers of pleasure rather than lovers of God."[42]

Some just live for the moment. For what excites them. For many this might involve putting their whole focus on sensual or sexual pleasure. The problem with this is that once you've tried one thing, you soon tire of it and want more. Or "different." The unrestrained sensual appetite invariably becomes more perverse, deviant, and twisted. An unholy sensual desire cannot be satisfied legitimately.

Sadly, we could all think of some graphic examples of that, and yet Scripture tells us that it's "shameful even to speak of those things which are done by them in secret."[43]

Living for pleasure is a dead-end street. As Paul wrote, "She who lives in pleasure is dead while she lives."[44]

I'm amazed by the length the Holy Spirit goes to in order to keep us off this road of destruction. The life of Solomon has been captured for us in Scripture, so that we won't have to run down every heartbreaking dead-end street that he did. And when you read the following passage, you'll realize he ran down just about all of them.

I also tried to find meaning by building huge homes for myself and by planting beautiful vineyards. I made gardens and parks, filling them with all kinds of fruit trees. I built reservoirs to collect the water to irrigate my many flourishing groves. I bought slaves, both men and women, and others were born into my household. I also owned great herds and flocks, more than any of the kings who lived in Jerusalem before me. I collected great sums of silver and gold, the treasure of many kings and provinces. I hired wonderful singers, both men and women, and had many beautiful concubines. I had everything a man could desire!

So I became greater than any of the kings who ruled in Jerusalem before me. And with it all, I remained clear-eyed so that I could evaluate all these things. Anything I wanted, I took. I did not restrain myself from any joy. I even found great pleasure in hard work, an additional reward for all my labors. But as I looked at everything I had worked so hard to accomplish, it was all so meaningless. It was like chasing the wind. There was nothing really worthwhile anywhere. (Ecclesiastes 2:4-11, NLT)

After all of that...after unlimited job opportunities...unlimited wealth... unlimited creative fulfillment...unlimited sensual pleasure, Solomon sums it up by saying, in essence, "It was all a big zero. I've wasted my life."

You see, that's why Solomon said at the end of Ecclesiastics, "This is the end of the matter, all has been heard. Fear God and keep His commandments, for this is the whole of man."

This is the whole of man, and this is what makes man whole.

Of Moses it was said, "He chose to be mistreated along with the people of God rather than to enjoy the pleasures of sin for a short time" (Hebrews 11:25, NIV).

When Jesus met the woman at the well in Samaria, He knew that she had spent her life trying to fill the void inside with romance, sex, men. He said to her, "If you drink of this water you will thirst again...."

That is true of common well water...and possessions, pleasure, the perfect body, and everything else out there that would try to fill the vacuum in our soul meant for God alone.

SOME WORSHIP PEOPLE

At one time or another, we've probably all referred to a certain actor or musician as our "idol." We want to be just like them. Or it could even be a godly man or woman we admire and want to emulate. The problem with idols—all idols—is that they will invariably disappoint you. You can make an idol or god out of a boyfriend, girlfriend, a gang, whatever. This person or these people become more important to you than God Himself. This is shown by the fact that you will do anything to keep your relationship with these people—*even deny the Lord and abandon your faith.*

It happens all the time. "If I really give my life to Jesus Christ I might lose this person...."

Yes, you might.

Jesus said, "If anyone comes to Me and does not hate his father and mother, wife and children, brothers and sisters, yes, and his own life also, he cannot be My disciple."[45]

The fact is, everything about this world is changing. Even the people we love most will one day pass away. The only real security in this whole universe is in our eternal God.

Thank God for absolutes! Thank God that His Word never changes... and neither does His love.

Chapter Nine

ENCOUNTER AT SINAI, PART 2:
FINDING THE ROAD TO HAPPINESS

A re you a happy person? You may have all the things a person ought to have to make them happy and content, and yet...you're not.

Why is that?

Because there is a right and wrong way to find happiness. There are two ways we can live in life, two paths we can take. Jesus says there is narrow way that leads to life, and the broad way that leads to destruction.

There are two foundations on which we can build: the rock, or the sinking sand. And the result is we can either live the happy and holy way or the miserable and unholy way.

When most people think of that narrow way, the life of obedience to God, they foresee misery, restrictions, and rules, rules, rules. The picture most non-believing people have of the Christian is one of gloom, pessimism, and—worst of all— extreme boredom. No drinking, smoking, partying, or sex (at least outside of marriage). In essence, *no fun!* Instead, they imagine every spare hour spent in Bible studies, prayer, or hanging out with other dull people.

In fact, the very opposite is true.

Jesus told the story of a young man who ran away from home—and it was a picture of what happens when we run away from God.[46] Have you ever noticed that the prodigal son found everything he was looking for in his father's house? What did he look for in the prodigal land to make him happy? Apparently nice clothes, fine food, and parties. Yet what did his father give to the rebellious son when he returned? Nice clothes, *bring out the best robe.* Fine food, *bring out the fatted calf.* And parties, *let's be merry!*

Everything that he needed in life he ultimately found in his father's house. And everything we need in life to make us truly happy is found there, too, in the realm of our heavenly Father.

You hear people talk about "what they gave up" to follow Christ, but honestly, what have they really lost? Addiction to drugs or alcohol? Hangovers? Unhappy, unhealthy relationships? Guilt? Emptiness? Fear of death?

Paul said, "Everything else is worthless when compared with the priceless gain of knowing Christ Jesus my Lord. I have put aside all else, counting it worth less than nothing, in order that I can have Christ" (Philippians 3:8, TLB)

The word "blessed" that we see so often in the Bible actually means "happy."

Literally, it means *happy, happy!* But where are we to find this double-happy state the Bible promises? By doing what God tells us to do.

The psalmist wrote: "Blessed is the man who fears the LORD, who delights greatly in His commandments" (Psalm 112:1). In other words, "Happy, happy the man or woman who takes great delights in the commandments of God."

Happiness is always connected to holiness. That's why the non-believer will never know true happiness. Sure, they will have moments of temporary happiness, but it will be short-lived. The Devil has his cheap counterfeits, but they are shallow because they have no deep well from which to draw. Our holy God, however, is the very headwaters of joy.

Ironically, you'll find that the most unhappy people are the people living for happiness! Happiness isn't something that we should seek outright, as an end in itself, it is a *by-product* of seeking and serving God. Happiness sneaks up on you when you're not looking as you seek to follow Christ and help people in His name. As Christians, we should not seek to be happy, we should seek to be holy—and we'll find happiness thrown into the bargain.

Psalm 1 says:

Blessed [happy, happy] is the man
Who walks not in the counsel of the ungodly,
Nor stands in the path of sinners,
Nor sits in the seat of the scornful;
But his delight is in the law of the Lord....
(vv. 1-2)

Happy-twice-over is the man who *walks not*.... His happiness isn't springing from what he does, but what he chooses not to do! The Ten Commandments aren't bars of a cage to keep us in, as much as they are barriers to keep evil out. Have you ever seen those underwater photographers who are lowered in cages into a shark-infested sea? Do you think their dominant emotion is frustration over being "hemmed in"? I doubt it! I think they are probably thanking God for the protection.

The Ten Commandments, remember, can be divided into two sections. The first four deal with my relationship with God, and the next six with my relationship with man. When we love God with all our heart, soul, and mind, we will be better able to love our neighbor as ourselves.

We have already looked at the first two commandments. For the next few pages, we'll be considering the third.

COMMANDMENT 3: DON'T TAKE HIS NAME IN VAIN

Here is one of the most misunderstood of the commandments—and one which can so easily be broken. How do we take His name in vain?

1. Through Profanity

God's last name is not "damn." It's always been curious to me how many who claim to be atheists invoke the name of God and Jesus so often. Even the non-believer, in his spiritually deadened state knows there is something different, something powerful, something special about invoking the name of God or the name of Jesus Christ.

The Bible makes it very clear that there is no higher, more honored, more powerful name in all of the universe.

> Therefore God also has highly exalted Him and given Him the name which is above every name, that at the name of Jesus every knee should bow, of those in heaven, and of those on earth, and of those under the earth, and that every tongue should confess that Jesus Christ is Lord, to the glory of God the Father. (Philippians 2:9-11)

God's name is important to Him.

Names are important to us, too.

Parents anguish over what name to give their child. At this writing, the five most popular names for girls at this writing are: Emma, Madison, Emily, Kaitlyn and Hailey. (Whatever happened to Debby, Sandy, Carol, or Susie?) Stone or gem names are hot choices for girls, leading to names such as Amber, Jade, Diamond, and of course, Crystal. The five most popular names for boys are: Jacob, Aidan, Ethan, Ryan, Matthew, and...Greg Laurie! (Just kidding.) Geographic names are also popular for boys, like Austin, Dakota, Zaire, Dallas, Sky, and Ridge.

Then there are those parents who think it's clever to stick their kids with a name that is a humorous play on words. These names are for real: Paige Turner, Warren Piece, Justin Case, Carl Arm, Chris B. Bacon, Eileen Dover, Gene Pool, Douglas Fir, and Cookie Cutter.

Names are important to God, too, especially His own name. God is very, very serious about His name. We have laws against slandering someone's personal name, and you can be taken to court for that offence. In the same way, there is a penalty for those who hold God's name in contempt and drag it through the mud. The Bible says, "For the LORD will not hold him guiltless who takes His name in vain."[47]

This is no idle threat, it's simply a statement of fact. God is setting forth an unchanging truth, something that's hardwired into Creation, not unlike the Law of Gravity. If you step off a thirty story building, you will fall to your death. That's not a threat, it's simply a statement of fact, a statement of *what is*. In the same way, if you take God's name in vain, you will not be held guiltless or go unpunished.

I shudder when I hear people go out of their way to insult or blaspheme God. The Bible tells us, "Do not be deceived, God is not mocked; for whatever a man sows, that he will also reap."[48]

We must never forget the holiness of our God. It is one of the most important, most repeated facts in all of Scripture. The angels around His throne do not say, "Eternal, eternal, eternal," or "faithful, faithful, faithful," or "mighty, mighty, mighty" (though He is all of those things). What they say is "Holy, holy, holy is the Lord God Almighty—the one who always was, who is, and who is still to come."[49]

So we want to always have reverence and respect for His holy name. What are some other ways that we take His name in vain?

2. Through Needless Oaths

Sometimes we may say, "I swear to God this is true...."

Okay, so it's true. But why do we have to bring God into it?

Probably because our word is not normally reliable. People who make commitments they don't keep or say things that aren't true think that by invoking the name of God, their promise will have more credibility. So we drag God's honor into the conversation to try to buttress our own. Jesus spoke directly to this practice in His Sermon on the Mount.

> "Again, you have heard that it was said to the people long ago, 'Do not break your oath, but keep the oaths you have made to the Lord.' But I tell you, Do not swear at all: either by heaven, for it is God's throne; or by the earth, for it is his footstool; or by Jerusalem, for it is the city of the Great King. And do not swear by your head, for you cannot make even one hair white or black. Simply let your 'Yes' be 'Yes,' and your 'No,' 'No'; anything beyond this comes from the evil one." (Matthew 5:33-37, NIV)

Don't bring God or heaven into your promises. Your word should be enough. To strengthen your promise with a vow shows that you have a credibility problem, and need to take steps to change that. What kind of steps? Let me list a few.

First, if you say that you're going to do something, *do it!* Don't make commitments you don't intend to keep. Don't say, "Oh sure, we'll meet you for dinner," and then cancel at the last minute because someone you like better called. Watch out! You may go out to dinner with the second person who called and then bump into the person you cancelled!

Don't say, "Oh yeah, I'll help you move out of your house this weekend," and then neglect to show up and call later with an excuse. We have a word for people who do things like these: *flakes.*

Second, if you're hired to do a job, do it. Get it done. Christians should be the hardest-working, and most diligent workers, and we should never use our faith as an excuse for laziness. ("I can't sweep the floor now, I need to *pray.*")

Third, when two people commit themselves to each other in marriage, they should honor those vows for the rest of their lives. People today—even

Christians—follow the trend of our times and just bail out of a marriage when it gets hard. They will cite "irreconcilable differences."

Jesus says, "Don't be like that." Let your yes be yes and your no, no.

3. By Using His Name For Personal Gain

Then there are those who misuse His name to further their business transactions. You can look in the Yellow Pages and see the sign of the fish on ads for car dealers, landscaping services, and Realtors.

Sadly, it goes much, much further than that. We have many people today involved in what is called "Christian retailing," who essentially market Christian products. You can purchase a Christian version of just about anything out there.

At what used to be called the CBA, or the Christian Booksellers Association conventions, you'll find everything from outstanding Christian books and music to ashtrays and lighters with the holy name of Jesus emblazoned them. You can get Christian bird feeders, body lotions, luggage, lamps, scones, mud flaps, wallpaper, candy bars, Frisbees, and mouse pads.

Do I have to have Christian mud flaps to be spiritual? Or Christian luggage? If you ask me, some of this is taking the Lord's name in vain. They are exploiting the name of Jesus to make a buck.

4. By Being Flippant Or Careless

It is possible that even sincere believers take His name in vain, without intending to. The phrase "in vain" describes that which is empty, idle, insincere, or frivolous. God's name must never be used in an empty, frivolous, or insincere way. When we say, "God bless you," "Praise the Lord," "Hallelujah," or "I'll pray for you," let those be heartfelt, sincere statements, not empty clichés.

The J. B. Phillips paraphrase of Romans 12:9 says, "Let us have no imitation Christian love." Another translation says, "Don't just pretend that you love others. Really love them."[50]

Perhaps the most subtle form in which this law is broken is by sheer hypocrisy: The man who claims Jesus as Lord but does not keep His commandments. Jesus said, "Why do you call Me 'Lord, Lord,' and not do the things which I say?" (Luke 6:46).

I'm going to make a statement that might shock you, but I believe it to be true: *The hypocrisy of the church is far worse than the profanity in the street.* To pray and not to practice, to believe and not to obey, to say, "Lord, Lord," and not do what He says…this is to take His holy name in vain! Now we come to the Fourth Commandment.

COMMANDMENT 4: REMEMBER THE SABBATH DAY

This command has produced more confusion, misunderstanding, and hard feelings than perhaps any of the others. Let's find out what it is…and what it *isn't*.

The original context of this command, of course, was a word to the Israel-ites, instructing them to set aside the seventh day as a day of total rest.

And now I'll make another statement that may shock you (two in one chapter): This command doesn't mean much for Christians living under grace. Let me tell you why I believe this. Here are some fast facts about the Fourth Commandment.

It Is The Only Commandment Not Repeated In The New Testament

Every one of the other Ten Commandments is repeated in the pages of the New Testament, and most are made more stringent. However, in all the New Testament lists of sins, breaking the Sabbath is never mentioned. Why? Because it was given to the Jews, not the non-Jews.

JESUS Never Taught Anyone To Keep The Sabbath

Jesus actually broke the Sabbath Law as it was followed in His day (Matthew 12:1-14). By perverting and twisting the meaning of the Sabbath, the Jewish leaders had turned it into a miserable, religious mess. Because Jesus healed people and made them whole on the Sabbath day they accused Him of breaking it! That's when He reminded them that man was not made for the Sabbath, but the Sabbath for man.

It's sad how religion takes the place of a relationship with God. It becomes all about going through rituals and rules with no real thought of a relationship with God Himself.

The Apostles Never Taught Anyone To Keep The Sabbath

In fact, they deliberately began meeting on the first day of the week, Sunday, because Jesus rose on Sunday. They spoke against turning the Sabbath into a religious law for Christians. Paul taught specifically on this subject:

> So don't let anyone condemn you for what you eat or drink, or for not celebrating certain holy days or new-moon ceremonies or Sabbaths. For these rules were only shadows of the real thing, Christ himself. (Colossians 2:16-17, NLT)

The apostle pointed out that all the Sabbath had been pointing to in the Old Testament scrolls was fulfilled in Jesus Christ!

The book of Hebrews underlines this wonderful truth:

> So there is a special rest still waiting for the people of God. For all who enter into God's rest will find rest from their labors, just as God rested after creating the world. Let us do our best to enter that place of rest. For anyone who disobeys God, as the people of Israel did, will fall. (Hebrews 4:9-11, NLT)

Other religions teaching on salvation say "Do," while Jesus Christ says *"Done."*[51] I am not under command to keep just one day special for the Lord, any more than I am required to approach God by means of animal sacrifices. There is no need! Those were signposts pointing me to Jesus, and full salvation in Him.

Knowing then, what the Sabbath is not, does it have any message to us as Christians? I believe there are two primary purposes behind the Sabbath principle.

A DAY OF REST

The Sabbath was to be a day of rest. God wants us to know that we need at least one day off out of seven to rest and recharge. Most of us are in a hurry. Have you noticed that life moves faster every day? We are the only nation in the world with a mountain called *Rushmore*. Many of us live constantly on the edge, our schedules jam-packed. And suddenly one day we wonder how so much of life passed us by!

We keep trying to cram more living into increasingly limited lives. That's the life principle behind the Fourth Commandment, we need *rest*. Our homes are filled with labor saving devices intended to make our lives easier than ever, and yet we have never worked harder. No wonder we're stressed out! We need a day to unplug the computer, turn off the cell phone, and *chill*.

As I quoted earlier in the book, the Lord says, "Be still and know that I am God."[52] Most of us can quote that verse—or even write it in calligraphy and frame it on the walls of our home. But it has to move beyond nice words into a definite, disciplined plan of action. We *need* to be still sometimes. God speaks to us in the stillness. David spoke of how the Lord led him into green pastures by still waters...and restored his soul. If we want the restoration, we have to be willing to walk with Him into the quiet place and sit down for awhile.

Even Jesus took time off.

> The apostles gathered around Jesus and reported to him all they had done and taught. Then, because so many people were coming and going that they did not even have a chance to eat, he said to them, "Come with me by yourselves to a quiet place and get some rest." So they went away by themselves in a boat to a solitary place. (Mark 6:30-32, NIV)

Our emphasis always seems to be on doing, but God is interested in our rest. He knows we need it. During the next 24 hours let me show you how hard your body will work. Your heart beats 103,689 times, your blood travels 168,000,000 miles, you breathe 23,040 times, you inhale 438 cubic feet of air, you eat 3 and a half pounds of food, you drink 2.9 quarts of liquid. You speak 4,800 words (that's one phone call for most girls!). You move 750 muscles, and you exercise 7,000,000 brain cells.

Whew! I feel tired just writing this stuff. We need a day to rest our bodies and be recharged spiritually. For many, Sunday is that day. Sunday is not the Sabbath, but a good day to honor the principle. It can be a time to get together with God's people to worship, pray, look at Scripture, and enjoy each other's company.

This is not an "option" for a believer, it's a *necessity*. If you fail to do this you will soon become a casualty in the race of life.

Now that we've considered the first four commandments covering our vertical relationship with the Lord, we need to shift gears to look at the following six commandments, speaking to our horizontal relationships with one another.

COMMANDMENT 5: HONOR YOUR FATHER AND MOTHER

Before a word is spoken about how you treat others, God starts with the family. Few things can give us as much pleasure in life as our families. Then again, few things can give us as much *pain* in life as our families.

Kids have problems with parents, parents have problems with kids. Husbands have trouble with wives, and wives have trouble with husbands. But God starts with the family because He created it.

In fact, our very existence as a society is contingent on the success of the family. That's probably why Satan hates it so, and has declared war on families all over the world.

Tragically, in today's twisted times, mothers and fathers aren't even around to honor—especially fathers. A man and a woman, married faithfully and raising their children is becoming less and less the norm. Currently, one million teenagers—12 percent of all women ages 15 and 19—become pregnant each year. Of those, 70 percent are unmarried. *The New York Times* has reported that unmarried pregnant teenagers are beginning to be viewed by some of their peers as role models. Research has found that a majority of Americans agree that single mothers can raise children as well as married couples.

They *can't*. Not even close.

And 70 percent of Americans between ages 18 and 34 think having children outside of marriage is "morally acceptable."

It *isn't*. It is neither moral nor acceptable, and it breaks the heart of the God who created marriage.

It has even come into vogue in Hollywood for actresses to have kids out of wedlock. They are the "new, liberated people."

Then you have homosexuals adopting kids—so incalculably destructive to God's order. God says, honor your father and mother—not honor your father and father or honor your mother and her live-in lover or partner. We tamper with God's order at our own peril!

Consider these statistics: 70 percent of juveniles in state–operated institutions come from fatherless homes; 63 percent of youth suicides are from fatherless homes; 90 percent of homeless and runaway children are from fatherless homes.

The Hebrew in this command for honoring your mom and dad comes from a verb *to be heavy*, or *to give weight.*

Children, obey your parents in all things, for this is well pleasing to the Lord. (Colossians 3:20)

Respect for parents is certainly something we have lost sight of in our culture. It's interesting that one of the signs of the last days will be a lack of respect for one's parents. Paul tells Timothy, "For men will be lovers of themselves, lovers of money, boasters, proud, blasphemers, disobedient to parents. ..." (2 Timothy 3:2).

You might say, "Greg, my mom and dad aren't even Christians. Should I still honor them?" *Yes.* In fact, in doing so you might win them to the Lord. The hardest people to reach are the members of your own family. Even Jesus' family members didn't believe in Him until His resurrection. They thought He was crazy![53] And who was a better example than Jesus?

What if my parents tell me to do something that's a sin?

Like what? Making your bed? Taking the trash out? Doing your homework? If it was a clear cut issue—such as your parents telling you not to believe in Jesus—then you must obey God and not man. But that is rarely the case. The fact of the matter is, most parents have their children's best interests at heart. Most of us would not be here today if it were not for our parents' warnings and protection.

It's easy for kids to think their parents don't know what they're talking about. Just wait until the shoe is on the other foot, and you hear yourself saying things to your kids that your parents said to you (and you vowed you would never say). *We didn't have it so easy when I was a kid. ...Do you think I have a money tree somewhere?.... If your friends told you to jump off a cliff, would you do that, too?*

What great joy it brings to a parent when the lessons they have taught their children have been learned and followed. When the God of the parents also becomes the God of their children.

Let's look at the second of the commandments pertaining to our relationships with people.

COMMANDMENT 6: YOU SHALL NOT MURDER

If ever there was a commandment that was ignored, it's this one. Nearly two million people a year become victims of violent crimes. Or contemplate the horrific act of mass murder on 9/11.

This commandment obviously forbids the taking of another human life for no justifiable reason. Without going in to a lot of depth in this brief fly-over, suffice it to say that the Bible does not condemn *all* killing. Numbers 35 plainly states the difference which God sets between killing and murder.

All murder, of course, is killing, but not all killing is murder. There are times when death is permissible, though not desirable. Self defense is one example. If someone were to break into your house with the intent of killing you or your family, Scripture allows you to defend yourself. Jesus told the disciples to take a sword with them on their travels. Why? Self defense!

When our military struck out at the wicked terrorists who attacked our nation, that is justifiable. It is not murder. (Murder is what *they* did.) It's self defense on a national scale.

We have all been aware of known killers condemned to death in different states across our country, and it is certainly biblical to do this.

Yes, you must execute anyone who murders another person, for to kill a person is to kill a living being made in God's image. (Genesis 9:6, NLT)

There is always a group of people who see it another way, holding vigil outside the prison where a murderer faces execution. They protest, they pray, and they usually hold up at least a few signs saying, "Thou shalt not kill."

Some would have a hard time understanding why we Bible-believing Christians would condone the execution of a murderer, and yet strongly oppose abortion. Yet you will find many who actually support abortion, and strongly oppose capital punishment. *That* to me is illogical, not the other position. They want to kill the innocent and spare the guilty. I want to spare the innocent and see justice brought to the guilty.

There are certainly good and sincere people on both sides of the issue of capital punishment. But there is something else to consider in this whole matter. In the Sermon on the Mount, Jesus takes the idea of murder one giant step further.

"You have heard that the law of Moses says, 'Do not murder. If you commit murder, you are subject to judgment.' But I say, if you are angry with someone, you are subject to judgment! If you call someone an idiot, you are in danger of being brought before the high council. And if you curse someone, you are in danger of the fires of hell." (Matthew 5:21-22, NLT)

Many people in the depths of their heart have anger and hatred to such a degree that they actually desire the death of another person. This is clearly forbidden in Scripture. In the book of First John, the apostle says, "Anyone who hates another Christian is really a murderer at heart. And you know that murderers don't have eternal life within them."[54]

The word used for *hate* in this passage means to habitually despise someone. It's not just a transient motion of the affections, but a deep rooted loathing.

Sometimes we will say, "I just hate her," "Or I can't stand him." God doesn't want His children to hate like that. Scripture tells us, "Get rid of all bitterness, rage and anger, brawling and slander, along with every form of malice. Be kind and compassionate to one another, forgiving each other, just as in Christ God forgave you."[55]

WALKING IN THE LIGHT

The Ten Commandments were given to *shut our mouths and open our eyes*. To drive us into the open arms of Jesus! Maybe you have had another god before Him. Perhaps you have taken His name in vain, dishonored your parents, or allowed yourself to hate someone.

James makes it clear that "whoever keeps the whole law and yet stumbles at just one point is guilty of breaking all of it."[56]

The Ten Commandments are a searing hot light that exposes reality. You might say, "I didn't realize what a sinner I was until reading these chapters."

Not long ago when I was driving, I came to an intersection and went straight through a red light. The truth is, I was daydreaming, and not paying attention to my driving. It wasn't intentional, but I still broke the law. And (wouldn't you know it?) right behind me was a cop. When those inevitable blue lights started flashing, I pulled over, and got out my driver's license and registration.

As soon as the officer walked up to the car, I told him, "I was wrong, I wasn't paying attention. It was crazy. I did that and it was my fault!" I was fully prepared to be ticketed. But the policeman said, "Most people don't admit it when they're wrong. Since you did, I'm going to let you go with a warning."

Listen, we all break the laws of God, intentionally and unintentionally. God wants us to come clean and admit failures and sin.

If we will turn to Jesus, He will forgive us of all our sin.

If we make it a habit to keep turning to Him at our first awareness of sin, we will "walk in the light, as He is in the light."

And that's a formula for a happy-happy life.

Chapter Ten

ENCOUNTER AT SINAI, PART 3:
GUARDING YOUR HEART

COMMANDMENT 7: YOU SHALL NOT COMMIT ADULTERY

A little boy who attended Sunday school one day where the Ten Command-ments had been the topic. He came away a little confused about the mean-ing of the Seventh Commandment. After church he asked his father, "Daddy, what does it mean when it says, 'Thou shalt not commit agriculture'"?

There was hardly a beat between the question and the father's wise reply: "Son, that just means you're not supposed to plow the other man's field." The boy seemed satisfied with that response.

There is no need for us as Christians to have any doubt or confusion about God's prohibition against adultery. Simply stated, adultery is when you have sex with someone beside your spouse. Fornication is sex with someone you are not married to. According to the Bible, these are sins.

Sadly, every one of us knows at least one person, if not many more, who have fallen into this sin. If men and women across the world simply obeyed this one commandment, imagine what a different world it would be today. How many divorces would have been avoided? How many murders would disappear from the books? And emotional breakdowns? And suicides? How many families would be still together? How many fathers would still be at home to raise their children?

What an awesome destructive force is released by this sin! Lives beyond counting have been destroyed by it—or at the very least, rendered desperately unhappy.

Jesus once described his time as "a wicked and adulterous generation." If that was true then, how much more so now? Historians looking back at our time would have to say it was characterized by an obsession with things sexual. The sins of adultery and immorality are at the root of so many of our social ills today. You would think from watching and listening to our media today that adultery is now viewed as a recreational sport.

This year 10 million teenagers will engage in 126 million acts of sexual intercourse, resulting in 1 million pregnancies, 496,000 abortions, 134,000 miscarriages, and 490,000 births.

Maybe you've heard questions like these—or even asked them yourself: *"Why is it so wrong to have sex with someone anyway? So what if you're not married to them? As long as two consenting adults agree, what's the problem? Why has God laid down a law like this in the first place? Doesn't He know that young people have raging hormones? Why is God out to spoil all our fun? What's His problem anyway?"*

Know this: God gave us this law for our *good.*

Think about a couple of basic traffic laws. Stoplights, for instance. Don't you hate them? Whenever you have all the time in the world, you seem to hit green after green—for miles. But when you're in a rush...? You can't buy a green light!

Sometimes, it would be nice to just forget about them, wouldn't it?

Sure, but you'll pay the price.

You will eventually be injured or even die—and so will others.

Oh sure, you'll feel that initial rush when you sail through the red light in that first intersection while everyone else is waiting their turn. You might even make through two or three intersections. But it's only a matter of time. You're going to hit someone broadside, or they will smash into you...and the fun will be over.

Those traffic laws are there for your own good—not to make your life miserable. And you could say the same thing about the commandments of God. He gave them to us in His love.

Let's remember something very important: *God created sex.* Sometimes we may lose sight of that fact. Sexual intercourse is not evil. In fact, in it's proper, God-ordained, God-blessed context, it is very good. And that context is within a marriage relationship. Period!

> Give honor to marriage, and remain faithful to one another in marriage. God will surely judge people who are immoral and those who commit adultery. (Hebrews 13:4, NLT)

> Drink water from your own well—share your love only with your wife. (Proverbs 5:15, NLT)

Outside of its proper context, sex becomes unbelievably destructive—spiritually, emotionally, and even physically.

What is the real purpose of sex? Through the years, the Christian position on this issue has been mischaracterized as, "Sex is only for procreation, childbearing." But that's not what the Bible really says. While it is certainly the process through which procreation takes place, God also gave us sex as a way to create unity between a man and a woman. When a man and woman have sexual relations, a oneness takes place.

> Don't you realize that your bodies are actually parts of Christ? Should a man take his body, which belongs to Christ, and join it to a prostitute? Never! And don't you know that if a man joins himself to a prostitute, he becomes one body with her? For the Scriptures say, "The two are united into one." (1 Corinthians 6:15-17, NLT)

Run away from sexual sin! No other sin so clearly affects the body as this one does. For sexual immorality is a sin against your own body. Or don't you know that your body is the temple of the Holy Spirit, who lives in you and was given to you by God? You do not belong to yourself, for God bought you with a high price. So you must honor God with your body. (1 Corinthians 6:18-20)

That is why there is no such thing as a quick, one night fling that doesn't mean anything.

It means plenty.

Sex is not some casual toy. It is a gift from God to be saved for that person with whom you want to become one.

"But wait," some might protest. "This doesn't hurt anyone."

Doesn't it? *It hurts you!*

A University of Tennessee study among young women found that "There seems to be a direct correlation between illicit sexual behavior and serious emotional problems."

Sex outside of wedlock can hurt the future marriage. The University of Oregon did a study among young men, and found that those who engage in premarital sexual relationships make poor marital risks.

It doesn't hurt anyone? What about the teen pregnancies? Each year more than 1 million teens become pregnant. Many of these babies never make it to term. One out of every five abortions is performed on a woman under age 20, and 4 out of every 10 teenage pregnancies ends in abortion. In other words, about 400,000 of the 1.6 million abortions occurring annually are performed on teenage mothers.

You don't think *that* is hurting someone? What about the innocent baby being killed? What about that young mother who (no matter what pro-abortion propaganda claims) will carry that guilt for years to come?

Free sex doesn't hurt anyone? What about AIDS? Did you know that AIDS is the leading killer of Americans between the ages of 25 and 44? Twenty-five percent of all HIV infections are found in people under the age of 22. The rate of infection from sexually transmitted diseases: syphilis, herpes, gonorrhea, and AIDS has reached epidemic proportions.

How do we deal with this? We are told to have "safe sex." The federal government has spent almost 3 billion of our taxes since 1970 to promote contraceptives and safe sex among our teenagers. Condoms, however, have a failure rate ranging from 15 to 36 percent!

Think of it like this. Imagine you find yourself on a flight where the captain announces, "Ladies and gentlemen, we are having some mechanical difficulties. The mechanics tell us there is a 15 percent chance we will not make it to our destination, but not to worry. After all, this is a safe flight!" Would you stay on board or head for the door? Or what if he said, there was a 36 percent chance the plane wouldn't make it?

Does that sound safe or sane to you?

I have a better idea than safe sex. *Save sex.* God has told us not to involve ourselves in illicit sexual relationships for very good reason! That is why this pervasive and powerful sin made the top 10.

> Listen to me, my sons, and pay attention to my words. Don't let your hearts stray away toward her. Don't wander down her wayward path. For she has been the ruin of many; numerous men have been her victims. Her house is the road to the grave. Her bedroom is the den of death. (Proverbs 7:24-27, NLT)

The passages concerning this sin are every bit as clear in the New Testament as those of the Old.

> Do you not know that the wicked will not inherit the kingdom of God? Do not be deceived: Neither the sexually immoral nor idolaters nor adulterers nor male prostitutes nor homosexual offenders nor thieves nor the greedy nor drunkards nor slanderers nor swindlers will inherit the kingdom of God. (1 Corinthians 6:9-10, NIV)

> Marriage is honorable among all, and the bed undefiled; but fornicators and adulterers God will judge. (Hebrews 13:4)

> God wants you to be holy, so you should keep clear of all sexual sin. Then each of you will control your body and live in holiness and honor. (1 Thessalonians 4:3-4, NLT)

You might say, "I've never committed this sin." That's great, but remember how Jesus said if you hated someone, it was the same as killing him? He also said something similar about the sin of adultery.

> "You have heard that the law of Moses says, 'Do not commit adultery.' But I say, anyone who even looks at a woman with lust in his eye has already committed adultery with her in his heart. So if your eye—even if it is your good eye—causes you to lust, gouge it out and throw it away. It is better for you to lose one part of your body than for your whole body to be thrown into hell. And if your hand—even if it is your stronger hand—causes you to sin, cut it off and throw it away. It is better for you to lose one part of your body than for your whole body to be thrown into hell." (Matthew 5:27-30)

"Looks at a woman." Obviously, Jesus doesn't mean a casual glance here, or all the men in the world would have to go around with blinders on. In the Greek, this term refers to the *continuous* act of looking. In this usage, the idea isn't that of an incidental or involuntary glance, but of intentional and repeated gazing.

Jesus isn't speaking here of unexpected and unavoidable exposure to sexual temptation. It's almost everywhere! It is the person who intentionally puts himself in the place of vulnerability, or if he is exposed, gives the Devil a foothold by allowing it into his thought processes. This is why Job said, "I made a covenant with my eyes not to look lustfully at a girl" (Job 31:1, NIV).

Some would say you just can't resist it. It's impossible for a man or a woman with a sex drive in this day and age not to fall.

That's simply not true. It takes more of a ramp-up to commit adultery than you might think. What we must recognize is that this aspect of human nature is combustible, and no one is immune to the flames. Keep your hand near enough to the fire, and hold it there long enough, and it *will* burn.

> But each one is tempted when he is drawn away by his own desires and enticed. Then, when desire has conceived, it gives birth to sin; and sin, when it is full-grown, brings forth death. (James 1:14-15)

One time I came upon my young son Jonathan playing video games before school started—and he knew very well he was breaking the rules. With a guilty look on his face he said, "I couldn't resist myself."

That's not a bad way to define temptation. When we get tempted and give in to it, we like to place the blame on someone or something else.

The Devil made me do it.

That person enticed me—trapped me.

I'm not responsible.

You remember the story of David and his fall with Bathsheba. David wasn't at fault for happening to see Bathsheba bathing. One wonders if Bathsheba knew he would be there, and intentionally put herself in a place where she would be seen. Remember this is a two way street! If lustful looking is bad, then those who dress and expose themselves with the desire to be looked at and lusted after are not less guilty—and perhaps more so!

Girls, ladies...think about what you are wearing (or not wearing) before you leave your house. How would you feel if it was Jesus who would be taking you out somewhere? That doesn't mean you can't wear stylish clothing. But don't dress in such a way as to encourage a guy to lust after you. And you know what that means better than I do.

"But Greg, you might protest, some guys would lust after a *tree!*" True. But that doesn't excuse you from having some modesty! David's sin was a continuous look, and then taking dramatic action as he misused his considerable power as king and had her brought to his bedroom.

What we must do to the best of our abilities is to *guard our minds*. If you're sitting in a theater or watching a movie at someone's house with some friends and a scene comes up that offends you, get up and walk out. If something sexually suggestive pops up on TV (seemingly once every two minutes or so), turn the channel or turn it off. Be careful where you go surfing on the net. Chat rooms, too. If a conversation with a member of the opposite sex becomes sexually suggestive, terminate it.

Check out something before you watch it, read it, or listen to it. Simply telling yourself, "I can handle it," could be nothing more than self deception.

Scripture urges us to bring "every thought into captivity to the obedience of Christ" (2 Corinthians 10:4-5).

How seriously did Jesus treat this temptation to lust? As you will see in the following passage, He doesn't recommend kid gloves.

> So if your hand or foot causes you to sin, cut it off and throw it away. It is better to enter heaven crippled or lame than to be thrown into the unquenchable fire with both of your hands and feet. And if your eye causes you to sin, gouge it out and throw it away. It is better to enter heaven half blind than to have two eyes and be thrown into hell. (Matthew 18:8-9, NLT)

With these strong words, Jesus points out the way of deliverance from this sin. Obviously, He's not speaking literally. If the problem is in the heart, what good is gouging out an eye or cutting off a hand? If the right eye were gone the left one could still look lustfully. If the right hand were cut off, the left one could still carry on sinful acts.

In the Jewish culture, "the right hand" represented a person's best skills and most precious faculties. The right eye represented one's best vision, and the right hand one's best skills.

Here's our Lord's point: *We should be willing to take strong action—to give up whatever is necessary—to keep us from falling into sin.* Anything that morally or spiritually traps us, that causes us to fall into sin or stay in sin, should be eliminated quickly and totally.

Commandment 8: You Shall Not Steal

Stealing runs rampant in today's culture, becoming far more commonplace than we may realize. We live in such a thieving culture we don't even notice how bad it is. We've become accustomed to it.

But think about it. Many of us think of alarm systems as standard options on a new car. Clerks at many gas stations and convenience stores take our money from behind bulletproof glass. Signs tell us that cashiers can't open safes. Tiny red lights blink on our car doors and dashboards indicating the alarm system is on. We place little signs in prominent positions on our front lawns, warning of a home alarm system.

Even the look of the one hundred dollar bill has changed. To thwart high-tech counterfeiters, the Treasury Department began phasing in a new design earlier this year, the first change since 1921. Why? Because people steal everywhere!

Consider these statistics: Although 1 in 5 homes have burglar alarms, 16 million homes were burglarized last year, with losses totaling up to 19.1 billion dollars. Bandits robbed people in the streets 20 million times last year. There is a robbery in our nation every 48 seconds Two million cars are stolen every year. In New York City, theft has become so common that the police won't even take a report.

A *Newsweek* article titled *The Thrill of Theft*, states: "Each year, ordinary people shoplift $13 billion of lipsticks, batteries and bikinis from stores.…Retailers like Brandy Samson, who manages a jewelry and accessories store in the Sherman Oaks, California Fashion Square, uses shoplifting as a guide to taste. "We know what's hot among teens by seeing what they steal," she says.[57]

In a recent article in *USA Today*, the reporter states that nearly half of U.S. workers admit to taking unethical or illegal actions in the past year. Those include one or more from a list of 25 actions, including cheating on an expense account, paying or accepting kickbacks, secretly forging signatures, and trading sex for sales. Workers say it's getting worse, with 57 percent saying they feel more pressure toward unethical behavior than 5 years ago, and 40 percent say it's gotten worse over the last year.

And check this out! Retail stores lose more to employee theft than to shoplifting, according to a University of Florida survey. Most employee theft goes unreported, but employee screening company guards mark estimates at $120 billion a year. Even though most instinctively know that stealing is wrong, many couldn't tell you *why*.

In a recent study by Ohio State University, researchers learned that 90 percent of teens agreed that stealing was wrong, yet 37 percent of high schoolers say they have stolen from a store in the last 12 months. Those who had not stolen anything in that time period were asked why. The number one reason? "I might get caught." The number two reason: The other person might try to get even. The number three reason? I might not need the item.

Newsflash! *How about because God says "You shall not steal?"* Here are some actual excuses used by people who were caught stealing.

"I was going to come back and pay for it."

"I got cheated at this store last week and I'm only evening the score." "It was just a prank."

"You mean this isn't a free sample?"

I read about a man named Natron Fubble who tried to rob a Miami deli, but the owner broke Fubble's nose by hitting him with a giant salami. Fubble fled and hid in the trunk of a parked car. The car, however, belonged to an undercover police team that happened to be trailing a different criminal. After five days, the officers heard Fubble whimpering in the trunk and arrested him.

In Belmont, New Hampshire a teenager robbed a local convenience store. Getting away with a pocket full of change, the boy walked home. What he didn't realize, however, was that he had holes in both of his front pockets! A trail of quarters and dimes led police directly to his house.

Police in Wichita, Kansas, arrested a 22 year old man at an airport hotel after he tried to pass 2 (counterfeit) $16 bills!

When two service stations attendants in Ionia, Michigan refused to hand over the cash to an intoxicated robber, the man threatened to call the police. They still refused, so the robber called the police and was arrested.

But it's not just people robbing stores or holding up service stations. The temptations to steal are constant: When you receive too much change at the store and keep it. When you take those office supplies home for personal use. When you take that help from the government you don't need.

Stealing has become epidemic in our society. We're shocked today when someone actually returns a lost wallet. (Unless the honest individual happens to be a Christian.)

I received a letter from a man who lost his wallet at one of our services. There was $1,700 cash in it. A young man brought it to his home and asked nothing in return. He wrote me, wanting to track him down to give him a reward.

Here is what God says about stealing: "Let him who stole steal no longer, but rather let him labor, working with his hands what is good, that he may have something to give him who has need" (Ephesians 4:28).

I see three principles in this verse.

1. Steal No Longer

Don't ever take anything that belongs to another individual, business—or whomever. Don't try to justify it in your mind because of "extenuating circumstances." It's wrong before God, and His eyes miss nothing! Scripture says, "God is closely watching you, and he weighs carefully everything you do" (Proverbs 5:21, TLB).

If you have taken something, if at all possible, *give it back*.

Remember the story of Zacchaeus? He had made his living taking advantage of others, overcharging them in their taxes. But one day Jesus saw him up in that tree and invited Himself over for a meal. The two disappeared behind Zacchaeus's closed door.

When they reemerged, Zacchaeus stood up and said: "Look, Lord! Here and now I give half of my possessions to the poor, and if I have cheated anybody out of anything, I will pay back four times the amount."[58]

2. Do Something Useful

Renew your commitment to work for everything you have. Like it or not, man is to earn his bread by the sweat of his brow. Paul minced no words on this point:

> For even when we were with you, we commanded you this: If anyone will not work, neither shall he eat. (2 Thessalonians 3:10)

Earn your own living. The world doesn't owe you one, and your parents can't support you for the rest of your life. Get a job, and learn a work ethic!

And whatever you do, do it heartily, as to the Lord and not to men. (Colossians 3:23)

3. Share What You Have

Sharing is the opposite of stealing. God wants us to help others who are in need, and we need to be gainfully employed to have resources to do that.

I'll tell you one another person we steal from...*God.*

"Will a man rob God?
Yet you have robbed Me!
But you say,
'In what way have we robbed You?'
In tithes and offerings."
(Malachi 3:8)

The Bible teaches that each Christian should give to God on a regular basis. "Well," you might say, "I *would* give, but I just don't have any money left over for God." That's why the first check you write every pay period needs to go to the Lord, trusting Him to meet all your other needs. Our obedience and faithfulness in this matter is a pretty accurate barometer of our relationship with the Lord.

This brings us to the Ninth Commandment.

COMMANDMENT 9: DO NOT BEAR FALSE WITNESS

Strictly speaking, this commandment was originally focused against perjuring oneself in a judicial trial. Yet it certainly applies to lying in all its forms.

To know what a lie is, I must first understand what truth is. George Barna conducted a poll and asked adults if they agreed with the following statement: *There are no absolute standards for morals and ethics.* Seven out of ten said they agreed with it! With this kind of outlook, it's easy to see why lying and deception are so much a part of our culture.

Another survey reported that 65 percent of high schoolers admitted to cheating on an exam within the previous 12 month period. On the college level, 24 percent of college students said they would lie to get or keep a job, and 47 percent of adults would accept an auto body repairman's offer to include unrelated damages in insurance claim. The book, *The Day America Told The Truth*,[59] pointed out the following:

Americans lie. They lie more than we had ever thought possible before the study. But they told us the truth about how much they lie. Just about everyone lies! 91% of us lie regularly. The majority of us find it hard to get through a week without lying. 1 in 5 can't make it through a single day without lying. And we're talking about conscious, premeditated lies. When we refrain from lying, it's less often because we think it is wrong (only 45%), than for a variety of other reasons, among them the fear of being caught (17%). We lie to just about everyone, and the better we know someone the likelier we are to have told them a serious lie.[60]

The Bible has a lot to say about this. In Proverbs 6, God speaks of the seven things He hates.

These six things the Lord hates,
Yes, seven are an abomination to Him:
A proud look,
A lying tongue,
Hands that shed innocent blood,
A heart that devises wicked plans,
Feet that are swift in running to evil,
A false witness who speaks lies,
And one who sows discord among brethren.
(Proverbs 6:16-19)

Hates in the passage above means to "hate personally a personal enemy." I certainly wouldn't want to be doing something God specifically says He hates, would you? It's worth noting that two of the seven things God hates refer to dishonesty.

Why does God speak so strongly about lying? Because it's so *destructive*.

Like a club or a sword or a sharp arrow is the man who gives false testimony against his neighbor.
(Proverbs 25:18)

The Living Bible renders the passage like this: "Telling lies about someone is as harmful as hitting him with an axe, or wounding him with a sword, or shooting him with a sharp arrow."

From passages like these, we could safely conclude that God hates lying in any form. He hates it because He is the source of truth. In fact, He used that very word to describe His character. Jesus said, "I am the truth."

Scripture tells us that it is impossible for God to lie.[61] In dramatic contrast, Jesus calls Satan "the father of lies" (John 8:44). When we lie, we are behaving more like children of the Devil than children of God.

Have you been telling lies about others lately? God says of the liar, "He who works deceit shall not dwell within My house; he who tells lies shall not continue in My presence" (Psalm 101:7). This means that if you are telling lies (and there really are no "little white ones"), you are in sin against God.

Paul writes, "Do not lie to each other, since you have taken off your old self with its practices and have put on the new self, which is being renewed in knowledge in the image of its Creator" (Colossians 3:9, NIV).

We know it's wrong...so why do we do it? Often because we have been caught doing something wrong. The classic example of "whoppers of all time" was Aaron with the golden calf.

[Moses] turned to Aaron. "What did the people do to you?" he demanded. "How did they ever make you bring such terrible sin upon them?"

"Don't get upset, sir," Aaron replied. "You yourself know these people and what a wicked bunch they are. They said to me, 'Make us some gods to lead us, for something has happened to this man Moses, who led us out of Egypt.' So I told them, 'Bring me your gold earrings.' When they brought them to me, I threw them into the fire—and out came this calf!" (Exodus 32:21-24, NLT)

Isn't that amazing? You happen to throw a bunch of earrings into the pot, and out leaps a golden calf!

A survey on lying in the *Washington Post* magazine cited the two principle reasons people tell falsehoods are to save face, and to keep from offending someone else.

We've all been faced with those situations when telling the truth is uncomfortable, to say the least.

A wife asks her husband, "Honey, do I look *fat* in this?"

The wisest answer here is an incomplete one. "Wow, I think you look great tonight." You don't have to go into detail!

Or you've just choked down a horrible meal as a guest in someone's home, and they ask, "How was it?"

"Umm..." you say, "I've never eaten anything like that in my life!"

Or someone sings a solo and just butchers the song. They come up to you afterward and say, "How'd I do?" What do you say? Well, you try not to state the obvious, while not telling an outright lie.

"It was one of the most fascinating performances I have ever heard. Your voice was distinct and stood out from all the rest."

An outright lie, however, is an outright lie. And the "little" ones can easily lead to more serious ones.

You say, "I'm not home," when you really are.

Or, "I forgot," when you really didn't.

Or, "It's good to see you!" when you don't feel that way at all.

Or, "I love your outfit," when you really hate it.

Or, "I was just getting ready to call you," when you had no intention.

Or, "I'll be praying for you," when you know you probably won't.

So you say you never lie? Maybe you lie more than you realize! Deception wears a number of different guises.

1. Gossip

There's another manifestation of bearing false witness that often tries to cover itself with a cloak of respectability. But it's poison through and through.

Gossip.

It topples governments, wrecks marriages, splits churches, ruins careers, destroys reputations, causes nightmare, spawns suspicion, and generates grief. Even its name hisses. *Gosssssip.*

> A gossip betrays a confidence;
> so avoid a man who talks too much.
> (Proverbs 20:19, NIV)

Within my circle of friends, there are certain people whom I know can keep a confidence. And then there are others…. If I tell them, "Don't tell anyone," it will be on CNN that night!

Gossip often veils itself in "acceptable ways," such as….

"Have you heard?"

"Did you know?"

"I don't believe it's true, but I heard that…."

"I probably shouldn't tell you this, but I know you'll pray…."

There's nothing wrong with conveying accurate information in appropriate situations. But the question is, are you *sure* that what you're about to say is true? Have you checked your facts? Have you gone to the person you're intending to talk about?

There's a little acrostic I came across that's helped a lot of people think twice about talking behind someone's back. In fact, it's the word T.H.I.N.K.

(T) Is it True? (H) Will it Help? (I) Is it Inspiring? (N) Is it Necessary? (K) Is it Kind?

"But Greg," you say, "if I applied those standards, 90 percent of what I say should never be said!" So be it. Maybe you're like the guy who told his friend, "I will never repeat gossip…so please listen carefully the first time!"

2. Flattery

This is one of the most subtle forms of deceit. One definition of flattery is saying things to a certain person's face that you would never say behind his or her back.

It's tempting to flatter someone to get something from them—so you tell them something you think they want to hear. You tell them they are better than they really are, saying things to them you don't actually believe yourself. It is a form of lying, and as with all lies, can be very damaging.

3. Exaggeration

Would it be an exaggeration to say we all do this?

We talk about that Alaskan King salmon that got away ("It must have been fifty pounds...."), or we tell someone "You've been on my mind all day" (would you believe ten minutes?).

We may exaggerate our skills to get a promotion. Or just stretch the facts to make the story we're telling more interesting or juicy. Harmless, you say? Not really. In the first place, it begins to erode your credibility, causing people to doubt your character. And more significantly, any form of lying opens the door to the Father of Lies...and that's a door you want to keep firmly closed.

4. Keeping Silence

How could saying nothing be a lie? This could be on those occasions when we hear somebody say something we know for a fact is not true, and we remain silent. Someone may be slamming a friend or an acquaintance, and you know what they are saying is off base. But you don't say a word; you let the destructive words stand. This is slander by silence, complicity by passivity. And it is as deceitful as if you had said it yourself.

And now we come to the final commandment in God's top ten. While the previous commandments we've discussed focus mostly on externals, this one has to do with our heart. The other commandments focus on actions, while this one deals with a state of mind.

COMMANDMENT 10: YOU SHALL NOT COVET

This Tenth Command reminds us that God cares about what goes on between our ears. We're kidding ourselves if we think God only takes note of external behavior.

> "You shall not covet your neighbor's house; you shall not covet your neighbor's wife, nor his male servant, nor his female servant, nor his ox, nor his donkey, nor anything that is your neighbor's." (Exodus 20:17-18)

Coveting isn't simply desiring something you don't have. *It is to be devoured by desire for something that is not yours.* The New Testament Greek translation of the Hebrew word for "covet" means to lust, to pant after something. It means to set the heart or to eagerly desire that which belongs to another.

A Roman Catholic priest, who had heard the confessions of some 2,000 persons, said he had heard men confess iniquities of every kind—including adultery and even murder—but he had never heard any man confess to committing the sin of covetousness.

How does coveting work? It begins with the eyes. The eyes look at an object, the mind admires it, the will goes over to it, and the body moves in to possess it.

Let's not misunderstand: You may admire your friend's car—and even buy one like it—but that is not coveting. Copying, maybe, but not coveting. Now if you were to find his car in a parking lot, jimmy the lock, hot wire the car, and drive away with it, that's coveting—and stealing, too. If you look at it, admire it, and your will desires it, the your body moves over to possess it, you have violated the Tenth Commandment. That is coveting which has led to action. In this case, to grand theft auto!

It's not wrong to desire a wife, either, but to desire the wife of another man is coveting. Coveting is a powerful and often underestimated sin. It can cripple you spiritually and ultimately destroy you. It must not be simply shrugged off or left unchecked.

Paul wrote this strong warning to Timothy: "For the love of money is a root of all kinds of evil, for which some have strayed from the faith in their greediness, and pierced themselves through with many sorrows" (1 Timothy 6:10). Judas betrayed the Savior of the world for thirty pieces of silver—that he never enjoyed for a moment!

It's not a sin to want to be successful in business, and make a good living. But when you become obsessed with it, when you are willing to do whatever it takes to get there, when it becomes the most important thing in life to you, coveting has become idolatry.

> Therefore put to death your members which are on the earth: fornication, uncleanness, passion, evil desire, and covetousness, which is idolatry. (Colossians 3:5-6)

The story of King David's great sin in 2 Samuel 12 is a classic case of a man who started with coveting—and slid straight down from there into sins that were far worse. *He coveted another man's wife...he stole her...he committed adultery...he was an accomplice to murder...he tried to cover it up.*

Have you ever stolen, lied, or coveted? Of course you have. We've all broken God's Ten Commandments. And we all would be without hope and without God in the world if He had not provided a remedy for our sins, a way back into intimacy and fellowship with Him.

You need to repent, change your direction, and ask God to forgive you right now.

Sometimes reading things like this can be a bit uncomfortable. We know very well we have violated some of these commands, and we don't like to have it pointed out to us—even in private. It's like going to the dentist with a killer toothache, and he tells you he needs to drill, and maybe do a root canal. You initially feel like getting out of that chair and walking out the door. But if you want to stop the pain and not have it get even worse, you must do it.

In the same way, God convicts us of our sin not to drive us to despair, but rather to send us into the open arms of Jesus. He knows what you've done. He has already paid for it at Calvary's cross.

He says "Come unto me...."

There isn't a single sin or broken command beyond His forgiving, restoring, healing power.

That's why we call Him the Savior.

Chapter Eleven

ENCOUNTER AT THE SUMMIT:
EXPERIENCING HIS GLORY

We've all walked our way through the different stages of friendship. When you first meet someone, you're very polite. You actually listen when they speak, give eye contact, and even laugh at their lame jokes.

But once you become real friends the formalities begin to fade, and the real business of friendship begins. You're more honest. You feel more freedom to speak your mind, to show your emotions. In fact, you let your guard down, and take the risk of letting your friend see what's going on inside your heart.

This progression might be symbolized by free access into your friend's kitchen. If he or she takes you there, that in itself is a mark of progress. Why? Because if you really don't want someone to stay very long, you usher your guest into your front room.

If you're new friends, you might be hanging out in your buddy's kitchen and see something good to eat—like a nice, ripe peach—on the counter. But since you still don't know each other all that well, you don't ask for the peach... you wait for it to be offered. (Maybe stare at it for a minute or two, so they get the idea!) But if you've known that individual for a long time, you might just pick up that peach and bite into it without asking. Why? Because your friend has invited you to make yourself at home—and means it.

Obviously, there are stages of intimacy and understanding in marriage, as well. Do you remember when you first met your spouse-to-be? Remember working so hard to make the best possible impression? You wanted to put your best foot forward, and always say "the right thing." I remember having a big crush on a girl in high school, and was so anxious about calling her that I made up a written list of things to talk about in advance. A script!

Finally, you popped the big question to the love of your life (I kind of slipped it in). During engagement you got to know each other even better. And finally your wedding day arrived.

When you've been married for awhile, you can actually begin to anticipate what your spouse wants—what he or she might be thinking. You can walk into a room and feel the vibes, knowing immediately whether your mate is in a good or bad mood. Sometimes in conversation, you even finish each other's sentences.

Most husbands—at least the wise ones—have figured out that women don't always say what they really mean. You need to learn to interpret. And because you love your wife, you're willing to take the time to do that...to find out what she's really thinking and how she's really feeling. It might take you awhile to draw it out, but if you are lovingly persistent, you'll come to an understanding.

But women need interpretation skills, too. Let me give you a few "for instances."

- When a man says to a woman, "It's a guy thing," what he really means is: There is no rational thought pattern connected with this, and you have no chance at all of making it logical.

- When a man says to a woman, "Can I help with dinner?" what he really means is: Why isn't it already on the table?

- When he says, "Uh-huh...sure, honey," or "Yes, dear," what he really means is: Absolutely nothing! It's a conditioned response.

- When he says, "It would take too long to explain," what he really means is: I have no idea how it works.

- When he says, "Take a break, honey. You're working too hard," what he actually means is: I can't hear the game over the vacuum cleaner.

- When he says, "That's interesting, dear," what he really means is: Are you still talking?

- When he says, "You know how bad my memory is," what he really means is: I can remember the theme song to "F-Troop," the address of the first girl I ever kissed, and the vehicle identification numbers of every car I've ever owned—but I forgot your birthday!

- When he says, "I can't find it," what he means is: It didn't fall into my outstretched hand, so I'm completely clueless.

- When he says, "You look terrific!" what he really means is: Oh please don't try on one more outfit, I'm starving!

- When he says, "I'm not lost! I know exactly where we are," what he really means is: No one will ever see us alive again!

In this chapter, we'll encounter the story of a man in the book of Exodus who truly knew the Lord personally—not only as God, but as a close friend. And there was no communication breakdown here.

"A Great Sin"

Moses was on intimate terms with the Lord of the universe, and could freely speak his mind. Scripture says that "the LORD spoke to Moses face to face, as a man speaks to his friend" (Exodus 33:11).The Lord revealed things to him He had never revealed to a human being before.

Then one day, deep in prayer, Moses asked the unthinkable—a request almost without parallel in human history to this point.

Moses asked to actually see God.

Shocking? Yes. But friends can ask special favors of friends. And God wasn't offended! In fact, He had been in the process of drawing Moses out, showing him what prayer was really all about.

In the last few chapters, we considered the Ten Commandments, given by God. They were personally delivered from the Lord to His friend Moses, up on Mount Sinai. Aaron had been left in charge of the people in his brother's absence. But instead of waiting with baited breath for the Word of the Lord, the Israelites had turned to full-tilt idolatry and gross immorality.

After seeing this debacle for himself, Moses told the people, "You have committed a great sin."[62] This raises an interesting question: Are some sins greater or worse than others? Some might say, "No, sin is sin. It's all the same." But that's not totally true. According to Scripture, there are some sins that truly are worse than others.

Now, in a broad sense, all sin—from the smallest infraction to the most grievous crime—separates us from God. Jesus made this clear in the Sermon on the Mount, when He pointed out that lusting was a sin as well as committing adultery, and hating was a sin as well as murder.

They won't send you to jail for hating someone, but count on it, you'll go to prison for murder—and maybe to death row. And though it's wrong and sinful to coddle lust in your heart, it doesn't have the same life-blasting ramifications of adultery.

Jesus drew a distinction between sins when He was speaking to Pontius Pilate. He told the Roman governor, "You could have no power at all against Me unless it had been given you from above. Therefore the one who delivered Me to you has the greater sin."[63]

Jesus was either referring to Caiaphas, the High Priest, or to Judas, the betrayer. Both of these men knew very well Jesus was innocent, and that what they were doing was dead wrong. When we have been schooled in the Scripture as Caiaphas had been schooled or exposed to the truth and power of God like Judas, we are essentially without excuse.

This leads to the "unforgivable sin," which is blasphemy against the Holy Spirit. The work of the Holy Spirit is to show us our need for Jesus, our need for a Savior. To "blaspheme" Him means to reject or disregard Him—in essence, to "blow Him off." It is to say, "I know the gospel is true, but I refuse to accept it or to follow Jesus."

This is the greatest sin of all.

Israel had committed a great sin in the shadow of Mount Sinai. Why was it a "great" sin? Because, like Caiaphas, they *knew* better. They were God's chosen, covenant people. They had seen His fearsome power demonstrated on their behalf.

Who could forget...

...the ten devastating plagues that shook the nation of Egypt to the core?

...that wild wind that split the Red Sea down the middle, making an escape route for Israel, and creating a watery grave for the pursuing Egyptians?

...the manna sent from heaven to sustain millions of people cut off from provision in the wilderness?

And on top of all that, the people of Israel had solemnly promised to obey the Lord on three separate occasions. In Exodus 19, for instance, there was this exchange:

Moses returned from the mountain and called together the leaders of the people and told them what the Lord had said. They all responded together, "We will certainly do everything the Lord asks of us." So Moses brought the people's answer back to the Lord. (vv. 7-8, NLT)

Jesus said, "From everyone who has been given much, much will be demanded; and from the one who has been entrusted with much, much more will be asked."[64]

Not only are some sins worse than others, but *all* sin must be dealt with. And Moses was about to deal with the shocking sin in the camp of Israel.

We already know of the guilt of the people worshiping a golden calf combined with an unbridled sexual orgy. But what made it all so much worse was the utter failure of Israel's leadership in the whole affair. While Moses was up on the mountain meeting with the Lord, Aaron, Hur, and the Levites had full authority to quell this uprising—and should have! Aaron heard the people clamoring for an idol. But instead of stopping this surge of popular sentiment cold, he figured he would make the best of it. He tried to justify it before God by throwing a burnt offering into the equation and calling it "a feast to the LORD."[65]

This lame attempt at "compromise," however, only outraged the Lord even more, and He came within a hair's breadth of wiping out the whole nation (or so it seemed), sparing Moses alone.

Moses was angry, too, but he interceded for his rebellious people, and God turned away from His wrath.

This is why I have a problem with a ministry philosophy that centers around "meeting people's felt needs." Here was a nation that had no idea what they really needed. Their "felt need" was for an idol. But what they really needed was faith in the God who had brought them this far.

TRUTH AND CONSEQUENCES

Though God pardoned Israel, there was still a price to be paid for their sin. This reminds us that God *in His grace* forgives our sins, but God *in His government* allows sin to work out its consequences in human life.

For instance, God forgave David for his sin of adultery with Bathsheba. But He also warned David that "the sword shall never depart from your house...."[66] And it didn't. To his lasting grief, David saw his own behavior repeated in the lives of his children.

Sin will have its pound of flesh. It will cost, and cost *big*. When Paul wrote that "the wages of sin is death," he meant more than physical death and the grave. It is also a principle of death that casts a shadow over life itself—over every worthwhile thing in our lives, robbing us of joy, peace, and contentment.

Moses came down from the crown of Mount Sinai and saw the people completely given over to idolatry and immorality. And when he confronted Aaron—the High Priest!—he got one of the lamest excuses anyone has ever scraped together.

Angry to the core, Moses gave the people an ultimatum. He cried out, "'Whoever is on the LORD's side—come to me!' And all the sons of Levi gathered themselves together to him" (Exodus 32:26). Moses commanded these loyal Levites to slay the offenders without pity, and 3,000 people were slain that day.

REMOVING THE CANCER

Some will say, "That's not fair! How could a God of love do something like that?"

We only show our ignorance when we make statements like that. Here's a newsflash. God doesn't owe you an explanation as to why He does or doesn't do certain things. He doesn't even owe you the time of day! And even if He did give us His reasons, we can't assume we would even begin to understand them. A finite human mind trying to grapple with the thoughts of God would be like wiring the full power of Bonneville Dam to a five-watt flashlight bulb. We couldn't handle them for an instant.

> "For as the heavens are higher than the earth,
> So are My ways higher than your ways,
> And My thoughts than your thoughts."
> (Isaiah 55:9)

> Oh, what a wonderful God we have! How great are his riches and wisdom and knowledge! How impossible it is for us to understand his decisions and his methods! For who can know what the Lord is thinking? Who knows enough to be his counselor? (Romans 11:33-34, NLT)

One thing we can be very sure of is that God hates sin, and it cannot be tolerated. It must be dealt with swiftly, lest it spread and do even more harm. The Bible compares it to leaven, something that grows quickly. It is like a cancer that left untreated will metastasize, spread, and kill.

It's hard for us to fathom a God of righteousness and judgment in this day of unconditional "tolerance" and political correctness. Some would even try to differentiate between the "God of wrath" in the Old Testament, and the "God of love" in the New. As if He had somehow evolved and changed, seeing things from a different point of view.

Not so! He is the same God, who is just and loving in both testaments of the Bible. He declares, "For I am the LORD, I do not change" (Malachi 3:6).

And believe me, you wouldn't want it any other way.

Some might say *"I don't believe in a God of judgment, just a God of love."* That may be true, but the God you are choosing to worship *is not real*. The French philosopher Voltaire once wrote, "God made man in His image, and man returned the favor."

Have you heard of "The Temple of the Thousand Buddhas."? It's an unusual place of worship in Kyoto, Japan, where worshipers can literally design their own deities. The temple is filled with more than a thousand likenesses of Buddha, each one a little different from the next, allowing worshipers to pick and choose which they like best. Devotees of Buddha often try to find the likeness they feel most resembles themselves.

And that's exactly what we do when we say, "Well, *my* God would never do thus and so...." Or maybe, "I agree with this part of what the Bible says, but not that *part*."

What you are doing, whether you intend to or not, is remaking God in your own image, and that is idolatry. It's no different from Aaron forming a golden calf and declaring, "This is your god, O Israel, that brought you out of the land of Egypt!"

STANDING IN THE GAP

The Lord told Moses He was fed up with the Israelites: "I have seen this people, and indeed it is a stiff-necked people! Now therefore, let Me alone, that My wrath may burn hot against them and I may consume them. And I will make of you a great nation" (Exodus 32:9-10).

God was testing Moses. I don't believe it was His intention to annihilate the whole nation, but to see if Moses would pray, intercede, and stand in the gap for the Israelites.

It's the same today. God is still looking for intercessors...people who are willing to stand in the gap.

The gospel of John tells the story of a desperate father whose son was at death's door. Though part of a royal family, this man found Jesus and humbled himself before Him—imploring and begging Him to touch his dear son.

Jesus' response was a little unusual—maybe not what you'd expect: "Unless you people see signs and wonders, you will by no means believe."[67]

As with Moses, Jesus was testing this distraught father. In reality, Jesus was not directing these words of rebuke to the man, but to the fickle crowd standing around observing these things.

That father patiently waited. Not to be deterred, he again petitioned Jesus. "Sir, come to my house before my child dies."

This man had passed the test, and stood strong as both a godly father and a true intercessor. And Jesus replied, "Go your way, your son lives."

Many times we pray and don't see the results we so desperately want. This is especially true as we pray for our children. But the story of that father, and the one of Moses crying out to God for his people, teaches us this important principle: When praying for the salvation of a soul, the intervention of God in a life, *don't give up!* You are praying according to the will of God. You can know that for sure, because Scripture says, "God is not willing that any should perish but that all should come to repentance" (2 Peter 3:9).

This is not unlike what the Lord said to Abraham when He told him, "Take now your son, your only son Isaac, whom you love, and go to the land of Moriah, and offer him there as a burnt offering on one of the mountains of which I shall tell you" (Genesis 22:2). It was never God's intention to take Isaac's life (God has never sanctioned human sacrifice), but rather to test and mature His servant Abraham.

Abraham passed his test with flying colors, and so did Moses. In fact, Moses offered himself in the place of his people—even willing to give up his hope of heaven if God would spare them.

Moses said to the Lord: "Oh, what a great sin these people have committed! They have made themselves gods of gold. But now, please forgive their sin—but if not, *then blot me out of the book you have written*" (Exodus 32:31-32, NIV).

This pleased the Lord, and He spared them. By offering himself as a sacrifice for a sinful nation, Moses was actually foreshadowing Jesus, who would give His life as a ransom for the world. And I can imagine God saying to him, "Moses, you remind Me of My Son."

Moses had come such a long way from the impetuous young Prince of Egypt, or the passive old man in the desert, watching the bush burn. He was now God's man, God's intercessor, and God's friend. He was beloved of the Lord.

But Moses' amazing conversation with the Lord wasn't over.

God told Moses that He would not destroy the people, but that He wouldn't go with them, either! Instead, He would send an angel to accompany them.

When Moses relayed this message to the nation, the people were devastated. They stripped off all the jewelry and ornaments and fancy trinkets they had packed out of Egypt and repented before the Lord.

And Moses, still in his role as intercessor for the people, went on negotiating with the Lord.

Moses said to the Lord, "You have been telling me, 'Take these people up to the Promised Land.' But you haven't told me whom you will send with me. You call me by name and tell me I have found favor with you. Please, if this is really so, show me your intentions so I will understand you more fully and do exactly what you want me to do. Besides, don't forget that this nation is your very own people."

And the LORD replied, "I will personally go with you, Moses. I will give you rest—everything will be fine for you."

Then Moses said, "If you don't go with us personally, don't let us move a step from this place. If you don't go with us, how will anyone ever know that your people and I have found favor with you? How else will they know we are special and distinct from all other people on the earth?"

And the Lord replied to Moses, "I will indeed do what you have asked, for you have found favor with me, and you are my friend." (Exodus 33:12-17, NLT)

The Lord was "drawing Moses out" as they spoke to each other. And He will do the same with us at different times in our lives.

We'll encounter a roadblock that stops us in our tracks. Bad news from the doctor...the job that didn't open...the deal that didn't close...the phone call that never came...the romantic relationship that never gelled...and sometimes you feel like you're losing hope.

Don't give up!

Press on. Press in. Keep praying, keep asking.

Remember Abraham, pleading with the Lord to turn back His impending judgment on the evil city of Sodom?

The Lord remained with Abraham for a while. Abraham approached him and said, "Will you destroy both innocent and guilty alike? Suppose you find fifty innocent people there within the city—will you still destroy it, and not spare it for their sakes? Surely you wouldn't do such a thing, destroying the innocent with the guilty. Why, you would be treating the innocent and the guilty exactly the same! Surely you wouldn't do that! Should not the Judge of all the earth do what is right?"

And the LORD replied, "If I find fifty innocent people in Sodom, I will spare the entire city for their sake." (Genesis 18:22-26, NLT)

Abraham kept the negotiating session going. If the Lord had responded to the number of 50, would He respond to 45? He would. And so it went, from 40 to 30 to 20...and finally to 10—as far as the patriarch dared to go.

It might almost seem irreverent the way Abraham "dickered" with the Lord in this conversation. In reality, however, it reveals the closeness of their friendship. It's also a reflection of the way business was done in the Middle East. You always bargained for a deal, never paying the original asking price.

Abraham was doing business with the Lord, and the most significant point about this conversation was that *he already knew he had the heart of the Lord in this prayer.* He could pray and plead with God in confidence, knowing that He was just and merciful, a God who truly didn't want to bring calamity on people.[68]

Moses was doing business with the Lord, too—and he also understood the heart of God with his requests.

1. He Asks For Divine Direction

> "Now therefore, I pray, if I have found grace in Your sight, show me now Your way." (Exodus 33:13)

This is really a prayer for every believer. In Moses' case, he needed further revelation about God's intentions for the future. *What next, Lord?*

God's reply in verse 14 is beautiful in its simplicity: "My presence will go with you, and I will give you rest."

The Hebrew term for "presence" here is especially vivid. God literally said, *"My face will go with you."* To give rest doesn't mean that Moses and Israel would cease from activity, but rather that they would enjoy God's protection and blessing. A loose paraphrase might read, *"Don't sweat the small stuff. I will take care of you."*

Just think how much time we waste in worry and fretting about things that never happen—how much needless energy we expend striving in our own strength to do what God has already promised to do for us.

It is said that worry is the interest paid on trouble before it's due! Worry does not empty tomorrow of it's sorrow…it empties today of its strength.

2. He Asks For Confirmation

> Then he said to Him, "If Your Presence does not go with us, do not bring us up from here. For how then will it be known that Your people and I have found grace in Your sight, except You go with us?" (Exodus 33:15-16)

This may sound like Moses was lacking in faith, but it was really a good thing for him to express to the Lord. In essence, he was saying, "Lord, I don't want to make this journey without You. *I must have this assurance.*" Though the Lord had promised to send His angel before them, Moses wouldn't settle for that. He didn't want angels—whether one or a thousand—he wanted *God.*

I think this was pleasing to the Lord.

There was an occasion in the gospel of John where Jesus laid out what it really meant to follow Him. May of His so-called "disciples" bailed that day. As

He watched these former followers walk away, Jesus turned to Peter and the others and said, "Will you also leave Me?"

> Simon Peter answered him, "Lord, to whom shall we go? You have the words of eternal life. We believe and know that you are the Holy One of God." (John 6:68-69, NIV)

"Lord, we don't know all that much, but this much we do know—we're staying with You!"

Do you want Jesus Christ to go with you in all you say and do? Sure, we might ask Him to accompany us when we're taking that long plane flight. We figure that if He's on board, we won't go down! Or we may want Him to go with us to that job interview...or into the operating room...or through that dangerous part of town after dark.

But do we also want Him to go with us on our vacation...or our night out with friends? Do we want Him to accompany us to that party or movie? If we would be ashamed or embarrassed for Him to see what we are seeing or doing, we shouldn't be doing it in the first place.

God reassured His friend Moses with these words: "I will also do this thing that you have spoken; for you have found grace in My sight" (v. 17).

By this time Moses figures he's on a roll. Everything he's asked for he has received. So he figures he may as well go for the gold.

3. He Prays For The Glory Of GOD To Be Revealed To Him.

And he said, "Please, show me Your glory." (v. 18)

Do you understand what Moses was asking for here? "Lord, I want to *see* Your glory. *I want to see You!*"

Did Moses overstep his bounds here? Did he take too many liberties with the Lord? Was God about to squash him like a bug against the rocky walls of Sinai?

Not at all. Not only was this not a bad thing for Moses to seek, it was a very good thing. Jesus Himself said, "If anyone loves me, he will obey my teaching. My Father will love him, and we will come to him and make our home with him" (John 14:23, NIV). Again, in the book of Revelation, He declared: "Look! I have been standing at the door, and I am constantly knocking. If anyone hears me calling him and opens the door, I will come in and fellowship with him and he with me" (Revelation 3:20, TLB).

Moses was a man who came to understand the principle objective of prayer. It's not just about "getting things" from the Lord, it's about getting *the Lord Himself.*

In Chapter 5, we saw how the conniving, scheming Jacob finally met his match when the Lord Himself "wrestled with him until the breaking of day."

Needless to say, Jacob lost that match, but in the process, an amazing thing happened to him. Jacob went from resisting to resting, from cunning to clinging. He had the Lord in the best wrestling hold he could think of, and he said to Him, "I will not let You go until You bless me!"

Here was a man who had come to understand prayer's true objective.

"Lord, whatever You want is fine by me—I just want You! I don't want to go even one step further in life without You right beside me."

Have you come to a point in your life where you are able to say to Jesus, "Your kingdom come, Your will be done, on earth as it is in heaven"? Or are you essentially praying, "Not Your will, but *mine* be done"?

We must never be afraid to place an unknown future into the hands of a known God. D. L. Moody counseled, "Spread out your petition before God, and then say, 'Thy will, not mine, be done.'" Later in life, Moody reflected, "The sweetest lesson I have learned in God's school is to *let the Lord choose for me.*"

God could not grant Moses all that he wanted, because seeing God in all His glory would have vaporized him. So the Lord worked out a special arrangement for His friend.

Then He said, "I will make all My goodness pass before you, and I will proclaim the name of the Lord before you. I will be gracious to whom I will be gracious, and I will have compassion on whom I will have compassion." But He said, "You cannot see My face; for no man shall see Me, and live." And the Lord said, "Here is a place by Me, and you shall stand on the rock. So it shall be, while My glory passes by, that I will put you in the cleft of the rock, and will cover you with My hand while I pass by. Then I will take away My hand, and you shall see My back; but My face shall not be seen." (Exodus 33:19-23)

I can't begin to imagine what that experience must have been like. Moses must have felt like the apostle Paul, who after being caught up into heaven for a brief time, "heard inexpressible things, things that man is not permitted to tell."[69]

We think of Paul and Moses and Jacob, and we're awed by such a relationship with the living God. But do you realize that if you are a believer in Jesus Christ, you have a relationship with God that's *even closer?* Under the old covenant, only specially chosen men like Abraham and Moses had this kind of access into God's presence. Then, with the giving of the Law and the establishment of the Tabernacle—and later the Temple God was to be approached only through the High Priest at particular times of the year by means of animal sacrifices.

Not just any person could stroll into the Holy of Holies and offer their prayer. If they tried, they would be struck down where they stood. Clearly, God did not *live in* His people at that time.

But all this changed with the death and resurrection of Jesus. He became our sacrifice, spilling His own blood on our behalf, and He is now interceding for us at the Father's right hand as our great High Priest.[70] When He died, the thick, heavy veil in the temple was ripped from top to bottom, because a new covenant had gone into effect...and the door into God's presence was thrown open wide.

We saw how, because of Moses, the people of Israel were spared. He interceded for them, and God turned away His wrath. In the same way, because of Jesus, we were spared. And now, because of His sacrifice, we have open access to God.

> And so, dear brothers, now we may walk right into the very Holy of Holies, where God is, because of the blood of Jesus. This is the fresh, new, life-giving way that Christ has opened up for us by tearing the curtain—his human body—to let us into the holy presence of God. And since this great High Priest of ours rules over God's household, let us go right in to God himself, with true hearts fully trusting him to receive us because we have been sprinkled with Christ's blood to make us clean. (Hebrews 10:19-22, TLB)

Yes, Moses was God's friend.

But so are you.

Jesus said, "No longer do I call you servants, for a servant does not know what his master is doing; but I have called you friends, for all things that I heard from My Father I have made known to you" (John 15:15).

He is a Friend who walks with you through all of life. Let that thought strengthen you to resist the folly and sorrow of a compromised life. And let that thought strengthen you and give you courage as you walk step by step into an unknown future.

In the pages of this book, we've been considering "the greatest stories ever told." It's good to look back on lives that God has touched, transformed, refined, and used mightily for His kingdom. But it's even more important to realize that *your life* is a story—a story you're either beginning, right in the middle of, or about to finish. But no matter where you are in that journey, as you allow Jesus to transform you and His Holy Spirit to fill you, empower you, and use you, your life will also be a great story.

And the best is yet to come!

THE GREATEST
STORIES
EVER TOLD

VOLUME TWO

Chapter One

MOSES' STORY: WHAT GOD IS LIKE

*"Surely blessing I will bless you, and multiplying
I will multiply you." —Hebrews 6:14*

Man is incurably religious. Down through the ages, most people have believed in the existence of God or gods. It may be that most human beings have given more attention to this idea of a supreme being or beings than all other concerns—food, clothing, housing, work, pleasure—put together.

The Greeks and Romans had a whole pantheon of gods, with familiar names like Jupiter, Mars, Mercury, and Venus. All of those multiple gods and multiple altars troubled the heart of the apostle Paul on one occasion when he was passing through Athens on his way to Corinth.

With a little time on his hands, the apostle decided to take a walk through town. That's when he saw that the city was filled with images and idols erected to various deities. And it distressed him.

It's easy to understand why. Paul had been a champion of the one true God from childhood. And Athens in that day probably had more temples, shrines, and altars than Los Angeles has McDonalds.

But as common as this belief in some kind of deity or supreme being might be, the nature of who God is and what He is like is a mystery to most people. The first-century Athenians hedged their bets by erecting an altar "to an unknown god." In other words, if there is a god out there that we've missed or overlooked in the religious life of our city, we want to make sure we're covered... even though we have no idea of who that particular deity might be.

In Acts 17, Paul seized on that altar to a mystery and set out to declare to them the Good News about this unknown god. With that idea as his on-ramp, he spoke to them about the true and living God who had sent His Son to redeem the world.

MAKING GOD KNOWN

God is still unknown to many people today. They don't know His name, they don't understand His nature, and they can't comprehend His holiness, power, and love.

And that's why God gave us the Bible. From one cover to the other, it was written to tell us what He is like. In fact, that was one of Jesus' principle objectives when He walked on this planet.

John tells us that "No one has ever seen God, but God the One and Only, who is at the Father's side, has made him known." Jesus said, "No one has seen the Father except the one who is from God; only he has seen the Father."[1]

To help people grasp a God they didn't really know or understand, Jesus told stories that illustrated His Father's nature and heart of compassion. In the story of the prodigal son, for example, Jesus tells of a father who longs for fellowship with his ungrateful runaway son, and runs to meet him when the boy comes straggling back home. It's a story that has touched people all over the world for thousands of years.

"THE LORD BLESS YOU . . ."

Some would suggest that the God of the Old Testament is different from the God of the New Testament. Nothing could be further from the truth. From one end of the Bible to the other, we see a God who loves, cares, and remains vitally interested in the course of our lives.

Way back in the book of Numbers, the fourth book of the Bible, we come to a passage that reveals God's heart for His people and gives us yet one more clue of what He is like.

> And the LORD spoke to Moses, saying: "Speak to Aaron and his sons, saying, 'This is the way you shall bless the children of Israel. Say to them:
>
> "The LORD bless you and keep you; The LORD make His face shine upon you, And be gracious to you;
>
> The LORD lift up His countenance upon you, And give you peace." '
>
> So they shall put My name on the children of Israel, and I will bless them." (Numbers 6:22-27)

The book of Numbers is a record of the wanderings of the Israelites in the wilderness. It tells us of the trials they faced and the mistakes they made as they traveled to the Promised Land. It chronicles their rebellion, stubbornness, ingratitude, and complaining—and the ramifications of their disobedience. But it also shows God's incredible longsuffering and patience with them.

We, too, live in a wilderness. We're travelers passing through from one place to the next. And we also face our trials and make our mistakes. In addition to that, we face threats each and every day. Since 9-11, we all look over our shoulders a bit more. With the government uncovering more and more terrorism attempts—and evil plots so hateful and destructive that it boggles the mind—it can be a bit frightening sometimes.

Then there are all the normal concerns of our lives: our livelihood, health, marriage, children, and future. These concerns only increase as you get older. The fact is, we are a fallen people living in a fallen world in need of a little help. Actually, a lot of help.

We need the blessing of our God every bit as much as the ancient Hebrews needed it. That's why God instructed the Israelite priests to pronounce a special blessing on His people, a people wandering in the wilderness. He wanted that blessing spoken again and again. The Lord was saying, "I want this ingrained in their brains, etched in their hearts. I want them to know this blessing by memory and be able to recite it at a moment's notice."

Why? Because it reminds us of who God is, what He is like, and how He sees you and me. There are six truths that shine out from these verses; six statements that reveal God's heart toward His own. I am indebted to my friend Damian Kyle for his excellent outline on this text.

TRUTH 1: GOD LOVES TO BLESS YOU

"The Lord bless you…" (Numbers 6:24)

Christians like to toss around the words "bless" and "blessing." We say it quite a lot, and most of the time we mean it.

We also abuse the term. Sometimes as Christians we use the word to let people know the conversation is over, and that it's time for them to leave. We stand up from our desk, or if we've met someone out in public and we get tired of talking to them, we'll smile and say, "God bless you!" Which, being translated, means: Good-bye. Go away!

Blessing, however, is truly a spiritual term. The world may try to hijack it, but they really have no idea of what it means. In fact, true blessing is something only a child of God can experience.

Jesus both began and concluded His earthly ministry blessing people. After His resurrection, when He met the two downhearted disciples on the road to Emmaus, He blessed them. When children came to Him He took them in His arms and blessed them. Just before He ascended into heaven, Jesus lifted His hands and blessed His followers. Jesus loved to bless people. In a portion of the Sermon on the Mount we call the "Beatitudes," He tied together a whole string of blessings.

> Then He opened His mouth and taught them, saying: "Blessed are the poor in spirit, For theirs is the kingdom of heaven…."
> (Matthew 5:2-3)

Our word for "blessed" comes from the Greek word *makarios*. In fact, this was the Greek name for the Mediterranean island of Cyprus. Because of its geographical location, balmy climate, and fertile soil, the Greeks believed that anyone who lived on this island had it made in the shade. As far as they were concerned, everything anybody needed for happiness and fulfillment could be found right there, on that sunny island. A self-contained place of happiness. There was no need to import anything, because if you lived in Cyprus, you had it all.

In other words, *makarios* was a metaphor for complete blessedness or happiness. From this, we learn two important things about God and blessings.

First, God wants us to be blessed and happy. He truly does. In the opening chapter of Genesis we read: "So God created Man in His own image; in the image of God... He created them." And the very next words are, *"God blessed them."*[2] So just know that the Lord loves to bless us.

Second, blessedness or true happiness is independent from circumstances. The point Jesus is making in Matthew 5 is that blessedness, the happiness that God has for us, is independent of what may be happening in our life at the moment.

So here in Numbers, the Lord tells the priest to do this for His people—to stand before them and say, "the Lord bless you."

Some might feel as though this benediction ought to read, "The Lord curse you..." That's because they have lived apart from God's blessings, and feel that they're dealing with His curse on their lives. Is it true that God cursed certain people or places? Yes, it is. But there was always a reason for that. His blessings could not fall on people who rejected His kindness and love. For all practical purposes, they had chosen to be cursed instead.

God cursed Cain because of his disobedience (Genesis 4:11-12). God said there would be a curse on the person who worshipped false gods (Deuteronomy 27:15), and on the person who lived immorally (Deuteronomy 27:20). The list goes on.

But there is one key passage in the book of Deuteronomy that shows us we have a choice between God's blessing or curse.

> I call heaven and earth as witnesses today against you, that I have set before you life and death, blessing and cursing; therefore choose life, that both you and your descendants may live; that you may love the LORD your God, that you may obey His voice, and that you may cling to Him, for He is your life and the length of your days...
> (Deuteronomy 30:19-20)

For those of us who have chosen life, who have chosen to love Him, cling to Him, and obey His voice, there is blessing. *Blessing in abundance.* Your Father loves to bless you! Jesus said, "Do not fear, little flock; for it is your Father's good pleasure to give you the kingdom."[3]

As a father, it was my joy to bless (some would say spoil) my sons. Looking back, I have to say that it never felt like a "task" or a heavy burden for me to feed or clothe them. You would have never heard me say, "What? More baby food? Do you have any idea how much this is costing?" Or, "Are you kidding? I have to pay for diapers for this kid again?"

It was a privilege and a joy to have my boys in the house, and now I get to experience it all over again as a grandfather (and I don't even have to mess with diapers!).

Truth 2: God Has Promised to Keep You

"The Lord Bless You And Keep You..." (Numbers 6:24)

God wants us to be constantly reassured that He will keep us and care for us. The Israelites needed to hear that as they moved from place to place in a desolate wilderness. And in the twenty-first century, in such an evil and uncertain world as this, we need this reassurance too.

Sometimes we worry about our safety and security, not only for ourselves but for our families. At other times we worry about our relationship with God, and our personal salvation. Even mature believers experience seasons of doubt. Elijah did. So did Moses, Gideon, Hezekiah, Thomas, and others.

But God promises to keep us.

I will lift up my eyes to the hills—
From whence comes my help?
My help comes from the LORD,
Who made heaven and earth.

He will not allow your foot to be moved;
He who keeps you will not slumber.

Behold, He who keeps Israel
Shall neither slumber nor sleep.

The LORD is your keeper;
The LORD is your shade at your right hand.
The sun shall not strike you by day,
Nor the moon by night.

The LORD shall preserve you from all evil;
He shall preserve your soul.
The LORD shall preserve your going out and your coming in
From this time forth, and even forevermore.
(Psalm 121:1-7)

The Hebrew word used for *keep* means "to keep, to watch, to guard, to hedge about."

Remember the story in Job when the angels came to present themselves before the Lord, with Satan among them? God started bragging on His beloved servant, and Satan challenged Him.

Then the LORD said to Satan, "Have you considered My servant Job, that there is none like him on the earth, a blameless and upright man, one who fears God and shuns evil?"

So Satan answered the LORD and said, "Does Job fear God for nothing? Have You not made a hedge around him, around his household, and around all that he has on every side? You have blessed the work of his hands, and his possessions have increased in the land."
(Job 1:8-10)

Those things are true for you, too. God has put a hedge or wall of protection around your life, one that Satan can neither scale nor penetrate. And if he tries to go in the front door, he has to face the Great Shepherd! Jesus said "I tell you the truth, I am the gate for the sheep... .Yes, I am the gate."[4]

Many passages remind us of the keeping power of God.

- 2 Thessalonians 3:3: But the Lord is faithful, who will establish you and guard you from the evil one.

- Jude 1:24: Now to Him who is able to keep you from stumbling, and to present you faultless before the presence of His glory with exceeding joy.

- 1 Peter 1:5: ...Who are kept by the power of God through faith for salvation ready to be revealed in the last time.

- Jude 1:1: ...To those who have been called, who are loved by God the Father and kept by Jesus Christ.

When expressing the keeping power of God, the original language uses what Bible scholars call the perfect tense; the nearest equivalent in English is *continually kept.* It is a continuing result of a past action. Because He has decided to keep us, He will carry that commitment forward through all the days and years of our lives.

Whatever your difficulties may be, you need to know that you are preserved in Christ! The apostle John tells us that "Jesus knew that His hour had come that He should depart from this world to the Father, having loved His own who were in the world, He loved them to the end."[5]

You don't lose something that you love. You don't carelessly toss aside your favorite hat or sunglasses or latest cell phone... you keep your eye on what you value. You know where it is. You don't go to Disneyland with your kids only to leave them behind and completely forget them. (Although you may be tempted!)

God never forgets what He loves. In the book of Isaiah He says: "Can a mother forget her nursing child? Can she feel no love for the child she has borne? But even if that were possible, I would not forget you! See, I have written your name on the palms of my hands."[6]

He has invested heavily in finding you, saving you, and adopting you into

His own family, and He will protect His investment! Were it not for the preserving grace of God, not a single one of us would make it. I don't care how strong you think you are, you would "spiritually vapor-lock" on the spot.

The Bible leaves no doubt: Jesus is always there loving, preserving, and praying for those who belong to Him.

> Therefore he is able to save completely those who come to God through
> him, because he always lives to intercede for them.
> (Hebrews 7:25, NIV)

Scripture makes it abundantly clear: You and I are preserved, protected, and continually kept by the power of God.

"So Greg," someone will inevitably ask, "does that mean I can never really fall away from my faith?"

No. Actually, you can fall away. In the book of Jude, we are warned and encouraged to "keep yourselves in the love of God."[7] Though God's love is unsought, undeserved, and unconditional, it is possible for you to turn away and fall out of harmony with that love. Here's the way the writer of Hebrews puts it:

> See to it, brothers, that none of you has a sinful, unbelieving heart that
> turns away from the living God. But encourage one another daily, as
> long as it is called Today, so that none of you may be hardened by sin's
> deceitfulness. We have come to share in Christ if we hold firmly till the
> end the confidence we had at first. (Hebrews 3:12-14, NIV)

So what does Jude mean when he tells us to "keep ourselves in the love of God"? Simply put, it means this: *Keep yourself from all that is unlike Him.* Keep yourself from any influence that violates His love and brings sorrow to His heart. Keep yourself in a place where God can actively demonstrate His love toward you. That means staying away from certain people, places, and activities that make it easier for us to fall into temptation. Now that we've been delivered from the kingdom of Satan, we want to make sure we never place ourselves in his clutches and back under his control.

When we pray (as Jesus taught us), "Lead us not into temptation," we're asking the Father to help us so we won't deliberately place ourselves in volatile situations. Bottom line, if you truly *want* to be kept safe, preserved, and enjoy God's hedge of protection around your life, it's there for you.

Okay, you say, I'm enclosed in the hedge. Does that mean God will keep me from trials, sorrows, and difficulties?

No, not at all. If we think the road to heaven is all sunlight and daisies, we'll be thrown for a loop when hardships or tragedies come into our lives. We will incorrectly conclude that God has somehow failed in His promise to keep us.

The truth is, God has never promised to keep us from all the bumps, bruises, and heartaches of life in this world. However, even though He may not keep us *from* the hardships, He will keep us through the hardships. He will be with us. He will give us His grace. He will see us through.

> When you pass through the waters,
> I will be with you;
> and when you pass through the rivers,
> they will not sweep over you.
> When you walk through the fire,
> you will not be burned;
> the flames will not set you ablaze.
> For I am the LORD, your God,
> the Holy One of Israel, your Savior.
> (Isaiah 43:2-3, NIV)

The Lord didn't say, "*If* you pass through the waters... *if* you pass through the rivers ... *if* you walk through the fire..." He said those things will be a part of our lives during our short stay on earth. I'm sure you have already had your personal share of waters, rivers, and fire. And if not, hold on, because you will.

But what a difference to face those things knowing that God is watching over your every step and will keep you in His power and love! He is no less our keeper for allowing difficulty to come our way.

And if we trust Him, He will walk with us and keep us through that difficulty until we reach the other side of it.

When the Israelites came up against the dead end between Pharaoh's army and the Red Sea, they had already been walking in a miracle. With a mighty hand, God had delivered them from centuries of slavery and brought the whole nation out of captivity. When had such a thing ever happened in history?

So the sea stretched out before them, and they could hear the rumble of horses and chariots behind them, as a vengeful Pharaoh and his army were in hot pursuit. Terrified, the Israelites pointed the finger of blame at Moses, crying out, "Why did you bring us out here to die in the wilderness? Weren't there enough graves for us in Egypt? Why did you make us leave? Didn't we tell you to leave us alone while we were still in Egypt? Our Egyptian slavery was far better than dying out here in the wilderness!"

You know the rest of the story. God parted that Red Sea, and the Israelites passed through safely to the other side. Then those same parted waters crashed down on the Egyptian army, drowning them.

Why didn't God just lift up the whole nation and teleport them to the other side? Because then they (and we) wouldn't have learned a priceless lesson: While God may not keep us *from* the trial, He will show His power and love by keeping us *through* the trial.

The same is true with those three courageous Hebrew teens, Shadrach, Meshach, and Abendego. They not only had to face the possibility of execution by fire in the king's blazing furnace, they actually had the experience of being tossed alive into those hungry flames.

I love what happened next. It has to be one of my favorite stories in the Bible:

> Then King Nebuchadnezzar was astonished; and he rose in haste and spoke, saying to his counselors, "Did we not cast three men bound into the midst of the fire?"
>
> They answered and said to the king, "True, O king."
>
> "Look!" he answered, "I see four men loose, walking in the midst of the fire; and they are not hurt, and the form of the fourth is like the Son of God." (Daniel 3:24-25)

It wasn't just three individuals walking through the fire that day; there was a fourth, and that fourth was the Son of God. In the same way, He will keep us through our trials, no matter how fiery.

There are so many illustrations of this principle. Right off the top of the head we could name Noah and the flood, Jonah and the great fish, Daniel and the lion's den.

"Yes," you say, "but it isn't always a happy ending. John the Baptizer got beheaded. Herod killed James with a sword. Stephen was stoned to death. Where was the keeping power of God for them? Or what about when a godly man or woman is hurt or killed in a terrible accident, or stricken with a massive heart attack? Has God failed to keep them?

In even asking a question like that, we are assuming it is somehow our right to live long, easy, and relatively tranquil lives and die peacefully in our sleep one day. But that's not what the Bible says. Jesus did not say, "In this world you will only have blue skies and sunshine." Rather He said, "In this world you will have tribulation, but be of good cheer…"[8]

Whatever happens in our lives, "our times are in His hands." Our life is a gift to us from God right now, and that breath you just took was a gift as well. Don't take that for granted. Even death doesn't mean God has somehow failed in His promise to keep us. Barring the Rapture, that great event in which Jesus Christ will return for His Church, there will come a time for each one of us to make that journey home to Heaven.

And when that moment comes, *however* it comes, God will be right there, taking us by the hand and guiding us from one life to the next.

So far we've seen that God wants to bless you, and that He will keep you. But there's a third truth to consider here.

TRUTH 3: GOD SMILES ON YOU

"The Lord make His face shine upon you..." (Numbers 6:25)

God wants us to be reminded daily that when He looks on us, He smiles! That's what this text means.

That's not the picture many people have of the Lord. They see Him as a frowning, glowering Father in Heaven, looking down on us with arms folded and one foot impatiently tapping, rarely if ever pleased by us. But that is not the picture God gives us of Himself.

God's face shines with pleasure toward us as His people. When He sees you, His face just lights up with joy! He isn't angry with you and He isn't disappointed with you.

> He is merciful and tender toward those who don't deserve it; he is slow
> to get angry and full of kindness and love. (Psalm 103:8, TLB)

He isn't a God who is by nature grumpy and unhappy with us until we do something nice to change His mood. He loves us, and the very thought of us, the very sight of us, puts a smile on His face.

When you read about the ancient religions, you encounter angry, fickle deities. There was no pleasing them. They always had a chip on their shoulders, and you had to walk on eggshells around them. You never knew on what side of the bed they'd be getting up from morning by morning.

But through this blessing in the book of Numbers, the Lord was basically saying, "I want my people to know on a regular basis that I am not like that!"

Paul writes: "What then shall we say to these things? If God is for us, who can be against us? He who did not spare His own Son, but delivered Him up for us all, how shall He not with Him also freely give us all things?"[9]

Not only does God's smiling, shining face look at you, but He sings over you as well! Consider this amazing passage:

> The LORD your God in your midst,
> The Mighty One, will save;
> He will rejoice over you with gladness,
> He will quiet you with His love,
> He will rejoice over you with singing.
> (Zephaniah 3:17)

I wonder what God's voice sounds like. As the prophet Ezekiel was describing a vision of the glory of the Lord, he wrote that "His voice was like the roar of rushing waters."[10]

I've always loved the ocean. The very sound of it calms me. God's voice is like the roar of rushing waters, or maybe the crash of the surf on a moonlit beach.

TRUTH 4: GOD IS GRACIOUS TO YOU

"The Lord make His face shine upon you, And be gracious to you…"
(Numbers 6:25)

This is also something He wants us to be reminded of. It's important that we understand what grace is—God's unmerited favor. We might better understand it by contrasting it with two other words: *justice* and *mercy.*

Justice is getting what I deserve.

Mercy is not getting what I deserve.

Grace is getting what I don't deserve.

Let's say I loaned my Harley to a friend one weekend, and he crashed and totaled it. Well, that friend of mine owes me a new bike! That's what justice demands. But let's say I decided to be merciful instead of demanding justice. In that case, I would ask for nothing in return; I would simply pardon him. But if I dealt with him in grace, I would take him out to dinner, then go to the Harley dealer afterwards and *buy him* a brand new Harley of his own.

You say, that sounds a little extravagant. And yet it is *nothing* compared with what the Lord has done for you and me.

We deserve hell, and we get heaven.

We deserve punishment, and we get rewards.

We deserve wrath, and we get love.

We deserve exile, and we get adopted into God's own family.

The Lord is gracious unto you! How we need His grace on a daily, even moment by moment basis. Why? Because we sin each and every day. Sins of omission and commission—things I've done that I shouldn't have done, and things that I should have done but didn't! That is why Jesus taught us to pray in the Lord's Prayer: "Forgive us our sins as we forgive those who sinned against us."

We know that prayer is a daily prayer because it includes, "Give us this day our daily bread." Just as surely as we need God's physical provisions every day, so we also need His forgiveness every day. We are essentially praying, "Lord, extend Your grace to me today."

This is how we are saved in the first place …by His grace.

> For by grace you have been saved through faith, and that not of yourselves; it is the gift of God, not of works, lest anyone should boast.
> (Ephesians 2:8-9)

His grace is also that which surrounds us and preserves us each day. When Paul felt he couldn't go on, praying and pleading for the removal of an agonizing burden in his life, God replied, "My grace is sufficient for you, for My strength is made perfect in weakness."[11]

At the beginning of this chapter, I mentioned the story of the prodigal son. I think it must be one of the most beautiful illustrations of God's graciousness in all of Scripture. If the father in Jesus' parable had been just, he would have had the boy stoned to death. If he was merely merciful, he would have taken him on as a hired hand, as the young man requested. But the father's response went beyond justice and beyond mercy...all the way to grace. He ran to meet the dirty, emaciated young man, and walked him back home again with a smile of pure joy on his face.

So God blesses, keeps, smiles, and is gracious to us. And if all of those things weren't enough, there's yet another truth here.

TRUTH 5: GOD IS ATTENTIVE TO YOU

"The LORD lift up His countenance upon you..." (Numbers 6:26)
What does that mean, that He lifts up His countenance? It literally means that He lifts up His face to look at me, to see my situation, to have a keen interest and give full attention to what's going on in my life.

Incredible! God is saying, "I watch out for you each and every day, and you have My full attention."

Have you ever been speaking to someone and pouring out your heart and suddenly you notice that they're looking right past you? Now, that is disheartening. It makes you feel a little bit devalued, doesn't it? Sometimes we may imagine that's how it is with God. He seems to be looking our way, but then we begin to wonder if His eyes are roaming somewhere else in the universe. Maybe there's a huge supernova going on in the Andromeda galaxy, and He wants to check it out. Or maybe something big is coming down in the Middle East, and His attention is diverted. Finally He looks back at us and says, "Now, what were you saying?"

Does He truly pay attention to me? Does He really know what's happening in my life right now—what I'm feeling, what I'm wondering, what I'm worried about?

The Lord doesn't want us to be concerned about such things. God is a Father who "lifts up His countenance" to us. He looks at us face to face, eye to eye. He gives us His full attention.

Isn't that one of the essential messages of Christmas? As Matthew recorded for us: "'Behold, the virgin shall be with child, and bear a Son, and they shall call His name Immanuel,' which is translated, God with us."[12]

He is *your* Immanuel...He is the God with *you*.

You may be at a place in your life where you've convinced yourself that no one really cares about what you think or feel or dream. But God does. You have His full attention.

Do you suppose Joseph felt God was attentive to him as he sat for two years in that Egyptian dungeon, falsely accused of rape? As the days ran on and on, it must have seemed at times that God didn't care at all. But the fact is, God was watching and attentive every moment. The Lord had incredible plans for this young man's life. Although Joseph couldn't have known it at the time, the Lord was about to make him the second most powerful man on Earth.

In order to prepare Joseph for this crucial role on the world stage, God allowed some time, some disappointment, and some adversity to toughen him up.

Yes, God wants to bless us, but we must learn to handle those blessings. Even if it doesn't feel like it right now, know that God is paying attention to you. He is out in front of you, going before you, preparing future blessings for you, and He has not forgotten about you, not even for a moment. He is attentive to you, and when the time is right, He will deliver you from your trials.

TRUTH 6: GOD WANTS TO GIVE YOU PEACE

"The LORD lift up His countenance upon you, And give you peace."
(Numbers 6:26)

As we consider the fact that the Lord wants to bless us, keep us, and smile on us, it should give us personal peace. When we consider that God is both gracious and attentive to us, a deep contentment should settle over our hearts. This is how Paul could write words like these:

> Don't worry about anything; instead, pray about everything. Tell God what you need, and thank him for all he has done. Then you will experience God's peace, which exceeds anything we can understand. His peace will guard your hearts and minds as you live in Christ Jesus. (Philippians 4:6-7, NLT)

Remember, Paul wrote these words in prison. These weren't the words of a madman, but a man who was at peace, a man fully convinced that God was in control of the details of his life. And Paul practiced what he preached, for when he and Silas were beaten severely and thrown into prison at midnight, they sang praises to God.[13]

What if they had been executed instead of released? No problem! God would keep and deliver them safely to heaven. And if they were freed, which they were, they would faithfully serve the Lord until He was done with them. Paul summed it all up by writing, "For to me, to live is Christ, and to die is gain."[14]

TAKE IT TO THE BANK!

"So they shall put My name on the children of Israel,
and I will bless them." (Numbers 6:22-27)

As He wrapped up this blessing, God was saying to the priests, "You have spiritual oversight over the people. And I want you to remember to pronounce this blessing on My people over and over. I will live up to it in their lives! Don't make excuses for Me, don't soft sell this or be afraid that you're going to put expectations upon Me that I won't be able to fulfill. I will do this, so tell them!"

For the same reason, my reader, I'm telling you these things today. God has told me to tell you that He will bless you, He will keep you, He will smile on you, He will be gracious to you, He will be attentive to you, and He will give you His peace.

You can take that to the bank.

But remember, this series of promises is only for the child of God. The nonbeliever cannot claim these things. They have no right or portion in this, because blessing is really only for the believer.

There's a reason for that. The only reason we can enjoy such blessings is because Christ took the curse that belonged to us! Galatians 3:13 tells us that "Christ has redeemed us from the curse of the law, having become a curse for us (for it is written, 'Cursed is everyone who hangs on a tree')."

Jesus was cursed so you could be blessed.

Jesus died so you could live.

Jesus was forsaken that you might be forgiven.

So, the choice is yours. Do you want to experience this blessing in your life? Then you will, because it's already yours. It's like finding out you have a whole lot more in your bank account than you realized. So make a withdraw instead of going through withdrawals! Remember, God is blessing you today, smiling on you, listening to you, being gracious to you, and giving you peace.

Or, you can choose a curse.

I don't mean anything mystical by that, and I'm not speaking of any so-called "generational curse" here. I simply mean that if you do not choose His blessings, you will remain outside the circle of His blessings, facing the full penalty and repercussions of your own sins.

The choice is entirely yours.

Choose wisely, my friend!

Chapter Two

Joshua's Story, Part 1:
It's All in How You Look at Things

*"For by thee I have run through a troop; and by my
God have I leaped over a wall."* —Psalm 18:29, KJV

And the Lord spoke to Moses, saying, "Send men to spy out the land of Canaan, which I am giving to the children of Israel; from each tribe of their fathers you shall send a man, every one a leader among them."

So Moses sent them from the Wilderness of Paran according to the command of the LORD, all of them men who were heads of the children of Israel. ...

Then Moses sent them to spy out the land of Canaan, and said to them, "Go up this way into the South, and go up to the mountains, and see what the land is like: whether the people who dwell in it are strong or weak, few or many; whether the land they dwell in is good or bad; whether the cities they inhabit are like camps or strongholds; whether the land is rich or poor; and whether there are forests there or not. Be of good courage. And bring some of the fruit of the land." Now the time was the season of the first ripe grapes.

So they went up and spied out the land from the Wilderness of Zin as far as Rehob, near the entrance of Hamath. ...Then they came to the Valley of Eshcol, and there cut down a branch with one cluster of grapes; they carried it between two of them on a pole. They also brought some of the pomegranates and figs. ...And they returned from spying out the land after forty days.

Now they departed and came back to Moses and Aaron and all the congregation of the children of Israel in the Wilderness of Paran, at Kadesh; they brought back word to them and to all the congregation, and showed them the fruit of the land. Then they told him, and said: "We went to the land where you sent us. It truly flows with milk and honey, and this is its fruit. Nevertheless the people who dwell in the land are strong; the cities are fortified and very large; moreover we saw the descendants of Anak there. The Amalekites dwell in the land of the South; the Hittites, the Jebusites, and the Amorites dwell in the mountains; and the Canaanites dwell by the sea and along the banks of the Jordan."

Then Caleb quieted the people before Moses, and said, "Let us go up at once and take possession, for we are well able to overcome it."

But the men who had gone up with him said, "We are not able to go up against the people, for they are stronger than we." And they gave the children of Israel a bad report of the land which they had spied out, saying, "The land through which we have gone as spies is a land that devours its inhabitants, and all the people whom we saw in it are men of great stature. There we saw the giants . . . and we were like grasshoppers in our own sight, and so we were in their sight."
(Numbers 13:1-3; 17-21; 23-33)

Some time ago, I read an article in *USA Today* about how people view or see God. The article was entitled "View of God can predict Values and Politics."

The survey, conducted by Baylor University, identified four viewpoints of God—or, as they put it, "four Gods." Baylor researchers determined the "four Gods" breakdown by analyzing questions about God's personality and engagement. The survey asked respondents to agree or disagree with any of ten descriptions of their personal understanding of what God is like, including phrases such as "angered by my sins" or "removed from worldly affairs."

The respondents could check off sixteen adjectives they believed describe God, including words such as absolute, wrathful, forgiving, friendly, or distant.

FOUR GODS?

Here are the so-called "four Gods" the Baylor researchers came up with:

1. The Authoritarian God

This God seems ticked off most of the time. He is angry at humanity's sins, and stays very engaged in both world affairs and the life of every creature. He is ready to throw the thunderbolt of judgment down on the unfaithful or ungodly. Those who call themselves "fundamentalist" or "evangelical" (say the researchers) would subscribe to this view.

2. The Benevolent God

This God is still in the business of setting absolute standards for mankind, as detailed in the Bible. But those who identify with this group, drawn primarily from mainline Protestants, Catholics, and Jews, see a forgiving God, more like the father who embraces his repentant prodigal son in the Bible. They're inclined (68.1 percent of them) to say caring for the sick and needy ranks highest on the list of what it means to be a good person.

3. The Critical God

This God has a judgmental eye on the world, but He's not going to intervene, either to punish or to comfort. Those who identified themselves with this point of view are less likely to go to church, and are significantly less likely to draw absolute moral lines on hot-button issues such as abortion or gay marriage.

4. The Distant God

Followers of this God see a cosmic force that launched the world, then left it spinning on its own.

The problem I have with the definitions of God espoused by the groups listed above is that they're *all* wrong. Am I expected to choose between these four views of God—Authoritarian, Benevolent, Critical, or Distant? Which one do you believe in? None of these are working for me. I propose a fifth category.

5. The Biblical God

Yes, He is angry at humanity's sins, as those who believe in the Authoritarian God say. But He is not ready to throw thunderbolts at our every misstep, or we would have all been fried eons ago! He is also kind and full of mercy, as those who believe in the so-called Benevolent God say. He cares about the sick and needy in the world, and in His wisdom and love, He certainly intervenes in the lives of men and women—contrary to what those who believe in the Critical God claim. He is not an impersonal "cosmic force," as proponents of the Distant God would claim. He not only has a personality, He is the very fountainhead of personality.

In our last chapter we considered what God is like—what characterizes Him. We saw that He is both just and loving, exercising judgment as well as mercy. He loves to bless us, keep us, smile on us, listen to us, protect us, and give us peace.

How we view God is important, because it will determine how we view life as well. It will affect you in every important choice you make, including who you marry, how you live, and how you will vote.

There is really no area of your life that will not be impacted by how you view God. Take crises and problems, for instance. If you have a big God you will have small problems. If your problems seem huge and overwhelming, then you have a small God.

Obviously, some problems are very serious—in fact, really big! But how big are they in comparison with Almighty God? He is much, much bigger. It's all in how you look at things.

A Ticket to the Wilderness

Many of us have heard the Biblical account of how the Israelites ended up wandering in the wilderness for forty years. In this chapter, we're going to find out why. (And no, it wasn't because men were in charge and refused to ask for directions!)

From their first step out of Egypt en transit to the Promised Land, the Israelites had the Ultimate GPS system. God Himself led them by day and protected them by night.

The Lord's plan for His people was a quick trek from the slavery of Egypt into the freedom and bounty of Canaan—a land God had prepared for them, flowing with milk and honey. But right out of the gate the Israelites began to murmur and complain.

I heard the story of a man who decided to join a monastery, where he took a vow of silence. More specifically, he was allowed to speak two words a year. So after the first year of complete silence, he came before the abbot of the monastery and said, "Bed's hard!"

The second year went by, and in his second two-word interview with the abbot he said, "Food's cold!" After the third year of silence, he said, "I quit!"

The priest in charge responded, "Well, it's no wonder! All you've done since you came here is complain!"

And that's all some people do ...complain, complain, complain. Israel, like a sprinter bursting out of the starting gates, began complaining almost *immediately*. For years and years, decades and decades, the captive nation had cried for someone to deliver them. Seeing their cruel bondage and hearing their cries, God sent them Moses as a deliverer. So how did they respond to this chosen savior? For the most part, they opposed him. *Hey, who died and made you king?* (Who made you a prince and ruler over us?)[15]

Then, even after they had miraculously crossed through the Red Sea on dry ground and God had wiped out their enemies, they turned on Moses (and the Lord) yet again.

Their version of GPS was God Himself, appearing as a pillar of cloud by day and a pillar of fire by night. All they had to do was follow Him—to move when He moved, and to stop when He stopped. In the meantime, God graciously fed His people with a supernatural substance called manna. (Someone told me that the Hebrew is *"Krisp-Kremo." But I have my doubts about that.*)

Coming with the sweet morning dew, the manna was waiting for them every morning. All they had to do was walk out through their tent doors and begin picking it up in baskets. The Bible describes it as a wafer with a sweet, nutty flavor—and it fulfilled their every nutritious need. The psalmist said:

They ate the food of angels! God gave them all they could hold.
(Psalm 78:25, NLT)

But they soon grew bored with God's provision for them. They had tried all of Moses' recipes—manna muffins, manna sandwiches, manna-cotti. They said, "We remember the good old days back in Egypt. We had meat given to us free each and every day! We want meat again!" So God told Moses He was going to answer their prayer—and give them so much meat it would be coming out of their ears.

And sure enough, one day it began to rain meat! You've heard of it raining cats and dogs? This time it rained birds! Quail came dropping out of the sky, and as Israel began to gorge on raw meat, they brought a curse down on themselves. Commenting on this incident, Scripture says:

> They soon forgot His works;
> They did not wait for His counsel,
> But lusted exceedingly in the wilderness,
> And tested God in the desert.

> And He gave them their request,
> But sent leanness into their soul.
> (Psalm 106:13-15)

Be careful what you pray or wish for . . . you might get it! One Bible paraphrase renders Psalm 106:15 like this: *"He gave them exactly what they asked for— but along with it they got an empty heart."*[16]

I don't know about you, but I'm glad God has *not* seen fit to answer all my prayers with a "yes." Sometimes I shudder to think about some of the things I've told God I wanted or needed in years gone by. I thought I knew what would be best for me in those days, and sometimes I missed it by a mile. God knew so much better, and He wisely only gave me those things that were best for me.

There is a lot said in this story about how we are to approach the Lord in prayer. Some would tell us that we must demand of God what we want, name-it-and-claim-it, blab-it-and-grab-it . . . whatever.

Here's my bottom line on the whole issue: I would never presume to think that I know what I truly need. That is why Jesus taught us to pray "*Your* kingdom come, *Your* will be done." So we can certainly pray for whatever it is we think we want or need, but add these words— "Lord, if this is somehow outside of Your will, overrule it! Your kingdom come."

Why would I do this? Because I might be praying for the wrong thing at the wrong time, or even the right thing at the wrong time, and God alone knows what is best for me. He loves me—enough to die for me! If God says "no" to you, believe me, you wouldn't want yes! He says no to your request for your own good. He is protecting you from yourself. And God's plan for us is infinitely better than we could ever plan for ourselves. Paul describes this as the good, acceptable, and perfect will of God (see Romans 12:2).

So instead of being satisfied with God's provision, Israel griped and complained, whining and moaning at the doors of their tents. As a result, God answered their prayer just the way they prayed it, and "sent leanness to their souls."

As a pastor for over thirty years now, I have seen what happens when people take what God has blessed them with for granted. A wife tires of her husband . . . who happens to be a loving, hard-working man. Sure he has his flaws and short-comings, and he's not particularly flashy, but he is a good provider and tries to be a good companion. But she has her eye on some other guy, or wants to be "free" again.

Her pastor and all her Christian friends tell her to stay in the marriage and appreciate her hubby. She disregards all of them, the Bible, and everything else. The Lord even puts obstacles in her path and seeks to stop her. Still she persists.

Eventually the Lord says, in so many words, "Is this what you want? Is this what you're determined to have at all costs? All right, here it is!"

At first she is elated, but then a month or two pass, and the novelty wears off. The New Mr. Right begins to look like Mr. I'm-Not-So-Sure, and she begins to have second thoughts. Her husband, however, may feel so betrayed he doesn't want to reconcile.

So what did this woman end up with? She got the desires of her heart, but God sent leanness to her soul.

Don't for a moment take any of the blessings God has poured out in your life for granted—your husband or wife, children, career, health, church, or friends. Don't ever find yourself saying, "I'm tired of this manna, and I want something else." Be careful! God may give you what you want, and you won't like it one bit.

This is also true of a person who is looking back at his or her old life, "BC," Before Christ. The devil whispers, "Remember the good old days in the world, the parties, the pleasures, the fun?" He never seems to bring up the misery, emptiness, and guilt, does he? A few random table scraps have been magnified to a royal feast in your imagination.

If you go back, if you turn away from Christ, let me warn you: All those things that you thought were so sweet and tasty will turn to ashes and bitterness in your mouth. The apostle Peter describes this unhappy return to the world in graphic terms:

> And when people escape from the wickedness of the world by knowing our Lord and Savior Jesus Christ and then get tangled up and enslaved by sin again, they are worse off than before. It would be better if they had never known the way to righteousness than to know it and then reject the command they were given to live a holy life.

> They prove the truth of this proverb: "A dog returns to its vomit." And another says, "A washed pig returns to the mud."
> (2 Peter 2:20-22, NLT)

Solomon wrote: "The backslider in heart will be filled with his own ways, but a good man will be satisfied from above."[17] Being filled from now on with your own ways, cut off from the satisfaction that can only come from heaven, is a definition of hell-on-earth.

MAJORITY AND MINORITY REPORTS

You would think the Israelites would have learned their lesson with the quail. Not so. In fact, their relationship with God was about to take a sharp turn for the worse. And it was a turn they would regret for many, many years.

The Israelites had now come to the brink of the Promised Land and were ready to enter. As a first step, God commanded them to send in twelve spies to check things out and bring back a report. And everything went downhill from there.

> After exploring the land for forty days, the men returned to Moses, Aaron, and the whole community of Israel at Kadesh in the wilderness of Paran. They reported to the whole community what they had seen and showed them the fruit they had taken from the land. This was their report to Moses: "We entered the land you sent us to explore, and it is indeed a bountiful country—a land flowing with milk and honey. Here is the kind of fruit it produces. But the people living there are powerful, and their towns are large and fortified. We even saw giants there, the descendants of Anak! The Amalekites live in the Negev, and the Hittites, Jebusites, and Amorites live in the hill country.
>
> The Canaanites live along the coast of the Mediterranean Sea and along the Jordan Valley."
>
> But Caleb tried to quiet the people as they stood before Moses. "Let's go at once to take the land," he said. "We can certainly conquer it!"
>
> But the other men who had explored the land with him disagreed. "We can't go up against them! They are stronger than we are!" So they spread this bad report about the land among the Israelites: "The land we traveled through and explored will devour anyone who goes to live there. All the people we saw were huge. We even saw giants there, the descendants of Anak. Next to them we felt like grasshoppers, and that's what they thought, too!"
>
> Then the whole community began weeping aloud, and they cried all night. Their voices rose in a great chorus of protest against Moses and Aaron. "If only we had died in Egypt, or even here in the wilderness!" they complained. (Numbers 13:25-14:2, NLT)

As many times as I have read this story, it still amazes me. Twelve spies were sent in, ten brought an evil report, two brought a good one. They all saw the same thing, but they reacted differently—each according to the way he saw God.

First, there was the majority report. These men did not see God for who He is; all they could see were the obstacles. Their eyes were filled with roadblocks, challenges, giants, and defeat. The very idea of entering the Promised Land terrified them, and their wide-eyed, melodramatic report created a near riot. *"The land we traveled through and explored will devour anyone who goes to live there!"* What a way to describe God's provision for their lives and plans for their destiny.

Next came the minority report. Two of the spies sent into the land saw God for who He was. Yes, they also saw the obstacles and challenges, but because they kept God in their view, the obstacles looked like opportunities. They could already foresee the great victories Israel would enjoy as they moved into the land under God's protection.

Joshua and Caleb, two faithful men, represented the minority view. And though they reasoned and pleaded with the people, they were shouted down. It really all comes down to how you look at things, doesn't it? There will always be people who have no vision, no faith, and no interest in change.

I heard the story of an American shoe company that sent a salesman to a foreign country. He had hardly arrived before he cabled for money to come home. His reason? "No one here wears shoes!" The company brought him back and sent another salesman over.

Soon a cable arrived from this second salesman: "The market is absolutely unlimited," he exulted. *"No one here has shoes!"* Again, it's all how you look at things. It's not that Joshua and Caleb were "positive thinkers" or glossing over real problems with a Pollyanna glaze. They were simply men who had faith in God and trusted His plan completely. God would never lead them into a land without a plan to protect and provide for them!

MOUNTAINS ALONG THE WAY

We may feel our faith isn't strong enough to see miracles and move mountains in our lives. Some well-meaning friends may tell us we need "more faith" or "greater faith." But this is backwards thinking. It's not so much great faith in God that's required, as it is *faith in a great God.*

From the very beginning of my ministry, I have had people tell me to turn back, that we "couldn't do" what we felt the Lord had called us to do as we sought to take steps of faith.

When I began preaching, people told me, "You're not qualified. You're way too young." I took comfort, however, from Paul's words to Timothy: "Let no one despise your youth, but be an example to the believers in word, in conduct, in love, in spirit, in faith, in purity."[18]

After our fellowship of young people outgrew the building we were meeting in, we felt God had raised up a church, and that we needed to separate ourselves from the larger body and create our own church home.

I was told, "If you leave this facility, your group will completely fall apart!" Obviously, it didn't. We continued to grow and experience God's blessings.

When we began our evangelistic crusades, the naysayers all told us, "This will never work! It's an outmoded model. Large crusades will die with Billy Graham." (By the way, a young Billy Graham was told that large evangelistic crusades would die with Billy Sunday!) Yet in spite of the predictions of doom, we had overflow crowds and broke the attendance record at the Pacific Amphitheatre.

Outgrowing that venue, we wanted to move our crusades to Angel Stadium in Anaheim. Again, "the experts" told us that the stadium was much too big, that not many people would come, and that we would be embarrassed.

When we filled the stadium, people said, "Well, this is a Southern California thing. It won't work outside of L.A." Then we went to Oregon and Washington State, filling stadiums there. "It's a West Coast thing," people said.

Then we went to Philadelphia—about as far culturally from Southern California as you can get. When our crusade succeeded there, the response was, "Well, it's a West Coast/East Coast thing; it would never work in the South."

Wrong again. The Lord blessed our meetings in Georgia and North Carolina. The response of our critics? "It's a U.S. phenomenon. Only in America!" Then we went to Australia and New Zealand. And finally people began to say, "This must be a *God* thing."

None of this would have happened if we had listened to "the majority report" and not taken steps of faith.

The twelve spies were blown away by the sheer immensity of things in the new Promised Land. Texas-sized grapes. Texas-sized cities with Texas-sized walls. Not to mention Texas-sized warriors walking the walls of those cities. The opponents were large, but two of the spies thought the opportunities were even larger.

So what kept them from entering the Promised Land? And what keeps us from entering the Land of Promises? Once again, it comes down to how you look at things.

WHAT KEEPS US FROM THE PROMISED LAND?

What kept the Israelites out of God's land of promise?

1. They Focused Their Attention On The Obstacles Instead Of The Objective

> "But the people living there are powerful, and their towns are large and fortified. We even saw giants there, the descendants of Anak! The Amalekites live in the Negev, and the Hittites, Jebusites, and Amorites live in the hill country. The Canaanites live along the coast of the Mediterranean Sea and along the Jordan Valley."
> (Numbers 13:28-29, NLT)

Powerful people ...fortified towns ...giants ...Amalekites ...Hittites ... Jebusites ...Amorites ...Canaanites. (Lions and tigers and bears, oh my!) The majority report was a string of one obstacle after another.

When you fix your attention on the obstacles rather than the objective, fear will always eclipse your faith. The objective—the reason the spies were sent into the land in the first place—was to get a strategy to conquer the land, not to determine if they could do it. God had already told them they could do it!

Obstacles are the frightening things you see when you take your eyes off the objective. The Israelites were not looking at their problems in the light of God, but at God in the light of their problems.

2. They Allowed Themselves To Be Gripped With Fear

> Their voices rose in a great chorus of protest against Moses and Aaron. "If only we had died in Egypt, or even here in the wilderness!" they complained. "Why is the LORD taking us to this country only to have us die in battle? Our wives and our little ones will be carried off as plunder! Wouldn't it be better for us to return to Egypt?" Then they plotted among themselves, "Let's choose a new leader and go back to Egypt!"
> (Numbers 14:2-4, NLT)

Fear stirred them into a tizzy. Wailing, moaning, weeping, whining. It wasn't a pretty picture. The fact is, trust and worry cannot coexist; when one comes in, the other goes out. In effect, they cancel each other out. When you trust you do not worry, and when you worry you do not trust.

Allowing themselves to be carried along on a wave of panic, the Israelites had talked themselves into going back to Egypt, back into bondage. Some Christians today aren't much different. A little discomfort, a few trials, a couple of dry days, and they're ready to retreat.

God will not force you into His blessing. When Gideon was putting together his army, he said to his recruits, "Anyone who trembles with fear may turn back and leave Mount Gilead."[19] In other words, General Gideon told the troops, *"Whoever is fearful and afraid, let him go home to Mommy!"* And Scripture tells us that 22,000 men took advantage of the dishonorable discharge and took to their heels.

The Christian life isn't a cakewalk, it's a conflict. It's not a playground, but a battleground. You can live in fear and unbelief and wander in the futility of your own self-imposed wilderness, or you can enter into all God has for you. It comes down to this: Do you have a big or small God?

3. God Didn't Want Them To Run From Giants, But Attack Them!

Joshua and Caleb reminded Israel that the Promised Land was everything God had told them it would be—a land flowing with milk and honey (not to mention grapes the size of oranges).

> "Do not rebel against the LORD, and don't be afraid of the people of the land. They are only helpless prey to us! They have no protection, but the LORD is with us! Don't be afraid of them!"
> (Numbers 14:9, NLT)

These two guys were ready to strap on the armor! *"Let's go get 'em! They don't have a chance against us. They're sitting ducks. They're as good as finished!"*

All of us have giants we face in life.

You might be facing a giant of fear as you read these words. Something has frightened you and continues to frighten you, robbing you of both peace and a good night's sleep. Every time you think of that thing (which is more often than you would like), you feel it grip you by the throat, and it seems as though it will never go away. You've become paranoid, constantly worried, and even crippled by this fear. That, my friend, is a giant.

It might be a giant of some kind of sinful habit you're struggling with. A certain area of your life is weak, and you fall into this same sin over and over again. You have victory for a few weeks—perhaps even a month—then it has you again. It could be pride, envy, gluttony, pornography . . . the list goes on and on.

In a related way, you may be facing a giant of addiction. You have tried to overcome this addiction again and again, but you have failed. It has now become a towering monster in your life, something that taunts you day in and day out.

You might be a facing a giant of personal threat. Someone keeps slandering you—or they have a lawsuit out against you. Perhaps someone has actually threatened to kill you or harm your family.

On the other hand, the giant in your life might be a heartbreaking situation that just seems to go on and on . . . an unsaved husband . . . a prodigal child . . . a crushing financial situation . . . an ongoing health concern. A giant is anything that seeks to control, hurt, torment, or destroy you.

So what do you do? *Force your giant into the light of day, and go on the attack.*

Let's say it's the giant of addiction—alcohol, drugs, pornography, overeating . . . whatever it might be. First, recognize you have a problem. Stop rationalizing and excusing it. Realize you *cannot* defeat it in your own strength. Then call on God and pray for His power. Gather some godly brothers or sisters around you and pray until you have a plan. Don't let this thing keep taunting you and mocking you. Attack it!

We see this principle of attacking giants in the life of David. The entire army of Israel was paralyzed by fear as the Philistine giant Goliath prowled the battle line between the two armed camps, taunting Israel and daring them to fight. David, hardly more than a shepherd boy at the time, was on an errand for his father and happened upon this scene. The young man's blood boiled when he heard the nine-foot-tall freak belching out threats and blasphemies against God. Without hesitation, he volunteered to face off against Goliath, *mano a mano.*

But it really wasn't a one-on-one contest, and David knew it. Far from it!

The God of Israel was with him, so what did it matter if there was a whole army of nine-foot, six-toed giants? David knew this was a spiritual battle that had to be won with spiritual weapons. So he prayed, and Scripture says that he *ran* out to the battle line to meet Goliath—and brought the giant down with a single stone.

You and I must do the same. Rather than cowering before those lumbering giants in your life, *attack* them. In God's strength and enabling, draw lines, make yourself accountable to others, and stay away from people or situations where you know you might be hammered with excessive temptation. Don't let that giant back in your life again.

Or let's say it's the giant concern in your heart regarding an unsaved loved one. The weeks and months go by, and that family member of friend seems as hardened to spiritual things as ever. Remember, the battle belongs to the Lord. *Attack*. Get your Christian friends together and pray about this. Commit it to the Lord each day, each hour if necessary. Then wait on Him, avoiding the temptation to force the situation and try to "help God out."

Again, don't look at God in the light of your giant. Look at your giant in the light of God!

Paul uses the wilderness wanderings of the Israelites as an allegory of the Christian life—an encouragement and a warning for last-day believers, like you and me. Like the Israelites, we were delivered from bondage. Theirs was a bondage under Pharaoh to slavery, ours was a bondage under Satan to sin. Moses came and delivered them, as Christ did for us. God's plan for them was to enter a Promised Land—a land of blessing and yes, conflict. It was full of both serious challenges and magnificent rewards.

There is a direct correlation to our lives here. We can choose to follow Jesus Christ as Savior and Lord and embrace this life one hundred percent—even in the face of difficulties, temptations, and towering giants. (But there will also be blessings galore!) Or we can turn back from that exciting, challenging life and live in a self-imposed wilderness of struggle and halfheartedness. The choice is indeed ours.

Are you in a wilderness right now? Do you find yourself always complaining about practically everything? Have you been taking your salvation for granted? Have you been thinking about going back to your old life?

Please don't even consider that—your loss would be unimaginable! So how can you change your outlook? Start with the rebellion of the Israelites and their refusal to trust God and move on into the land of His provision. Then fast-forward forty years. The wilderness wanderings are over, Moses has passed away, and only two men remain from that whole generation: Joshua and Caleb. They're both getting up in years now, but they are clear-eyed and ready to tackle whatever awaits them. Listen to the strength in Caleb's voice!

"Now, as you can see, the LORD has kept me alive and well as he promised. ...Today I am eighty-five years old. I am as strong now as I was when Moses sent me on that journey, and I can still travel and fight as well as I could then. So give me the hill country that the LORD promised me. You will remember that as scouts we found the descendants of Anak living there in great, walled towns. But if the LORD is with me, I will drive them out of the land, just as the LORD said." (Joshua 14:10-14, NLT)

Wow! There's no way this guy is ready for a rocking chair and shuffleboard. He's telling Joshua, *"Let me at those giants. With God going before me, I'll mow 'em down."*

What kept Caleb going all those years? How did he keep his focus when so many did not? What is the secret of spiritual longevity?

Look back at Joshua 14:8. Reflecting on that fateful day when the spies returned from the Promised Land, he said, "My brothers who went with me frightened the people from entering the Promised Land. For my part, *I wholeheartedly followed the LORD my God"* (NLT).

Wholeheartedly following God like Caleb means you give one hundred percent to God. So many want to get all of God's gifts and blessings, but give so little of themselves. Caleb's strength never weakened. He kept God as the first love in his life, and grew in strength through the years.

It's all in how you look at things. How do you see God? Little or big? This will determine the course your life will take. If you see Him for who He is, you will long to know and walk with Him. If you see Him for who He is, you will see this world for what it is ...empty, pathetic, and on its way to destruction.

On the other hand, when you are only giving the Christian life your bare minimum, and your love for Jesus is not burning brightly, this world and its temporary pleasures will look more and more appealing. When that happens, you, too, will take your manna for granted and try to live in the past.

Sure, the Promised Land had obstacles and giant problems.

But Israel served a big God and so do we! The Christian life will always have its share of obstacles, challenges, and even a giant or two, but if we are *following the Lord completely,* we will have our priorities straight. We will see those obstacles as opportunities. No matter how large your problem, Your God is more than equal to the task.

It's all in how you look at things!

Chapter Three

JOSHUA'S STORY, PART 2:
OVERCOMING OR OVERCOME?

*"For every child of God defeats this evil world, and we
achieve this victory through our faith." —1 John 5:4,* NLT

Have you ever had one of those days when you were on an absolute roll in your spiritual life? God was blessing and using you in such a powerful way. You could tangibly see your steps were being ordered by the Lord.

Then, suddenly, you just blew it big time. You fell so hard you couldn't believe you had done it. You certainly didn't see it coming. In effect, you snatched defeat out of the jaws of victory.

Why does that happen? The answer to this question is found here in the book of Joshua.

The book of Joshua is the book of new beginnings for the people of God. The wilderness wandering of forty years had finally come to an end. It was time to enter in. Though challenging and exciting, this wasn't going to be easy. In fact, it was shaping up to be a full-blown war with the Canaanites, the inhabitants of the land.

We might ask, why is such a place given in the Word of God to record the military victories (and sometimes defeats) of the Israeli army in the conquest of Canaan? Why are we given detailed accounts of armed conflicts where blood was shed?

Because we, too, are at war.

It's not a war of flesh and blood, but a spiritual battle. It started on the day of your conversion and will rage until the day you go to heaven. You will be tempted, harassed, hassled, and attacked.

Simply put, Satan does not want you to follow Jesus Christ.

Thankfully, God knows our breaking point and won't give us more than we can handle. It's really not a choice of fighting or not fighting. It's a choice of victory or defeat …winning or losing …advancing or retreating …staying in the wilderness or entering the Promised Land.

In the Christian life, you are either an overcomer or you are overcome. He brought us out that He might bring us in!

"We were slaves of Pharaoh in Egypt, and the Lord brought us out of Egypt with a mighty hand; and the Lord showed signs and wonders

before our eyes, great and severe, against Egypt, Pharaoh, and all his household. Then He brought us out from there, that He might bring us in, to give us the land of which He swore to our fathers."
(Deuteronomy 6:21-23)

As we saw in the last chapter, when the people came to Kadesh Barnea, Joshua and Caleb said, "Let's go up now and possess it, for the Lord is with us!" That's faith! But the people said, "No way! We're not able!" That's unbelief, and it cost an entire generation the opportunity to experience God's provision and rest. Instead, they wandered through a desolate wilderness for forty years.

SURROUNDED

Unbelief says, "Let's stay back where it's safe." Faith says, "Let's go forward to where God is working!" The apostle John put it like this: "For whatever is born of God overcomes the world. And this is the victory that has overcome the world—our faith. Who is he who overcomes the world, but he who believes that Jesus is the Son of God?" (1 John 5:4-5).

Sometimes, however, we can feel a bit overwhelmed in this spiritual battle. I read a story from the Korean War that illustrated the kind of attitude we should cultivate in our daily warfare with the evil one. As enemy forces advanced, Baker Company was cut off from the rest of the regiment.

For several hours no word was heard, even though headquarters repeatedly tried to communicate with the missing unit.

Finally the command center received a faint signal. Straining to hear each word, a corpsman asked, "Baker Company, do you read me?"

"This is Baker Company."

"What is your situation?"

"The enemy is to the east of us, the enemy is to the west of us, the enemy is to the south of us, and the enemy is to the north of us." Then, after a brief pause, the sergeant from Baker Company said, "And we're not going to let them escape this time!"

Maybe you feel like that embattled military unit sometimes. Everywhere you look, it seems like the enemy is at work, wrecking havoc in the lives of countless people and still finding time to attack, tempt, and generally harass you.

Why is that? Because Jesus Christ is coming back! Even if some liberal theologians don't believe it, the devil knows all too well that Jesus is returning to earth soon. That's good news for us—and an incentive to share our faith and live holy lives. For the evil one, it's an incentive to attack our faith and try to make us stumble and fall. He wants to take as many down with him as possible.

We need to wake up to the reality of all of this, because the devil is never too busy to rock the cradle of a sleepy saint. Paul writes, "Do this, knowing the time, that now it is high time to awake out of sleep; for now our salvation is nearer than when we first believed. The night is far spent, the day is at hand. Therefore let us cast off the works of darkness, and let us put on the armor of light" (Romans 13:11-12).

We are at war, and the sooner we recognize that fact, the better off we'll be. God had deeded the Promised Land to the children of Israel, but they still had to enter in and *possess* what was rightfully theirs.

The same is true for us. There is no power apart from Jesus Christ that you have to submit to, no addiction that needs to control your life, and no lifestyle you cannot break free from. He whom the Son sets free is free indeed.

ENTERING IN

The book of Joshua, besides being accurate history of Israel conquering the Promised Land, is also a beautiful picture of warfare and victory in the Christian life. The previous four books in the Bible—Exodus, Leviticus, Numbers, and Deuteronomy—feature Moses as a symbol of the Law. Israel's wilderness years picture our needless wanderings when we don't obey God.

But Joshua pictures Jesus bringing us into a new land. The city-by-city battle with the Canaanite kings in this book has a great deal to say about the spiritual battles in which we're all engaged day by day. Commenting on all the Israelites went through, the apostle Paul wrote these words to the church at Corinth:

These things happened to them as examples and were written down as warnings for us, on whom the fulfillment of the ages has come. So, if you think you are standing firm, be careful that you don't fall! (1 Corinthians 10:11-12, NIV)

Let's set the scene. Forty years have passed since that fateful day when Israel turned back in unbelief, refusing to enter the Promised Land. All of those original doubters who refused to trust God have passed away, and the wilderness wanderings are finally at an end.

The time had come, and God told Joshua to lead the people into the land He had prepared for them. Reminding them to obey the Word of God and to be courageous, the Lord promised that every place the sole of their foot touched was theirs to possess.

There was only one problem with crossing over into Canaan. It was the small matter of the entire nation crossing the Jordan River ...at flood stage. From earliest memories, the Israelites had heard about their parents crossing the Red Sea. But that was forty years ago! Now it was time for the Lord to show His power to a new generation. And once again, the Lord showed His mightiness, causing the river to dry up when the foot of the first priest who led the way stepped over the bank.

On the other side stood the ominous city, Jericho, with its massive, towering walls and thousands of armed inhabitants. It could have been incredibly intimidating to realize that this huge fortress city was to be their first military objective.

God understands the way we see things. The psalmist tells us, "For He Himself knows our frame; He is mindful that we are but dust."[20] Bearing that in mind, He prepares us for those seemingly overwhelming challenges we encounter in life. And that's what He did for Israel.

The first thing He did was to block a rushing, overflowing river at the moment when the nation needed to cross. That ought to have put some courage into every heart!

By the way, that's another good reason to make sure you meet with the Lord every morning, spending time in His Word and in prayer. You and I have no idea what the day before us will bring. We might find ourselves facing one of the greatest crisis moments in our lives—or one of the most wide-open opportunities we've ever experienced. The Lord wants to prepare us for those moments, giving us direction and filling us with His Spirit. And He will ...if we are faithful to seek Him and meet with Him.

But He wasn't done preparing General Joshua's heart for battle. Within sight of Jericho's great walls, a mysterious visitor showed up at Joshua's campsite.

> When Joshua was near the town of Jericho, he looked up and saw a man standing in front of him with sword in hand. Joshua went up to him and demanded, "Are you friend or foe?"
>
> "Neither one," he replied. "I am the commander of the Lord's army."
>
> At this, Joshua fell with his face to the ground in reverence. "I am at your command," Joshua said. "What do you want your servant to do?"
>
> The commander of the Lord's army replied, "Take off your sandals, for the place where you are standing is holy." And Joshua did as he was told. (Joshua 5:13-15, NLT)

Joshua asks, "Are you friend or foe?" (Please say friend!) This commander was the Lord Himself! He was saying, in effect, "Joshua, I didn't come to take sides ...I came to take over!"

Moses experienced the presence of the Lord in a burning bush at a turning point in His life. This was Joshua's moment, but this face-to-face encounter with God was completely different from Moses'. God came to Joshua in a way He could understand. Joshua was a soldier, so that's how the Lord appeared to him.

This reminds us that God makes Himself known to each generation—and He's not bound by how He appeared to the last generation. Our children can't live off of our faith or descriptions of our past experiences. We can teach them what we have learned, but they need their own encounter. God gave that to Israel. He was leading them a step at a time, and the challenges would grow with intensity.

STRANGE BATTLE PLANS

So the nation of Israel crossed the Jordan in the midst of a miracle, and their leader had a personal encounter with God and a promise of heaven's might in upcoming battles.

All of this was preparing them for the mighty city of Jericho. The only way this city was coming down was by the power of God. So the Lord gave Joshua the battle plan. . . .

Throw up massive ladders on the walls, scale them, and attack!

Cut off food supplies and starve the inhabitants out.

Shoot arrows over the walls.

No, none of the above. God had a more novel plan.

Now the gates of Jericho were tightly shut because the people were afraid of the Israelites. No one was allowed to go out or in. But the Lord said to Joshua, "I have given you Jericho, its king, and all its stromg warriors. You and your fighting men should march around the town once a day for six days. Seven priests will walk ahead of the Ark, each carrying a ram's horn. On the seventh day you are to march around the town seven times, with the priests blowing the horns. When you hear the priests give one long blast on the rams' horns, have all the people shout as loud as they can. Then the walls of the town will collapse, and the people can charge straight into the town." (Joshua 6:1-5, NLT)

Does it ever seem to you like God is just having a little fun at our expense? Of course, that's not the case, but it does seem that He is always coming up with all sorts of unusual and diverse ways to accomplish His purposes. And why does He do that?

So we will stay dependent on Him.

What if the angel of the Lord had visited Joshua and given him a basic straight-up battle plan for conquering Jericho? Joshua could have said, "Thanks, Lord. That's what I thought. I'll check in with You after it's all over."

No, one reason God gives us fresh strategies and unusual methods is so that we will simply place ourselves entirely in His care and keeping and say, "Lord, that blows my mind. I would have never thought of that. I have no idea what to do next—I'm just going to follow You step by step."

Whether it's Joshua with trumpets or Gideon with torches and pitchers or David with the "sound of marching feet in the tops of the balsam trees," God loves to use weakness to show His strength, and though it might at times seem random, it never is. Pardon the expression, but there is a method to the madness. It's really not madness at all, but God's way of keeping us looking to Him.

Do you want a classic example? Recall how God healed Naaman, the mighty Syrian general. This famous, decorated soldier had leprosy and heard of a prophet in Israel.

When he approached Elisha's residence, however, loaded with gifts and goodies, the prophet barely gave him the time of day. He said, "Go, dunk yourself seven times in the Jordan."

Why this unusual and humbling prescription? Because Naaman was a proud man, and God wanted him to strip off his armor and his finery and all he normally hid behind and expose himself for what he was: a leper ...a diseased man who was helpless to change his condition. [21]

It's the same reason God wants us to confess our sin. It's not, *"Lord I'm already a good person, please make a little bit better."* Not that, but, *"O Lord, I'm a helpless sinner! Save me, for I have no other hope!"*

Consider the various ways Jesus healed people. He healed with a word. He healed with a shout. He healed with two touches. He spat on some dirt and made mud. You see this pattern throughout Scripture; God will often do His work in ways that seem unusual—even upside down.

Do you want success? Don't seek it, but seek the Lord instead.

"But seek first the kingdom of God and His righteousness, and all these things shall be added to you." (Matthew 6:33)

You want to be happy? First learn to be sad!

"Blessed are those who mourn, for they shall be comforted." (Matthew 5:4) [Literally, "Happy are the unhappy!"]

You want to be great? Learn to be a servant of others.

"Whoever wants to be first must take last place and be the servant of everyone else." (Mark 9:35, NLT)

So the Lord revealed the plan to Joshua on how Jericho would fall. March around it each day in total silence, and on the seventh day do it seven times— and then shout for all you're worth! Each day, the whole Israelite nation got into formation and quietly marched around that massive city.

Each day may have been more difficult than the last as they saw the immensity of this challenge. Those walls—how thick and high and imposing they must have seemed.

We all have Jerichos in life, problems that loom large and make our spirit tremble within us. What is the Lord seeking to accomplish in such times? Sometimes He just wants us to see how impossible the situation is apart from Him. He will march us around and around it, driving home the point that we cannot handle this in our own strength or wisdom.

For many of us, the greatest difficulty is simply coming to that place where we finally admit the whole thing is simply too big for us to tackle. *The walls are too high ...the obstacles are too great ...the enemy is too strong ...the situation is too complex ...and I'm too weak to lift a finger. If this Jericho is going to fall somehow, it is God and God alone who must bring it about.*

It was British preacher Alan Redpath who used to say, "When you get to the end of yourself, you get to the beginning of God." And that is so true. Is that where you are right now? You've been marching around your Jericho—that incurable illness, that unsolvable problem, that unsaved spouse, that failing business, that prodigal child. You think about your future and it feels like your wheels are spinning in the sand, and you don't know what to do. It's your Jericho, and God is the only one who can help you overcome it.

Just remember that His ways probably won't line up with yours.

THE DAY OF RECKONING

The inhabitants of Jericho were very wicked people. They used their children as prostitutes for their false gods or even sacrificed them on pagan altars. They were into every kind of idolatry, sin, and gross perversion. In His mercy, God had given them plenty of time to repent before their day of reckoning.

The reputation of Israel and Israel's mighty God had certainly preceded them. They may not have had Fox News or CNN in those days, but word got around. Most of Canaan would have heard the stories about the ten plagues, the parting of the Red Sea, and the destruction of Egypt's army, the military superpower of the day. "And you say those Israelites are on their way ...where?" They certainly could have seen the handwriting on the wall and made their peace with God, but they didn't.

God patiently endured the evil of the Canaanites from the time of Abraham to Moses, a period of over four hundred years. From the Exodus to the crossing of the Jordan was yet another forty years in Israel's history. *And the Canaanites knew what was going on!* Every miracle and wonder was known, right up to the parting of the Jordan so the entire nation could walk through without even getting their sandals wet.

Do you think the Canaanites didn't hear about the manna, the water from the rock, the cloud by day and the pillar of fire by night? They'd heard. They knew. But they resisted turning to God to the bitter end. They didn't so much as lift a finger to believe, but in fact opposed Israel.

Why did God mandate that Joshua and the army utterly destroy Jericho? Because the Lord knew that living in proximity to these Canaanites would pollute and corrupt His people. The spiritual principle we can apply from this is that God will not tolerate compromise with sin in our lives!

After six days of silent marching, the day of battle finally arrived. On this seventh day, in obedience to God's explicit instructions, the people marched around the city seven times—followed by a mighty shout! Immediately, the walls of the city collapsed, and Israel's soldiers charged in to take care of business.

What a glorious story this is. Truly, one of the greatest stories ever told. But as striking as this historical account may be, what follows in the very next chapter interests me even more. We read in amazement how Israel goes from the lofty heights of victory to the lowest dregs of defeat.

A STUNNING FAILURE

The Bible is a brutally honest book. If our hero does the right thing, we have the full account to read and celebrate. If our hero turns out to be a zero or a villain, however, the Bible doesn't varnish it. The pages of Scripture are the only true "no spin zone." After taking down Jericho, the rest of Canaan's land was going to be a cakewalk. Yet chapter 7 opens with an ominous word.

> But Israel violated the instructions about the things set apart for the LORD. A man named Achan had stolen some of these dedicated things, so the LORD was very angry with the Israelites.
> (Joshua 7:1, NLT)

It had been God's plan for Israel to roll from one victory to another, overtaking their enemies in Canaan. Instead, they suffered a crushing, humiliating defeat at a little place called Ai.

Victory unto victory. That is God's desire for His sons and daughters. We need not fail in the Christian life if we don't want to. Defeat may happen in the life of a believer, but it doesn't have to. Yes, there will be opposition and attacks from the enemy as we march forward in obedience to God's will. Those who are making a difference for God's kingdom can count on gaining the attention of the dark side. Anyone who determines to be content with nothing less than God's best has a target on his or her back. Why? Because they are a threat!

Here's how Israel failed so quickly after one of her greatest victories.

> Joshua sent some of his men from Jericho to spy out the town of Ai, east of Bethel, near Beth-aven. When they returned, they told Joshua, "There's no need for all of us to go up there; it won't take more than two or three thousand men to attack Ai. Since there are so few of them, don't make all our people struggle to go up there."

> So approximately 3,000 warriors were sent, but they were soundly defeated. The men of Ai chased the Israelites from the town gate as far as the quarries, and they killed about thirty-six who were retreating down the slope. The Israelites were paralyzed with fear at this turn of events, and their courage melted away. (Joshua 7:2-5, NLT)

So why did they fall? And for that matter, why do *we* fall?

#1 Reason for Falling: Self-confidence

Ai was only a small city compared to Jericho, which now lay in smoldering ruins. They could do this one in their sleep! They wouldn't even need the whole Israeli army, just a few thousand men. Now, this argument was based on the supposition that *Israel* had captured Jericho. Actually, all they had done was march around its walls and shout. God had given them that victory!

Sometimes you face your greatest dangers after you have won a battle. As we will see later in this book, it was after his spectacular success on Mount Carmel that the great prophet Elijah panicked and ran away in fear. Andrew Bonar said, "Let us be as watchful after the victory as before the battle."

Remember Simon Peter's words in the upper room?

> "You will all fall away," Jesus told them, "for it is written: 'I will strike the shepherd, and the sheep will be scattered.' But after I have risen, I will go ahead of you into Galilee."
>
> Peter declared, "Even if all fall away, I will not."
>
> "I tell you the truth," Jesus answered, "today—yes, tonight—before the rooster crows twice you yourself will disown me three times."
>
> But Peter insisted emphatically, "Even if I have to die with you, I will never disown you." And all the others said the same.
> (Mark 14:27-31, NIV)

Peter heard the Lord's warning, but he couldn't believe *he* would fall. Other people might stumble, other people might turn timid, but not *him*. The big fisherman had no idea what spiritual danger he was in.

Pride, the Bible warns us, goes before a fall. Self-confidence is at the core of many sins that people commit. We tell ourselves, *I can handle this. … I'll know when to stop. …I would NEVER become an alcoholic …or adulterer … or embezzler …or pornography addict.*

It's like when you're at a dinner party and at the end of the meal someone orders a big dessert with four forks. If I don't take the first bite, I'm okay. But once I've taken it, I'm like a shark who smells blood in the water!

We demonstrate dangerous self-confidence when we imagine we can do what we want, when we want, with whom or against whom we want, and not suffer any repercussions. No one is above the law—especially God's law. So if you hear of someone stumbling into sin, don't be arrogant and condemning. *"How could they be so stupid! I would never do anything like that."*

Maybe …and then again, maybe not. Listen to the warning of Scripture:

> Dear brothers and sisters, if another believer is overcome by some sin, you who are godly should gently and humbly help that person back onto the right path. And be careful not to fall into the same temptation yourself. (Galatians 6:1, NLT)

#2 Reason for Falling: Neglect of Prayer

It's clear that Joshua did not go to the Lord for a fresh battle plan for Ai. Flushed with the victory at Jericho, he thought Ai would be a walk in the park. Instead, it was a Waterloo.

Here's something to remember: If you pray in a time of victory, you will never have to plead in time of defeat. Thinking back to Simon Peter, he went from boasting that he would never deny the Lord during the last supper, to the Garden of Gethsemane, where he was told to watch and pray but took a nap instead.

Then, when the guards came to arrest Jesus, Peter woke up with a start and started swinging his sword ...just before taking to his heels and running away. He was boasting when he should have been humbling himself, sleeping when he should have been praying, and fighting when he should have been trusting.

So how did Joshua respond to the disaster at Ai? His first response was to blame the whole thing on God!

> Then Joshua cried out, "Oh, Sovereign LORD, why did you bring us across the Jordan River if you are going to let the Amorites kill us? If only we had been content to stay on the other side! Lord, what can I say now that Israel has fled from its enemies? For when the Canaanites and all the other people living in the land hear about it, they will surround us and wipe our name off the face of the earth."
> (Joshua 7:7-9, NLT)

He said *what?* "If only we had been content to stay on the other side"? After all God had done for him and Israel? How quickly we forget the blessings of God.

I love the Lord's response.

> But the LORD said to Joshua, "Get up! Why are you lying on your face like this? Israel has sinned and broken my covenant! They have stolen some of the things that I commanded must be set apart for me. And they have not only stolen them but have lied about it and hidden the things among their own belongings." (Joshua 7:10-11, NLT)

The Lord is essentially saying, "Stop already! You guys brought this on yourselves! It's time to take action!" How often we disobey God, and then when we reap the consequences we blame Him for our troubles. That brings us to the third reason for defeat at Ai.

#3 Reason for Falling: Disobedience

Someone in the camp had directly disobeyed God's solemn command. One man named Achan had stolen property which belonged to God. Ordinarily the soldiers shared the spoils of war, but in this case, God specified that everything—people, houses, animals, goods—was to be utterly destroyed. There would be plenty of goodies for the Israelites in the future, but in this particular conquest, God told them all of the bling belonged to Him! It was a small request considering the fact that He gave them the victory to begin with.

This brings up a very important point. The Bible tells us that we, too, belong to God—life, career, family, body, health, possessions, and future. It is the Lord's! The Bible says "You are not your own; you were bought at a price."[22] Yet so often we forget that, and neglect God.

Is it too much for us to dedicate time each day to pray and read His Word? It's God who gives us each and every twenty-four hour day—our every breath is in His hand. Is it too much for us to remember the Lord in our giving of finances? Scripture tells us we rob God when we fail to give! (More about that later.)

It's interesting—and very sobering—to note that the sin of one man had an impact on the whole congregation. It's still that way. Sometimes I hear people complain about the church, or why they do this or that. Let me ask you a question. *What if your church was just like you?* What if everyone attended as often as you do? Would the church be empty or full? What if everyone worshipped as you do in song? Would your church be full of praise and singing, or would it be silent? What if everyone shared the gospel as faithfully as you do? Would your community be reached for Christ? What if everyone studied their Bible like you do? Would you have a biblically literate or illiterate church?

You affect the church—whether you want to believe that or not. And no individual Christian can go his or her own way and commit sin without affecting the whole body. As Alan Redpath used to say, "No child of God can grown cold in his spiritual life, without lowering the temperature of everyone else around him." The victory of the church as a whole depends on the victory of each individual member. That is why we should want to build up and help one another, rather than berating each other and tearing each other down.

Achan's sin affected his family, his people, and his nation. One man outside of the will of God is a menace to everyone else! Look at the prophet Jonah. God had sent him to Nineveh to warn the city of impending judgment. But instead of heeding the clear call of God, he disobeyed and caught a ship headed in the opposite direction. As a result, God sent a storm to shake that ship and everyone on board . . . until Jonah repented.

Are you outside of the will of God and dragging others down? What kind of spiritual influence do you have on those you rub shoulders with every day? You are being watched, and you do have influence, whether you realize it or not.

If find yourself getting continually knocked down spiritually, maybe it's because there is unconfessed sin in your life. The Bible says, "If I regard [hold onto or cling to] iniquity in my heart, the LORD will not hear me" (Psalm 66:18, KJV).

Speaking of the forbidden items Achan had stolen, the Lord told Joshua, "You will never defeat your enemies until you remove these things from among you" (Joshua 7:13, NLT).

How did the sin of Achan go down? Pretty much the way all sin goes down!

Joshua told Achan to come clean, and the man confessed: "Indeed I have sinned against the LORD God of Israel, and this is what I have done: When I saw among the spoils a beautiful Babylonian garment, two hundred shekels of silver, and a wedge of gold weighing fifty shekels, I coveted them and took them. And there they are, hidden in the earth in the midst of my tent, with the silver under it" (Joshua 7:20-21).

This was a sin from the get-go, and Achan knew it.

THREE STEPS TO DISASTER

The First Step: He Saw

Most temptation starts right here. This is the way merchants get you into their stores. I read an article in *USA Today* about how retailers encourage customers to shop in their stores. Apparently, it's not only with displays and mannequins wearing the latest styles.

At the SonyStyle store they have developed a signature fragrance of vanilla and mandarin orange that wafts down on shoppers, relaxing them and encouraging them to hang around.

Other retailers use different scents in different departments. Bloomingdales uses baby powder in the baby store, suntan lotion in bathing suit area, and, well, you get the idea. We are drawn toward temptation through our senses.

It's not always the first look that gets us into trouble, but the second! Jesus mentioned this in the Sermon on the Mount when He warned of lustful looking. You can't help seeing what you see, but you can help following that mental pathway toward lust. I like the old quote from Martin Luther. He said that he couldn't stop the birds flying over his head, but he could stop them from building a nest in his hair!

The Second Step: He Coveted

Coveting is a powerful and underestimated sin that can cripple you spiritually, and ultimately destroy you. It must not be downplayed or left unchecked. Think of some of the people in the Bible who threw everything away—their life and possibly their eternity—because of greed and covetousness. Judas betrayed Jesus for thirty pieces of silver. And as we just read, Achan's unrestrained act of coveting led to the death of at least thirty-six of his fellow soldiers, his own life, and the lives of his wife and children. *For a new robe and some money?* What a price!

Paul said it so well to his young associate, Timothy:

But godliness with contentment is great gain. For we brought nothing into the world, and we can take nothing out of it. But if we have food and clothing, we will be content with that. People who want to get rich fall into temptation and a trap and into many foolish and harmful desires that plunge men into ruin and destruction. For the love of money is a root of all kinds of evil. Some people, eager for money, have wandered from the faith and pierced themselves with many griefs. (1 Timothy 6:6-10, NIV)

It's not a sin to want to be successful in business and make a good living. But when you become obsessed with it ...when you are willing to do whatever it takes to get there ...when it becomes the most important thing in life to you, coveting has become idolatry.[23]

The Third Step: He Took

Achan thought that, somehow, he could get away with breaking God's command. Didn't he understand that the God who could split the Jordan River for His people to walk across, the God who pushed down the mighty walls of Jericho with the flick of His little finger, would see what he was doing? Did he really think he would somehow pull one over on God and slip by?

The Lord once asked Jeremiah, "Can anyone hide himself in secret places, so I shall not see him? ...Do I not fill heaven and earth?"[24]

Scripture warns, "Your sin will find you out!"[25] By the way, that statement was issued to God's people, not lost people.

We all have our Jericho's and Ai's. Our victories and defeats. Are you facing a Jericho right now? Put it in God's hands. Ask Him for His wisdom and direction, and wait on Him to show you what to do. His methods may surprise you, but the end result will be infinitely better than you could have planned for yourself.

Are you recovering from an Ai? Get up off the ground, face up to the sin, own up to the disobedience, receive God's forgiveness, and move on to the next battle.

God's grace will get you moving, and God's power will push down your walls.

Chapter Four

GIDEON'S STORY:
WHEN A LITTLE IS A LOT

"Go in this strength that is yours. . . .
Haven't I just sent you?" —Judges 6:14, THE MESSAGE

Sometimes it seems like our nation's language has been turned upside down. If you were to take someone from the late 1950s, put them in a time machine, and drop them off in the middle of today's culture, they would be hopelessly confused.

Just look at the expressions we use. Certain slang expressions have not stood the test of time; words like "groovy" and "far out" have seen their day. But other expressions going back to the fifties—I'm thinking of the word "cool"—are still in use today.

Then there's the word "hot," as in "that's hot." What's strange is that something can be both cool and hot at the same time!

If something is good we say "that's bad!" We'll look at a hot (cool?) car and say, "How fast will that *bad boy* go?" That's because bad is good. Then if something is *really* good we say, "That's killer!"

So good is bad, and really good is killer, and really, really good is *sick*. (You need to be or know a teenager to get this one, and it will most likely be out of date by the time this book is in print!)

Now in the old days, if someone was doing drugs, sexually loose, and partying, you would say "that's bad." And that's exactly what we meant. The person who was principled, moral, and didn't use drugs was "good." We said what we meant.

But how do you say it now? Is he so good he's bad, or is he so bad he's good? Is he so hot he's cool, or is he so cool he's hot?

Hollywood, through music, movies, and TV, has only reinforced this confusing state of affairs. Does God have anything to say about this confusion of terms? Yes, He does. In the book of Isaiah, the Lord says,

Woe to those who call evil good
and good evil,
who put darkness for light
and light for darkness,
who put bitter for sweet
and sweet for bitter.

Woe to those who are wise in their own eyes
and clever in their own sight. (Isaiah 5:20-21, NIV)

The cultural confusion and anything-goes attitude of this twenty-first century is certainly nothing new. In fact, in the book of Judges, the seventh book of the Bible, the state of things in the nation of Israel was really turned upside down.

One verse in that book summarizes the whole situation:

In those days there was no king in Israel; everyone did what was right in his own eyes. (Judges 17:6)

God raised up thirteen judges—twelve men and one woman—to guide His people through this chaotic, roller-coaster period of Israel's history. When we think of "judges" here, we must not think of Supreme Court judges in black robes. These were more like Wyatt Earp or one of the lawmen of the Wild West. The country needed someone to keep a semblance of law and order in the land ... but even so, these were wild and crazy times in Israel.

A SAD CONTRAST

As the book of Judges begins, Joshua has died. What a sad contrast between Judges and Joshua! Though they are right next to each other in the Bible, they are worlds apart. Joshua is primarily the record of the adventures and exploits of Israel as they obeyed God and entered into the Promised Land.

Joshua is the story of conquest, while Judges is a book primarily about defeat. Joshua is a book of faith, while Judges is a book of unbelief and disobedience. Joshua is a book about people uniting around one man to lead them, and Judges is about everyone doing what was right in their own eyes.

It was the year 1256 BC, and approximately 200 years had passed since Joshua had led the Israelites on their famous march around the walls of Jericho. By God's power, Israel saw those walls implode, and they went on to conquer many of the inhabitants of Canaan, including the Amorites, Hittites, Ammonites, and Jebusites. There were many battles over many years, but they didn't finish the job. They failed to drive all the Canaanites out, and lived to regret it.

There's a parallel here to our lives as Christians. We may commit ourselves to the Lord and give Him the master key to multiple doors. At the same time, however, we keep a couple of closets for ourselves ... dark, hidden, and locked. We may think our secret sins are closed off from the rest of our lives, but it's only a matter of time before the contents of those hidden closets begin to haunt us.

As Judges chapter 6 opens, we see the tribes of Israel living under the cruel dominion of the Midianites. This occupation of the nation was God's discipline in their lives as a direct result of their disobedience. Israel did evil in the sight of the Lord, so He handed them over to the Midianites (Judges 6:1).

The Midianites were the first in history to domesticate the camel, giving them a huge military advantage. Have you ever checked out a camel? They are big, fast, ugly, and can go days without water. And they spit, too! Can you imagine seeing your enemies swooping down on you riding these things—by the thousands? It would be terrifying.

Every year at the time of harvest, these Midianites would invade Israel like a plague of locusts and appropriate all the crops for themselves. Nearly in despair, Israel finally remembered they had an Almighty God and called on Him to deliver them.

In answer to those prayers, the Lord Himself showed up, picking out a candidate for national hero and deliverer.

God's choice for the job of champion would have surprised everyone. It certainly surprised the candidate himself!

"WHO ... ME?"

As our story begins, we find a man named Gideon trying to prepare the little bit of wheat that he'd managed to glean, hiding behind the walls of a small winepress. Hardly a picture of heroism and courage. Like the rest of Israel, he was hungry, hurting, and humiliated. But in Gideon's story we will discover the kind of qualities God is looking for in the person He will use for His glory.

> Now the Angel of the LORD came and sat under the terebinth tree which was in Ophrah, which belonged to Joash the Abiezrite, while his son Gideon threshed wheat in the winepress, in order to hide it from the Midianites. And the Angel of the LORD appeared to him, and said to him, "The Lord is with you, you mighty man of valor!"
>
> Gideon said to Him, "O my lord, if the LORD is with us, why then has all this happened to us? And where are all His miracles which our fathers told us about, saying, 'Did not the LORD bring us up from Egypt?' But now the LORD has forsaken us and delivered us into the hands of the Midianites."
>
> Then the Lord turned to him and said, "Go in this might of yours, and you shall save Israel from the hand of the Midianites. Have I not sent you?" (Judges 6:11-14)

Gideon's response is interesting. He's essentially saying, "If God has chosen me, why is everything going wrong and where are all the miracles we heard about in days gone by?"

I heard the story of a mother who was telling some Bible stories to her little girl, talking about Creation, the parting of the Red Sea, and the miracles in the lives of men like Moses, Joshua, and Daniel. The little girl turned to her mom and said, "Mommy, you know, God was much more exciting back then!"

That's how Gideon felt. He'd heard about the good old days, but where was God now? It's a valid question. In Gideon's case, it could have been answered with a rebuke. *You're suffering because you and your people have forgotten Me and worshipped false gods!* But the Lord was very patient with Gideon.

Verse 14 says that "the LORD turned to him." It could better be translated "The Lord looked at him." After making eye contact, He simply said, "Go in this might of yours, and you shall save Israel from the hand of the Midianites. Have I not sent you?"

God could have taken the time to rehearse the whole situation going back to Joshua's day, but He's basically telling Gideon, "Let's not get into that right now. It would take too long. Here's how I plan to resolve the crisis you're in right now."

This wasn't a time to question or criticize, but to take some action! There is a time to pray and there is a time to move. I've always been a pretty practical guy. I tire of long, drawn out meetings where people philosophize about this and that. I am more the kind of person who wants to identify the problem, come up with the best solution, and get after it!

Gideon, however, wasn't seeing this at all.

He replied to the Lord, "O my Lord, how can I save Israel? Indeed my clan is the weakest in Manasseh, and I am the least in my father's house." (Judges 6:15)

In other words, "I'm the runt of the litter!" It reminds me of another young man in Scripture who was the youngest and least in his father's house. That young man's name was David, and God had big plans for him.

GOD USES PEOPLE WHO ARE HUMBLE

This gives hope to all the people out there who are not extraordinary, but ordinary. They weren't the best students, or class president, or homecoming queen. They weren't the first chosen for the team, but the last. They didn't make the cover of *People's* "World's Most Beautiful People." They don't have great natural talents.

God can do amazing things through people like this—people who see their shortcomings, but also the greatness of God.

When Jesus called Simon Peter, Peter responded, "Depart from me, for I am a sinful man!" *Don't waste your time on me Lord; I'll only let You down!* But Jesus saw Peter for who he would become, not just who he was.

God tells Gideon He will do the work through him. "And the LORD said to him, 'Surely I will be with you, and you shall defeat the Midianites as one man'" (Judges 6:16).

"Who am I?" Gideon asks in verse 15.

"That's not the issue!" the Lord says in verse 16. "It doesn't matter who *you* are, for I have said *I* will be with you!"

"If God be for us, who can be against us?" the Scripture asks.[26] Notice how God addressed Gideon: "The LORD is with you, you mighty man of valor!" I love this! Another translation says, "Mighty hero, the LORD is with you!"[27]

It could almost sound like mockery. In Joshua, the expression refers to brave soldiers marching into the heat of battle. It would be like going up to a scrawny little guy and saying, "Hey, you buffed-out bodybuilder!"

If there was anything Gideon was *not* at that moment, it was a mighty hero. He was more like a pathetic zero! God sees us for who we can become, not who we are.

We see a lump of clay, God sees a beautiful sculpture.

We see a blank canvas, God sees a Rembrandt.

We see a lump of coal, God sees a sparkling diamond.

We see a Gideon hiding in a winepress, God sees a mighty man.

We see a vacillating, unsure Simon, God sees a rock like Peter.

We see a persecuting Saul of Tarsus, God sees a mighty apostle Paul.

We see failure, God sees potential.

By the way, some of the greatest successes come from failure. The doorway of success is often entered through the hallway of failure. Sometimes failure functions simply as a process of elimination. Thomas Edison once said, "Many of life's failures are people who did not realize how close they were to success when they gave up."

Gideon felt unworthy of such a privilege and responsibility and needed some reassurance from the Lord, so God gave him a miracle.

Gideon replied, "If you are truly going to help me, show me a sign to prove that it is really the LORD speaking to me. Don't go away until I come back and bring my offering to you."

He answered, "I will stay here until you return."

Gideon hurried home. He cooked a young goat, and with a basket of flour he baked some bread without yeast. Then, carrying the meat in a basket and the broth in a pot, he brought them out and presented them to the angel, who was under the great tree.

The angel of God said to him, "Place the meat and the unleavened bread on this rock, and pour the broth over it." And Gideon did as he was told. Then the angel of the LORD touched the meat and bread with the tip of the staff in his hand, and fire flamed up from the rock and consumed all he had brought. And the angel of the LORD disappeared. (Judges 6:17-21, NLT)

God had done His part, and now it was time for Gideon to get started. God usually leads us one step at a time. He wants us to be faithful in the little things before He will give us more to do. Some may want to journey to faraway lands and speak to isolated people groups. That's an excellent goal. But maybe the first thing God would have you do is talk to the coworker who works beside you all day.

In the gospel of Luke, Jesus said, "Whoever can be trusted with very little can also be trusted with much, and whoever is dishonest with very little will also be dishonest with much. So if you have not been trustworthy in handling worldly wealth, who will trust you with true riches? And if you have not been trustworthy with someone else's property, who will give you property of your own?" (Luke 16:10-11, NIV).

We all would like to be used of God. But start with small things. All of our pastors at Harvest Christian Fellowship started in our Helps Ministries, including the parking lot crew, ushering, counseling, and teaching Sunday school. They proved themselves faithful in the little things before they were given greater responsibilities.

What opportunities has God set before you right now? It's interesting that when Jesus spoke about faithfulness with small things, He began with money! "And if you are untrustworthy about worldly wealth, who will trust you with the true riches of heaven?"[28]

You talk about all you want to do for God. But let me ask you this: Do you give regularly of your finances to God as He commands? If you can't be faithful in something as simple as that, why would you expect you would do more if you had more? "No," you say, "if I had more money I would give more to God." It's all relative. The fact is, if you had more money, you might spend more money and still not give! Wherever you are in life, you need to honor the Lord with your finances. God will bless you for it.

> Honor the LORD with your wealth and with the best part of everything you produce. Then he will fill your barns with grain, and your vats will overflow with good wine. (Proverbs 3:9-10, NLT)

Gideon had a test for God, but God also had a test for Gideon. His first task was to tear down the altar his father had built to Baal. The Lord told him to take the second best bull from his father's herd and barbeque it on the remains of this altar. Gideon did as God commanded.

Gideon did what the Lord commanded, but it wasn't exactly like he did it at high noon. In fact, he waited for the middle of the night. Some commentators criticize him for that, but I think it's still admirable. Sure, he did it under cover of darkness, but at least he did it! Again, I admire people who get the job done!

There are a lot of critics out there who may argue around and around about the best way to do something, and never actually accomplish anything at all. Then there are the Gideons and Simon Peters of life who fumble here and there, but still get the job done. I would rather try and fail than never try at all.

Yes, Gideon did it at night. But that was no true indication of where he would end up as a warrior and leader for the Lord. Just because someone doesn't start out with great promise, doesn't necessarily mean they won't come around in the end. We all remember the devoutly religious man Nicodemus who came to Jesus by night. This is mentioned a few times in Scripture, so it's noteworthy. He probably did that because he was afraid of what others would think.

Nicodemus was a famous man, a household name. Jesus asked, "Are you the teacher in Israel and you don't know these things?" So though he may have had a weak beginning, he had a much better ending. For instance, Judas Iscariot was a full-fledged apostle in good standing while Nicodemus was still groping his way in. Yet at the end of our Lord's ministry, Judas betrayed Jesus and went and hanged himself. But old Nicodemus stepped forward when all the disciples had forsaken the Lord and fled Him. In company with Joseph of Arimathea, they boldly approached Pilate to take and care for the body of Jesus. [29]

So you may have a feeble beginning but a strong finish. Better that than a strong beginning and no finish (because you gave up and turned back!).

Gideon tore down the altar of Baal his father had erected. When everyone discovered it the next morning, they were aghast! They called for the execution of Gideon. Instead of turning on his son, the father defends him, and seems to have his own faith rekindled.

Listen, the hardest people to reach will always be your own family. As Jesus said, "A prophet is not without honor except in his own town." Even Jesus' mother and siblings did not believe in Him till his death and resurrection!

And can you imagine being one of Jesus' siblings? He was flawless! He never sinned, was never a poor witness. Can't you just hear Mary saying, "Why can't you be more like your brother Jesus? He always does the right thing!"

"But Mom ... Jesus is perfect!"

"I know, honey," Mary might have responded. "But you need to ask yourself the question each day, 'What would Jesus do?'"

Don't give up on your family. You don't need to preach sermons to them all day long. You need to show your faith by the way you live and the decisions you make.

Gideon, however, still had his doubts. So he laid more tests before God, including his infamous fleece before the Lord. God accommodated Gideon's doubt and unease, and confirmed His word again and again.

Finally, this reluctant "man of valor" was reassured, and relatively ready for the task at hand: to deliver Israel from the Midianites. For that, of course, he needed an army, and Gideon was able to rally 32,000 men. Not nearly enough to take on a superpower like Midian, but a good enough beginning.

And that's about the time the Lord took out His pruning shears.

> The LORD said to Gideon, "You have too many warriors with you. If I let all of you fight the Midianites, the Israelites will boast to me that they saved themselves by their own strength. Therefore, tell the people, 'Whoever is timid or afraid may leave this mountain and go home.'"

So 22,000 of them went home, leaving only 10,000 who were willing to fight. (Judges 7:2-3, NLT)

Of all the upsets celebrated by military historians or sports fans, none is more stunning than the one God accomplished through Gideon. He was basically outnumbered 450 to 1, and yet Gideon's army won a crushing victory over the Midianites. It would be like a Pop Warner Team going up against the New York Giants. Or a little league team taking on the Los Angeles Angels. The Midianite army was huge!

The armies of Midian, Amalek, and the people of the east had settled in the valley like a swarm of locusts. Their camels were like grains of sand on the seashore—too many to count! (Judges 7:12-13, NLT)

God wants to get the glory for the work He does. So He will often let things stack up in such a way that there is *no way out but Him*. There will be that insurmountable obstacle like the Red Sea He wants us to get through. There will be the towering walls of a Jericho He wants us to fell. There will be the frightening giant Goliaths He wants us to defeat.

But it's not us doing it for God, but God doing it through us and sometimes for us. There is always His part and our part.

The Red Sea parted, but Israel had to march through.

The walls of Jericho fell, but Israel still had to march around them.

The giant Goliath fell, but David still had to attack.

Peter pronounced the crippled man at the Temple gate healed, but he still had to pull him to his feet.

Are you overwhelmed by the odds right now? There's no way out of your situation but God! Believe it or not, that's a good place to be.

I love the prayer of Jehoshaphat when facing huge odds as an enemy army approached. He prayed, "O our God, will You not judge them? For we have no power against this great multitude that is coming against us; nor do we know what to do, but our eyes are upon You" (2 Chronicles 20:12).

Literally, he prayed, *"We are looking to you for help."*

So Gideon tells the cowards to go home. Why? Because fear is contagious. In the same way, if you're looking for life on Easy Street with no conflict or challenge, go home! But if you want to be used by God, and want your life to make a difference, move forward!

Gideon was probably expecting a few to turn tail and run for home. *But 22,000?* That was two-thirds of his army! There was one final test now for Gideon and Israel. This was to be a secret test.

But the LORD told Gideon, "There are still too many! Bring them down to the spring, and I will test them to determine who will go with you and who will not." When Gideon took his warriors down to the water, the LORD told him, "Divide the men into two groups. In one group put all those who cup water in their hands and lap it up with their tongues like dogs. In the other group put all those who kneel down and drink with their mouths in the stream." Only 300 of the men drank from their hands. All the others got down on their knees and drank with their mouths in the stream. The LORD told Gideon, "With these 300 men I will rescue you and give you victory over the Midianites. Send all the others home." (Judges 7:4-7, NLT)

This test revealed the soldiers' attitude toward the enemy. One group just thought about water. They were the lappers. Basically, they forgot about the Midianites and just satisfied their thirst. They could have been easily ambushed and killed.

God said, "Send 'em home, Gideon."

Then there were the cuppers. These kneeled, bringing the water to their lips while still watching. They were alert, cautious, not letting down their guard. And there were only 300 of them in the whole bunch.

So Gideon is now down to the top three percent of the 10,000. He's down to the cream of the crop, the Delta Force, the Seals, the Green Berets, the SWAT team!

Then God gave the battle plan to Gideon. He was to divide his force into three groups, instructing them to take a burning torch covered by a clay jar in one hand, and to carry a trumpet in the other.

What kind of a battle plan was that? It was beginning to sound as strange as God's plan for taking Jericho—marching silently and then shouting!

So Gideon's elite force of Israeli warriors crept up on the vast Midianite camp without knife, sword, spear, or slingshot. They had clay jars, they had shielded torches, they had trumpets, and they had a battle plan.

Then he said to them, "Keep your eyes on me. When I come to the edge of the camp, do just as I do. As soon as I and those with me blow the rams' horns, blow your horns, too, all around the entire camp, and shout, 'For the LORD and for Gideon!' " (Judges 7:17-18, NLT)

It's so crazy it's classic. But that's just what they did. In the middle of the night, the Midianites were startled by the sudden flaring of three hundred torches, the blast of three hundred ram's horns, and the shouts of three hundred men filled with faith and adrenaline.

Utterly panicked, the enemy soldiers drew their swords and began slicing and stabbing at each other. In the end, the Midianites were utterly routed.

THINNING OUT THE RANKS

So what does a story like this have to say to us today? More than we may realize.

In John chapter 6, just when Jesus seemed to be riding the crest of popular fame and acclaim, He delivered a tough sermon that perplexed and disgusted the crowds of followers.

The apostle John tells us that after that time, "many of His disciples went back and walked with Him no more" (v. 66).

Why did Jesus do this? Why did He intentionally thin out the ranks of His followers—on more than one occasion? Because He knew the hearts of those followers and hangers-on. He knew that many of them—perhaps most of them—were there to see a big show, some dramatic miracles, and maybe collect a free meal or two. Those who truly loved Him and were devoted to Him were relatively few.

That was the dynamic behind the thinning of Gideon's army. After the reluctant, the fearful, and the careless went home, only 300 remained. But with this 300, God gave to Gideon and the Israelites the victory.

God said to Gideon, "By the 300 I will save you …" Why did God impose this test? He wanted to get rid of the halfhearted people, the fair-weather followers, those who had no real heart for Him. Listen, God can do more with 300 committed people than 10,000 reluctant followers!

God was and is looking for men and women who will love Him more than anyone or anything else. English evangelist John Wesley once said, "Give me a hundred men who love God with all of their hearts and fear nothing but sin, and I will move the world."

Once, when the crowds kept growing and growing, following Him everywhere, Jesus turned to them and spoke very directly.

> "If anyone comes to Me and does not hate his father and mother, wife and children, brothers and sisters, yes, and his own life also, he cannot be My disciple. And whoever does not bear his cross and come after Me cannot be My disciple." (Luke 14:26-27)

Jesus laid out the cost of discipleship to the curious, the hangers-on, the casual followers. The groupies, if you will. In describing true discipleship, Jesus said some of the most solemn and searching words that ever fell from His lips. In the course of this message, He said three times, "cannot be my disciple." In other words, these are absolute prerequisites to true discipleship. Let's look at them together.

HATE LOVED ONES?

"If anyone comes to Me and does not hate his father and mother, wife and children, brothers and sisters, yes, and his own life also, he cannot be My disciple." (Luke 14:26)

What's this all about? Christians are supposed to "hate"?

Jesus was using a form of speech that would have been very familiar to His audience. He used the oriental method of sharp contrasts, and the word "hate" is used as the opposite of "love." If there is ever a time when the highest, most noble of earthly loves comes into conflict with Christ and His cross, the call of Christ must prevail!

But why would Jesus say such things to all those people who followed Him? It was almost like He was intentionally trying to get rid of them.

In a sense, He was. At least some of them.

Jesus wanted to winnow out the casual, non-committed followers, those who had no real heart for Him. Looking back to Gideon's story, we find that God can do more with 300 alert, committed men than he can with 32,000 who are halfhearted. God is still looking for men and women who will shake their world. Men and women who will be true disciples. If you're looking for a life of ease, with no conflict or sacrifice, then the life of a disciple is not for you.

Remember, God *will* test us as Christians. Do you remember when you were in school and the teacher would make a dreaded announcement something like this? "Class, today I'm giving a pop quiz."

That rather bizarre group of diligent students with too many pens in their pockets and tape wrapped around the bridge of their glasses would actually smile with glee at such an announcement! (We used to call these people geeks and nerds; now we call them boss!)

The teacher might add, "If you've been paying attention, you have nothing to worry about!" Well, of course my stomach sank because I *hadn't* been paying attention. And needless to say, I failed many a test.

Sooner or later we have to learn the material or we will never advance. Well, God gives pop quizzes too, and he rarely, if ever, announces them ahead of time. They just come. We think we know certain truths so well. We love to tell others how to do it. And then the Lord, through a test in our lives, says, in essence, "Let's see how well you've been listening."

A true disciple will be one who is drinking in his Master's every word, marking every inflection of voice with an intense desire to apply what's been learned.

So Jesus was testing the people. Looking for real disciples. What was that first test? What did Jesus mean when He spoke about "hating" family members? He chose this analogy to show how our love for God must take preeminence over all others.

The point is, you will either have friction in your relationship with the Lord and harmony with people, or harmony in your relationship with the Lord and friction with people! Jesus warned, "Beware when all men speak well of you." You can't have it both ways! It's one or the other! Your love for others must be like hatred when laid alongside your love for God.

Are you a wholehearted follower of Jesus Christ, loving Him so passionately that all other loves in your life pale by comparison? Is there someone in your life you are putting ahead of the Lord today? It may be a person in your family that you love more than God Himself. It may be a relationship

you're involved in right now. You know you are compromising God's standards and risk losing God's best for your life, but you're afraid of displeasing
that someone. It may be that you've put your career ahead of the Lord, or
maybe there's some other pursuit that you won't give up no matter what.

Will you become a true disciple of Jesus today, and love Him more than anyone or anything else? Will you step out from the "fickle multitudes" and "fair-
weather followers" to walk with Him through the rest of your life? Will you be
like one of Gideon's 300 and volunteer to join in great exploits for your Lord?

If that's your commitment today, get ready for an exciting life.

And watch those Midianites scatter.

Chapter Five

Samson's Story:
He—Man with a She—Weakness

"Get her for me, for she looks good to me."
—Judges 14:3, NASB

Life is full of surprises.

Many are unexpected pleasures and blessings that come our way. Others are tragic and sad.

I have been greatly surprised by the way certain people's lives have turned out. I can think of people I've met through the years who seemed to have no potential whatsoever. You never expected these guys or girls to amount to much of anything. Maybe you even made fun of them in school. Then, five or ten years after graduation, you hear one of these "geeks" is the president of a multi-million-dollar software company!

Then there are those whose lives seemed to be brimming over with promise and potential. They had something special, and you just knew they would make their mark in life. Blessed with multiple talents, giftedness, and personality, they seemed to stand out from the crowd. Perhaps it was someone who was unusually gifted spiritually. And sure enough, their star began to rise, and you're thinking, "Well, at least I can say I knew them back when."

Then suddenly, seemingly without warning, the bottom seems to drop out of this individual's life. Or you watch in perplexity as The Golden Boy, The Golden Girl, are slowly sidetracked by foolish, life-marring decisions.

Stories like that are always very sad, because God has a unique, custom-designed plan for each of our lives. And when we stubbornly turn from His path to follow our own ways or the impulses of our flesh, our personal loss is incalculable.

The prophet Jeremiah tells the story of his trip to the potter's house, where he watched as the craftsman molded clay into useful vessels. On the potter's wheel, the pliable, shapable clay could be made into something both useful and beautiful.

That is a picture of our lives. We're the ones who determine if we will be flexible and moldable in God's hands. We make ourselves that way by our openness to His plans and our willingness to obey. I believe the steps of our lives are allowed by God before our conversion, and ordered by the Lord after. God knew the day you would receive Christ, and He has allowed your life experiences in order to do a unique and never-to-be-duplicated work in your life.

At this very moment, even as you read these words, you can be pliable and shapable in God's hands, or you can continually resist Him. He gives you that choice.

For instance, after all the tragedies and setbacks in young Joseph's life (read his story in Genesis 37–50), he could have adopted a victim mentality and become bitter. Instead, he chose to be *better*. After many years of watching God work through the ups and downs of his life, he could still say to his brothers, "As for you, you meant evil against me, but God meant it for good in order to bring about this present result, to preserve many people alive. So therefore, do not be afraid."[30]

Outside of the potter's house described in the book of Jeremiah[31] was a field littered with cracked, broken pots and vessels. Wreckage. Lives that could have been objects of beauty and great usefulness to God—but would not yield. These broken shards represent wasted potential.

Before us in this chapter is the story of a man who had off-the-charts potential that was largely wasted. Gifted with unbelievable physical strength, Samson had God's blessing and anointing on his life. He could have been one of the greatest leaders in the history of Israel. But instead, his life became a proverb, an example of how not to live.

When you think of Samson's life, you think *waste*. A life of squandered resources and untapped potential and ability. He threw it away because of some subtle but ultimately fatal errors in judgment. His life stands as a warning to all of us.

Time and again in Scripture, however, the streams of tragedy and hope run side by side. Samson's story also speaks of second chances . . . and the grace of God.

THE DEVIL IN THE DETAILS

The life of Samson illustrates the ancient truth that a good beginning doesn't necessarily guarantee a good ending. That's basically what Solomon wrote: "The end of a thing is better than its beginning" (Ecclesiastes 7:8). The American poet Henry Wadsworth Longfellow said, "Great is the art of beginning, but greater is the art of ending."

When we think of Samson's tragic fall, our minds race to his encounters with Delilah. But the fact of the matter is, it was a series of smaller compromises that ultimately proved to be his undoing.

Many of us vividly remember the explosion of the space shuttle Challenger on January 28, 1986. Seven crew members died in that tragic mishap. After weeks of careful research, technicians revealed that the primary cause of the explosion was a failure of something called an "o-ring."

O-rings are rubber rings used as mechanical seals or gaskets. When an o-ring failed on Challenger's rocket booster, it allowed the super-heated gasses from the burning rocket to escape, ultimately resulting in the explosion.

It's mind-boggling to think of that shuttle—something so large, so powerful, so incredibly expensive, so carefully designed—being brought down by something as small and seemingly insignificant as an o-ring.

Samson's life was similar. We can trace a breakdown in the smaller areas of his life . . .leading to an explosion.

Some of you who read these pages are young, with tremendous potential to make a difference for God in this very dark world at this crucial time in history. Through the life of Samson, God warns you to walk with great care so that you don't repeat this mighty man's mistakes. But the story isn't just a red flag for young people. All of us need to attend to the details of our lives, seeking to walk before God with a whole heart.

A GREAT PARADOX

Samson's life stands as one of the greatest paradoxes in the Bible. He had such magnificent potential to do something truly great for God, and to lead his people out of the state of backsliding into which they had fallen.

Humanly speaking, Samson had superhuman qualities. Physically, there was none stronger. Mentally, he was sharp, clever, and alert.

And spiritually? He had an admirable start in life. He was one of the two men in the Old Testament whose birth and mission were foretold by angels. Of Samson it was said, "The boy is to be a Nazirite, set apart to God from birth, and he will begin the deliverance of Israel from the hands of the Philistines."[32]

He certainly *began* that job, and he may have been able to *finish* the task had he allowed that potential to reach full bloom. For this calling, he was given a special anointing of the Holy Spirit that gave him strength like no other.

These were extremely dark days in Israel's history. As the Bible describes it, everyone did what was right in his own eyes, and the Word of the Lord was scarce. The people of God had been living compromised lives and didn't want to rock the boat with their enemies, the Philistines. So as God always does when the times turn spiritually and morally dark, He raised up a deliverer. Someone to turn the light on.

As prophesied before his birth, Samson chose to live a life separated to God, taking the vow of a Nazirite. Among other things, the provisions of that vow included the following restrictions:

1. A Nazirite was to separate himself from all wine and liquor.

2. He was to avoid all contact with a dead body.

3. He was to be holy unto the LORD.

4. No razor was to ever touch his head.

When we think of Samson, we remember his long hair. In fact, his supernatural strength was symbolized by those untrimmed locks. If it was the same today—if hair still represented physical strength—some of us bald guys wouldn't get on very well!

But it wasn't his hair that gave Samson strength, it was his wholehearted commitment to God, symbolized by the hair.

From the very beginning, it was clear that God was with this young man in a special way. Scripture tells us that "he grew and the LORD blessed him, and the Spirit of the LORD began to stir him. ..."[33]

But no sooner does this promise begin in Samson's life than he flatly disobeys God's commands and marries a Philistine woman. Clearly, this was what Scripture calls an "unequal yoke." God tells us to avoid such relationships for very good reasons. For every case where that nonbeliever has come to faith, there are probably a hundred cases of the believer being dragged down and spiritually compromised. Ignoring his parents' objections, Samson did what he wanted and married her. Why did he do that? Because she looked good. As he told his parents, "Get her for me, for she looks good to me."[34]

HOOKER, LINE, AND SINKER

A series of mishaps followed, resulting in the breakup of that potential marriage. In conflict after conflict, Samson used his God-given superhuman strength to achieve victory over Israel's Philistine overlords.

The troubles and trials in this young man's life should have been a divine wake-up call for him. It was an opportunity for him to learn from his mistakes and turn around before it was too late.

Instead, he went the other way.

Refusing to heed God's warnings, Samson went from the frying pan into the fire. The devil got the mighty Samson hooker, line, and sinker!

> One day Samson went to the Philistine town of Gaza and spent the night with a prostitute. Word soon spread that Samson was there, so the men of Gaza gathered together and waited all night at the town gates. They kept quiet during the night, saying to themselves, "When the light of morning comes, we will kill him."
>
> But Samson stayed in bed only until midnight. Then he got up, took hold of the doors of the town gate, including the two posts, and lifted them up, bar and all. He put them on his shoulders and carried them all the way to the top of the hill across from Hebron.
> (Judges 16:1-3, NLT)

What was a Nazirite doing in a Philistine city's red light district? Certainly no one forced him to do it. He deliberately made this choice and crossed the line. As far as he was concerned, no ambush could hurt him, no trap could hold him. So in his supreme self-confidence, he blatantly took this radical step.

Clearly he was not walking with the Lord at this point, for we read of no spiritual struggle, either before or after he headed for the land of his enemies to consort with a prostitute.

No one talks much about this first part of Samson's downfall. But in this episode with the harlot in Gaza, we discover all the seeds of his future destruction. What he sowed in Gaza with the prostitute he later reaped with the devious Delilah.

When his enemies discovered Samson was in the city, they laid plans to trap him inside the walls. Posting a guard by the house, the Philistines set up an ambush by the city gates. Studded with nails and covered with metal, these massive gates were virtually fireproof. And once locked, there was no way out of the city . . . for an ordinary man, at least.

The ambushers went to sleep, confident their nemesis could not escape. In the middle of the night Samson left the prostitute's house, put his arms around the gateposts—timbers driven deeply into the earth—and tore out the gates, posts and all, dumping them some twenty miles away!

Needless to say, no one attacked Samson that day.

But when you think about it, this display of God-given might was just another chapter in a tragic story. Samson had power without purity. Strength without self-control. For twenty years he had experienced the thrill of victory—without once tasting the agony of defeat! That should have kept him thankful to God. Instead, it produced a deadly complacency about his spiritual life.

Some may even think because God doesn't discipline or exercise His judgment immediately, that He doesn't see or doesn't care about our sins. That's a big mistake! As Paul made clear, "Don't be misled: No one makes a fool of God. What a person plants, he will harvest."[35]

Samson demonstrated he had no integrity in his life when it came to women . . . and that did not escape the notice of Satan. Having found his "in," the devil moved in for the kill. He custom-designed a delectable little dish named Delilah.

Desperate Measures

Some time later Samson fell in love with a woman named Delilah, who lived in the valley of Sorek. The rulers of the Philistines went to her and said, "Entice Samson to tell you what makes him so strong and how he can be overpowered and tied up securely. Then each of us will give you 1,100 pieces of silver."

So Delilah said to Samson, "Please tell me what makes you so strong and what it would take to tie you up securely."

Samson replied, "If I am tied up with seven new bowstrings that have not yet been dried, I would become as weak as anyone else."

So the Philistine rulers brought Delilah seven new bowstrings, and she tied Samson up with them. She had hidden some men in one of the inner rooms of her house, and she cried out, "Samson! The Philistines have come to capture you!" But Samson snapped the bowstrings as a piece of string snaps when it is burned by a fire. So the secret of his strength was not discovered. (Judges 16:4-9, NLT)

These Philistines were desperate. Samson seemed to slaughter them for sport. On one occasion he killed thirty of them, seemingly without effort, to settle a bet. Then, finding himself surrounded, he killed a *thousand more with a mere bone he had found.* What can you do with a guy who rips lions apart and walks off with city gates on his shoulders? It was intolerable. Determined to bring Samson down, the Philistine leaders offered Delilah big bucks to find the secret of his strength.

No doubt Delilah was an attractive woman.

But what kind of bait would you expect Satan to use?

Temptation often comes in attractive packages ...desirable, appealing, and very costly. It promises life but brings death. Is there a "Delilah" in your life now?

Once again, Samson had involved himself with the wrong person. First there was the Philistine woman, then the prostitute, and now Delilah. Samson had blatantly ignored every warning shot that God fired across his bow ...and Satan was about to cash in on this he-man's she-weakness.

Realizing he couldn't bring this warrior down on the battlefield, Satan switched to the bedroom and found a willing victim. Did Samson ever realize the stakes of the game he was playing, toying with Philistine women? He must have thought he could just laugh it off and walk away from it all. But he was about to walk into a trap he couldn't shrug out of. (The tip-off for Samson should have been that Delilah worked at Super-Cuts!)

For temptation to do its damage, there must be a desire on our part. The apostle James wrote: "But each one is tempted when he is drawn away by his own desires and enticed. Then, when desire has conceived, it gives birth to sin; and sin, when it is full-grown, brings forth death."[36]

In other words, for Satan to succeed, we must listen, yield, and, most importantly, desire what he offers. Our adversary will use different types of bait to tempt us. But remember, it's not the bait that constitutes sin, it's the bite!

Delilah definitely plied her seductive charm on Samson. But one thing must be noted. The lady was certainly up front with her intentions!

So Delilah said to Samson, "Please tell me where your great strength lies, and with what you may be bound to afflict you." (Judges 16:6)

This would be the first indication that this was not a healthy relationship! Couldn't Samson have realized what was going on? Did he think it was all a big game?

Sin is so intoxicating. And it leads us to lie to ourselves. ("I can quit anytime I want to.") Samson thought he could handle it. Famous last words!

You've heard the rationalizations—and maybe even used them in times past. "I'll just go so far and then stop. Just this one time, and I'll never do it again." In response to statements like these, the Bible asks a very relevant question: "Can a man scoop fire into his lap without his clothes being burned?" (Proverbs 6:27, NIV)

Answer? Probably not, unless he's wearing asbestos.

Can you believe how blunt Delilah was? "Will you please tell me exactly how I can trap you so the Philistines can come in and capture you?"

How many wake-up calls did God give Samson? Sadly, Samson had already taken the bait. And you've got to hand it to Delilah, she was persistent! As the pretty lady kept begging and pouting and crying, Samson came closer and closer to revealing the true secret of his strength.

The story of Samson highlights some very important truths for our survival in the midst of the spiritual warfare that rages all around us.

1. Moral Compromise Always Makes Us Vulnerable

If Samson had not begun this sinful relationship with Delilah and the other Philistine women, he would not have found himself in this deadly situation.

Nobody falls suddenly into sin. It may look that way to an outside observer. It may even seem that way to the one who falls. But the truth is, each major compromise is preceded by a series of small compromises.

And those small compromises? They may appear to be so insignificant to you that "playing the edge" seems like no big deal.

—*What's wrong with a little soft pornography?*
I can handle it.

—*Why shouldn't I go out for a few drinks with the old gang?*
I know when to quit.

—*Who really cares if I fudge a little on my expense account?*
It's almost expected.

—*Why shouldn't I date a nonbeliever?*
It's not like we're getting married.

Is there any moral compromise in your life right now? If so, deal with it. Because someday, in some way, shape, or form, Delilah will show up on your doorstep.

And you may find yourself in a trap that has no back door.

2. Temptation Comes In Attractive Packages

The Philistines didn't go out and hire some homely woman to ensnare the Hebrew champion, they hired a fox! When sin comes, it will not come as something ugly and destructive, but rather as something desirable, seemingly good, and fulfilling.

The Bible says that the fruit of the tree in the Garden was pleasant to look upon. In other words, it looked more like a ripe, succulent peach than it did a pinecone!

3. Temptation Comes When We Choose The Wrong Friends

Samson had a consistent ability to choose the wrong people to hang out with. First it was the Philistine girl that so distressed his godly parents, then the prostitute from Gaza, and finally Delilah . . . who was pure poison.

Paul nailed it when he wrote: "Do not be misled: 'Bad company corrupts good character.'"[37]

After following several false leads, Delilah turned up the heat and went in for the kill.

> Then Delilah pouted, "How can you tell me, 'I love you' when you don't share your secrets with me? You've made fun of me three times now, and you still haven't told me what makes you so strong!" She tormented him with her nagging day after day until he was sick to death of it.
>
> Finally, Samson shared his secret with her. "My hair has never been cut," he confessed, "for I was dedicated to God as a Nazirite from birth. If my head were shaved, my strength would leave me, and I would become as weak as anyone else."
>
> Delilah realized he had finally told her the truth, so she sent for the Philistine rulers. "Come back one more time," she said, "for he has finally told me his secret." So the Philistine rulers returned with the money in their hands. Delilah lulled Samson to sleep with his head in her lap, and then she called in a man to shave off the seven locks of his hair. In this way she began to bring him down, and his strength left him.
>
> Then she cried out, "Samson! The Philistines have come to capture you!"
>
> When he woke up, he thought, "I will do as before and shake myself free." But he didn't realize the Lord had left him.
>
> So the Philistines captured him and gouged out his eyes. They took him to Gaza, where he was bound with bronze chains and forced to grind grain in the prison. (Judges 16:15-21, NLT)

What a sad story. Delilah had said to him, "If you really love me, you will do this." Now that's just about the oldest line in the book. Listen, any person who asks you to compromise your principles as a believer to prove your love *doesn't really love you*. And you would do well to get out of such a relationship as fast as you can.

If you love me, you'll go all the way with me.
If you love me, cover for me! Lie for me this one time.
That's not love at all!

What's so amazing to me is that Samson felt comfortable enough with Delilah to fall asleep in her lap! Talk about "sleeping with the enemy." And within this passage, we can find one of the saddest statements in the Bible.

"He didn't realize the LORD had left him" (v. 20).

He had lost his once-close connection with God, but wasn't even aware of it. This is so typical of someone trapped in sin. Everyone else sees, everyone else knows, and several brave people may even take the risk to warn that individual. But he or she responds with defensiveness, indignation, and hostility. *Everyone's against me. No one understands me. What right do they have to judge me?* And on and on it goes.

Then one day they wake up and it's too late. Life has changed forever, and there is no going back.

When Satan finally nailed God's champion, he tossed Samson aside like yesterday's garbage. The text says, "He was bound with bronze chains and forced to grind grain in the prison."[38]

And out of this last verse, we see several tragic characteristics of sin.

SIN BLINDS, FINDS, AND GRINDS

First, Sin Blinds You

You find yourself doing completely irrational things. Insane things. I know of men with great families—loving wives and adoring children—who left it all for some stupid fling with another woman. I know of many women who have done the same, leaving devoted husbands—even their children—in some mindless quest to "find themselves."

This is insanity, and words can't even describe how deeply they will regret it one day. Ah, but that prospect of sin is so very promising at the outset. You start by fantasizing about it. *What would it be like if I did thus and so with so and so....* Maybe you move from there to a little "harmless" flirting. That can easily lead to sharing intimate problems, even discussing your marital woes with that individual.

When someone questions you, you say, "Relax. We're just good friends, nothing more." Or maybe, "He really understands me," or "She really listens to me."

If you're that deep into self-justification, it's obvious that you've been blinded by sin. And if you think you can get yourself entangled and just walk away, you'd better take a page out of Samson's notebook. That's what he thought too

Second, Sin Finds You

You may very well experience a euphoric-like excitement the first time you cross the line in an extramarital relationship ...or indulge in that sexual encounter ...

or visit that elicit Web site ...or get away with that lie ...or experiment with those drugs. You feel somehow above the normal constraints others face. It will be different for you, you tell yourself. You'll have your cake and eat it too. No, you won't. Your sin will find you out!

And what's that sound you hear?

"The Philistines are upon you!"

Third, Sin Grinds You

Satan is all about selling you an experience, but keeping quiet about the price tag. And don't kid yourself—you *will* pay a terrible price. I want to go back to a no-nonsense passage of Scripture I partially quoted earlier. Paul wrote:

> Don't be misled—you cannot mock the justice of God. You will always harvest what you plant. Those who live only to satisfy their own sinful nature will harvest decay and death from that sinful nature. But those who live to please the Spirit will harvest everlasting life from the Spirit. (Galatians 6:7-8, NLT)

The price tag for an adulterous affair includes broken marriages, betrayed trust, a damaged witness, a shattered reputation, and devastated children with deep wounds they will most likely carry for the rest of their lives.

That's a pretty steep bill. And that's without mentioning the possibility of AIDS, venereal disease, and depending on what you've done, maybe even jail time! But who cares about all that? It's all about your "needs," right?

Samson found out the hard way what a horrible, devastating thing unconfessed sin can be. But even in this mess there was hope!

Judges 16:22 says, "However, the hair of his head began to grow again after it had been shaven." This is the "life verse" for all of us folically-challenged guys (otherwise known as bald men).

Samson was now a blind slave of enemies who desperately hated him. How could life sink much lower than that? But even then, well beneath the Philistine's radar, God was working again in Samson's life ...*as his hair began to grow back.*

This passage tells us God holds out hope to us even if we have failed. God did indeed give Samson another chance. The truth is, we're all going to have our stumbles and failures.

But here's the underlying question: How will we respond to those disappointing letdowns and setbacks? What will we learn that will enable us to "fall forward," laying hold of the forgiveness of God and avoiding that trap in the future?

If, we continue to repeat the same mistakes and excuse our sins, blaming them on circumstances, people, or whatever, we seal our own fate! And in time, we, too, will end up with a wasted life.

As Samson's hair began to grow, strength trickled back into his body. He could feel it! One night the Philistines were having a drunken feast to their vile god, Dagon. Sometime during the festivities, someone came up with the bright idea of dragging the sightless Samson out of the dungeon to make fun of him.

It turned out to be a very bad idea ... for them.

A servant guided the now-blind champion to the foundational pillars of the temple, where the Philistines were partying away. Israel's one-time hero asked God for one final surge of strength and pushed those pillars apart, collapsing the temple and killing more Philistines in that one action than he had in his entire lifetime.

Poetic justice? Certainly that. But tragically, Samson went down with them.

We can't look at the wreckage of Samson's life without thinking about another young man who was temped sexually, but with a very different conclusion than Samson.

A Life in Contrast

His name was Joseph, a godly young Hebrew slave serving in the household of an Egyptian official named Potiphar. Joseph was a handsome and well-built man, and Potiphar's wife laid eyes on him from the first time he entered the household. As the days went by, she pressured young Joseph to have sex with her *every single day.* This woman was more relentless than Delilah! Finally, tired of waiting, she grabbed hold of his tunic and pulled him down onto her bed.

So what did Joseph do?

He did what any reasonable person should do under such circumstances. He ran like the wind!

Though he lived hundreds of years before the Paul, Joseph did exactly what the apostle counseled young Timothy: "Run from anything that stimulates youthful lusts. Instead, pursue righteous living, faithfulness, love, and peace. Enjoy the companionship of those who call on the Lord with pure hearts" (2 Timothy 2:22, NLT).

Unlike Samson, who thought he could play with sin and not be hurt, Joseph knew his limits and simply didn't trust himself to dabble with immorality. Wisdom beyond his years!

Paul told the Corinthians: "Therefore let him who thinks he stands take heed lest he fall."[39] Joseph knew he was vulnerable, so he fled!

I'm reminded of an old Chinese proverb that says, "He who would not enter the room of sin must not sit at the door of temptation."

Fleeing sexual temptation is a no-brainer. It would be like walking across a field and coming upon a coiled rattlesnake looking at you through those glazed eyes, ready to strike. What do you do? Try to negotiate with the rattler? Reach some sort of compromise, perhaps? Do you just stand there, trying to stare it down, or even approach it to show how strong you are?

If you do, I hope your will is in order. No, if you have half a brain you back off and run as fast as you can. It is better to shun the bait than to struggle on the hook!

Flee temptation, and don't leave a forwarding address. Every temptation is an opportunity to flee to God. Are you squandering your life right now on something or someone that's destroying you from the inside out? Are you flirting with sin? Watch out!

Learn the lesson of Samson. It isn't enough to know what is right, or even to be used by God in a powerful, earth-shaking way.

You have to finish the race. So let's get on with it. Don't neglect the small things in your life—like those little o-rings—lest you crash and burn.

Samson may have had more muscle than Joseph, but who was stronger? The man or woman who leans heavily on the Lord will never live to regret it.

Chapter Six

DAVID'S STORY, PART 1:
THE MAN AFTER GOD'S HEART

*"I have found David the son of Jesse, a man after
My own heart, who will do all My will." —Acts 13:22*

Have you ever felt unloved and under-appreciated? Has it ever seemed to you as though your faithful work always goes unnoticed in life? Have you ever faced a problem so large it seemed like it could never be overcome?

Then keep reading...because you'll find encouragement in this chapter.

The Old Testament book of 1 Samuel introduces us to David, one of the Bible's most significant people. In battle, he was fearless. In leadership, he was discerning and wise. Yet David was more than some action-movie macho-dude. He had a tender heart toward God, and was both a poet and musician.

Most significantly, he is the only man in all the Bible to be called "a man after God's own heart." And it's one thing to have someone else say that about you—maybe your pastor or your best friend or your brother-in-law. But when God Himself declares that about you...that's a milestone for anyone.

I have found David the son of Jesse, a man after My own heart, who will do all My will. (Acts 13:22)

David is mentioned in the New Testament more times than any other Old Testament character. When we think of David, two other names spring to mind.

David and Goliath...and David and Bathsheba. In many ways, those two names sum up his life. One signifies his greatest victory, the other, his most devastating defeat.

Sometimes in horse racing or politics, they talk about a "dark horse" coming from somewhere back in the pack to win the race. The title has never fit anybody better than this young son of Jesse. No one in Israel could have imagined or expected that this shepherd boy would rise to the throne of Israel.

This was a period of history, following the era when Israel was ruled by judges, when the people began demanding a king so they could "be like the other nations." They wanted someone inspiring and noble to lead them in battle against their enemies.

So God gave them the perfect candidate. If David was the man after God's own heart, than Saul was the man after *man's* own heart. Saul had it all going.

He was from a good family, tall, strikingly handsome, and in the beginning at least, modest and humble. In addition to all of that, Scripture says that "the Spirit of God came upon him in power"[40] to accomplish the tasks at hand and save the nation from its enemies.

Saul started off very well...but all too soon began to self-destruct. His offenses started somewhat small, then snowballed. By the time 1 Samuel 16 rolls around, Saul was already finished. He would stay on the throne for forty more years, but God had rejected him and no longer blessed his reign.

But God had another plan. God *always* has a plan. He had already selected a new man for the job and set the wheels in motion to bring David to throne of Israel. It was as though the Lord was saying, "All right, I gave you a king after your own heart, just like the other nations. You asked for him, and you got him. Now it's My turn!"

To say God's selection was a surprise would be a classic understatement. No one, not even the great prophet Samuel, saw it coming.

Why did God pick David, the youngest son of Jesse? We need to pay careful attention to this choice, for in His selection of David the Lord is showing us the kind of person He is looking for...the kind of person He will use in His kingdom.

And yes, God is actively looking for people to use! Never doubt it. In the book of Ezekiel the Lord said, "I looked for a man among them who would build up the wall and stand before me in the gap on behalf of the land so I would not have to destroy it, but I found none" (Ezekiel 22:30, NIV).

In years to come, the prophet Hanani told a fickle king of Judah, "The eyes of the LORD search the whole earth in order to strengthen those whose hearts are fully committed to him" (2 Chronicles 16:9, NLT).

God found in David a man who would stand in the gap, a man whose heart was fully committed to Him. Will He find a heart like that in you?

David was really just a boy at this point, but one with seemingly limitless potential. So the Lord sent the prophet Samuel to go anoint a new king of Israel.

The timing couldn't have been better for Samuel. The old prophet had slipped into a depression over the failure of Saul. He had probably come to think of the young man like a son. (His own sons were corrupt and a deep disappointment to him).

So God spoke to Samuel, told him to shake off his funk, and directed him to an obscure little village called Bethlehem.

Now the LORD said to Samuel, "You have mourned long enough for Saul. I have rejected him as king of Israel, so fill your flask with olive oil and go to Bethlehem. Find a man named Jesse who lives there, for I have selected one of his sons to be my king."

But Samuel asked, "How can I do that? If Saul hears about it, he will kill me."

"Take a heifer with you," the LORD replied, "and say that you have come to make a sacrifice to the LORD. Invite Jesse to the sacrifice, and I will show you which of his sons to anoint for me."

So Samuel did as the LORD instructed. When he arrived at Bethlehem, the elders of the town came trembling to meet him. "What's wrong?" they asked. "Do you come in peace?"

"Yes," Samuel replied. "I have come to sacrifice to the Lord. Purify yourselves and come with me to the sacrifice." Then Samuel performed the purification rite for Jesse and his sons and invited them to sacrifice, too. (1 Samuel 16:1-5, NLT)

Interestingly, the Lord did not reveal to Samuel (at that point) who the man was to be. This is typical of the Lord. He leads us one step at a time. As much as I've wanted it at times, God rarely gives me a detailed blueprint of all that He wants me to do. More often, He just tells me to take a certain step of faithful obedience, and I am to act on it. God's way becomes plain when we start walking in it. Obedience to revealed truth guarantees guidance in matters unrevealed.

Remember the story of Philip's unexpected journey in the book of Acts? A powerful evangelist, Philip had been experiencing wide open doors and hearts in Samaria. Signs and wonders shook the city, and people were almost lining up to hear the gospel. Evil spirits were beating a path out of town, and Dr. Luke tells us that "there was great joy in that city."[41]

Right in the middle of the big Samaritan crusade, however, Philip suddenly received puzzling new marching orders.

But an angel of the Lord spoke to Philip saying, "Get up and go south to the road that descends from Jerusalem to Gaza." (This is a desert road.)[42]

Okay, Philip might have been thinking. *I'm in the biggest evangelistic campaign of my life and the Lord tells me leave town and head south ...into the desert. What is this all about? Does He want me to preach to lizards?*

Actually, there is no indication Philip thought anything of the sort. He simply obeyed the word of the Lord and hit the road. The Holy Spirit didn't give him any explanation, and Philip didn't ask for one.

So he started out, and on his way he met an Ethiopian eunuch, an important official in charge of all the treasury of Candace, queen of the Ethiopians. This man had gone to Jerusalem to worship, and on his way home was sitting in his chariot reading the book of Isaiah the prophet. The Spirit told Philip, "Go to that chariot and stay near it." (Acts 8:27-29, NIV)

What followed was the dramatic conversion of an important foreign official—possibly the very first African convert to Christianity. Philip had been successfully serving the Lord in a city ...but because he obeyed God's word step by step, he had the opportunity to touch a continent!

In Samuel's case, he knew that he was supposed to go to the village of Bethlehem and crown the next king of Israel—whoever it was. So the great prophet suddenly showed up, and Scripture says, "the elders of the town trembled at his coming."[43] Why were they shaking in their sandals? A guilty conscience, maybe? Maybe it was like seeing a highway patrolman in your rearview mirror, and your heart beats a little faster. You're thinking, "What did I do?"

Bethlehem, close as it may have been to Jerusalem, was definitely off the beaten path. Years later, in the book of Micah, God would say:

> But you, Bethlehem Ephrathah,
> Though you are little among the thousands of Judah,
> Yet out of you shall come forth to Me
> The One to be Ruler in Israel....(Micah 5:2)

This was not only David's home, but because Jesus was of the lineage of David, it would be His birthplace as well. Samuel tells the town elders that he's there to offer a sacrifice, and that he wants everyone to show up. This would give him a chance to check out Jesse's sons.

Immediately, Samuel is drawn to Eliab, the pick of the litter.

When they arrived, Samuel saw Eliab and thought, "Surely the LORD's anointed stands here before the LORD."

But the LORD said to Samuel, "Do not consider his appearance or his height, for I have rejected him. The LORD does not look at the things man looks at. Man looks at the outward appearance, but the LORD looks at the heart."

Then Jesse called Abinadab and had him pass in front of Samuel. But Samuel said, "The LORD has not chosen this one either." Jesse then had Shammah pass by, but Samuel said, "Nor has the LORD chosen this one." Jesse had seven of his sons pass before Samuel, but Samuel said to him, "The LORD has not chosen these." So he asked Jesse, "Are these all the sons you have?"

"There is still the youngest," Jesse answered, "but he is tending the sheep."

Samuel said, "Send for him; we will not sit down until he arrives."

So he sent and had him brought in. He was ruddy, with a fine appearance and handsome features.

Then the LORD said, "Rise and anoint him; he is the one."

So Samuel took the horn of oil and anointed him in the presence of his brothers, and from that day on the Spirit of the LORD came upon David in power. Samuel then went to Ramah. (1 Samuel 16:6-13, NIV)

What a fascinating story this is! Father Jesse proudly parades his seven sons before the visiting prophet. The magnificent seven!

But the Lord said, "No ...not that one...not him either ...no ...no ...next." So Samuel asks, "Do you have any other sons?" Take note of Jesse's reply: "There remains yet the youngest, and there he is, keeping the sheep."[44] This phrase "the youngest" doesn't just mean David was less in years than the others. It means that he was least in his father's estimation. So much so, Jesse would not have even included him had Samuel not asked if there were any others.

How sad it is when parents show favoritism to one child over another. Isaac and Rebekah both did this, with Isaac favoring Esau and Rebekah favoring Jacob. It ended up tearing their family apart.

Perhaps you felt unappreciated by your parents. They rarely expressed their affection toward you or had an affirming word for you. Or perhaps they divorced, and you never really knew their love.

Know this: Those who are rejected of men are beloved of God. You need to know that in spite of your parent's lack of love for you, you have always had a heavenly Father who deeply loves you.

David later wrote, "Though my father and mother forsake me, the Lord will receive me."[45]

Alan Redpath once wrote: "The thought of God toward you began before He even flung a star into space, then He wrote your name on His heart. It was graven in the palm of His hands before the sky was stretched out in the heavens."

So the magnificent seven have been paraded before Samuel, and to his chagrin, not one of them is God's candidate. So he asks to see this last son, the youngest, who wasn't even invited to the party.

Imagine David at that moment. He's out with the sheep in the field like any other day. Someone says, "Hey, David, they want you back at the house!"

David comes sprinting in, smelling like the sheep he had been keeping company with. He was a teen with reddish hair and a pleasant way about him. God says to the prophet, *That's My boy.* The next thing David knows, this old prophet is pouring oil on him and saying, "This is the next king of Israel!"

Those watching these proceedings probably thought Samuel was going senile! *David? King?* It was too ridiculous to contemplate. Imagine the shock, and then the jealousy, of David's brothers. Especially Eliab!

But there was no mistaking it. David was clearly God's choice, reminding us yet again that God sees things differently than we do. This brings us to the first principle about the people God uses.

1. God Uses Ordinary People

David was in many respects the polar opposite of King Saul. Where Saul came from a family where he was loved and doted on, David apparently came from one where he was neglected, even disliked. While Saul was the most handsome man in Israel, David was just an ordinary shepherd boy, though a good-looking one. Saul was attractive on the outside; inside he was vain, shallow, and devoid of true integrity. In contrast, though very young, David had a deep spiritual life and intense devotion to God.

But why does God seem to go out of His way to use ordinary people? A paraphrase of 1 Corinthians 1:26-28 records these words of the apostle Paul:

> Take a good look, friends, at who you were when you got called into this life. I don't see many of "the brightest and the best" among you, not many influential, not many from high-society families. Isn't it obvious that God deliberately chose men and women that the culture over-looks and exploits and abuses, chose these "nobodies" to expose the hollow pretensions of the "somebodies"?[46]

You always hear the excited buzz when some famous athlete or celebrity embraces faith in Christ (or at least appears to). We want to say to nonbelievers, "Look, we have Celebrity X on our side now!" And then we want to put them on Christian TV and rush them out into the public to represent us, disregarding the warning from Scripture that tells us to not elevate a new convert.[47] But so often that celebrity falls short and we are embarrassed.

God seems to go out of His way to choose the unexpected person. Why? "So that no man may boast before God."[48]

When the religious elite of Jerusalem encountered Peter and John after the resurrection of Jesus, they didn't know what to make of them. Weren't these men just common, uneducated fishermen? Where did all the boldness and the penetrating speech come from? Why were these men so different? Then they acknowledged that these men *had been with Jesus.*

You see, God wants the glory for what He has done and is doing. And the recruits He looks for to carry His work forward will probably look very different from the people we might have picked. Just like Samuel, we get hung up on a person's appearance. But God looks right past that into the heart.

Dwight L. Moody once had a man say to him, "Moody, the world has yet to see what God can do with and in and through the man who is wholly dedicated to Him!" Moody replied, "I want to be that man!" And God took a shoe sales-man and made him one of the greatest evangelists in human history. He went from selling soles to saving souls!

2. God Looks For Truly Spiritual People

I'm not speaking here of some pompous "holier-than-thou" spirituality, but the real thing. The most spiritual people I have met have been very down-to-earth. I have no interest in some phony head-in-the-clouds mysticism, but rather a genuine day-by-day relationship with the living God.

Knowing and walking with God is essentially a *practical* matter, and those who really know Him will be some of the most real and touchable people you will ever meet.

Real people? We've certainly met them in the pages of this book, haven't we? Men like Jacob, Moses, and Gideon weren't cardboard cutouts or representations in a stained glass window. They put their sandals on one foot at a time like the rest of us. They were human through and through.

That's the kind of spirituality I'm talking about with David; it was practical, but it was also deeply committed to God. For insight into who David really was, one only has to read the Psalms. He had a deep hunger for God and a strong commitment to what was right.

In Psalm 57:7 (KJV), he wrote, "My heart is fixed, Oh God, my heart is fixed." That was David's heart: focused, not fickle; meditative, yet brave and courageous. In Psalm 27 he really laid out the whole purpose of his life:

One thing I have desired of the Lord,
That will I seek:
That I may dwell in the house of the Lord
All the days of my life,
To behold the beauty of the Lord,
And to inquire in His temple. (v. 4)

David was saying, "Wherever You are, Lord, that's where I want to be—just as close as I can get. That's the chief desire of my life."

It sounds a little like the apostle Paul, doesn't it? He, too, had that clear, singular aim and objective: "One thing I do, forgetting those things which are behind and reaching forward to those things which are ahead, I press toward the goal for the prize of the upward call of God in Christ Jesus."[49]

Mary had singleminded devotion as she sat at Jesus' feet, drinking in every word. At that point, her sister Martha did not have that singular focus, leading Jesus to say, "Martha, Martha, you are worried and troubled about *many* things. *But one thing is needed,* and Mary has chosen that good part, which will not be taken away from her."[50]

Do you have this clear focus and aim in your life? Or do you have double vision as you find yourself trying to live in two worlds? Our greatest danger in life is in permitting the urgent things—those pressing, insistent details of life—to crowd out the important.

What was this one thing that David desired?

To behold the beauty of the LORD,
And to inquire in His temple.

Perhaps you have felt the same way. You love being with God's people at church, and you wish you could set up camp under the nearest pew and just live there.

That is a God-given desire. It means you have come to see the value and blessing of fellowship with God and His people. For David, the meeting place of God was in the Tabernacle. But today, for us as believers, the Holy of Holies is open 24 hours a day, 365 days a year.

> Therefore, brothers, since we have confidence to enter the Most Holy Place by the blood of Jesus, by a new and living way opened for us through the curtain, that is, his body, and since we have a great priest over the house of God, let us draw near to God with a sincere heart in full assurance of faith. (Hebrews 10:19-22, NIV)

What an unbelievable privilege. You and I have a privilege that David and the great saints of the Old Testament could scarcely even imagine—confidence to enter the most holy place ...drawing near to God.

You and I can worship and call on the Lord anytime, anywhere. Even a place like your car can become a sanctuary of sorts, with Bible teaching CDs, mp3 players, and worship music.

When you meditate on psalms like Psalm 27, you have to think, "No wonder God called this a man after His own heart!" His heart seemed to beat in time with the Lord's. If you want to be a man or woman after God's own heart, you would do well to learn from the priorities of David.

Not long ago, a question in a magazine advertisement caught my attention: *Is it an alarm or a calling that gets you out of bed in the morning?*

I like that question. I think it's something we need to ask ourselves often. What gets your blood pumping? What makes you tick? What is the "one thing" in your life right now? Everybody has that one thing. It might be career, money, possessions, success, or relationships.

By the way, there's nothing wrong with any of the things I just mentioned, but they should never, never become the focus and driving purpose of your life. That pursuit should be reserved for God alone. If you will order your life so that you "seek first his kingdom and his righteousness ...all these things will be given to you as well."[51]

Is that some kind of guarantee that you will obtain all you long for on this earth? No, He doesn't promise that. But then again, He may give you more! God knows what's right, so just seek Him. You'll never be a loser for it.

David was an ordinary man and a spiritual man—both qualities that God looks for in the man or woman He uses. And there was also a third important quality....

3. God Uses Faithful People

At this particular time in David's life, his primary responsibility was for his sheep.

Not armies. Not battles. Not kingdoms. Not alliances.

Just sheep. A flock of woolies in the wilderness.

But it was a responsibility he took very seriously. He later mentions that he went one-on-one with both lions and bears to protect those sheep—and he took them down! Out there in the open country, he would spend hours worshipping the Lord while he watched that little flock. No doubt, that is when Psalm 23 must have come to him.

The Lord is my shepherd, I shall not want....

Just because God has called you to be a leader doesn't mean you are ready. There are always a series of tests first. It was this way before Elijah anointed Elisha ...before Moses passed the baton to Joshua ...before Joseph was prepared to step into a huge position of responsibility.

Young Joseph, you may remember, had been filled with visions of grandeur. He had a dream and rightly envisioned his brothers bowing before him. But some things are best kept to yourself. Perhaps God has given you a dream, a vision of what you will be.

Don't go boasting of it to everyone; just be faithful in what He has set before you. If it is really from Him it will happen, but not through your manipulation and conniving.

As we have seen, David had already been anointed. And yet instead of allowing that to change his life, he just kept on faithfully doing what he had been doing previously.

As Chuck Swindoll points out in his excellent book on David, "he didn't go down to the nearest department store and try on crowns. He didn't order a new set of business cards, telling the printer 'Change it from Shepherd to King-elect' He didn't have a badge saying, 'I'm the new Man.' Didn't shine up a chariot and race through the streets of Bethlehem yelling, 'I'm God's choice ... You're looking at Saul's replacement!' No, he just waited for further orders."[52]

And now those orders had come. But those instructions from God didn't drop out of heaven in a golden envelope. As far as we know, there had been no dramatic vision or dream pointing the young shepherd toward the Valley of Elah and a confrontation with a Philistine champion.

It didn't happen like that. David was simply sent by his dad to carry some bread and cheese to his big brothers on the battle line. And obedient son that he was, David accepted the task without question and started on his way.

Sometimes it's funny how God works. It was faithfulness on an errand for his dad that would result in David's first big victory. David could have protested and said, "Don't you know that I'm the future king of Israel? I'm above such things! Let them find their own cheese sandwiches."

No, David was a spiritual man, a faithful and humble man, and he did what Jesse asked.

So often, that's the way God's directions come. We may be looking for some spectacular sign in the heavens or a mysterious voice in the night. More likely, however, God will call us and direct us through the simple, everyday occurrences of life. If we are walking with God and faithfully taking care of our responsibilities, He will guide our steps.

David's brothers were on the battle lines because the Israelites were facing off with their longtime enemies, the Philistines. The two armies, occupying opposing sides of the Valley of Elah, had been in a virtual standoff for days.

The main attraction during those days had been a Philistine warrior by the name of Goliath. He was a hulking freak, a giant of a man, who had been a warrior from his youth. Every day he would bellow over to the Israeli side, "What's the matter with you guys? Are you chicken? Send someone to fight me right now and this will be over. In fact, I'll make you a deal you can't refuse. If your guy can beat me, we Philistines will serve you. But if I win, Israel becomes our slaves. What do you say? Deal?"

If Goliath had been trying to get inside the Israelites' heads and psych them out, he was successful. The giant had them all—King Saul included—trembling with fear.

Enter David, the-shepherd-boy-anointed-king. And that is how David "happened" to hear the bellowing of Goliath, challenging Israelite warriors to single combat. History was about to be made, and it all started with an errand by a faithful young man.

In my life, I've found that divine opportunity usually—if not almost always—comes unexpectedly. I think of the wonderful doors God has opened for me over the years, and they always seemed to happen suddenly.

David looked at the oversized Philistine with amazement. He couldn't believe his ears. The giant was actually blaspheming the God of Israel—and no one was doing anything about it!

Goliath would have been a fear-inspiring sight. He wore a suit of armor over his nine-foot-six-inch frame—and the armor alone weighed in at 200 pounds. His massive head was covered with a bronze helmet, and he carried a huge javelin, with a head that weighed 25 pounds!

Every day this freak yelled his challenges across the valley, and every day the Israelites sank deeper into despair. This had gone on for *forty days* by the time David arrived. Israel's army was virtually paralyzed by fear.

And then the red-headed stranger showed up.

The young man who had taken on lions and bears in the wilderness couldn't believe the soldiers—including his brothers—could sit there and listen to that mockery and blasphemy day after day. David became righteously indignant. He was ready to take on Goliath right then and there.

But there was some opposition to David fighting the Philistine. So, who opposed David? The enemy? No, his own brother, Eliab. The elder son of Jesse laid into his little brother with a vengeance.

> "What are you doing around here, anyway?" he demanded. "What about the sheep you're supposed to be taking care of? I know what a cocky brat you are; you just want to see the battle!"
> (1 Samuel 17:28, TLB)

"What's the matter, little boy?" he mocked. "Did you get bored at home and want to play with the big boys?" Eliab was probably still smarting from the fact that God had rejected him and chosen his red-headed freckle-faced younger sibling instead.

There was Goliath, like a mouthpiece of the devil himself, taunting Israel and mocking God …and Eliab wanted to fight with his little brother!

This is so typical of some in the church today. Even in the face of a lost world all around us and with the end times upon us, so many in the church want to quibble over such insignificant things! When are we going to realize who the real enemy is?

David basically ignored Eliab and went to talk to the king. Saul—whom Scripture tells us was head and shoulders above everyone else in the country—should have stepped forward as Israel's champion. Standing in the presence of this failed king, David volunteered to take on Goliath singlehandedly.

Saul and his soldiers laughed at the thought of a youth like David taking on Goliath. But since they really had no other options, they finally agreed. Maybe Saul was thinking, "This kid might buy us some time. Or maybe Goliath will laugh himself to death, or trip over little David. Who knows? If nothing else, it will be pure entertainment. Go David! We're behind you one hundred percent!"

If David knew they were smirking at him, he didn't let it faze him. Instead, he prepared himself to go to war for the God he loved. And this brings us to fourth quality God looks for in the people He uses.

4. God Uses People Who Are Bold and Courageous

There is a time for faithfulness, humility, and persevering through a long string of normal days. As Eugene Peterson titled one of his books, we need "a long obedience in the same direction."

But we must also remember that when God opens a door of opportunity, it can be very quick and unexpected. In our walk with Him, we will encounter situations where something must be done, said, attempted, or accomplished quickly—a divine moment that must be seized or lost forever.

When those moments come …*Carpe Diem.* (Seize the day!)

Maybe you are at such a place right now. You've encountered a wrong that needs to be righted. A person who needs to be spoken to. A moment that must be seized to step out in faith. There is both a time to pray and a time to get up off your knees and *move.*

David knew that Goliath had ridiculed the living God long enough. It was time to move. So he gathered five smooth stones and walked directly over to Goliath with his sling.

As the Philistine paced back and forth, his shield bearer in front of him, he noticed David. He took one look down on him and sneered—a mere youngster, apple-cheeked and peach-fuzzed.

The Philistine ridiculed David. "Am I a dog that you come after me with a stick?" And he cursed him by his gods.

"Come on," said the Philistine. "I'll make roadkill of you for the buzzards. I'll turn you into a tasty morsel for the field mice."

David answered, "You come at me with sword and spear and battle-ax. I come at you in the name of GOD-of-the-Angel-Armies, the God of Israel's troops, whom you curse and mock. This very day GOD is handing you over to me. I'm about to kill you, cut off your head, and serve up your body and the bodies of your Philistine buddies to the crows and coyotes. The whole earth will know that there's an extraordinary God in Israel. And everyone gathered here will learn that GOD doesn't save by means of sword or spear. The battle belongs to GOD—he's handing you to us on a platter!"

That roused the Philistine, and he started toward David. David took off from the front line, running toward the Philistine. David reached into his pocket for a stone, slung it, and hit the Philistine hard in the forehead, embedding the stone deeply. The Philistine crashed, facedown in the dirt.

That's how David beat the Philistine—with a sling and a stone. He hit him and killed him. No sword for David!

Then David ran up to the Philistine and stood over him, pulled the giant's sword from its sheath, and finished the job by cutting off his head. When the Philistines saw that their great champion was dead, they scattered, running for their lives.
(1 Samuel 17:41-51, THE MESSAGE)

God is still looking for men and women—ordinary people—willing to do extraordinary things. But as with David, you must be a truly spiritual person and have a heart that is fixed on God. You must be willing to be faithful in the little things, but also bold and courageous.

And when the moment comes ... seize it!

Chapter Seven

DAVID'S STORY, PART 2:
THE POWER OF FORGIVENESS

"Who am I that you pay attention to a stray dog like me?"
—2 Samuel 9:8, THE MESSAGE

We've all experienced it. When the holidays come, we suddenly find ourselves thrown into close quarters with relatives we may not have seen for months, even years. We're rubbing shoulders with cousins we didn't know we had, in-laws we wanted to forget, aunts who drive us nuts, and uncles who always tell the same dumb stories.

You may have some issues of genuine pain in your family. You've been wounded at some point—deeply hurt—by the people who should have loved you most, and the holidays only remind you of that. Children have been disappointed with parents, and parents with children. Husbands have been let down by wives, and wives by husbands. Petty squabbles turn into long-standing rivalries and feuds. The bitterness at times can run very deep.

Maybe it was the way someone handled family money.

Maybe it was some angry words—spoken long ago, and long remembered.

Maybe someone deliberately slandered you, telling lies and hurting your reputation.

So how should you handle this?

In a word, *forgive.*

You say, "But they don't deserve forgiveness!" That may be true. But since when did what we "deserve" enter the equation? Would you really like to be judged by God on the basis of what you deserve?

C. S. Lewis wrote that "everyone says forgiveness is a lovely idea, until they have something to forgive." But by harboring resentment and refusing to forgive, we grieve the Holy Spirit.

> And do not bring sorrow to God's Holy Spirit by the way you live. Remember, he has identified you as his own, guaranteeing that you will be saved on the day of redemption.
>
> Get rid of all bitterness, rage, anger, harsh words, and slander, as well as all types of evil behavior. Instead, be kind to each other, tenderhearted, forgiving one another, just as God through Christ has forgiven you. (Ephesians 4:30-32, NLT)

God's command to forgive should be enough, but let me give you an additional reason ...you may live longer! A new field of research has been developed on the subject of forgiveness. Recent studies suggest that those who do not forgive are more likely to experience high blood pressure, bouts of depression, and problems with anger, stress, and anxiety.

Charlotte van Oyen Witvliet of Hope College in Holland, Michigan has found that there are robust physiological differences between non-forgiving and forgiving states in those she has studied. "If you are willing to exert the effort it takes to be forgiving," says Witvliet, "there are benefits both emotionally and physically."

As many of these studies are beginning to illustrate, forgiveness is not about absolving the perpetrator; it is about healing the victim. "Forgiveness isn't giving in to another person, it's getting free of that person" said Frederic Luskin, director of the Stanford Forgiveness Project.

God knew what He was talking about when He told us to forgive!

Many people think that the Old Testament is all about vengeance and harsh justice, while the New Testament owns the concept of forgiveness. And yet the Old Testament book of 1 Samuel relates one of the most moving stories of forgiveness in the Bible. It's a story of how David dealt with his enemies when "payback time" finally came.

A SURPRISE CHOICE

Saul, as we have already seen in an earlier chapter, was the ruler God gave to Israel after they had begged and whined for a king so they "could be like all the other nations." So the Lord gave them just what *they* wanted (not always such a good thing), a tall, handsome, charismatic man after their own heart.

All too soon, however, Israel's first king became paranoid and vengeful, misusing his office and dishonoring the Lord who had elevated him to such prominence. Before his reign was really up and rolling, he'd already forfeited the kingship.

David, a youthful, clear-eyed shepherd who loved the Lord with all his heart, was God's surprise choice for Saul's successor. After slaying Goliath in the Valley of Elah, the youngest son of Jesse became an instant folk hero with the people. If Israel had radio in those days, a new song about David would have topped the charts. Everyone was singing it ...and particularly the women!

So the women sang as they danced, and said:

"Saul has slain his thousands,
And David his ten thousands."
(1 Samuel 18:7)

David struck up a very strong friendship with Saul's son Jonathan. Prince Jonathan, a good and valorous young man, knew very well that God's hand was on David. Under normal circumstances, Jonathan could have expected to receive the kingship from his father. But these weren't normal circumstances, and the young prince could see the handwriting on the wall. Rather than being filled with resentment and jealousy, however, Jonathan simply asked his friend to remember his decedents after his death.

Meanwhile, Saul was on a collision course with his destiny. Overcome with hatred and jealousy, he tried to kill David over and over.

In other words, once David was selected by God, his troubles began! It's often the same for you and me. There's no doubt that making a conscious decision to follow Jesus Christ transforms any life for the better, filling the emptiness in your life and washing away sin and guilt. You're given an entirely new dimension of life to live. You now have a God who will guide and counsel you and direct you through all the ups and downs of life, and best of all, you have the hope of heaven!

But while one complete set of problems ceases to exist, an entirely new set of problems begins! Conversion makes our heart into a battlefield. But the good news is that God will be with us, never giving us more than we can handle.

Can anything ever separate us from Christ's love? Does it mean he no longer loves us if we have trouble or calamity, or are persecuted, or hungry, or destitute, or in danger, or threatened with death? (As the Scriptures say, "For your sake we are killed every day; we are being slaughtered like sheep.") No, despite all these things, overwhelming victory is ours through Christ, who loved us.

And I am convinced that nothing can ever separate us from God's love. Neither death nor life, neither angels nor demons, neither our fears for today nor our worries about tomorrow—not even the powers of hell can separate us from God's love. No power in the sky above or in the earth below—indeed, nothing in all creation will ever be able to separate us from the love of God that is revealed in Christ Jesus our Lord. (Romans 8:35-39, NLT)

For absolutely no reason beyond Saul's insane jealousy, David was forced into exile—and this after the king had twice tried to pin him to the wall with a spear.

As Saul and his army chased David from one end of Israel to the other, David had a couple of golden opportunities to kill this crazy man. Once, at a place called Engedi, Saul entered a dark cave to "answer the call of nature." The king laid aside his robe and there he was, as vulnerable as can be, within easy reach of David's sword (and what a humiliating way to go).

Instead of running Saul through, however, David used his sword to cut off part of his royal robe. After Saul left the cave, David called to him, "Do you feel a draft, King Saul? I could have killed you but I didn't! The Lord judge between you and I and the Lord avenge me of you!"[53]

Saul, suddenly realizing how close he had been to his doom, called back to David.

> "Is this your voice , my son David?" And Saul lifted up his voice and wept. Then he said to David: "You are more righteous than I; for you have rewarded me with good, whereas I have rewarded you with evil.... Now I know indeed that you shall surely be king, and that the kingdom of Israel shall be established in your hand."
> (1 Samuel 24:16-17, 20)

But in spite of such assurances, Saul tried again and again to eliminate his perceived rival. The once promising king utterly threw away his life, ending up so desperate and spiritually bankrupt that he sought counsel from a witch.

Finally, the wicked Saul reaped what he had sown. He died on the battlefield alongside his son Jonathan. The words on his tombstone could have very well read, "I have played the fool!" Actually, Saul committed suicide on the battlefield, falling on his own sword.

A short time later, some fool approached David, claiming to have killed the king. Outraged, David had this man executed. The House of Saul and the House of David, however, continued in war for a number of years. Saul had another son named Ishbosheth, and Abner, Saul's general, made him king.

Not long after this, Abner and Isbosheth had an argument, and the general threatened to defect. Sure enough, he went to David and offered to unite the kingdom under him. After all the misery Abner had caused David, he could have struck the military man dead. But instead David accepted the offer and gave Abner and his men a great feast.

David was simply tired of the fighting, and he longed for peace. When Joab, David's general, returned, he was outraged. He hunted Abner down and murdered him. Stunned by this vicious act of violence, David went into deep mourning.

The plot continued to thicken! Later, a couple of men loyal to David assassinated Ishbosheth, Saul's son. Coming to David with the news and expecting to be rewarded, the king dealt as harshly with them as he had with the man who had claimed he killed Saul.

Here's where all of this is leading.

David did not deal with his enemies the way they dealt with him. He believed in justice and mercy. He dealt with those who wanted to exploit the situation with justice, but he dealt with those who were innocently caught in the crossfire with forgiveness.

Without the benefit of psychologists or intensive academic and university studies, David understood the power of forgiveness.

Maybe you, too, have been persecuted wrongfully by someone, or have an enemy who has tried to do you harm. Perhaps you still feel the bruises from someone who turned against you or spread lies about you.

How would you feel about these adversaries if their personal attacks against you—totally undeserved—affected your life for *years?* Now ...imagine yourself emerging on the other side of the dark tunnel after all this hurt and harassment. Would your first thought be of how you could show kindness to that person or to any of their family?

Well, that's exactly what David did.

REMEMBERING HIS PROMISE

Some time after David had been established on his throne over all Israel, firmly in power, he remembered something. It was a promise he had made to both King Saul and Prince Jonathan. On different occasions, he had sworn an oath to both men to show kindness and mercy to their descendants. But were any of them still alive?

What follows in Scripture truly is one the greatest stories ever told!

(David) summoned a man named Ziba, who had been one of Saul's servants. "Are you Ziba?" the king asked.

"Yes sir, I am," Ziba replied.

The king then asked him, "Is anyone still alive from Saul's family? If so, I want to show God's kindness to them."

Ziba replied, "Yes, one of Jonathan's sons is still alive. He is crippled in both feet."

"Where is he?" the king asked.

"In Lo-debar," Ziba told him, "at the home of Makir son of Ammiel."

So David sent for him and brought him from Makir's home. His name was Mephibosheth; he was Jonathan's son and Saul's grandson. When he came to David, he bowed low to the ground in deep respect. David said, "Greetings, Mephibosheth."

Mephibosheth replied, "I am your servant."

"Don't be afraid!" David said. "I intend to show kindness to you because of my promise to your father, Jonathan. I will give you all the property that once belonged to your grandfather Saul, and you will eat here with me at the king's table!"

Mephibosheth bowed respectfully and exclaimed, "Who is your servant, that you should show such kindness to a dead dog like me?"

...And from that time on, Mephibosheth ate regularly at David's table, like one of the king's own sons.... And Mephibosheth, who was crippled in both feet, lived in Jerusalem and ate regularly at the king's table. (2 Samuel 9:2-8, 11, 13)

This story may not have the dramatic elements of Samson's story—or the sagas of Gideon or Joshua, either. It's more subtle, but beautiful and tender. Here is David, who after years of struggle with the house of Saul is finally crowned king of Israel—perhaps fifteen years after he was anointed in Bethlehem.

Under normal circumstances, kings in that era would seek to eliminate any potential rivals to the throne. What would you have done in similar circumstances? Is your motto, "I don't get mad, I get even"? Even though he was disabled, Mephibosheth, grandson of Saul and the son of Prince Jonathan, would have been next in line for the throne if Saul's family was still ruling. As a matter of fact, this young man was still a potential threat to David's crown as long as he was alive. Yet David reached out to a potential rival, even an enemy, and loved him.

No wonder David was called "a man after God's own heart"!

A SHADOWED LIFE

Mephibosheth was only five years old when his father and grandfather were killed. Imagine, if you will, the life he had known up until then. The privilege and potential of his present could not have prepared him for the hard life he would have to face in his future.

Raised as a young prince in the royal residence by a brave and godly father, Mephibosheth had no inkling of the dark clouds gathering all around his small world. And then, in just one moment of carelessness and through no fault of his own, his life was changed forever.

When the news hit the palace of his father and grandfather's deaths, the nurse in charge hurried to take Mephibosheth—heir to throne—into hiding. In her haste, however, she would add even more tragedy to the story. Somehow she dropped the young child, crippling his legs for the rest of his life.

His name, literally translated, means "a shameful thing." There was nothing little Mephiposheth had done to earn this name, but he was looked down upon. Now crippled, with no hope of gaining the throne, he was regarded as a worthless person.

Maybe sometime in your growing-up years you were dropped too. As a child you were mistreated, neglected, abused, and forgotten, like so many kids today who have basically been left to themselves. Maybe people haven't given you much hope. You've been written off by parents, coaches, and teachers.

I have some good news for you today. God specializes in taking people who have been dropped in life and picking them back up again!

I read about how Walt Disney, as a young man, was fired from his job at a newspaper. When Disney asked why, his supervisor bluntly replied, "Walt, you're not creative enough. You never have any new ideas. We're sorry, but we're going to have to let you go."

Disney got dropped in life. But instead of giving up and withdrawing into himself, he moved to California, borrowed $500, and started a graphics arts company in a garage. Shortly after, he came up with a little character he named Mortimer Mouse...later to become Mickey. And the rest is history.

Mephibosheth was dropped in life. And all through his years he may have lived as a fugitive in fear of King David. No doubt he had been told the circumstances of his crippling fall. Maybe he blamed all his woes on the upstart king. If it weren't for David, he would be whole and complete and seated on his grandfather's throne. Perhaps he lay awake some nights, wondering if the king knew about his existence. Would he wake up to the sound of soldiers some night, banging on the door where he lived? That would be the end for him and his family. He would be called to the palace to pay with his life for the actions of his grandfather.

Mephibosheth would have been taught to hate David. How could he have ever imagined that the king was seeking the welfare of someone from Saul's family?

David asked Saul's former servant, "Is there still anyone who is left of the house of Saul, that I may show him kindness for Jonathan's sake?" (2 Samuel 9:1).

The word "kindness" in this verse could better be translated *grace*. David was saying, "Is there someone of Saul's household I could show grace to?" Grace is positive and unconditional acceptance in spite of the other person. It is a demonstration of love that is undeserved, unearned, and un-repayable.

"Is there any relative of Jonathan I can show unconditional love to?"

A man named Ziba mentions Mephibosheth. But notice what he says. "There is still a son of Jonathan; he is crippled in both feet" (2 Samuel 9:3, NIV). I don't think it's reading too much into the text if I paraphrase Ziba's words to say: "Yes, O King, there is someone. But you many want to reconsider your offer. He is crippled. Disabled. Handicapped. He can't reciprocate your kindness."

It's never easy to be disabled. But in this era of history, it was just plain awful. There were no wheelchairs, no handicapped access to buildings, no reserved parking places. Mephibosheth would have had to be carried everywhere. To the table. To the restroom. To his bedroom. To wherever he wanted to go! In essence, Ziba is saying, "Do you really want to take on this responsibility? This isn't your problem, King!"

Do you think that mattered to David? Not at all! Love is not based on the worthiness of the object. So Ziba complies with David's request and tells him where Mephibosheth lives; a place called Lo-debar, located in a relatively obscure spot on the east side of the Jordan River.

The former of prince of Israel was living in some barren corner in the middle of nowhere. This wasn't a fit place for a child of a king to be living. Lo-debar means literally, "the place of no pasture." What a pathetic picture we have of Jonathan's son. Isolated from worship at the Tabernacle, cut off from fellowship, unable to walk or live an independent life, and living out his life in a barren place. It wasn't an easy life—nor a happy one.

It's also a picture of each of us before we gave our lives to Jesus Christ. Hanging out in Lo-debar …living like lowlifes …feeling unloved, unwanted, undeserving, and unneeded. But just as David reached out in grace and kindness to Mephibosheth, so God reaches out to us. The Bible says that "while we were still sinners, Christ died for us."[54]

So King David sent for the forgotten Prince Mephibosheth and brought him from Makir's home to Jerusalem. David was persistent, not giving up on this young man. He didn't just send for him, but *brought* him.

Here is a reminder of how persistent we should be when reaching out with the gospel. Jesus told us to "Go out to the roads and country lanes and make them come in, so that my house will be full."[55]

Remember the story of the four men who brought their paralyzed friend to Jesus, practically ripping the roof off the house where He was speaking because they couldn't get in the door? Remember how Andrew brought his brother Peter to Jesus? God shows the same loving persistence toward you and me.

In this story of the crippled prince, David, like Jesus, shows forgiveness and love instead of judgment. Though Mephibosheth had personally done nothing wrong (that we know of), his grandfather had tried to murder David—for years and years!

But David had made a promise he intended to keep.

So how did Mephibosheth react when he heard David wanted to see him? He was afraid! Under normal circumstances, he would have been justified to have that fear. After all, Mephibosheth's point of reference was his wicked grandfather. It was customary for eastern kings to not only kill all rivals to their throne, but to exterminate their heirs as well. Bottom line, Mephibosheth simply didn't know David. If the young prince had known this man of God, he wouldn't have been afraid. This was a new king with a new heart. He was a man who began as a shepherd boy, became a giant-killer, then endured long, lean years of struggle and hardship as a fugitive. But he was man who grew into his calling and title, "a man after God's heart."

In the same way, there are many people who are afraid of God today. We think He's out to get us or make our lives miserable. We imagine that His main purpose toward us is imposing a bunch of restrictive rules and regulations that will hem us in and turn our lives from living color to black-and-white. What a false and warped perception of God! A. W. Tozer writes, "Nothing twists and deforms the soul more than a low or unworthy conception of God."

David brought Mephibosheth into his royal family, "and Mephibosheth lived in Jerusalem, because he always ate at the king's table" (2 Samuel 9:13, NIV).

In just thirteen verses in 2 Samuel 9, the Bible mentions the word "eat" or "ate" four times. Yes, eating is a necessary biological function to sustain life. But in Scripture, it's often much more than that; it is a time of fellowship, sharing, and rejoicing.

Jesus' first miracle was performed at a wedding feast. The last thing Jesus did after His resurrection and just before His ascension was to cook fish over coals and eat a meal with His disciples. None of us wants to go to dinner with a person we really don't know or don't like. (It can give you indigestion). That's why blind dates are such a drag! Most of us like to dine with family and friends, people we're comfortable with and enjoy.

Listen to the Lord's invitation in the book of Revelation:

> Look! I stand at the door and knock. If you hear my voice and open the door, I will come in, and we will share a meal together as friends. (Revelation 3:20, NLT)

When the day finally came for Mephibosheth to meet David, he was gripped with apprehension. For the first time in his life, he would see the man whom his grandfather hunted mercilessly for years and regarded as Public Enemy Number One.

After David's kind words and incredibly generous offer, Mephibosheth bowed down, realizing he had been dead wrong in allowing the prejudice of others to influence his own attitude.

Let's draw a few lessons from this story as we wrap it up.

WHAT WE LEARN FROM THE STORY

Lesson 1: Don't Let Others Form Your View Of God

Find out for yourself who God is. Mephibosheth allowed the prejudice and bias of others to keep him from a generous king and provider. So many are kept from a relationship with God by what others say. I recently spoke to a young woman struggling with drugs. She placed the blame for her problems on her parents. In the course of our conversation, I warned her not to form her view of God based solely on the attitudes and actions of her mother and father.

We parents will inevitably disappoint, make mistakes, and get it wrong many times. But not God. He always gets it right. And when He looks on you as His child, He smiles with delight!

God loves you, and His plan for you is better than any you could ever come up with for yourself. Don't run from Him, but to Him. Sit at His table and enjoy His company. Nobody has a greater interest in your life than He does, and He has all the time in the world for you. He says to you, "I know the plans I have for you. ... They are plans for good and not for disaster, to give you a future and a hope" (Jeremiah 29:11, NLT).

Lesson 2: Forgive Your Enemies

Forgive them whether they deserve it or not.

David could have engaged in payback, big time, hunting down everyone who had ever been associated with Saul and his reign. But he did the very opposite, endearing him to all of Israel.

Abraham Lincoln was once criticized by an associate for his attitude toward political enemies. The associate asked, "Why do you always make friends of them? You should destroy them!" Lincoln replied, "Am I not destroying my enemies when I make them my friends?"

Paul writes:

> Repay no one evil for evil. Have regard for good things in the sight of all men. If it is possible, as much as depends on you, live peaceably with all men. Beloved, do not avenge yourselves, but rather give place to wrath; for it is written, "Vengeance is Mine, I will repay," says the Lord. Therefore, "If your enemy is hungry, feed him; if he is thirsty, give him a drink; for in so doing you will heap coals of fire on his head" (Romans 12:17-20).

When the right time came, God took care of the enemies of David. He didn't have to lift a finger.

Lesson 3: Leave The Past In The Past

David could have spent the rest of his life stewing over what had happened or what others had done to him. He lost at least fifteen prime years of his life hiding in caves and running from Saul—and he was totally innocent!

Think of what could have happened as a result of all those injustices. David could have shriveled up inside, becoming a bitter, negative man. But he didn't, as the story in this chapter reveals. He came through those dark days with a kind and tender heart still intact. He could have become angry at God, turning away from the Lord because He didn't rescue him and elevate him sooner. But we all know that didn't happen either. All you have to do is open up the Psalms, and you see that David's love and heart for the Lord just grew and grew.

In fact, it was those lonely years of hiding in the wilderness where David would experience God as his Refuge, Rock, Deliverer, and Strong Tower.

As a man after God's heart, David knew God was in control of his life, no matter how difficult the circumstances. He wrote:

> But as for me, I trust in You, O LORD;
> I say, "You are my God."
> My times are in Your hand;
>
> Deliver me from the hand of my enemies,
> And from those who persecute me.
> (Psalm 31:14-15)

Even though he didn't enjoy suffering any more than you and I enjoy it, David knew the Lord was allowing what he was experiencing to prepare him for the future, both good and bad.

The funny thing about life is that what we initially think is "good" may turn out in time to be "bad." And that which seems so bad right now may turn out to be very, very good.

The Bible says of God: "He has made everything beautiful in its time. Also, he has put eternity into man's heart, yet so that he cannot find out what God has done from the beginning to the end."[56]

Bottom line, even though he had been victimized, David refused to be a victim. Through everything that happened to him in his life, he kept his focus on the Lord, giving Him his trust and devotion.

The story of David and Mephibosheth is a picture of what God has done for us.

First, out of sheer love for Jonathan, David lavished his grace on his friend's handicapped son. It reminds me of how God, out of love for His Son, Jesus Christ, paid the price for our sin at Calvary. He's still seeking those who are spiritually handicapped, people locked in destructive lifestyles of sin. God has sought us out, calling us to His table.

Second, Mephibosheth had nothing, deserved nothing, and could repay nothing. In fact, He was hiding from the king. The same is true of us. We were willful, intentional sinners, yet Jesus sought us out and called our name.

Third, Mephibosheth was adopted as a son and invited to eat at the king's table for the rest of his life. We have been adopted into God's family. We have not received the spirit of bondage again to fear, but one of adoption.[57]

God has made us a part of His eternal family. We are invited to be near Him, to be with Him, to find purpose and joy in His service, and to share in the bounty of His table.

That, my friend, is grace.

Chapter Eight

DAVID'S STORY, PART 3:
THE GOD OF SECOND CHANCES

"Then Nathan said to David, 'You are the man!'"
—2 Samuel 12:7

Retailers make it *so* easy for you to part with your money.

You can buy furniture and not pay a dime for a year.

You can buy a car for no money down and with easy monthly payments …
for the next seventeen years.

And of course you can charge everything under the sun—from a cheeseburger, to your groceries, to your new high-powered laptop, to your dental work, to your pet vaccinations.

It's so easy. It's so convenient. In years past, people actually had to set money aside and save up for things they wanted. Can you imagine? They didn't buy something until they had enough money, then they went in and laid the cash on the counter. What an archaic notion!

But in all of that retail ease and convenience to which we've become accustomed, there is something we tend to forget.

The bills *will* come due.

We *will* still pay.

In our third look at King David in this book, we come to the story of a man who made a big grab for gratification …and then paid a very, very steep price. King that he was, David found out that no one is above the law—God's law, that is. He may have thought he could sin and never pay, but he was wrong. And when the bills came due, he owed more than he ever dreamed.

Plucked from obscurity, David became the greatest king in the history of Israel. Who can forget his dramatic rise from shepherd boy to giant-killer?

When the years of running and hiding from jealous King Saul were finally over, David stepped into his destiny, ruling first over his own tribe of Judah, and then over the whole nation of Israel.

Recognizing God's hand on their leader, the people loved him. And David, at least in the beginning, was humble enough to recognize that God was the source of his success. He truly loved the Lord and wanted to stay close to Him and serve Him. In all of this, David lived up to the Lord's description of him as a man after God's own heart!

Everything was going so beautifully.

But then he got sloppy.

It started with a lustful look and ended up as a nationwide scandal. Though David's initial sin with Bathsheba lasted only minutes, the repercussions of it lasted for the rest of His life. No sin, except perhaps the original sin of Adam and Eve, has received as much press as David's adultery with Bathsheba. But we must not forget as we read this story, sordid as it is, that David was still called a man after God's own heart.

That is not in any way to justify David's actions, for it was a terrible wrong and broke the heart of God. But it is a reminder to us that if someone as beloved of God as David could fall, so could anyone ...including you or me.

SATAN SETS THE TRAP

In the spring of the year, when kings normally go out to war, David sent Joab and the Israelite army to fight the Ammonites. They destroyed the Ammonite army and laid siege to the city of Rabbah. However, David stayed behind in Jerusalem.

Late one afternoon, after his midday rest, David got out of bed and was walking on the roof of the palace. As he looked out over the city, he noticed a woman of unusual beauty taking a bath. He sent someone to find out who she was, and he was told, "She is Bathsheba, the daughter of Eliam and the wife of Uriah the Hittite."

Then David sent messengers to get her; and when she came to the palace, he slept with her. She had just completed the purification rites after having her menstrual period. Then she returned home. Later, when Bathsheba discovered that she was pregnant, she sent David a message, saying, "I'm pregnant." (2 Samuel 11:1-5, NLT)

David was about fifty years old when this incident took place. He had ruled Israel for twenty years, moving from victory to victory, with success and God's favor at every turn. He had distinguished himself as a wise and compassionate ruler, a man of God, a fierce general, a skilled musician, and a gifted poet, writing beautiful psalms of praise to God.

No doubt about it, King David was on a roll, and paradoxically ...that's a time when we really need to be on our guard. When we're walking through a time of crisis, we naturally look to the Lord for help and guidance. But when life sails along smoothly on a calm sea, with no clouds on the horizon, we tend to become careless. We lower our guard ...and the devil pounces.

Remember when Jesus faced that period of intense temptation when he went one-on-one with the devil in the wilderness? When did that happen? Right after His baptism, where the heavens opened, the Spirit descended upon Him like a dove, and a voice from the deep blue said, "This is my beloved Son...."

After the dove came the devil.

After the blessing comes the trial.

The two often go hand in hand. So when you walk out of church feeling blessed, encouraged, and spiritually well fed, don't be surprised if you find temptation and testing waiting in the wings.

Odd as it may seem, Satan usually hits us when we're enjoying God's rich blessings. He waits for that moment when we are the most vulnerable—though we may imagine it to be a time in our lives when we're at our strongest and best!

David had already set the scene for his defeat by actions he had done in direct disobedience to God. This reminds us that the sins we commit today may not have their full impact on us until much later. David didn't fall suddenly; as with everyone, it was a process.

Second Samuel 5 tells us that in defiance to God's laws, David took concubines after he became king. God specifically said in Deuteronomy 17 that the future king was never to do this. The reason: "Neither shall he multiply wives for himself, lest his heart turn away...."[58]

That was exactly what was happening to David—his heart was slowly but surely turning away from God.

David was allowing lust to consume his life. He might have thought it was justified because he had such a strong sexual drive. He may have thought, "Having all these wives and concubines will satisfy me." But the truth is, it only stoked the fire.

There is a difference between a healthy, God-given sex drive and being gripped with lust. God has given sexual desires to every man and woman, to be fulfilled in a monogamous marriage commitment. Without such built-in sexual attraction, the human race would have died out!

But when a man is filled with lust, as David seemed to be, he cannot satisfy it with more lust. That's like throwing gasoline on a bonfire. You show me a person who is having a serious lust problem, and I'll show you someone who *feeds* it. It may be pornography, music with explicit lyrics, friends who are preoccupied with immorality, or all of the above.

Sometimes I counsel people who seem completely mystified by all the lustful thoughts they keep having. For some reason, they don't make the connection between what they allow themselves to see or hear and what keeps dominating their thoughts. The truth is, when you don't feed lust, you starve it! David had been feeding his lust with all these women he had at his beck and call. Godly people in the kingdom were no doubt becoming aware of this. Yet they may have whispered to one another, "Oh well, it could be worse. Besides, look at all the good he's done."

If David had only realized it, he had been fattening himself up for the kill. And of course it happened when he least expected it ...on a quiet, warm spring afternoon as he strolled on his rooftop.

THE TRAP IS SPRUNG

> Late one afternoon, after his midday rest, David got out of bed and
> was walking on the roof of the palace. As he looked out over the city, he
> noticed a woman of unusual beauty taking a bath.
> (2 Samuel 11:2, NLT)

Instead of leading his troops in war, David sent a proxy so he could kick back
and take life easy. He was in bed when he should have been in battle. There's
nothing wrong with a little R & R, as long as we remember that there *is* no rest
from spiritual battle. Hell never takes a vacation.

Our greatest battles don't usually come when we're working hard; they
come when we have some leisure time on our hands, when we're bored.

Alan Redpath once observed, "Times of leisure are to be more dreaded
than those of the most strenuous toil."

Late one afternoon David got up from a nap, stretched, and decided to
walk up to the palace rooftop for a little fresh air. It sounds like he had been
burning the midnight oil, allowing himself to sleep in.

While Israel's troops were in the field, David was lounging around in his
royal pajamas, catching some sun at the palace. And while he was out on his
rooftop, just idly looking down at the city, David saw a beautiful woman bathing herself.

To be honest, this would have been a temptation for any healthy man, but
for a man who had already fed the fire of lust, it was deadly. There's no record
that David even struggled over what to do. He swiftly took action to take this
woman for himself.

All rational thinking went out the door; he was like an animal driven by
his lust for what he wanted. Repercussions, reputation, even fear of God, went
by the wayside. He wanted this woman! So he dispatched a servant to find out
who she was.

> The man said, "Isn't this Bathsheba, the daughter of Eliam and the
> wife of Uriah the Hittite?"[59]

In other words, this courageous servant said, "King David, this is a married woman!" It seems that this servant could see what David was thinking
(perhaps even more than David). When deluded by sin, we are often the last to
realize what we are doing and where we are heading. Sin makes us stupid! We
manage to rationalize every step, convincing ourselves it's really okay.

Then some Christian comes along and says, "What in the world are you doing?
Why are you compromising your life like this?" Set back on our heels by such re-
marks, we're offended. *The nerve of that person! How judgmental can you get?*

As we read in an earlier chapter, Samson was the last to know that God's
hand was no longer upon him. When Delilah had finally worn him down and

he revealed the secret of his strength, she cried, "The Philistines are upon you, Samson." He rose up to cast off his enemies like rag dolls, as he had done before, but he didn't realize that the Spirit of the Lord had departed from him.

If David had been spiritually alert at all, he would have seen this servant's comment as a red flag. A warning. *"King David, this is a married woman. Married to one of your warriors who is fighting for his country at this moment."*

Probably at some later point in his life, David would write:

Let a righteous man strike me—it is a kindness;
let him rebuke me—it is oil on my head.
My head will not refuse it.[60]

There would come a time when David would realize the value of strict accountability—a friend who would be willing to hit him with the truth, even if it felt like a blow to the head. (You have to wonder how it would have been for David if Prince Jonathan had lived.) But at this point in his life, he blew right on past all of God's red flags, and David had Bathsheba brought to the palace.

Don't Become a Stumbling Block

Scripture says of Bathsheba, "The woman was very beautiful in appearance," and the Bible does not exaggerate. This means she was a knockout, drop-dead stunning! It's important to note that she shared in this sin, too. We have no record of Bathsheba protesting or fighting the king's advances, nor do we read of David forcing himself on her. It appears that she was a willing accomplice.

A modest Hebrew woman would not bathe in a place where she could be seen. Could it be Bathsheba knew she was in eyeshot of the king and hoped he might look her way? It's not enough to simply avoid sin in our lives; we must also take care that we are not a stumbling block to others.

Yes, each of us will give a personal account to God. So let's stop condemning each other. Decide instead to live in such a way that you will not cause another believer to stumble and fall.
(Romans 14:12-13, NLT)

Another translation puts it like this: "Here's what you need to be concerned about: that you don't get in the way of someone else, making life more difficult than it already is."[61]

Granted, if David had attended to his duties and gone to war, he would not have seen Bathsheba that fateful afternoon. But at the same time, if she had given more thought to her actions, she would not have put temptation in his path. If lustful looking is bad, then those who dress and expose themselves with the desire to be looked at and lusted after are not less, but perhaps more, guilty!

Girls and women ...think about what you are wearing (or not wearing) before you leave your house. How would you feel if it was Jesus who was taking you out somewhere? That doesn't mean you can't be in style. But don't dress in such a way as to encourage a guy to lust after you.

You might protest, "But Greg, some guys would lust after a *tree!*" True. But that doesn't excuse you from practicing some modesty.

I think Paul nailed it for all of us when he wrote:

> Be very careful, then, how you live—not as unwise but as wise ...be-cause the days are evil. Therefore do not be foolish, but understand what the Lord's will is. (Ephesians 5:15-17, NIV)

Neither David nor Bathsheba walked carefully in this incident, and both, I believe, were at fault. As it is so often said, *It takes two to tango.*

Even so, David was clearly the aggressor here. He stopped, looked, lusted, and acted on his sin. And because he was king and had the power, he used it.

A TANGLED WEB

You have to jump through a lot of hoops to end up in adultery. You don't just fall into someone's bed. You have to go beyond mere lust, and begin to plot and scheme and lie. The awful betrayal in this sin is more than the act itself, it's in all the prep work and attempts to hide it.

David probably enjoyed himself on this night of sinful pleasure. It's just like that expensive toy you buy for yourself and play with for a week or two. Then the bill comes due, and you have already moved on to other conquests. And then to add insult to injury, the bill comes due with interest.

That's how sin works. There is that initial high, that rush of excitement. After all, the Bible says there is pleasure in sin for a time. But Scripture also reminds us that your sin will find you out!

Not long after his one night stand with Bathsheba, she sends him a note that says, "David, I'm pregnant!"

Here now is the second obstacle or red-flag warning David should have paid attention to. When it dawned on him that he had actually impregnated another man's wife, he should have repented before God and come clean. If he had confessed before God and men *right then*, there certainly would have been some pain and anger and messy complications. But the end of the story might have turned out very differently. I can imagine Uriah taking his wife, moving to Beersheba, and raising the child as his own.

But instead, David did what most people try to do when they're caught in sin. *They try to cover it up.* But there is something about sin that just doesn't want to stay covered. Remember Moses murdering the Egyptian and burying him in the sand? All it took was a good stiff wind to reveal what he had done.

DEADLY COVER-UP

Of all the people caught in adultery over the years, I cannot think of one who willingly admitted it. They only admit it when confronted with the evidence—and even then they may try to deny it.

So the plot began to thicken right away. David asked his top general, Joab, to call in Bathsheba's courageous husband, Uriah, who had been fighting the king's battle at Rabbah. So the unsuspecting soldier was sent home and ordered to report to the king.

How excited he must have been! Why would the King of Israel, a man after God's own heart, summon someone like me? What a privilege and honor!

Poor Uriah. He would have never dreamed of David's true motives. After a little small talk, David asked Uriah how the battle was going. Then he told him to go home to his wife (nod, nod, wink, wink). But Uriah was such a man of integrity he could not justify this luxury when his fellow soldiers were still fighting for the king. So he wrapped himself up in his cloak and slept outside the palace.

Now what?

David found out what had happened, and invited Uriah to the palace again, this time getting him drunk. Still, Uriah slept outside the palace. This was the third red-flag warning on David's collision course with destruction. He should have seen it and repented. He had Uriah right there! What if he had confessed and rid his soul of that awful weight? It would have been initially very difficult and embarrassing, but what grief it would have saved!

Have you ever sensed God putting up roadblocks in your life to keep you from going a certain direction or pursuing a certain course? Perhaps you've been contemplating a certain sin—adultery, stealing, or cheating on your taxes. You've been rationalizing it in your mind, but God has not made it easy. That's because He loves you! That conviction, that guilt you feel in your heart, is actually a gift of mercy from God.

We have smoke detectors in our homes that sound the alarm when they sense smoke and chirp annoyingly when they need a battery. Sometimes—just to stop the racket—someone may foolishly pull out the batteries and disable the devices. And there are times when we want to do the same for our conscience.

David, instead of heeding God's red flags, dreamed up the most wicked scheme of all. At this point, David's sin had gone beyond lust, adultery, and deception.

Now he was planning a murder.

David sent Uriah back to battle with a letter he was to deliver to General Joab. No doubt Uriah felt proud and happy to be carrying a message from his king. How could he know that it was his death warrant? The orders were for the Israeli army to attack, and then for everyone to fall back, leaving poor Uriah standing alone.

I wonder what Joab thought when he read this letter. Strange how David could write such beautiful psalms and dance before the Ark of God with all his might—*and write a letter like this.* Man after God's own heart, my foot!

Brave Uriah died in battle that day, and after a brief period of mourning, Bathsheba married King David and came to live in the palace. It certainly looked as though everything was working out, and that David and Bathsheba had successfully covered up a potential scandal.

But David forgot to take God into account. And the Bible says that "the thing that David had done displeased the Lord" (2 Samuel 11:27).

David's Broken Heart

In spite of his extreme wickedness in this incident, David was still a believer—although a very disobedient one. Deep down, David had known this was a sin before God. In later years, he would write two psalms—Psalms 32 and 51—about the agony of guilt and regret he endured following his sin.

> Oh, what joy for those whose disobedience is forgiven,
> whose sin is put out of sight!
> Yes, what joy for those whose record
> the Lord has cleared of guilt,
> whose lives are lived in complete honesty!
>
> When I refused to confess my sin,
> My body wasted away,
> and I groaned all day long.
> Day and night your hand of discipline was heavy on me.
> My strength evaporated like water in the summer heat.
>
> Finally, I confessed all my sins to you
> and stopped trying to hide my guilt.
> I said to myself, "I will confess my rebellion to the Lord."
> And you forgave me! All my guilt is gone. (Psalm 32:1-5, NLT)

These words were written by a man who had walked and talked with God since childhood. He had known God's blessing and power in his life. But for twelve torturous months, he had fought the conviction of the Holy Spirit and was not experiencing God's presence as he had before.

He was in relationship with God, yes, but not in fellowship. And it was hell on earth for David. One paraphrase renders Psalm 32:4 like this:

> The pressure never let up;
> all the juices of my life dried up.[62]

The king's very life—everything that made David, David—was drying up like parched clay. Every bit of the joy and hope and excitement he had once known had drained out of his soul.

God will simply not allow His child to get away with sin. If you take away nothing else from this chapter, please mark that! David's tortured soul and the searing conviction he felt in his life were really signs of life. The discipline he was enduring was a sign that he was a child of God.

> If God doesn't discipline you as he does all of his children, it means that you are illegitimate and are not really his children at all. Since we respected our earthly fathers who disciplined us, shouldn't we submit even more to the discipline of the Father of our spirits, and live forever?
>
> For our earthly fathers disciplined us for a few years, doing the best they knew how. But God's discipline is always good for us, so that we might share in his holiness. No discipline is enjoyable while it is happening—it's painful! But afterward there will be a peaceful harvest of right living for those who are trained in this way.
> (Hebrews 12:8-11, NLT)

If you start to go the wrong way, find serious roadblocks in your path, and feel the heat of conviction kicking in, rejoice! And if you feel the vise of guilt and remorse closing in on you after you sin, celebrate that! All of these signs are indicators that you are indeed a child of God. I have neither the privilege nor the right to discipline someone else's child, but I must discipline my own children for their own good!

David had tried to cover up his tragic sins, but the evidence of his crime was everywhere. The Bible tells us, "He who covers his sins will not prosper, but whoever confesses and forsakes them will have mercy."[63]

I have personally witnessed this so many times. You see someone who seems to have their life together, walking with God and serving Him. But for some reason, the Lord doesn't seem to be blessing their life or ministry. It's one problem after another, crisis after crisis, really of their own making.

Then one day it all comes out. You find out they have been living a lie. And make no mistake about it, sooner or later your sin will find you out! It will catch up with you.

So one day in David's life the best thing that could possibly have happened, happened.

David got busted.

The prophet Nathan came to pay the king a visit. It's significant to note that the Bible says, "Then the LORD sent Nathan to David." When? Right after the act of adultery with Bathsheba? No. Right after Bathsheba revealed she was pregnant? No. Right after David had Bathsheba's husband sent to die? Again, no.

It was about twelve months after all this had taken place, and David could hardly live with himself. The prophet tells a parable about a man who had his lamb stolen.

"There were two men in a certain town, one rich and the other poor. The rich man had a very large number of sheep and cattle, but the poor man had nothing except one little ewe lamb he had bought. He raised it, and it grew up with him and his children. It shared his food, drank from his cup and even slept in his arms. It was like a daughter to him.

"Now a traveler came to the rich man, but the rich man refrained from taking one of his own sheep or cattle to prepare a meal for the traveler who had come to him. Instead, he took the ewe lamb that belonged to the poor man and prepared it for the one who had come to him."

David burned with anger against the man and said to Nathan, "As surely as the Lord lives, the man who did this deserves to die! He must pay for that lamb four times over, because he did such a thing and had no pity."

Then Nathan said to David, "You are the man!"
(2 Samuel 12:1-7, NIV)

David had become caught up in the story and felt hot anger toward that selfish rich man who had no pity. Who was this horrible person who would steal a poor man's ewe lamb? The fellow didn't deserve to live!

In so saying, David slipped his neck right into Nathan's noose. Strange how David could be so harsh toward a man who had merely stolen a sheep, when he had taken a man's wife and had that man killed.

Have you ever noticed that when you excuse sin in your own life, you become very critical of the very same thing in other people? This is what Jesus was referring to when He spoke of a speck in your brother's eye and a log in your own.[64]

Imagine how David must have felt when Nathan pointed a long, bony finger at the king and said, "You are the man!" At that moment, his cover was blown, his sin was exposed, and the truth was out. It was a mixture of shame, humiliation—and huge relief!

Hearing this bold declaration of his sin, David said, "I have sinned against the LORD."[65]

He had that right.

Yes, he had certainly sinned against Bathsheba, Uriah, and the women to whom he was already married. But the underlying issue was that he had betrayed and sinned against God, the One who had loved him, protected him, and blessed him since boyhood.

That's why in spite of all the wrong he had done, David was still a man after God's heart. I have read about people who have been caught in adultery. These are some of the actual things they have said:

"Nobody's perfect."

"Sorry, I didn't mean to hurt you."

"It happens to the best of us."

"If nothing else, I can always serve as a bad example."

"I'm only human."
"Doing stupid things is my way of making my life interesting."
"Everybody has the right to make mistakes."
"Tomorrow, no one will remember."
"Stupid is as stupid does."
And then the all-time classic, *"The devil made me do it."*

If you are a child of God, the devil didn't make you do anything! Sure, Satan played a role, but he needed your cooperation. The apostle James tells us: "Temptation comes from our own desires, which entice us and drag us away. These desires give birth to sinful actions. And when sin is allowed to grow, it gives birth to death" (James 1:14-15, NLT).

There is only one correct response to being caught in sin, and David had it right. "I have sinned against the LORD!"

Nathan then gives David this sober reminder of the effects of his sin. Because of what he had done, he had given occasion for the enemies of God to blaspheme. If only we would think of things like this when we start to fall into sin. The damage to our witness, our integrity, our reputation, and to the work of Christ in our world can't even be calculated.

The prophet went on to tell David that the sword would never leave his house. And that's exactly what happened, as David faced the repercussions of his sin for years to come. The child born from this encounter between David and Bathsheba died. Then as the years passed, David's own children repeated his very behavior. One of David's sons treated his half-sister as David treated Bathsheba, taking advantage of her. Then Absalom, another of David's sons, treated his brother as David treated Uriah and became a murderer, eventually leading a rebellion against his father.

As they say, the apple doesn't fall far from the tree.

Just because we have been forgiven doesn't mean we avoid the consequences of reaping what we have sown.

In spite of all that transpired, however, David was forgiven and restored to fellowship with God. As devastating as this story sounds, David actually did make a comeback. He got right with God and ended his race well.

Is this one of the "greatest stories ever told"?

Yes and no.

No, because it's the story of failure in the life of a child of God and a great spiritual leader. In that sense, it's one of the *saddest* stories ever told. But it is a great story in that it is also about forgiveness. Yes, David paid a heavy price for his sin. But God gave David a second chance, a new beginning.

And here is something even more stunning than that.

Out of that forgiven sin—a dreadful, sordid thing that never should have happened but did—God drew out something good. Not just good for David, but for the whole world, right down to you and me.

David was from the town of Bethlehem, and Jesus would one day be born as the root and offspring of David, both through the bloodline of Mary and the lineage of Joseph. That's why Joseph and Mary went to Bethlehem to be taxed.

But here's the shocker: *Bathsheba made it into the Messianic line of Jesus Christ (Matthew 1:6).* And she wasn't the only questionable person to make it into the Messianic line. So did Tamar and Rahab, one woman who tricked her own father-in-law into having sex with her, and the other woman a professional prostitute!

So, what does this mean?

Our God is the God of second chances! I wish I could turn back the clock for the girl who has lost her virginity before marriage. Or for the guy who has been unfaithful to his wife and lost his marriage and family. Or for the person who has polluted his or her mind with pornography. But I can't do that any more than I could unscramble an egg. Having said that, however, you can stop such behaviors here and now, even as you read these words.

Maybe you've been involved in some kind of sexual sin or adulterous relationship that hasn't yet been exposed. Now is the time to repent . . . to change your mind and head in a new direction. As Jesus said to the woman caught in the act of adultery, *"Go and sin no more."*

Every one of us has the capacity to fall in this area, and those who feel most secure and confident may be the very ones who are walking closest to the cliff.

But the *restorative* grace of Jesus Christ that pulls us out of the pit, giving us a second chance and working all things for good in our lives, is the same *protective* grace that can keep us from falling in the first place.

That's why we owe our praise "to him who is able to keep you from falling and to present you before his glorious presence without fault and with great joy" (Jude 24, NIV).

What a Savior!

Chapter Nine

Solomon's Story:
The Foolish Wise Man

*"I looked at everything I had tried, it was all so useless,
a chasing of the wind, and there was nothing really
worthwhile anywhere." —Ecclesiastes 2:11, TLB*

The next time your past tries to keep you from following God, just remember *you're in good company*. Stories of flawed people, people who did both right and wrong, fill the pages of the Bible.

Some seemed to *always* get it right, like Joseph.

Others *mostly* got it right, like David.

Others *sometimes* got it right, like Samson and Saul.

Today's chapter is about a man who finally got it right at the end of his life, after many sad and wasted years. He was a man who tried it all. If anyone was ever qualified to say, "been-there-done-that-bought-the-tee-shirt," it was this man.

The Bible says that as a young man he loved the Lord, yet he became the hedonist extraordinaire, a playboy who made Hugh Hefner look like a lightweight in comparison.

He was highly educated, yet he went on unbelievable drinking binges. He was an architectural genius, masterminding the building of incredible structures, and chased after women like there was no tomorrow. What a study in contrasts!

And he was worth *billions*.

No, I am not describing some contemporary billionaire like Bill Gates, Donald Trump, or Rupert Murdoch. Nor am I describing some Hollywood actor like Tom Cruise, Brad Pitt, or Tom Hanks.

This man lived thousands of years ago. Yet the lessons and experiences of his life are as current as tomorrow's newspaper. It was he who coined the phrase, "There's nothing new under the sun."

His name was Solomon, and his is one of the greatest stories ever told.

The son of David and Bathsheba, Solomon became the king of Israel after his father's death. No one, not even David, had such incredible potential to be a great king. He was given wisdom on a scale that had never been known up to that point, and had virtually unlimited power to do good. He had a godly heritage from his father, David, who in spite of his serious lapse recovered and became indeed a man after God's own heart.

Solomon started his reign beautifully.

But the joy and beauty began to fade all too soon, as this young king with so much potential turned away from the Lord who had so richly blessed him. In Ecclesiastes, written by Solomon, we have the story of that fall.

A SEARCH FOR MEANING

It wasn't enough for Solomon to hear about right and wrong from others. Like many young people, he wanted to know for himself.

It was a tragic decision. By the time he came to the end of himself, he had thrown away a life with unbelievable potential. Here's how he began his memoirs in Ecclesiastes.

> The words of the Preacher, the son of David, king in Jerusalem. "Vanity of vanities," says the Preacher; "Vanity of vanities, all is vanity." What profit has a man from all his labor In which he toils under the sun? (Ecclesiastes 1:1-3)

Solomon liked the word "vanity"; he used it thirty-eight times in Ecclesiastes as he wrote about life under the sun. The word vanity used here is not speaking of personal vanity, as in spending too much time in front of the mirror every day. The word here, in the original, means emptiness, futility, meaninglessness, a wisp of a vapor, nothingness, a bubble that bursts.

Ecclesiastes tells us that nothing on this earth will satisfy us completely. Nothing, no pleasure, no relationship, no accomplishment will bring enduring value in life.

It's like riding one of those stationary bikes. You pedal and pedal but never really go anywhere. They have high-tech ones now where you can watch a video of a road with a scenic landscape, but the fact is, you get off that bike in the very same place where you started.

Here are more of Solomon's conclusions:

> Smoke, nothing but smoke. ... There's nothing to anything—it's all smoke.

> What's there to show for a lifetime of work, a lifetime of working your fingers to the bone?

> One generation goes its way, the next one arrives, but nothing changes—it's business as usual for old planet earth.

> The sun comes up and the sun goes down, then does it again, and again—the same old round.

> The wind blows south, the wind blows north.

> Around and around and around it blows, blowing this way, then that—the whirling, erratic wind.

> All the rivers flow into the sea, but the sea never fills up.

The rivers keep flowing to the same old place, and then start all over
and do it again.

Everything's boring, utterly boring—no one can find any meaning in it.

Boring to the eye, boring to the ear.

What was will be again, what happened will happen again.

There's nothing new on this earth.

Year after year it's the same old thing.

Does someone call out, "Hey, this is new"?

Don't get excited—it's the same old story. Nobody remembers what
happened yesterday.

And the things that will happen tomorrow? Nobody'll remember them
either. Don't count on being remembered.
(Ecclesiastes 1:2-11, THE MESSAGE)

Well, that's certainly cheerful! Why was Solomon so depressed?

In the book of Ecclesiastes, Solomon was looking back on a life lived without God. He was reflecting on man's attempt to meet the deepest needs of
human life while leaving God out of the equation.

This is ironic when you consider his life story. Here was a man who for
all practical purposes was raised in a godly home, and more importantly, for
many years embraced the Lord. David gave godly advice to his son, and when
he was near death, he told young Solomon: "My son, learn to know the God
of your ancestors intimately. Worship and serve him with your whole heart
and a willing mind. For the LORD sees every heart and knows every plan and
thought. If you seek him, you will find him. But if you forsake him, he will reject you forever. So take this seriously."[66]

David was saying, "Son, you can't live off your dad's faith. You need to have
your own." This is something we all wish for our children and grandchildren—
that our faith would become theirs, our God their God. As Ruth said to her moth-
er-in-law, Naomi: "Your people shall be my people, and your God, my God."[67]

Initially Solomon followed his father's advice. But as time passed, the
young king forgot this commitment, allowing his heart to become at first divided, and then hardened. He began to love both the Lord *and* the world. According to Scripture, however, that will never wash.

The Bible reminds us that friendship with the world is enmity with God.
Whoever will be this world's friend will be God's enemy. And in this rebellion
against God, much like the prodigal son, Solomon broke away from his roots,
his foundation, and decided to take a crash course in sin.

He was prepared to try it all.

Solomon's "Experiments"

Sex, drinking, partying, unlimited materialism, the finest education, entertainment, collecting art, you name it, Solomon tried it. He actually did what most people only dream of. But in the end, it all turned into a nightmare. And bear in mind that he didn't just dabble in these things; as they say in the south, he went whole hog! He thought of it as something of a research project. He had to know for himself, so he would literally try and experience it all.

No stone would be left unturned.

No possession not acquired.

No pleasure not experienced.

The irony of all of this is that *he really knew better!* Solomon had met with God early in his reign and been blessed in a special way.

> That night the Lord appeared to Solomon in a dream, and God said, "What do you want? Ask, and I will give it to you!"
>
> Solomon replied, "You showed faithful love to your servant my father, David, because he was honest and true and faithful to you. And you have continued your faithful love to him today by giving him a son to sit on his throne.
>
> "Now, O Lord my God, you have made me king instead of my father, David, but I am like a little child who doesn't know his way around. And here I am in the midst of your own chosen people, a nation so great and numerous they cannot be counted! Give me an understanding heart so that I can govern your people well and know the difference between right and wrong. For who by himself is able to govern this great people of yours?"
>
> The Lord was pleased that Solomon had asked for wisdom. So God replied, "Because you have asked for wisdom in governing my people with justice and have not asked for a long life or wealth or the death of your enemies—I will give you what you asked for! I will give you a wise and understanding heart such as no one else has had or ever will have! And I will also give you what you did not ask for—riches and fame! No other king in all the world will be compared to you for the rest of your life!" (1 Kings 3:5-13, NLT)

God essentially offered Solomon a blank check. What would you ask for if the Lord came to you and said, "What do you want? Ask, and I will give it to you!" Because Solomon had his priorities in order (at this particular time at least), he asked for what God really wanted him to have—wisdom to lead his people.

When you boil it down, this is what prayer is really all about—bringing our will into alignment with His. Jesus said, "If you abide in Me, and My words abide in you, you will ask what you desire, and it shall be done for you."[68]

The fact of the matter is, if I'm truly living in communion with Him, and His words are at home within me, I will be asking for what He wants me to have anyway. Prayer isn't bending God my way, but my bending His way!

This is what Jesus was saying when He told us, "Seek first His kingdom and His righteousness, and all these things will be added to you."[69]

What things? Jesus had been previously speaking of the unbelievers who think of nothing more than what they will eat, drink, and wear. So essentially He is saying, "If you put My will, plan, and purposes first in your life, everything else you need will be there for you."

That doesn't necessarily mean everything you want.

But it does mean what He says ...everything you need.

As Paul wrote, "And this same God who takes care of me will supply all your needs from his glorious riches, which have been given to us in Christ Jesus" (Philippians 4:19, NLT).

Note that he said all of your needs, not all of your greeds. As it happens, many of the things we so desperately want don't turn out to be what we thought they would be. You've heard the saying, "Be careful what you wish for, because you might get it." There's a lot of truth in that. Because God truly loves us and wants our best, there will be prayers He doesn't answer with a "Yes."

He may say, "Wait," or He may say, "No."

But whatever He says is for our highest good and His ultimate glory.

As Garth Brooks has sung, "Thank God for unanswered prayers." When God does say no, it's always for a good reason—His good reason. You may not be able to see that at a given point in your life, any more than a child will see the value of homework or vegetables. But in time, you will.

The great British preacher C. H. Spurgeon said, "When you have a great desire for heavenly things, when your desires are such as God approves of, when you will what God wills, then you will have what you like."

Yes, God answered Solomon's prayer and gave him great wisdom. Solomon's discernment was so profound that people came from around the world to sit at his feet and drink in his words. An authority no less than the Queen of Sheba, after observing Solomon's accomplishments firsthand, could only shake her head and say, "The half has not yet been told!"[70]

Even at the peak of his magnificence and splendor, however, this wisest of men had already made a series of foolish decisions that would lead to his ultimate fall.

A SERIES OF COMPROMISES

1. He Compromised His Walk

As God had promised David, his son Solomon had the privilege of building a wondrous temple in Jerusalem for the worship of the one true God. His prayer of dedication in 1 Kings 8 is stunningly beautiful. After that address, he turned to the people and said,

May he give us the desire to do his will in everything and to obey
all the commands, decrees, and regulations that he gave our ancestors.... And may you be completely faithful to the Lord our God. May
you always obey his decrees and commands, just as you are doing
today. (1 Kings 8:58, 61, NLT)

But even as Solomon was uttering these true and glorious words, he was in the
midst of violating them. Solomon had disobeyed God and married a nonbeliever.

Solomon made an alliance with Pharaoh, the king of Egypt, and married one of his daughters. He brought her to live in the City of David
until he could finish building his palace and the Temple of the LORD
and the wall around the city. At that time the people of Israel sacrificed their offerings at local places of worship, for a temple honoring
the name of the LORD had not yet been built.

Solomon loved the LORD and followed all the decrees of his father, David, except that Solomon, too, offered sacrifices and burned incense at
the local places of worship. (1 Kings 3:1-3, NLT)

Because the Temple had not yet been completed, the people sacrificed as
their neighbors did, on the high places of the pagan gods. Tragically, Solomon
followed this practice too, all the while saying that he loved the Lord.

The king of Israel had become unequally yoked together with an unbeliever, and he began to compromise his singlehearted devotion to the Lord.
It's an old, old story, and one I've heard many times about relationships such
as these. To keep peace in the home, it is usually the believer who makes compromises to appease the nonbeliever. And this is precisely why God tells us
to "not be unequally yoked"![71]

2. He Compromised His Wealth

Solomon began amassing a huge fortune, as people paid very large amounts of
money to hear his wisdom. But as time passed, Solomon began to trust those
riches more than God.

Money, as they say, is a wonderful servant, but a hard task-master. We can
accomplish wonderful things of eternal value for the Lord with our money,
and that is why every believer should give as God instructs. There is no excuse
for withholding our giving, and it blocks God's blessings when we do.

Should people cheat God? Yet you have cheated me!

But you ask, "What do you mean? When did we ever cheat you?"

You have cheated me of the tithes and offerings due to me. You are under a curse, for your whole nation has been cheating me. Bring all the
tithes into the storehouse so there will be enough food in my Temple.

If you do ...I will open the windows of heaven for you. I will pour out a blessing so great you won't have enough room to take it in! Try it! Put me to the test! (Malachi 3:8-10, NLT)

Nearly every contemporary study on the subject indicates that American Christians give an average of two to three percent of their income. And nine out of ten give nothing at all. In the passage above, God challenges His people to step out in faith and be obedient with their finances—and watch what happens!

Is your money serving you, or are you serving it?

3. He Compromised His Morality

If it wasn't enough to marry a nonbeliever, Solomon started a collection! Seven hundred wives (can you imagine that many mothers-in-law?), and three hundred concubines on top of that. Not only was this wrong morally, but it would turn Solomon to other gods.

Scripture sternly warned against this very thing.

The LORD had clearly instructed the people of Israel, "You must not marry them, because they will turn your hearts to their gods." Yet Solomon insisted on loving them anyway.....

In Solomon's old age, they turned his heart to worship other gods instead of being completely faithful to the LORD his God, as his father, David, had been.... In this way, Solomon did what was evil in the Lord's sight; he refused to follow the Lord completely, as his father, David, had done. (1 Kings 11:2, 4, 6, NLT)

As an old man looking back on so much tragic waste in his life, Solomon wrote these words: "I set my mind to seek and explore by wisdom concerning all that has been done under heaven" (Ecclesiastes 1:13, NASB).

In Hebrew, the word translated "seek" means to investigate the root of a matter, as in doing a research paper. For all practical purposes, Solomon committed himself to research the roots of human behavior. *Why do people do what they do?* As he pursued this theme, he set aside all spiritual principles and truth and neglected both his family and the affairs of state as king. Whether it was passion, pleasure, philosophy, sex, or money, he was obsessed with finding out everything he possibly could about each.

To "explore" means to examine all sides. He was saying, "I will not only study these things, I will personally experience them."

In other words, he wanted to feel the full effects of alcohol himself. He wanted to participate in sexual immorality. He was prepared to try it all— unfettered sex, drinking, partying, unlimited materialism, entertainment, collecting art, and even great building projects. But in the end, it all turned into a miserable state of existence.

THE FAILURE OF EDUCATION

Somewhere in this long, weary odyssey, Solomon thought that if he could obtain the finest education money could buy, it would satisfy his heart.

But it didn't. Not at all.

In spite of his vast learning, there was still an emptiness, a hole in his heart.

I said to myself, "Look, I am wiser than any of the kings who ruled in Jerusalem before me. I have greater wisdom and knowledge than any of them." So I set out to learn everything from wisdom to madness to folly. But I learned firsthand that pursuing all this is like chasing the wind. The greater my wisdom, the greater my grief. To increase knowledge only increases sorrow. (Ecclesiastes 1:16-18, NLT)

This is not to say it's foolish to pursue an education; it's actually a wise and prudent thing to do. Solomon's problem here was that he looked to the pursuit of knowledge *without God*. And when God is left out of the picture, the result will always be empty, empty, empty.

So Solomon decided to shift gears from being an honors student to becoming a party animal. "All right," he said. "If academic pursuit is going to leave me empty, I'll just check my brain at the door and party!"

I said to myself, "Come on, let's try pleasure. Let's look for the 'good things' in life." But I found that this, too, was meaningless. So I said, "Laughter is silly. What good does it do to seek pleasure?" (Ecclesiastes 2:1-2, NLT)

That is why the Bible reminds us that she "who lives for pleasure is dead even while she lives," and that "even in laughter the heart may ache, and joy may end in grief."[72]

When Solomon went after pleasure, it was no holds barred. As mentioned, he had access to at least a thousand women. He chased after every sexual possibility his fertile mind could dream up, and still this emptiness persisted.

So what was next? How about hitting the bottle?

After much thought, I decided to cheer myself with wine. And while still seeking wisdom, I clutched at foolishness. In this way, I tried to experience the only happiness most people find during their brief life in this world. (Ecclesiastes 2:3, NLT)

After a few hangovers, and maybe waking up in bed with people he had never seen before, he saw the emptiness of all that. So he shifted gears once again, and with unlimited resources at his disposal, he thought he would build the finest palaces and homes money could buy. He also planted magnificent vineyards, likely beyond anything ever seen in Israel before.

And then, after many wasted years, Solomon finally came to his senses.

Solomon had learned the bitter lessons of life the hard way. But he really had no one to blame but himself. He came to a clear-eyed conclusion at the end of his memoirs in the book of Ecclesiastes.

Among other things, he deeply regretted wasting his youth, warning others not to make the same mistake.

Remember now your Creator in the days of your youth,
Before the difficult days come,
And the years draw near when you say,
"I have no pleasure in them."
(Ecclesiastes 12:1)

Another translation says, "Don't let the excitement of youth cause you to forget your Creator. Honor him in your youth before you grow old and say, 'Life is not pleasant anymore.'"[73]

In this, Solomon was so right.

Youth is such an important time in life. It is there, in our younger days, that we lay a foundation, establish our priorities, and dream our dreams. That is why I am so committed to reaching young people for Christ.

In some ways, it would be an easy thing for me to just kick back after thirty-plus years of ministry and enjoy all that the Lord has done. Now that I'm in my mid-fifties, I can see myself saying, "Maybe it's time to slow down a little and just focus on people my own age and older."

But I can't do that. My heart burns for young people who don't know the Lord. I don't want to be like others who curse the darkness, I want to turn on the light. With all the thousands of young people who have come to Christ at our Harvest Crusades or in one of our services at Harvest Community Church, I constantly run into them all over the country and receive many letters. I have the opportunity to hear what God has done in their lives and how He is using them, with many going into full-time ministry. As John said "I have no greater joy than to hear that my children walk in truth."[74]

Which brings us to Solomon's final conclusion about his search for meaning in life. Fasten your seat belt. Are you ready?

SOLOMON'S NOT-SO-AMAZING CONCLUSION

Here now is my final conclusion: Fear God and obey his commands, for this is everyone's duty. God will judge us for everything we do, including every secret thing, whether good or bad.
(Ecclesiastes 12:13-14, NLT)

Solomon wraps up his book by saying, "Look, take it from a seasoned pro! Believe me, I *know* what I'm talking about here! If you leave God out of the picture—no matter what else you may have going—your life will be empty, meaningless, and futile. Do you want to have a full life, a more abundant life? Do you truly want to live out your life as a whole woman, a whole man? Well, here's your answer: *Fear God and keep His commandments.*

Sadly, Solomon threw away his whole life figuring this out. Following God was the answer all along, and deep down, I think Solomon knew that from day one.

But he trashed his life anyway.

How many times have we heard this? How many more young men and women are going to step into adulthood telling themselves that submitting to the Lord really doesn't apply to them?

How many more marriages will be destroyed? How many more children deprived of both parents? How many more lives ravaged by substance abuse? How many more people living only to consume things and never thinking of others?

God only knows.

The bottom line is, don't waste your life like Solomon did. He had the potential to be a great man, and for a time he was. But he self-destructed. You would have thought that he would have learned from the example of his father, both good and bad. But he was determined to learn it all the hard way, becoming a *summa cum laude* graduate of the school of hard knocks.

Here was the wisest man who ever walked this earth, and he lived out his life like a fool.

Fear God and keep His commandments.

His father told him this early on. Solomon himself proclaimed this to his people at the dedication of the Temple, yet he completely disregarded it and lived the way he wanted to live. What he initially knew intellectually, he now knew experientially.

If only we would take God at His word! If only we would obey Him—even when it's difficult. To have the courage to say "no" when others are saying "yes," and "yes" when others are saying "no."

Listen, before you know it, you will have more life behind you than before you. I hope you and I will not have wasted a good part of our lives, as he did.

We all have two major dates in our lives. You can see them on the headstone of a grave, separated by a little dash: The date of our birth and the date of our death.

We can't choose our entrance, and we can't choose our exit.

But what we do with that little dash in between is all ours.

Chapter Ten

ELIJAH'S STORY, PART 1:
THE BATTLE OF THE GODS

*"Then Elijah told the people, 'Enough of that—
it's my turn. Gather around.'"* —1 Kings 18:30, THE MESSAGE

We live in troubled times. Sexual promiscuity and perversion proliferate on every side. Senseless and random acts of violence fill the daily news reports. Our nation has been rocked by terrorism as we have never seen before, and experts warn us it may get worse. Far worse.

It's enough to make us want to despair at times. To shrug our shoulders and say, "There's just no hope. There's nothing the church can do—there's nothing that I personally can do—to make any kind of difference."

That thought is simply not true.

The book of 1 Kings reveals an era of Israel's history where conditions were strikingly similar to our own—and in some ways even worse.

Yet one man made a difference.

His name was Elijah.

As a prophet of the living God, Elijah had an immense task before him. This prophet entered the scene at one of the darkest, most evil times in his nation's history. His story is introduced to us in 1 Kings 17, but the chapters leading up to that passage show just how godless and depraved the spiritual state of that once godly nation had become.

Throughout history, whenever a nation or a people abandon faith in the one true God, moral breakdown quickly follows. The northern kingdom of Israel had veered sharply from the Lord's commands immediately after the rebellion that severed them from Jerusalem and the southern kingdom of Judah. And once they had rejected the Lord, everything went downhill from there.

It's not that these Israelites were atheists. They just wanted to worship other gods alongside their worship of the Lord. Somehow, they imaged they could pay lip service to the God of their fathers and yet directly disobey Him by their actions.

Why shouldn't we have it all? They reasoned. Why shouldn't we have God and our idols too? Have you ever tried to imagine how this made God feel? How would *you* feel if your spouse left you for another lover? Hurt and betrayed, no doubt. But what if he or she left you for a *mannequin?*

You don't understand! This mannequin loves me! Besides, it never criticizes or nags me. Then again, it's a little on the quiet side, but that's why I love it!

Is it any more ridiculous when anyone—you and I included—turn from the living God to a false one? We, too, have our idols …we've just made them seem a little more respectable. You can hear the grief in God's voice when He told Jeremiah:

> For My people have committed two evils:
> They have forsaken Me, the fountain of living waters,
> And hewn themselves cisterns,
> broken cisterns that can hold no water.
> (Jeremiah 2:13)

Every person has a god—some altar he bows before, some philosophy he lives by, some pursuit, possession, or passion he gives his allegiance to. Some worship their bodies, some their intellects. But the greatest physique will eventually fail. The most brilliant mind will fade.

Others bow before the altars of power, pleasure, or possessions. When it all comes down, however, is that god going to help you in your hour of need, when you are facing tragedy, hardship, and uncertainty? When you're drowning, do you call out, "MasterCard, where are you? American Express, help me!"

Israel's false gods couldn't help them, either. And that's what led to the big showdown at Mount Carmel Corral.

PRELUDE TO BATTLE

Maybe you've heard of the big boxing matches in times past, with nicknames like "Thrilla in Manila," or "The Rumble in the Jungle." These over-hyped media events couldn't hold a candle to the Battle of the Gods!

A quick historical flyover may give us some perspective before we dive in. For over one hundred years, Israel had lived under the reign of three kings: Saul, David, and Solomon. Each had their flaws, some more than others.

When Solomon's son Rehoboam came to power, the nation was ripped down the middle, dividing into a northern and southern kingdom. At the time Elijah stepped onto center stage, the northern kingdom of Israel had known more than sixty years of blatant unbelief, assassinations, betrayals, idolatry, ungodliness, and cutthroat rulers.

Now there was a new king in town, and he was the most sinful of all. His name was Ahab. He was married to an extremely wicked woman named Jezebel, who was the real power behind the throne. A rabid idolater, she introduced Baal worship to Israel, and it was only a matter of time until her husband, Ahab, followed in her course.

Jezebel's evil reputation became so notorious that her name was used many years later by the apostle John to illustrate evil seeping into the church.

You allow that woman Jezebel, who calls herself a prophetess, to teach and seduce My servants to commit sexual immorality and eat things sacrificed to idols. (Revelation 2:20)

Ahab and Jezebel even planted a sacred grove of trees for the worship of Ashteroth, the goddess of sex and violence. This king and queen assumed they could do as they wished, openly flaunting God's standards with impunity. But God hadn't been sleeping while all this was going on. He was very aware of what Ahab and Jezebel had been doing, and He was angry!

Ahab did more to provoke the Lord God of Israel to anger than all the kings of Israel who were before him. (1 Kings 16:33)

Of all the thousands of Hebrews in the northern kingdom, only 7,000 remained who had not bowed the knee to Baal—but even those 7,000 were so paralyzed by fear that their existence was unknown to Elijah.

Suddenly, with no forewarning or fanfare, the mighty prophet Elijah burst onto that sordid scene. His very name was a rebuke to this wicked royal couple: *My God is Jehovah* or *the Lord is my God.* In other words, your God may be Baal, but mine is the Lord!

Elijah's origins also have a bearing on the story. He was a Tishbite from Gilead, a region east of the Jordan River. The people from that part of the land were a rough-hewn lot, tough and tanned from the sun—maybe like someone from the Australian outback. I'm not saying that Elijah was Crocodile Dundee, but dressed in animals skins as he was, he must have looked out of place in the capital city.

When we think of Elijah, we immediately think of powerful miracles such as raising the dead, stopping rain, and calling fire down from heaven. We know he was bold, courageous, and full of faith. We might say, "What good is it to look at a man like this? What principles could I possibly learn from his life to apply to my own? He was superhuman!"

But that's simply not true. James reminds us that "Elijah was as human as we are...."[75] He had moments of marvelous courage and determination. But there was also a time in his life when he became so afraid, so despondent, that he wanted to give up and die! Scripture records his story to remind us once again that God can and does use imperfect people, and that it's possible to live a godly life in an ungodly world, even if it seems like we're standing alone.

Seemingly out of nowhere, the prophet strode into the palace of King Ahab and walked right up to the throne.

And Elijah the Tishbite, of the inhabitants of Gilead, said to Ahab, "As the Lord God of Israel lives, before whom I stand, there shall not be dew nor rain these years, except at my word." (1 Kings 17:1)

Elijah flung down the gauntlet of his challenge at the very nerve center of the country and his people. Where did he get such boldness? We all know how difficult it can be to stand up for something that isn't popular, to go against the grain.

No one in King Ahab's court knew anything about Elijah at that point. He just walked in off the street, following no protocol, putting forward no introductions, and making no attempt to show deference to the king. Suddenly there he was, with fire in his eyes: a rugged, rough-around-the-edges, unsophisticated man from the outback of Gilead. Everyone must have stared in open-mouthed amazement. I can see the people around Ahab asking each other, "How did this guy get through security? Where did this wild man get such boldness?"

As time went on, the rulers of the northern kingdom would become even more curious. Who was this man, and how did he come by such confidence and power? Within the story itself, Scripture reveals a number of his secrets.

What were Elijah's secrets?

1. He Knew God

He stood continually in the presence of God.

> As the LORD God of Israel lives, before whom I stand... (1 Kings 17:1)

Elijah served a living God, not a dead one like Ahab and Jezebel. Like Job he could say, "I know that my Redeemer lives...."[76] The expression "Before whom I stand" is an interesting one. Though Elijah stood in the physical presence of Ahab, he was also supremely conscious of the presence of God. He understood what it meant to "dwell in the secret place of the Most High and abide under the shadow of the Almighty."[77]

When you stand in the presence of God, you will not bow before any man. The Bible says, "The wicked flee when no one pursues, but the righteous are bold as a lion."[78]

This awareness of God's presence gave Elijah the courage to stand his ground. We need to remember that wherever we go and to whomever we speak, God is with us! Elijah may have only been one person, but he was one person with God.

Do you ever feel that way? Like you are an army of one? The only person in your class, workplace, neighborhood, family who is an outspoken Christian? If so, are you willing to take a stand like Elijah did?

It's so easy even as a Christian to just blend into the woodwork. You don't want to come off as a prude, so you try to roll with it. You laugh at that dirty joke along with everyone else. You wink at an indiscretion for fear of coming off too goody-goody. You tell a lie to get that promotion, or make a compromise to be with the "in" Crowd.

But at what cost?

Elijah was no compromiser. God is looking for men and women today who are willing to stand up like Elijah. To stand in the gap.

In the book of Ezekiel, God told the prophet:

> So I sought for a man among them who would make a wall, and stand in the gap before Me on behalf of the land, that I should not destroy it; but I found no one. (Ezekiel 22:30)

As Chuck Swindoll observed, "Those who find comfort in the court of Ahab can never bring themselves to stand in the gap with Elijah."

2. He Was A Man Of Prayer

> Elijah was as completely human as we are, and yet when he prayed earnestly that no rain would fall, none fell for the next three and one half years! Then he prayed again, this time that it would rain, and down it poured and the grass turned green and the gardens began to grow again. (James 5:17, TLB)

It was Elijah's prayer in private that was the source of his power in public. Notice that Scripture says he prayed *earnestly*. When we see him on Mount Carmel, praying for God to break the drought and send rain, it was not a casual, laid-back request, "Well, God, it would sure be nice if it would rain." Rather, he passionately poured out his heart to heaven. While the words he prayed are not recorded, there was an indication of his intensity in his physical posture.

> Elijah climbed to the top of Carmel, bent down to the ground and put his face between his knees. (1 Kings 18:42, NIV)

Much of our prayer has no power in it because there's no heart in it! If we put so little heart in offering our prayers, we can't expect God to put much heart into answering them.

3. He Faithfully Delivered The Message

As society has changed over the last ten or twenty years, much of what we believe and declare about our Lord Jesus Christ has become "politically incorrect."

The Bible as absolute truth? *Outrageous.*

Jesus as the only way to God? *Narrow-minded!*

Clear standards of right and wrong? *Bigoted.*

The reality of heaven and hell? *Hate speech!*

The gospel is not a popular, culturally-approved message in twenty-first century America. But if we intend to be faithful to God, this is the very message we must proclaim—with as much grace, compassion, and discernment as we can. As Paul tells us:

> Let your speech always be with grace, seasoned with salt, that you may know how you ought to answer each one. (Colossians 4:6)

We're to be gracious and kind, yes, but it is not for us to edit the gospel or God's Word to make it more "palatable." Paul said he did not fail to declare the whole counsel of God.79 We cannot promise God's forgiveness without speaking of repentance. We cannot offer the hope of heaven without warning about hell. Moody said whenever you preach on hell you should always do so with tears in your eyes.

4. He Was A Man Of Faith And Obedience

After delivering the message of judgment to what must have been a stunned and incredulous Ahab, Elijah turned on his heel and walked straight out of the palace.

I can just imagine him stepping outside and saying, "That went great, Lord! What's next? How 'bout we take on those false prophets up on Mount Carmel?" And God replies, "Actually, I had a different plan in mind."

> Then the word of the LORD came to him, saying, "Get away from here and turn eastward, and hide by the Brook Cherith, which flows into the Jordan. And it will be that you shall drink from the brook, and I have commanded the ravens to feed you there."
>
> So he went and did according to the word of the LORD, for he went and stayed by the Brook Cherith, which flows into the Jordan.
> (1 Kings 17:2-5)

God wanted Elijah to disappear from the scene for a while. He directed the prophet to a little hidden ravine, to rest there and await further orders. To Elijah's credit, he offered no argument. He obeyed the Lord and slipped into total obscurity.

This is why God could so mightily use this man. He obeyed even if it didn't make sense in the moment. Perhaps this has happened to you. God has changed the course your life is taking. You may have left a successful career to spend more time with your young children. There may have been a cutback at work, and you were let go. Perhaps the Lord has redirected your ministry. He directed you to leave an effective work to start another. Maybe sickness has altered your plans, or you don't have the energy you once did and have had to make changes.

This may seem like The End, but it may be a New Beginning!

When God closes one door, He always opens another. We are always ready to follow when it's green pastures and still waters, but when one of those valleys-of-the-shadow appears before us we may panic and want to find another way.

At first, hiding in the ravine must have felt strange—maybe somewhat bizarre—for Elijah. There he was sitting alone by a brook day after day, waiting for the ravens' food service to deliver his breakfast and supper. I'm sure the isolation had its drawbacks. But I have a hunch Elijah knew the Lord was prepping him for something big up ahead.

And He was.

It would be Elijah's biggest test yet. The Lord was about to challenge the false gods of Israel in a direct confrontation before the watching eyes of the nation, and Elijah was going to be His representative!

> And it came to pass after many days that the word of the Lord came to Elijah, in the third year, saying, "Go, present yourself to Ahab, and I will send rain on the earth." (1 Kings 18:1)

After Elijah's bold announcement and the drought that followed, he became a wanted man. His face was on every post office wall and milk carton in Israel. He had been MIA, but now he was back in action.

Elijah and Ahab had their second face-to-face confrontation, and it was every bit as tense as the first one.

> Then it happened, when Ahab saw Elijah, that Ahab said to him, "Is that you, O troubler of Israel?"
>
> And he answered, "I have not troubled Israel, but you and your father's house have, in that you have forsaken the commandments of the LORD and have followed the Baals.
>
> Now therefore, send and gather all Israel to me on Mount Carmel, the four hundred and fifty prophets of Baal, and the four hundred prophets of Asherah, who eat at Jezebel's table." (1 Kings 18:17-19)

The word Ahab uses for *troubler* means "viper, snake in the grass." King Ahab was saying "You snake in the grass, where have you been keeping yourself?"

I'm not too sure I would say something like that to a person who could call fire down from heaven! Elijah could have responded, "Oh yeah, well you're toast, Ahab!"

Instead, with courage and great dignity, Elijah turned the insult back on Ahab, where it truly belonged. "I'm not the troubler of Israel, but *you are*!" He reminded the king of how he and his people had brought this calamity on themselves by their penchant for full-tilt idolatry, worshipping Baal and Ashteroth.

It's always amazing to me how people will break God's commandments over and over, stubbornly resisting His loving warnings, and then when hardship comes into their lives (usually of their own making) they blame it on God! Instead of taking responsibility for what they have done and how they have lived, they want to point their finger at heaven.

And of course, they take it out on God's people. "You're a Christian? Well, let me tell you how God messed up my life...." It's really a sad situation, because these people are blaming the only One who can help them.

None of this should surprise us. The Bible never promised us a rose garden in this life. Paul wrote, "Yes, and all who desire to live godly in Christ Jesus will suffer persecution."[80] In the Sermon on the Mount, Jesus said: "God blesses you when people mock you and persecute you and lie about you and say all sorts of evil things against you because you are my followers. Be happy about it! Be very glad! For a great reward awaits you in heaven."[81]

So Elijah issued God's challenge, proposing that Ahab and the prophets of Baal and Ashteroth meet him on the peak of Mount Carmel—with the whole nation watching!

This would be something much weightier than any heavyweight championship between mortal men. This was to be a battle of the gods, determining who was the true ruler of the universe …the Lord God of Israel or Baal.

This really wasn't to be a contest between Elijah and Ahab, but between God and Satan, light and darkness, good and evil. The king of Israel agreed to Elijah's terms and assembled the false prophets on Mount Carmel—calling out the whole nation to witness the event. Perhaps Ahab thought the drought might be broken as a result of the big doings up on Carmel. It could even be that he was hedging his bets …if God didn't come through, he might have reasoned, maybe Baal would send the rain.

The fact is, God was positioning the evil king to step into a trap. Scripture tells us that God moves the king's heart wherever He wants.[82]

The contest Elijah proposed was to be a straightforward test. Elijah would place a sacrifice on an altar to the Lord, and the prophets of Baal would do the same for their god. The god who answered by raining fire down from heaven on the sacrifice was the true and living God …the Genuine Article. It was more than a fair proposal, because Baal was supposedly the god of the sun and of the elements (even though he had failed to bring rain).

As the prophet surveyed the huge crowd at the summit of the 1,600-foot peak, he laid down a challenge. "How long will you falter between two opinions? If the LORD is God, follow Him; but if Baal, follow him."[83]

Even the true believers in Israel weren't willing to take a stand at this point. When this man of God spoke of faltering between two opinions, the picture is one of someone tottering back and forth, much like a person who is intoxicated.

It's not that the people didn't believe in the Lord God of Israel. They just wanted to believe in Baal and Ashteroth too. They wanted to straddle the fence and enjoy the best of both worlds. You see, it was unpopular to worship the Lord in that day and age. The king and queen did not approve. Besides, if you just went along with the Baal-Ashteroth program, there were benefits. If, however, you insisted on worshipping the God of Abraham, Isaac, and Jacob, you could lose your head.

The Israelites of Elijah's day didn't want to live under God's absolutes, with all the responsibilities that would bring, so they would follow some other god until things turned so bad they began to reap the results of their idolatry. Then they would turn back to the true God again. Each time they edged their way back from the brink of destruction God was merciful to them, forgiving them.

Moses saw the same tendency when the people worshipped the golden calf out in the wilderness. At one point he cried out, "Who is on the LORD's side? Let him come to me."[84] Joshua similarly realized a decision had to be made, and that a man or woman couldn't live in two worlds at the same time.

Serve the LORD! And if it seems evil to you to serve the LORD, choose for yourselves this day whom you will serve, whether the gods which your fathers served that were on the other side of the River, or the gods of the Amorites, in whose land you dwell. But as for me and my house, we will serve the LORD. (Joshua 24:14-15)

Jesus said essentially the same thing: "He who is not with Me is against Me, and he who does not gather with Me scatters abroad."[85]

It's no different today; there are still people who try to live in two worlds. It reminds me of swimming in a lake or the ocean when the water is cold. If you're going to swim at all, it's easier to just plunge in, rather than submerging yourself inch by freezing inch. Being in that "in-between" state is the most miserable of places.

Jesus said it like this to the church at Laodicea: "I know all the things you do, that you are neither hot nor cold. I wish that you were one or the other! But since you are like lukewarm water, neither hot nor cold, I will spit you out of my mouth!"[86]

Know this: Idols in our hearts cause God to refuse to listen to our prayers. The Lord told the prophet Ezekiel, "Son of man, these leaders have set up idols in their hearts. They have embraced things that will make them fall into sin. Why should I listen to their requests?"[87]

Finally, the stage was set.

The audience was in place.

The time had come for the battle of the gods.

THE BATTLE THAT WASN'T

So they took the bull which was given them, and they prepared it, and called on the name of Baal from morning even till noon, saying, "O Baal, hear us!" But there was no voice; no one answered. Then they leaped about the altar which they had made.

And so it was, at noon, that Elijah mocked them and said, "Cry aloud, for he is a god; either he is meditating, or he is busy, or he is on a journey, or perhaps he is sleeping and must be awakened." So they cried aloud, and cut themselves, as was their custom, with knives and lances,

until the blood gushed out on them. And when midday was past, they prophesied until the time of the offering of the evening sacrifice. But there was no voice; no one answered, no one paid attention.
(1 Kings 18:26-29)

Elijah almost seemed to be enjoying himself here. He was definitely having some fun at their expense, and began to mock them. The phrase "he is busy" seems to imply that Baal had taken a trip to the celestial men's room, or as the Living Bible puts it, maybe "he's out sitting on the toilet!" Now that's just flat-out funny!

But it was no laughing matter to the four hundred prophets of Baal. Why didn't their god hear them? Why didn't he answer? Almost as if they were taking Elijah's advice, they began to shout louder and louder.

Elijah wasn't the only one mocking them that day. Their own gods mocked them. Ahab and the people saw this too— the emptiness and futility of these gods the people had followed!

Sometimes when people are living in sin, they're happy there. Or at least they say they are. But as C. S. Lewis observed, "Even atheists have moments of doubt." The Bible teaches that non-Christians are blinded by the god of this world. We need to pray that God would open their eyes to reality—to their real state. They may think they are happy, but they are also on the way to hell. And if they will be honest, their so-called happiness is a shallow sort of thing, and short-lived at best.

The Israelites had to see the futility of their own gods before they turned to the Lord. Elijah allowed the false prophets to have their shot all day long— morning to evening. This hoarse, beaten, bloodied bunch had come to their wit's end. It must have been grotesque to see all those men groveling on the ground, screaming, moaning, and bleeding.

This is the world in all its glory and splendor! Satan can make a God-rejecting life seem so smart and sophisticated, so appealing, glossy, and attractive. But underneath it is filthy, destructive, and in the end ... just plain pathetic.

With the time for the evening sacrifice coming on, Elijah stepped onto center stage.

> Then Elijah said to all the people, "Come near to me." So all the people came near to him. And he repaired the altar of the LORD that was broken down. And Elijah took twelve stones, according to the number of the tribes of the sons of Jacob.... Then with the stones he built an altar in the name of the LORD; and he made a trench around the altar large enough to hold two seahs of seed. And he put the wood in order, cut the bull in pieces, and laid it on the wood, and said, "Fill four waterpots with water, and pour it on the burnt sacrifice and on the wood." Then he said, "Do it a second time," and they did it a second time; and he said, "Do it a third time," and they did it a third time. So the water ran all around the altar; and he also filled the trench with water. (1 Kings 18:30-35)

Why did Elijah soak the altar three times? Because he wanted there to be no doubt when God answered and set the sacrifice aflame.

Then Elijah lifted a simple prayer to the Lord. There was no screaming, dancing, moaning, bleeding, or theatrics. Elijah had a serene confidence in God's power. This reminds us that when we are in prayer and worship, we don't have to work ourselves up into some kind of frenzy to bring God's power down.

God is already here.

He dwells among His people.

He tells us that where two or three are gathered together in His name, He's right there in their midst. Scripture reminds us that He inhabits the praises of His people.[88] In other words, when we are praising Him, He is there ...as someone has said, "Closer than hands or feet, closer than breathing."

When we work so hard to bring God close to us, many times it's just our attempt to have an emotional experience where we can "feel" God.

Don't get me wrong. Emotions are great, and when the Lord touches you in that way, there's nothing like it. But you should never approach worship expecting such an experience every time, or conclude that you haven't encountered God because you haven't "felt" God. Just relax, know He is there, call upon Him, and let the emotions fall where they will.

God is here, and that is all that really matters.

And He was there that day on Mount Carmel, too, ready to answer Elijah's calm, dignified prayer. All of Israel was about to see a demonstration of His power.

THE FIRE FALLS

At the usual time for offering the evening sacrifice, Elijah the prophet walked up to the altar and prayed, "O Lord, God of Abraham, Isaac, and Jacob, prove today that you are God in Israel and that I am your servant.

Prove that I have done all this at your command.
O Lord, answer me! Answer me so these people
will know that you, O Lord, are God and that you
have brought them back to yourself."

Immediately the fire of the Lord flashed down from
heaven and burned up the young bull, the wood, the stones, and the
dust. It even licked up all the water in
the trench! And when all the people saw it, they fell face down on the
ground and cried out, "The Lord—he is
God! Yes, the LORD is God!" (1 Kings 18:36-39, NLT)

This truly is one of the greatest stories ever told!

And what do we learn from this man, Elijah—the man Scripture says was just like us? What were the secrets of His effectiveness?

Let's review them one more time.

He knew God. No matter where he was, whether in the palace of a godless king or sitting all alone by the brook Cherith as the long days of waiting slipped by, Elijah knew he was in the immediate presence of God. What confidence he drew from this assurance! Who could intimidate him when he stood in the continual presence of the Almighty?

He was a man of prayer. He prayed earnestly, putting it all on the line, and God answered.

He faithfully delivered the message. Elijah had a tough message from God in tough times. And he declared it just the way he heard it.

We, too, have a message to deliver—and marching orders from our Commander-in-Chief. It is not for us to update, popularize, or edit the gospel of Jesus Christ. We are to faithfully deliver it, plain and simple. And with love.

He was a man of faith and obedience. Elijah knew how to occupy a place of prominence, and also how to step out of the spotlight and patiently wait for God to act. What does that say to you and me? Be obedient to what the Lord has set before you today, and He will give you more to do tomorrow.

Perhaps as you read these words you realize that your passion in life—your "god," your idol—no longer satisfies as it once did. It's empty, even mocking you! There is no better day than today to call on the true and living God who loves you, giving Him a chance to answer the deepest needs in your life.

How will He answer? He may answer dramatically—with a great surge of relief, happiness, and emotion. Then again, the answer may come as a quiet confidence that grows and blossoms with the passing of time.

Either way, He *will* answer the truly searching person who comes to Him! Jesus said, "All that the Father gives Me will come to Me, and the one who comes to Me I will certainly not cast out."[89]

Chapter Eleven

ELIJAH'S STORY, PART 2:
THE LEGACY OF A LIFE

"Do you know that the Lord is going to take your master from you today?"
"Yes, I know," Elisha replied, "but do not speak of it." —2 Kings 2:3, NIV

It seems the older you get, the faster time flies by.

When I was in elementary school, time seemed to crawl like a snail. *When would the day be over? When would we get Christmas break? When would summer vacation start?*

Now, it's not just the years that zip by, it's entire decades! I read an interesting thing about what time it is in your life.

It goes like this:

If your age is 15, the time is 10:25 a.m.

...20, the time is 11:34 a.m.

...25, the time is 12:42 p.m.

...30, the time is 1:51 p.m.

...35, the time is 3:00 p.m.

...40, the time is 4:08 p.m.

...45, the time is 5:15 p.m.

...50, the time is 6:25 p.m.

...55, the time is 7:34 p.m.

...60, the time is 8:42 p.m.

...65, the time is 9:51 p.m.

...70, the time is 11:00 p.m.

I don't know where that puts you, but for me it's about 7:30 p.m. That's sad, because I've been going to bed at 9:30 these days!

Now that I'm a grandfather, it reminds me I have passed to another generation. But I am determined to be the *fun grandpa* for my grandbaby Stella (and others).

Have you heard about some of the telltale signs that age might be creeping up on you? You know you are getting old when ...

...your mind makes commitments your body can't keep.

...the little gray-haired lady you help across the street is your wife!

...everything hurts, and what doesn't hurt doesn't work!

...your little black book contains names ending only in M.D.

...you dim the lights for economic reasons, rather than romantic ones.

...your back goes out more than you do.

...your children begin to look middle-aged.

...you are warned to slow down by a doctor instead of a cop.

...your knees buckle and your belt won't.

...you have too much room in the house and not enough in the medicine cabinet.

...you sink your teeth into a juicy steak and they stay there.

Why am I bringing up all these cheerful things? Because in this chapter, we will be looking at the legacy of a life.

High Drama

As my parents' generation passes and my generation enters its final stage, we need to think about our legacy, our heritage, what we are passing on.

In one of the "greatest stories ever told," this chapter will consider the account of one man who passed his legacy to another. This is the story of the final days in the life of Elijah the prophet—and his departure was as dramatic as his entrance!

Elijah didn't just step onto the scene in Israel, he *burst* onto the scene—seemingly out of nowhere. His startling appearance and bold warnings shook up the godless status quo in the northern kingdom.

Elijah was a hairy, rough-hewn character who wore a leather belt and didn't back down to anybody. And when his work was over, God swept him up to heaven in a chariot of fire.

In what was probably his finest moment, Elijah stood boldly on the peak of Mount Carmel and yelled out to the people, "How long will you stagger between two opinions?" At the climax of that story, the fire of God fell in a dramatic fashion, and after three years of devastating drought, the rain returned—in buckets!

In spite of these great events, however, King Ahab and Queen Jezebel refused to turn to the Lord. Instead of being moved by the great miracle of fire from heaven, Jezebel only became firmer in her unbelief. Although given ample opportunity to turn from her evil ways, she only dug her heels in deeper. Like Pharaoh, she became harder each day until she paid the ultimate price—she was thrown out of a high window to her death. (Which is precisely what the Bible tells us ...sin pays a wage, and that wage is death).

Then there was the puppet king, Ahab. He was a lot like the fickle crowds on Mount Carmel, sliding back and forth between two opinions. On the one hand, Ahab was impressed with the miracles of Elijah. But on the other hand he was afraid to offend his wicked, manipulative wife. Ahab was ultimately killed on the battlefield—in disguise—manipulating to the very end. There are so many like Ahab who are impressed by God, yet are afraid to take a stand lest they offend someone.

Ahab witnessed "the battle of the gods" we looked at in the previous chapter, and then hightailed it back to his palace—in a driving rain.

But what happened to Elijah in the aftermath of that stunning victory? Did he celebrate? Relax? No, after such a great struggle, the prophet suddenly became vulnerable.

A LOW MOMENT AND A NEW FRIEND

As Scripture says, "Elijah was as human as we are."[90] After his great victory over the false prophets of Baal on Mount Carmel, Elijah allowed his fears to get the best of him. On word of a threat from Jezebel, he fled for his life into the desert, crawled under a scraggly tree, and asked God to take his life.

But God didn't condemn His battle-weary servant. Instead, He led him to a cave in a mountain . . . and an unforgettable experience of meeting with God.

Low lows often come after high highs.

Up in that cave, the Lord told Elijah his ministry was now coming to a close. His work was almost done, and he was about to leave the scene. But before Elijah's departure, he had to find someone to carry on the work God had called him to. It was time to pass the baton.

The Lord already had that successor picked out. Elijah was to anoint Elisha to take his place.

So he departed from there, and found Elisha the son of Shaphat, who was plowing with twelve yoke of oxen before him, and he was with the twelfth. Then Elijah passed by him and threw his mantle on him. And he left the oxen and ran after Elijah, and said, "Please let me kiss my father and my mother, and then I will follow you."

And he said to him, "Go back again, for what have I done to you?"

So Elisha turned back from him, and took a yoke of oxen and slaughtered them and boiled their flesh, using the oxen's equipment, and gave it to the people, and they ate. Then he arose and followed Elijah, and became his servant. (1 Kings 19:19-21)

Yes, Elisha was a servant to the prophet. But I have a hunch they became close friends, as well. How gracious the Lord is to provide us with fellowship and friendship in those seasons of life when we're battle-weary. That's a reminder that discouragement and depression should not keep us isolated from our brothers and sisters in Christ. That's the time when we need them most!

In the season before Elijah's dramatic homegoing, the older prophet would spend a great deal of time with Elisha, preparing him for the work at hand. How important this is for us to do as well—to take all that the Lord has done in our lives and invest it in the lives of others. It's called mentoring, or to be biblical, discipling others. Yet sadly, many of us have not made this a priority in our lives.

Which brings us back to the Great Commission.

"GO THEREFORE . . ."

> Then Jesus came to them and said, "All authority in heaven and on
> earth has been given to me. Therefore go and make disciples of all na-
> tions, baptizing them in the name of the Father and of the Son and
> of the Holy Spirit, and teaching them to obey everything I have com-
> manded you. And surely I am with you always, to the very end of the
> age." (Matthew 28:18-20, NIV)

That is what we do across the world with our Harvest Crusades. We have all
heard the "go preach the gospel" part, but we often miss the phrases "make
disciples" and "teaching them."

Making disciples and teaching. Jesus first calls us to be His disciples,
then directs us to lead others into the same life commitment.

Paul wrote: "So we tell others about Christ, warning everyone and teaching everyone with all the wisdom God has given us. We want to present them
to God, perfect in their relationship to Christ" And to Timothy: "You have
heard me teach things that have been confirmed by many reliable witnesses.
Now teach these truths to other trustworthy people who will be able to pass
them on to others" (Colossians 1:28; 2 Timothy 2:2, NLT).

Somewhere along the line, evangelism has been isolated from discipleship. But Jesus never made such a distinction! One should automatically
follow the other. The Great Shepherd never intended for newborn lambs to
be left alone in the pasture.

Next to actually leading an individual to faith in Christ, the greatest joy in life is
seeing that man or woman grow spiritually and begin leading others to the Lord!

You don't have to be a Bible scholar to play a vital role in a new believer's
life. For many new converts, the main problem seems to be acclimating to the
Christian life. They need teaching, but they also need a personal example.

In short, they need a friend.

Later in his life, Paul demonstrated this ministry of friendship-discipling with
his young associate, Timothy. In his final letter to the young man, he wrote: "But
you... know what I teach, and how I live, and what my purpose in life is. You know
my faith, my patience, my love, and my endurance" (2 Timothy 3:10, NLT). How
could Timothy know those things? Only by spending time with his mentor. That
was the apostle's model of bringing others along in their walk with Jesus Christ.

> And you know that we treated each of you as a father treats his own
> children. We pleaded with you, encouraged you, and urged you to live
> your lives in a way that God would consider worthy. For he called you
> to share in his Kingdom and glory. (1 Thessalonians 2:11-12, NLT)

Discipleship is not a new idea.

Moses did this with Joshua, Aquila and Priscilla with Apollos, Barnabas with John Mark, and Jesus with the Twelve. And of course, in the story before us, we see the same dynamic with Elijah with Elisha.

We've all heard about Simon Peter, but not as much about his brother, Andrew. Andrew never gets much press, and yet it was he who brought Peter to the Lord in the first place. If there were no Andrews, there would be no Simon Peters.

We hear about the great apostle Paul all the time. But we don't hear all that much about two men who played a key role at a crucial time in his life: Ananias and Barnabas.

These men didn't author any of the books in the New Testament, and—other than Ananias praying for Saul's eyes to be healed—they performed no dramatic miracles by the hand of God. We have no record of either of them preaching a sermon.

But both of these men touched the life of a man who in turn touched millions—perhaps billions—all over the world for two millennia! If helping Paul get started in the faith was all that they had accomplished in their whole lives, they would have still had a huge impact on the kingdom.

The fact is, we all need to be about the work of helping and encouraging those who are younger in the faith. It's important for our spiritual health. Every believer needs outflow in their lives as much as they need input. Do you know what you get when you have all input and no outlet? The Dead Sea!

We as believers could find ourselves in spiritual danger if, in our attendance at Bible studies and prayer meetings and intake of spiritual information, we do not have an adequate outlet for our newfound truths! By discipling others, we will not only save sinners from hell, we will also save ourselves from stagnation.

New believers need our wisdom, knowledge, and experience as mature believers. And by the same token, we as mature believers need their childlike simplicity of faith, their fresh love relationship with Jesus, and their zeal! As Solomon wrote, "The generous [or giving] soul will be made rich, and he who waters will also be watered himself."[91]

A NEW TEAM BEGINS

When Elijah found Elisha, he threw his mantle over the younger man's shoulders.

Although Elisha may not have understood the full significance of that calling in that very moment, he definitely knew it was a big turning point in his life.

What he did next would seal the deal.

Elisha then returned to his oxen, killed them, and used wood from the plow to build a fire to roast their flesh. He passed around the meat to the other plowmen, and they all had a great feast. Then he went with Elijah, as his assistant. (1 Kings 19:21, TLB)

Elisha saw himself as a servant and an assistant to the great prophet. Did he understand that he would be Elijah's successor—and actually double his master's miraculous ministry in Israel? Elisha may have felt he wasn't quite ready for that, but in reality, he was.

Over and over again through the years, I have found that God is not looking so much for ability as availability. Someone willing to step into the gap when they see a need in the church. People often ask me how they can "get into ministry." I feel like responding, "Just look around you!" Ministry opportunities are everywhere!

As Jesus said: "Do you think the work of harvesting will not begin until the summer ends four months from now? Look around you! Vast fields of human souls are ripening all around us, and are ready now for reaping."[92]

Look at the pattern of those God called in Scripture. *They were all busy in the Lord's work already!* They weren't just sitting around contemplating their navels. When God called David to slay Goliath, he was obediently running an errand for his father. When He called Paul and Barnabas to launch out on their first missionary journey, they were already active in a teaching ministry in the Antioch church. When Philip received the call to meet the Ethiopian eunuch on the desert road, he was in the middle of a big evangelistic meeting in Samaria.

In other words, all of the people I just mentioned *were already in motion for the Lord.* The Holy Spirit didn't have to jump-start them, He just had to direct them.

So what are you doing to serve the Lord right now? Any service to the Lord—demonstrating your servant's heart and your availability—is an on-ramp to even greater service. What kind of help does your local church need? Ushering? Counseling new believers? Help in the parking lot? Giving regularly of your finances?

I'll tell you about a foreign land where you can go right away. The natives of this land are small of stature and speak a different language. The region? *Sunday school.* The tribe of people? *Little kids.*

Teaching little ones to know the Lord and follow Him is a direct fulfillment of the Great Commission. And it doesn't require a plane ticket or a passport.

INITIAL RELUCTANCE?

Understandably, Elisha at first seemed reluctant to simply walk away from everything he had known to follow the man of God. He said, "Please let me kiss my father and my mother, and then I will follow you" (1 Kings 19:20).

His words sound familiar, don't they? In fact, they are very much like the words of a man who had been called by Jesus in the New Testament.

> Still another said, "I will follow you, Lord; but first let me go back and say good-by to my family."

Jesus replied, "No one who puts his hand to the plow and looks back is fit for service in the kingdom of God." (Luke 9:61-62, NIV)

Why did Jesus say that? Because He knew this man's heart through and through, and He saw the reply for what it was: an excuse to play for time. Jesus knew that once he went to say good-bye to the folks at home, he would never return. (Have you ever tried to say good-bye at a family reunion? It can take all day!)

Elijah was calling Elisha to be what *he* had been through the years: a true follower of God. As I said, he was reproducing himself. The prophet was saying, in essence, *"Elisha, if you want to be used of God, then you must make your move!"*

So it is with you. If you want to change your world, if you want to be used by God, then you must love God more than anyone or anything else! Are you willing to do that?

In Luke 14:26, Jesus said something that has puzzled many through the years: "If anyone comes to Me and does not hate his father and mother, wife and children, brothers and sisters, yes, and his own life also, he cannot be My disciple."

Obviously, Jesus wasn't counseling hatred of your loved ones here. He was saying, "Your love for God must be so strong, so intense, that all other loves in your life would be like hatred in comparison."

Elisha, realizing it was now or never, slaughtered his oxen and barbequed them on the wood of his plough. Elisha had made his commitment—and celebrated with filet mignon! There would be no looking back now. He had burned his bridges.

UNFINISHED BUSINESS

With his successor chosen, Elijah could have gone into early retirement …a little golfing, a little shuffleboard, and maybe just kicking back on the front porch in his rocking chair. But there were still a couple of matters of serious, unfinished business that needed his attention.

Israel's wicked "first couple," Ahab and Jezebel, had passed from the scene by this point, succeeded by their son, Ahaziah. Apparently not learning anything from the Lord's harsh judgment of his parents, Ahaziah had determined to live just like all the evil kings that had preceded him.

But all his fun and frivolity came to an end with a serious accident at his palace. Somehow he had fallen through the latticework of an upper room, critically injuring himself. Even with his life hanging in the balance, Ahaziah refused to turn to the Lord. Instead, he sent messengers to inquire at the temple of Baal, to see if he would live.

Meanwhile, God directed Elijah to intercept these representatives of the king with a message from the true and living God. Elijah stopped them and asked, "Why are you looking to Baal to see if the king will get well? Is there no God in Israel?"

In other words, after all that happened in that nation with the three-year drought and the great "battle of the gods" on the peak of Mount Carmel, hadn't they learned anything?

It reminds me a bit of the spiritual condition of our country right now. Right after the tragedy of 9/11, people flocked to churches en masse, looking for answers and reassurance, showing (for a short season) some spiritual hunger. But now things have pretty much gone back to the way they were. Many in our nation have no time or thought for God. In some ways, things almost seem worse than before our great national crisis.

But when that next hurricane, earthquake, or terrorist attack shakes and rattles us, many will be back. History teaches one thing, and it is that man learns nothing from history.

Elijah boldly told the king's emissaries: "You go tell the king that he will die in his bed!" So much for political correctness. Elijah had certainly lost none of his boldness. So the messengers returned to Ahaziah, and the king asked them, "Why are you back so soon?"

They replied "A man came up to us and asked us, 'Is there no God in Israel? Why do you go to Baal?'" Then he said, "Go tell the king he will die in his bed!"

The king gulped. "What did this man look like?"

The messengers replied, "He was a hairy man with a leather belt."

"It was Elijah!" the king replied. Ahaziah apparently still had enough strength to become very angry, and he sent a captain with fifty soldiers to arrest the prophet.

The first chapter of 2 Kings tells the incredible story of the king's attempts to arrest the prophet, who had settled himself on a hilltop.

The captain of Israel said "Man of God, the king has said come down...."

Elijah replied, "If I am a man of God let fire come down from heaven and consume you and your fifty men."

And that's just what happened. The arresting party was killed to the last man, their charred bodies lying at the base of Elijah's hill.

The exact same thing happened again! Finally, a third group came, and the captain knew he needed to take a different tack or he would be toast— literally. He basically said to Elijah, "O man of God, give me a break, I'm just doing my job!"

Elijah went with him, and then personally delivered his message to the king—face to face. If Ahaziah had been hoping for a softer answer this time around, he didn't get it. Elijah told him bluntly, "You're going to die." Age had not diminished the prophet's courage one iota. And the king died just as Elijah had said he would.

DEPARTURE DAY

When the time came for Elijah's final departure, it would prove to be a valuable time of testing for Elisha, his companion and successor. It's interesting to see how the old prophet seemed to be dissuading his disciple from coming with him.

> When the LORD was about to take Elijah up to heaven in a whirlwind, Elijah and Elisha were traveling from Gilgal. And Elijah said to Elisha, "Stay here, for the Lord has told me to go to Bethel."
>
> But Elisha replied, "As surely as the LORD lives and you yourself live, I will never leave you!" So they went down together to Bethel.
> (2 Kings 2:1-2, NLT)

This same exchange happened two more times: a quick trip to Jericho, and then the Jordan River. And Elisha stuck to his mentor like superglue.

Why was Elijah doing this? He could very well have been testing his disciple's commitment. Many of us will say to Jesus, "I'll do whatever You want me to do. I'll go wherever You want me to go." So the Lord tests us on that, asking us to do something difficult or go somewhere uncomfortable … and we begin to backpedal.

Jesus said, "You are my friends if you do what I command." And the apostle John tells us, "This is love for God: to obey his commands. And his commands are not burdensome."[93]

Whatever Jesus asks us to do, wherever He asks us to go—no matter how difficult or illogical it may seem at the time—the very best thing we can do is obey.

How would it be with Elisha? How would the apprentice fare in this test from Elijah? I think he was being given the opportunity to turn back, to change his mind, perhaps even to go home. A rough road lay ahead for Elisha. It wasn't easy being a prophet in a nation that had turned its back on God. As a highly visible representative of the living God, he would be hated and hounded by powerful people.

A similar case occurred when the fickle multitudes turned back from following Jesus. To His own disciples Jesus said, "Do you also want to go away?"

> But Simon Peter answered Him, "Lord, to whom shall we go? You have the words of eternal life. Also we have come to believe and know that You are the Christ, the Son of the living God." (John 6:67-69)

Jesus doesn't want fair-weather followers. He will intentionally thin out the ranks of those who aren't really committed. You see, God wants you to want Him. He won't force His way into your life.

Remember how the resurrected Christ appeared to the two disciples on the Emmaus Road? They hadn't recognized Him, and as they drew near the house, "He made as though He would go further …" before they prevailed on Him to stay.

Amazing! This is a God who responds to our invitation. That is why He gave us the ability to choose, to decide.

In Revelation 3:20, Jesus says, "Behold, I stand at the door and knock. If anyone hears My voice and opens the door, I will come in to him and dine with him, and he with Me."

He doesn't say, "Behold, I stand at your door, and if you don't open up, I'll break it down." He waits for an invitation.

Finally, just before he was to leave this earth, Elijah asked Elisha the big question.

> When they had crossed, Elijah said to Elisha, "Tell me, what can I do for you before I am taken from you?"
>
> "Let me inherit a double portion of your spirit," Elisha replied.
>
> "You have asked a difficult thing," Elijah said, "yet if you see me when I am taken from you, it will be yours—otherwise not."
> (2 Kings 2:9-10, NIV)

This moment was the real test of Elisha's motives and heart. What did the younger man want? Elisha simply wanted power to follow in Elijah's footsteps, faithfully and effectively carrying on his mentor's work. And God's blessing did come on him in a double portion.

What would you like the Lord to do for you today?

I heard a story about three men on a desert island who discovered a magic lamp. The genie they released from the lamp gave a wish to each of them.

The first man said, "I wish I were home with my family eating a big steak dinner." And *poof*, he was gone! The second man, encouraged by the first man's success, said, "I wish I were a billionaire living in a beautiful mansion." And *poof*, in an instant he was gone too. The third man was now all alone and feeling a bit melancholy. When it came time for his wish, he said, "I miss my friends. I wish they were still here with me!"

What do you want the Lord to do for you? Do you have a heart like Elisha, that wants more than anything else to serve God with all your heart and all your strength?

That's the kind of heart's desire that pleases the Lord, and those are the kind of prayers He delights to answer.

Elijah left a mighty legacy to his successor and friend. What kind of legacy are you leaving today? Are you discipling anyone? Do you have a life worth emulating? Or are you just a fair-weather follower?

Elijah was one of the two people in the Bible who never died (the other was Enoch). And there is a generation that will not see death, that will be caught up to be with the Lord in the air.

As the book of Hebrews tells us: "Christ was sacrificed once to take away the sins of many people; and he will appear a second time, not to bear sin, but to bring salvation to those who are waiting for him."[94]

Will you be watching and waiting like Elisha?

What a day that will be! But whether He calls us to meet Him in the air or we walk through the doorway of death, our first glimpse of heaven, our first moment in the presence of Jesus, will be—for us, forever—the greatest story ever told.

THE GREATEST
STORIES
EVER TOLD

VOLUME THREE

Chapter One

JOB: WHEN LIFE HITS BOTTOM

Have you ever had a really bad day?

Consider the plight of three janitors at Fowler Elementary School in Ceres, California. Alerted to the fact that there was a gopher loose in the building, these three vigilant custodians finally cornered the rodent in a utility room.

Some time later, after recovering from his injuries, one of them explained just what happened in that encounter. It seems that they tried to spray the rodent with several canisters of a solvent used to remove gum from floors, hoping to freeze it to death.

Believing their efforts successful, one janitor lit a cigarette in the poorly ventilated room. Sparks from the lighter ignited the solvent, and the ensuing explosion blew all three of them out of the room and injured sixteen students in the adjoining hallway.

Fortunately no one was injured seriously. Not even the gopher. The little animal survived the incident and was released in a field.

Now that is called having a really bad day. Maybe you're having that kind of day even as you read this book. How would you know? I came across this list somewhere.

You know you are having a really bad day...

- when your pacemaker comes with a thirty-day money back guarantee...
- when the pest exterminator climbs under your house and never comes out...
- when a copy of your birth certificate arrives in the mail marked "null and void"...
- when the restaurant gives you a senior discount without asking, and you're only thirty-seven years old...
- when your wife takes the dog on vacation and leaves you at the kennels...
- when your plants do better when you don't talk to them...
- when the bird singing outside of your window is a vulture...
- when your horn sticks on the freeway behind thirty-two Hell's Angels motorcyclists.

I'm reminded of a story of a woman whose husband was critically ill, and had been slipping in and out of a coma for several months. Through it all, his wife of many years had faithfully stayed by his side every single day. So one day he came to, and motioned for his dear wife to come closer.

She nestled close, her eyes filled with tears.

"You know what?" he rasped. "You've been with me through all of the bad times. When I got fired, you were there to support me. When my business failed, you were there. When I got shot, you were right there by my side. When we lost the house, you didn't leave me. And when my health started failing, you were still by my side."

And then the husband said, "You know what?"

The wife drew a bit closer, and said, "What?"

"I think you're bad luck."

We may laugh at that, but the fact is that you and I face trouble from the day we are born. It comes with the territory of life on a broken planet. In fact, if you ever find yourself experiencing a conflict-free day, you can chalk it up as one of the better and rarer days of your life.

Conflict is one thing. But what about those days when it seems like the bottom drops out? You know what I'm talking about. It's a day when what couldn't go wrong goes wrong, and then even more goes wrong beyond that. And you ask yourself, "*Why is this happening to me?*"

Or maybe we're watching the evening news, and it seems like events all over the world are spinning out of control. We hear about a deranged student shooting other students and teachers, and we ask the question, "Why?" Why would someone do something like this? How could anyone be given over so totally to evil?

Or maybe we hear of a natural disaster like a tsunami or an earthquake, wiping out thousands of lives in an instant. And again we say, "Why?"

Or maybe, just to bring it home a bit, a friend of ours, while driving home from church, gets killed in a head-on collision with a drunk driver. Later you learn that the inebriated person survived.

Why do things like that happen?

WHY DOES GOD ALLOW IT?

Why does God allow tragedy? We've all heard it stated in many ways. Why does He allow babies to be born with disabilities? Why does He permit wars to rage? Why does He seem to turn the other way when innocent people are being killed? What about all of those horrible injustices in our world? This hurricane. That epidemic. This wildfire. Why do these horrible things afflict our world? If God can prevent such tragedies, why does He allow them to take place?

Here is the classic statement of the problem. Either God is all-powerful but He is not all good, therefore He *doesn't* stop evil. Or He is all good but He is not all-powerful, therefore He *can't* stop evil. And the general tendency is to blame all of the problems of the world on God to say that God is the one who is somehow responsible.

"If God is so good and loving," people will say, "why does He allow evil?" Now the first part of that question is based on a false premise. By even stating it in that way, what I'm really saying is that I don't believe God to be good and loving.

By questioning God's goodness and love, I am in essence saying that I know more about it than He does. The fact is, God doesn't *become* good because that's my opinion of Him, or because I happen to personally agree with His actions or His words. Nor does He become good because we vote on it and all agree that is the case.

God is good because God says He is good. And it's not up for a vote.

Jesus said, "No one is good except God alone."[1]

You see, God is good whether I believe it or not, and He alone is the final court of arbitration. As the apostle Paul said, "Let God be true, and every man a liar."[2]

What, then, is "good"? *Good is whatever God approves.* And by the same token, bad is exactly what God says is bad.

Some might say, "That's circular reasoning." Yes, you could say that. But I would describe it as *biblical* reasoning. The Word of God is our source of truth, defining right and wrong, and what our values ought to be.

In Isaiah 1:18 we read: "'Come now, let us reason together,' says the LORD."

Or as another translation puts it, "Come let us argue this out, says the LORD."[3]

God is saying, "Here's the way I see things. You need to see it the way that I see it." And He goes on to tell us that His thoughts are above our thoughts and His ways are above our ways.

So God is good. Period.

Let's come back to the second part of that question. Why does He allow evil? The first thing we have to remember is that mankind was not *created* evil. Man and woman were created innocent...ageless...immortal. Their responsibility in the Garden of Eden was to tend it, watch over it, and discover all that God had created. But of course we know that our first parents made the wrong choice, ate the forbidden fruit, and everything changed down to this day.

But don't be too hard on Adam and Eve, because if you had been in the Garden, you would have done the same thing. And so would I. We might have fallen sooner or we might have fallen later, but we would have surely gotten around to it, as evidenced by the fact that we all make wrong choices throughout our lives.

The result of that original sin (we know all too well) was that death entered into the human race. As we are told in Romans 5:12, "When Adam sinned, sin entered the human race, and Adam or Adam's sin brought death and so death spread to everyone for everyone has sinned."

So we need to keep in mind that humanity, not God, is responsible for sin.

In light of that, one might then ask the question, "Why didn't God make us incapable of sin?" Answer: Because He didn't want puppets on a string. He didn't want windup robots. He didn't want preprogrammed people with neither choice nor will.

When my granddaughter Stella was about eight months old, I remember playing some little games with her—or, as much of a game as you can play with a baby. One of her toys played a little song, and Stella was kind of bopping to the beat (amazing child!).

As she was moving around, every few beats she would turn over and reach out her hand to me, and wait for me to grab it. After we touched hands, she would turn around a few more times and do it again...reaching her hand out to me. She did this about eight or nine times. And I loved it. I could have played that little game all day long. It was so cute, and it was just her little idea. She wouldn't stop reaching until I grabbed her tiny hand.

Now think about it. Stella didn't play that little game with me because I forced her to. She did it because I'm the greatest grandfather that ever was! (She doesn't know this yet, but she will.) This was something that came from her own will. She *wanted* to play a game and reach out her hand to me.

It's the same in our relationship with God. He doesn't want you relate to Him and talk to Him and love Him because you *have* to. He wants you to do it because you *choose* to. He gave you that ability.

In the Garden, Adam and Eve used that independent will to make a wrong choice. So do we. And so much of the evil in the world and the wrongs that are done are set in motion by people who simply make wrong choices...one after another.

"Okay," you reply, "I can accept that. But why does God allow bad things to happen to good people? And more to the point, why does God allow bad things to happen to *godly* people?"

I'm glad you asked. Because that brings us to one of the greatest—and most tragic—stories in all the Bible. The book of Job is in God's Word for a reason—actually many reasons. But one of the principle things this book does is to help us think through this whole issue of the goodness of God, and how it touches a world and a human race under the curse of sin.

Most of us can accept the idea of suffering in general, especially as an outcome or consequence of bad behavior. In other words, if someone lives a reckless, wicked life, committing horrible atrocities, and faces the repercussions of those deeds, we say, "They got what they deserved. It was poetic justice. They reaped what they sowed, and it finally caught up to them."

We can accept the idea of suffering in circumstances like those. But how does it strike us when an innocent and godly person suffers?

That was the case with Job, a man who not only avoided doing wrong, but also worked very hard to do what was right. So much so, in fact, that God actually bragged on his righteousness and integrity before the hosts of heaven.

That was right before the bottom dropped out of Job's life, and everything changed. Maybe you've heard people talk about "the patience of Job." In the next few pages, we're going to see exactly what that statement means.

THE MAN FROM UZ

Job was a real, historical, flesh-and-blood man who many scholars feel walked the earth during the time of the patriarchs, somewhere between 2000 and 1800 BC. Scripture says he lived in the land of Uz—which may sound like Oz, but Uz was a real place in the world, not an imaginary land of munchkins and talking scarecrows. It was most likely east of the Jordan, perhaps in northern Arabia. Many scholars tell us that the book of Job may be the oldest book of the Bible, possibly written by Moses himself.

The New Testament writer James validates Job's story, and the great lesson it teaches about patience and faith:

> We give great honor to those who endure under suffering. Job is an example of a man who endured patiently. From his experience we see how the Lord's plan finally ended in good, for he is full of tenderness and mercy. (James 5:11, NLT)

Uz was a real place and Job was a real man with real problems with a real God to whom he turned—the very same God you and I can turn to in our times of need.

Let's set the stage for this amazing account by picking up an introduction from Job chapter one.

> There was a man named Job who lived in the land of Uz. He was blameless, a man of complete integrity. He feared God and stayed away from evil. He had seven sons and three daughters. He owned seven thousand sheep, three thousand camels, five hundred teams of oxen, and five hundred female donkeys, and he employed many servants. He was, in fact, the richest person in that entire area.
>
> Every year when Job's sons had birthdays, they invited their brothers and sisters to join them for a celebration. On these occasions they would get together to eat and drink. When these celebrations ended—and sometimes they lasted several days—Job would purify his children. He would get up early in the morning and offer a burnt offering for each of them. For Job said to himself, "Perhaps my children have sinned and have cursed God in their hearts." This was Job's regular practice. (Job 1:1-5, NLT)

So right off the bat we learn some important things about the man named Job.

#1: He Was A Man Of Integrity And Character

Character may be the most important thing in any individual's life. How do you determine character? Here's what it comes down to. When you are all alone, when no one is looking, when there's no one around to impress, what does your life look like? *That* is who you really are. The measure of a man or woman's real character is what they would do if they knew they would never be found out.

What if I could give you a foolproof guarantee that you could get away with a certain sin? Would you do it? Would you cheat on your income taxes? Would you be unfaithful to your spouse? If that is the case, then that is who you most truly are.

It really comes down to what you think about most. What saddens you? What makes you mad? What makes you laugh? That is your character. A German proverb says that "a man shows his character by what he laughs at."

Bottom line, Job practiced what he preached. He was a man of true integrity. God Himself said so, and no one could have a higher endorsement than that.

#2: He Was A Wealthy Man

Success has turned many a head, and wealth has been a spiritual stumbling block to many. We are warned in Psalm 62:10, "If riches increase, do not set your heart on them."

Remember what Jesus said about wealth in the parable of the sower? He spoke of seed that was sown on the ground where it took root, but was eventually choked out by weeds. "The seed that fell among the thorns," Jesus explained, "represents others who hear God's word, 19 but all too quickly the message is crowded out by the worries of this life, the lure of wealth, and the desire for other things, so no fruit is produced."[4]

That is not to say it is wrong to desire success, a nice home, or a prosperous business. But it is wrong if you let it become the driving force in life. Don't let that become your obsession. Don't let that become your God. Because the Bible says, "Put to death, therefore, whatever belongs to your earthly nature: sexual immorality, impurity, lust, evil desires and greed, which is idolatry."[5]

Job had vast wealth and holdings, but it didn't turn his head.

#3: He Was A Family Man

Job raised his children in the way of the Lord and brought them before God in prayer every day without fail.

So even when his adult kids were having a celebration, he would pray for them. He would offer a sacrifice on their behalf, which was an Old Testament way of saying he was interceding for them. Here was a dad who was concerned about the spiritual lives of his kids, and he prayed every day that they would steer clear of sin and walk with God.

Our kids need our prayers—every day of their lives, in the culture in which we live today. While it's true that we need to work toward releasing our sons and daughters, and launching them into independent, self-sufficient lives, we'll always be their parents, and they will always need Mom and Dad's faithful prayers.

Job was a concerned parent, bringing his family before the Lord, praying for their protection and blessing.

#4: He Was A Prayerful Man

When Scripture says Job prayed for his adult children, it underlines the fact that "this was Job's regular custom." In other words, when it came to prayer, Job wasn't hit-or-miss. He had an established routine of coming before the Lord with his requests.

The Bible says that we should "pray without ceasing"...and "in everything give thanks; for this is the will of God in Christ Jesus for you."[6] Does that describe your life? Is God first in your list of priorities? Do you pray for your children? Do you set a godly example for them to follow? You've heard the expression, "The apple doesn't fall far from the tree." That is so often true when it comes to loving the Lord and following Him. Your sons and daughters will take their cues from watching how you relate to God, and the priority you give to your spiritual life.

Job set an outstanding example for his children. And as this story unfolds, we are given dramatic evidence as to why it's so vital to cover your family with prayer every day. In one of the most fascinating passages in all of Scripture, we are allowed to look behind the scenes and see what was happening in the spiritual realm that would directly affect Job's life, and every member of his family.

BEHIND THE SCENES

One day the angels came to present themselves before the LORD, and Satan the Accuser came with them. "Where have you come from?" the LORD asked Satan.

And Satan answered the LORD, "I have been going back and forth across the earth, watching everything that's going on."

Then the LORD asked Satan, "Have you noticed my servant Job? He is the finest man in all the earth—a man of complete integrity. He fears God and will have nothing to do with evil."

Satan replied to the LORD, "Yes, Job fears God, but not without good reason! You have always protected him and his home and his property from harm. You have made him prosperous in everything he does. Look how rich he is! But take away everything he has, and he will surely curse you to your face!"

"All right, you may test him," the LORD said to Satan. "Do whatever you want with everything he possesses, but don't harm him physically." So Satan left the LORD's presence.

(Job 1:6-12, NLT)

Talk about having friends—and enemies—in high places! God was so proud of Job He was bragging on him. Look again at verse 8. "Have you noticed my servant Job?...the finest man in all the earth—a man of complete integrity."

When I read that statement and then go on to read what happened to Job immediately after God made it, I feel a little nervous about the idea of God ever bragging on me! I almost feel like saying, "Lord if You're ever feeling proud of me just for a fleeting moment, could we kind of keep it between the two of us?"

I wonder if God would ever boast of His servant Greg, or would boast of you with all the angels standing around. I would tend to doubt it in my case. We often will see ourselves one way—maybe in a quick surface way—while God knows us through and through. Over in the book of 1 Samuel, we're told, "The LORD does not see as man sees; for man looks at the outward appearance, but the LORD looks at the heart."[7]

You and I can be way off in the way we evaluate one another. We might be in a worship service and find ourselves drawing conclusions about how spiritual that person next to us might be. If he's singing loudly, closing his eyes, and raising his hands up high, we might conclude, "Now that is a spiritual person." Then we look around a little more and see someone else who isn't singing at all. Maybe her head is bowed a little, but she's simply holding the chair in front of her and doesn't seem engaged in the worship. And we conclude, "She's not a very spiritual person. I wonder if she's even a believer."

The truth might be the very opposite of what we think!

We don't know what's going on in the heart of another person. So...we had better leave all such conclusions and evaluations with the Lord Himself, where they actually belong. We need to just concentrate on seeking to live a godly life.

So here is God bragging on the man from Uz. *"My servant Job."* There could be no higher endorsement, and no higher job description: a servant of the living God.

We're also introduced to Satan in this passage. We have to get rid of the world's stereotypical caricature of a devil in a red suit and pointed ears, wearing a goatee and carrying a pitchfork. (I especially take issue with the goatee part, as I have been known to sport one myself from time to time.)

I'm not sure where that came from, but it bears no resemblance to the description of our adversary in Scripture.

Satan is a powerful spirit being...not a myth, not a cartoon character, and not "the dark side of the force," lacking identity or personality. He is real, and Scripture calls him by name.

Satan the accuser came....(Job 1:6)

Satan answered.... (Job 1:7)

In verse 7 he describes his activities to the Lord, "going back and forth across the earth, watching everything that is going on." Then in verse 12 we read that Satan left the Lord's presence. You see, we're talking about an active personality with an agenda here, not an impersonal force. Satan has something he very much wants to accomplish.

And what is that? *The devil's single, consuming ambition is to turn you and me away from God and all that is good.* His ultimate agenda can be summed up in the statement of Christ in John 10:10, where Jesus said, "The thief's purpose is to steal and kill and destroy. My purpose is to give life in all its fullness."[8]

You can immediately see the contrast. Jesus is in effect saying, "I have come to give you life. Satan has come to give you death. I have come to give you freedom. He has come to give you bondage. I have come to build you up, to save you, to restore you. He has come to steal, kill, and destroy." And that is what he wants to do with you down to this very day, this very hour.

MASTER DECEIVER

The devil is very effective at what he does. Never doubt that. Never underestimate his capacity to package his wares, making bad things look good, and good things look bad. He is a master deceiver, and we should never dismiss him or treat him lightly.

One wonders, why did God create someone as wicked as the devil to begin with? He didn't! God did not create Satan as we know him today. In fact, he was created as a beautiful and high-ranking angel named Lucifer, or "son of the morning." Once serving the Lord in a place of exalted glory and responsibility, Lucifer was in an elite category with other high-ranking angels like Michael and Gabriel. The book of Isaiah gives us a quick peek at what happened to this mighty being.

> "How you are fallen from heaven,
> O Lucifer, son of the morning!
> How you are cut down to the ground,
> You who weakened the nations!
> For you have said in your heart:
> 'I will ascend into heaven,
> I will exalt my throne above the stars of God;
> I will also sit on the mount of the congregation
> On the farthest sides of the north;
> I will ascend above the heights of the clouds,
> I will be like the Most High.'
> Yet you shall be brought down to Sheol,
> To the lowest depths of the Pit."
> (Isaiah 14:12-15)

Lucifer, you see, was not satisfied with worshipping God. He wanted that worship for himself. So this once beautiful, powerful angel of God lost his exalted position in heaven. Lucifer became Satan when he fell to the earth. Satan means "accuser," which he now is. Jesus said, "I saw Satan fall like lightning from heaven."

Now an enemy of God, Satan—along with his hosts of fallen angels—has many strategies to seduce, subvert, and destroy the people of God. He may approach us in all his depravity, seeking to draw us directly into his web of wickedness and sin. But the Bible says he can also appear as "an angel of light," seeking to deceive us and lead us off into false directions and wrong paths.

So even though we shouldn't become overly preoccupied with our adversary and his activities, it is wise for us to understand his methods of operation. Paul wrote to the Corinthians that they should take a certain course of action "in order that Satan might not outwit us. For we are not unaware of his schemes."[9]

Being aware of his schemes and how he operates can help us to effectively resist him. And that is exactly what Scripture tells us to do: "Resist the devil and he will flee from you."[10]

It would be one thing to deal with this one powerful spirit being. But the Bible tells us that when the devil fell, he did not fall alone. We're told in Revelation 12:4 that he took one-third of the angels with him—untold thousands of them. And it is my belief that those fallen angels are what we would know of as demons today, doing his bidding and his dirty work. But though the devil lost his once-exalted position, we learn from this first chapter of Job that he still has access to heaven and the throne of God.

And what does he do with this access?

He comes before God to accuse us. In fact, the Bible calls him "the accuser of our brethren."[11] The devil's primary objective in coming before the God of heaven is to bring constant and specific accusations against you and me and all followers of Jesus Christ.

That seems to be what is happening as Job's story opens.

LOOKING FOR TROUBLE

God says to Satan. "Where have you come from?" The devil responds, "I have been going back and forth across the earth watching everything that is going on."

The Bible describes Satan as a roaring lion walking about seeking whom he may devour. He never takes a vacation. He never rests. Wouldn't it be nice if the devil took a day off? A devil-free day! But it isn't going to happen. He doesn't take a day off—or an hour off, or even a minute off. When he is defeated, he circles around and comes back for more. If you block him at the front door, he'll try to come in the back door, or sneak in through a window. If keep your doors and windows shut, he'll try to come down through the ceiling or tunnel up through the floor. He is so persistent! He doesn't back off. He is a lion constantly pursuing its prey.

We've all seen those programs on television where the zebras are running together, and there is that one little zebra lagging behind. As soon as you see him, you know he's a goner for sure. You feel so bad for him. "Oh no. Get away little zebra! Run faster!" But you know he's going to end up being a striped lunch for Leo the lion.

Satan walks to and fro, up and down, constantly sizing things up. He says, "There's a Christian who isolates himself from the other Christians. Maybe I'll go after him." Or, "There's someone filled with pride and arrogance. I know I can bring him down." Or, "Oh, that girl over there looks vulnerable right now. I know how I will defeat her. I'm moving in!"

He is always sizing you up. Always looking for a weakness. Always looking for a vulnerability of some kind. And so he is going back and forth across the earth just looking for trouble.

Jesus called Satan the father of lies. But he also tells the truth sometimes, as in Job 1:9-10: "Job fears God, but not without good reason. You have protected him and his home and his property from harm. You have made him prosperous in everything he does. Look how rich he is."[12] The King James Version translates it this way: "You have put a hedge around him."

This brings us to a very important truth. Despite his heartless, wicked agenda, Satan still has to ask permission before he can touch a child of God. Why? Because of the hedge of protection that God has placed around you as His child. In one story in the gospels, a host of demons even had to ask Jesus permission to enter a herd of pigs!

Satan cannot simply ride roughshod over you and do whatever he wants, because God has placed limits on his activities. God knows our breaking point, and He will never give us more than we can take. In 1 Corinthians 10:13, Paul writes these crucial words: "There is no temptation taken you but such as is common to man: but God is faithful, who will not allow you to be tempted above what you are able; but will with the temptation make a way to escape, that you may be able to bear it."

There is always a way out. There is always a back door. Sometimes even the front door, or perhaps a window. You may think you are trapped and that there is no way out of Satan's web. But there always is! The enemy may harass you, but he can never exceed what God in His grace and wisdom allows.

On another occasion Satan came asking for permission to assault Simon Peter. Jesus turned to the fisherman and said, essentially, "Simon, Simon, Satan has been asking for you by name that you would be taken out of the care and protection of God."

It's interesting that Satan asked specifically for Peter. Has he ever asked for me by name? I doubt it. I don't know that I have ever been tempted by the devil.

You may be saying, "What do you mean by that, Greg? That's a strange statement." Let me explain. I have certainly been hit with temptations orchestrated by the devil, but Satan can only be in one place at one time. Sometimes we think of him as roughly God's equal, only on the dark side. We know that God is all-powerful, all-knowing, and everywhere-present, and we may imagine Satan to have similar attributes.

He doesn't.

The devil is not God's equal. The devil is a powerful spirit being, but he has limitations. He can't be all over the world tempting and harassing everyone at the same time. That's why he employs his vast army of demons. So even though Satan himself may have never tried to tempt me and drag me down, he's had lots of help over the years. So in effect, it's the same thing. In the case of Peter, however, the devil didn't want to trust an attack to one of his underlings. He came knocking himself. Peter was a big fish, and a direct threat to Satan's kingdom.

Immediately aware of Satan's designs, Jesus warned Peter, assuring him, "I have prayed for you, Peter, that your faith would not fail."

Jesus prays for you, too. He is your Advocate, and speaks in your defense when the evil one tries to slander you before the Father.

One popular paraphrase puts it like this:

> I write this, dear children, to guide you out of sin. But if anyone does sin, we have a Priest-Friend in the presence of the Father: Jesus Christ, righteous Jesus. (I John 2:1 THE MESSAGE)

God has placed a hedge around you—an impregnable fortress—which Satan and his demons cannot penetrate. Whatever comes your way, then, must have God's permission. Just as God protected Job, so He will protect you.

You might ask the question, "Well, what if this or what if that happens? I saw this tragedy befall a friend of mine, and I couldn't handle that if that happened to me."

That's likely true. Right at this moment, you couldn't handle it. But if God allowed that particular circumstance in your life, He would also give you the strength to endure that trial.

ATTACKING JOB'S INTEGRITY

In the first chapter of Job, Satan says to God, in essence, "Job fears You, God, because You give him a lot of wonderful possessions. But if You took it all away, he wouldn't fear You anymore. In fact, he would curse You to Your face. I can prove it to You, if You let me."

The Lord replies, "All right. But you can't touch him physically—only those things that belong to him." Obviously, that's a loose paraphrase. But it does give us a clear picture of Satan in his role as "the accuser of the brethren."

"Job? He's just a mercenary! He's just in it for what he can get out of it."

Here's what that might look like in our lives. First, the devil whispers in your ear, "Go ahead and do it. You'll get away with it. No one will ever know. It'll be fun." So you do whatever it is he is enticing you to do. Then he comes back to you and says, "Why you pathetic, miserable, hypocrite! What a loser you are! You're worthless. God doesn't love you any more, and your salvation is out the window. Don't show your ugly face in the church again. And don't even think about praying or reading the Bible!"

It's very easy to fall for this. And we find ourselves with our chin on our chest, kicking dirt, and saying, "Oh Lord, I failed You. I'm not worthy to worship You and speak for You."

But wait. Hold on a minute here. You were never worthy. None of us were. None of us are. Even on your best day, when you were doing everything right and didn't commit any sins that you knew of, you weren't even close to "worthy" on that day.

The devil doesn't want you to know that. He wants you to think, "Well, I've got to work my way back to God. I've got to do a bunch of good things if I'm going to approach the Lord in prayer."

That is a lie.

You can approach God any time based on the sacrifice of Jesus on the cross, and His shed blood for you. It has never been about my worthiness. It has always been about His grace extended to me.

When it comes to that, how much do we really understand about God's grace in Christ? Can we even begin to wrap our minds around it? The psalmist tried, using the biggest picture he could imagine.

> As high as heaven is over the earth,
> so strong is his love to those who fear him.
> And as far as sunrise is from sunset,
> he has separated us from our sins.
> (Psalm 103:11-12, THE MESSAGE)

The book of Hebrews says, "Let us therefore come boldly to the throne of grace, that we may obtain mercy and find grace to help in time of need."[13]

Once again, Satan doesn't want you to know these things. He doesn't want you to think about verses like these. No. He will whisper in your ear and say, "You've committed that sin one too many times. How many times do you expect God to forgive you? You can't go to Him." And then the guilt and despair will come—guilt that can drive you crazy.

Is all guilt bad, then? No…even guilt has its purpose. You might think of it as a warning system. You're walking down the street barefoot and you step on a little sliver of sharp glass. The pain in your foot shoots right up to your brain, and the warning is instantaneous. *Stop! Don't step down any further.*

It's just a little cut, and not all that bad. But it hurt. It was uncomfortable.

It's not bad enough to have you check into emergency, but it's definitely reason to be careful, to back off a little. Yes, it slows you down for a minute or so, but it's definitely better than the alternative—which is putting your full weight on a large piece of glass, cutting your foot wide open, and having to go the hospital to get stitched up.

No, you don't like the discomfort of that initial pain, but it has served you well if it keeps you from more serious injury.

Guilt can be the same way. I say or do something wrong, and almost immediately, I know it. Guilt kicks in to say, "You are not right with God," or "You are not right with that person, and that needs to be rectified."

It's guilt. It's not enough to plunge me into despair or send me into depression, but it's enough to bring me to the cross, where I say, "Lord, I have failed, I have sinned in this, and I'm sorry. Please help me and forgive me."

As far as Satan is concerned, that's the worst. Everything in him wants to keep you from the cross, where Jesus paid the debt for our rebellion and sin with His own blood. It was the cross that sealed Satan's doom, and he doesn't want you anywhere near it. If he could, he would drive you far away from it. He wants you to feel guilty and condemned, separated from God. But God wants that guilt to bring you to Him, where you will find mercy, forgiveness, and healing.

Judas Iscariot sinned against Jesus, betraying Him, and then went out and hung himself. If Judas had sought forgiveness for his treachery, would Jesus have forgiven him? Yes, that's what I believe. And here's why. When Jesus was in the garden of Gethsemane, and Judas came with the temple guards to arrest Him, Jesus made this statement. "Friend, why have you come?"

Did Jesus know why Judas had come that night? Of course He did. He had already identified him as the betrayer and told him to go do what he was going to do quickly. But I believe in that final moment, Jesus was offering to Judas one last opportunity to repent. But Judas listened to the wrong voice, the voice of guilt, and took his own life.

What about Peter? After he had denied the Lord, and then had direct eye contact with Him, Peter went out and wept bitterly.

But here's the difference.

He came back.

Peter returned to Christ, was forgiven, restored, and offered an even wider, more significant ministry.

So here's the important lesson. If you fail the Lord (and you will), don't run from Him or try to hide. Come back to Him.

When Jesus said, "Simon, Simon! Indeed, Satan has asked for you, that he may sift you as wheat...," He added, *"But I have prayed for you, that your faith should not fail;* and when you have returned to Me, strengthen your brethren."[14]

You need to remember that your defense against the accusations of the devil is the Son of God Himself, who intercedes for you before the throne of the Father. He prays for you, He represents you, He defends you. Romans 8:33 says, "Who will bring any charge against those whom God has chosen? It is God who justifies. Who is he that condemns? Christ Jesus, who died, more than that, who is raised to life, is at the right hand of God interceding for us."

This is Jesus, our Savior. He is the One who saves us, justifies us, defends us, and preserves us. Yes, we believe and affirm these things. He is a faithful, merciful God, filled with lovingkindness.

But we're still left with a troubling question. Why would He allow righteous people to suffer?

That's the question before us in the next chapter.

Chapter Two

JOB: GOD'S PRESENCE IN THE STORM

"Have a nice day."

We hear it a dozen times a day. The phrase is an American classic, isn't it? It often comes at the end of a transaction at your local market, where the clerk will say, "Thank-you-for-shopping-with-us-and-have-a-nice-day."

Do they mean it? Probably not, but it's in the employee manual, so they have to say it. For all the emotion and sincerity they put into it, they might as well be saying, "Cows eat grass."

Maybe you've stood at the returns window of your local big-box store, trying to return a defective or unwanted item for a refund. The employee behind the counter may very well say, "I'm sorry. We cannot accept your return. Have a nice day."

How sorry are they? And how am I supposed to have a nice day when I'm stuck with an expensive but useless item?

So what does that even mean to "have a nice day"? Does it mean a day devoid of all problems? A day free of all sickness, conflict, hardships, or speed bumps? Is that a "nice" day?

Sometimes God gets portrayed as *nice*—sort of a glorified Santa Claus, smiling benignly from heaven. He just wants everyone to get along, plant a tree, eat organic, and have a happy life. We can almost hear Him saying from Mt. Sinai, "Have a nice day."

But is that really the picture that the Bible gives us? Is "niceness" one of His attributes as the true and living God? I'm not suggesting here that God can't or won't bless you with health or wealth. Nor am I suggesting that God is somehow reluctant to bring happiness into your life.

But that is not God's primary objective...for you to have a nice day. *God's objective in your life is to be glorified and to make you more like Jesus Christ.* Your goal in life should not be happiness, but holiness. The good news is that one will follow the other! Truly holy people are among the happiest people you will ever meet. *And to be a holy person means you will have to go through some trials, some hardships, and some suffering.* It simply comes with the territory.

Now some would suggest that if you suffer, if you're sick, or if you're enduring some kind of hardship, it is a result of your own sin, and if you just had more faith this would not be happening to you.

Those are wrong ideas. But they are not new ideas.

That sort of false teaching goes all the way back to the oldest book of the Bible, the book of Job.

We read about the "behind the scenes" dialogue between God and Satan concerning Job's integrity and character. God had boasted about His servant, and Satan was hot to challenge the Lord's boast. What happened next was a string of events this good man couldn't have dreamed of in his worst nightmare.

THE DARKEST DAY

One day when Job's sons and daughters were dining at the oldest brother's house, a messenger arrived at Job's home with this news: "Your oxen were plowing, with the donkeys feeding beside them, when the Sabeans raided us. They stole all the animals and killed all the farmhands. I am the only one who escaped to tell you."

While he was still speaking, another messenger arrived with this news: "The fire of God has fallen from heaven and burned up your sheep and all the shepherds. I am the only one who escaped to tell you."

While he was still speaking, a third messenger arrived with this news: "Three bands of Chaldean raiders have stolen your camels and killed your servants. I am the only one who escaped to tell you."

While he was still speaking, another messenger arrived with this news: "Your sons and daughters were feasting in their oldest brother's home. Suddenly, a powerful wind swept in from the desert and hit the house on all sides. The house collapsed, and all your children are dead. I am the only one who escaped to tell you."

Job stood up and tore his robe in grief. Then he shaved his head and fell to the ground before God. He said,

"I came naked from my mother's womb,
and I will be stripped of everything when I die.
The LORD gave me everything I had,
and the LORD has taken it away.
Praise the name of the LORD!"

In all of this, Job did not sin by blaming God.
(Job 1:13-22, NLT)

Job was not having a nice day.

His losses in those horrific few hours are almost incomprehensible. Think about it. In one day Job, one of the wealthiest men in the land, lost everything—all his assets, so wisely and carefully built up through the years. His trusted servants—what we might call loyal, longtime employees—had all perished in a string of (what we know to be) supernatural disasters.

Those things would have been difficult enough to endure. But it got much,

much worse. The worst news of all on this day was to hear that his children—his pride and joy—had all been killed. Seven sons and three daughters. Wiped out in a moment.

Having walked with parents through the death of a child, I can tell you that this is the worst thing that can happen to a mother or a father. No parent ever wants to outlive his or her children. We spend our lives caring for them, nurturing them, loving them, and investing our hopes and dreams in them. For most loving fathers and mothers, to lose a child is a fate literally worse than death.

Satan had challenged God, saying, "You just let me take away the things he holds dear and then see how loyal and faithful Job will be. He'll curse You to Your face!"

The Lord granted Satan permission to turn Job's world upside down—within limits. The evil one would not be allowed to lay a finger on Job himself.

And how did Job fare in that attack? Did he curse God as Satan suggested? No. He praised God. *"The LORD gave me everything I had, and the LORD has taken it away. Praise the name of the LORD!"*

No wonder the Lord was bragging on Job! You can almost hear the pride in the Lord's voice as He says to Satan,

> "Have you noticed my servant Job? He is the finest man in all the earth—a man of complete integrity. He fears God and will have nothing to do with evil. And he has maintained his integrity, even though you persuaded me to harm him without cause."

But Satan wasn't through yet (is he ever?), issuing one final challenge.

> Satan replied to the LORD, "Skin for skin—he blesses you only because you bless him. A man will give up everything he has to save his life. But take away his health, and he will surely curse you to your face!"

> "All right, do with him as you please," the LORD said to Satan. "But spare his life." So Satan left the LORD's presence, and he struck Job with a terrible case of boils from head to foot."

> Then Job scraped his skin with a piece of broken pottery as he sat among the ashes. (Job 2:3-8, NLT)

In times like these, you would like to think you could turn to your spouse for support. But it didn't work that way for Job.

> His wife said to him, "Are you still trying to maintain your integrity? Curse God and die."

> But Job replied, "You talk like a godless woman. Should we accept only good things from the hand of God and never anything bad?" (Job 2:9-10).

We have much to learn from this story of Job. In his letter to the church, the apostle James wrote, "As you know, we consider blessed those who have persevered. You have heard of Job's perseverance and have seen what the Lord finally brought about. The Lord is full of compassion and mercy."[15]

Persevere.

That's the key word here. The book of Job teaches us how to persevere—hang in there—when we go through heartaches and hard times. Because it's not a matter of *if* some kind of calamity, trial, sickness, or difficulty will strike you or someone you love. It's a matter of *when.*

From the pages of Job's story, we learn not only how to persevere in our own dark days, but also how to bring comfort to others who are enduring times of great difficulty.

Satan's Unwitting Role

When we read about Satan, this powerful and evil spirit being who hates God and despises mankind, we might wonder why God allows Satan to even exist.

As he says in his own words, he is restlessly going back and forth across the earth, looking for trouble…looking for lives to ruin…looking for saints to cause to stumble. In the last chapter we asked the question: "Why does God allow him to carry on? Why doesn't the Lord just take him out?"

Why? Well you might be surprised to know that Satan, in his own twisted way, serves the purposes of God.

You ask, *"How in the world could that be?"*

Just consider this. Satan unwittingly played a major role in the cross of Christ. In his enduring hatred for God's Son, the devil thought it would be a great idea to have Jesus betrayed, arrested, beaten within an inch of His life, and then crucified and put to death on a Roman cross.

Everything went according to Satan's plan. As Jesus told the mob who came to apprehend him, *"This is your moment, the time when the power of darkness reigns."*[16]

The power of darkness did indeed reign that day, and Satan's plan succeeded. But so did the plan of God.

What the evil one didn't realize was that it was the Father's plan all along that the Messiah would die for the sins of the world. In the book of Zechariah and in Psalm 22, God even mentioned that the Messiah would die by crucifixion (graphically described thousands of years before it had even been invented).[17] In the prophecy of Isaiah, we're told "It was the Lord's will to crush him and cause him to suffer."[18] Unaware that he was making the biggest blunder since his rebellion against God, Satan played into the plan and purpose of God (also prophesied in the book of Zechariah) when in his rage and hatred he inspired Judas Iscariot to betray Jesus for 30 pieces of silver.[19]

Satan's "best shot" against God and the people of God was the crucifixion of the God-man, Jesus Christ. And in that act he unwittingly not only sealed his own doom, he opened the door for Jesus to offer redemption and salvation to the whole world.

But that's not the end of the matter. Believe it or not, Satan can also accomplish God's purposes through the trials and afflictions that he throws our way. How? By helping us to cling to the Lord in dependence and prayer and, as a result, to grow stronger spiritually.

COMPANY SHOWS UP

But let's think about Job's situation. Here he is. He has lost his possessions. He has lost his children. He has lost his health. He might have wished he had lost his wife after what she said, but she was still around, which only added his misery. And on top of all that, he has broken out in ugly, painful boils. The onetime wealthiest, most influential man of his known world is reduced to sitting on an ash heap, scraping his scabs with fragments of a broken pot.

About that time, company showed up.

The Bible names three friends who came to "sympathize with him and comfort him."[20] As it turned out, Job would have been better off if these guys had just stayed home.

These three counselors apparently traveled a great distance, and when they arrived at Job's residence and caught sight of their old friend huddled out back on top of an ash heap, they were shocked right down to their sandals.

When they saw Job from a distance, they scarcely recognized him. Wailing loudly, they tore their robes and threw dust into the air over their heads to demonstrate their grief. Then they sat on the ground with him for seven days and nights. And no one said a word, for they saw that his suffering was too great for words. (Job 2:12-13, NLT)

Believe it or not, that was the perfect thing to do. What Job needed right then was just someone to be with him. These friends started out with the right idea when "no one said a word."

We need to learn from this example. When you spend time with someone who is suffering or grieving, don't feel that you need to necessarily say something "wise and profound," or try to explain the situation. To begin with, you don't know enough to explain anything, because that knowledge lies with God alone. And besides that, explanations have never healed a broken heart.

Sometimes the best thing to do is just be there.

And say absolutely nothing.

When our Lord was facing His imminent arrest and crucifixion, He was waiting with His disciples in the Garden of Gethsemane. To His three closest companions, Peter, James, and John, He said, "My soul is crushed with grief to the point of death." And then He said to them, "I want you to just stay with Me.

Stay with Me and watch with Me."[21]

Watch with Me.

He didn't ask for a sermon, He didn't want an explanation, and He wasn't looking for someone to step in and fix His situation. In His humanity and in His sorrow that night, He just wanted a few friends around, that's all. And they were with Him...at least in body. Unfortunately, they couldn't keep their eyes open and slept right through His great anguish and struggle.

When someone is hurting, you just need to go to them. One of the best things you can say is, "I don't know what to say." Then take your own advice and don't say anything! If you do say something, keep it simple.

"I love you."

"I'm here for you."

"I'm praying for you."

As a pastor, I frequently have to walk right into the middle of human suffering. And when I get that call that someone's child or spouse has died, or someone has found out they have cancer, it's very hard to deal with. Even pastors don't know what to say at times.

But most of the time, my words aren't all that important anyway. I have found that by simply showing up—showing love, and a readiness to listen—I've been able to bring comfort to these grieving ones. Sometimes, you ask the individual what he or she is facing, and then you just close your mouth and listen with both ears.

A number of years ago, a man I know fairly well lost his daughter in a car accident. A month had passed since the accident, and I hadn't seen him since it happened. I happened to find myself in a room with him and a group of other guys, and though everyone knew about his daughter, they all tiptoed around the subject. No one said a thing to him or even approached him. It's almost as though he was being punished for suffering.

Why did these men hold back? They may have thought, *"Well, if I say anything it might be real uncomfortable. He might even cry."* So no one was willing to even broach the subject.

I remembering thinking to myself, *"Something needs to be said."*

So I took him aside, and just bumbled out the words, "I am so sorry about what happened to your daughter."

He looked me in the eyes and said, "Thank you for mentioning it," and began to open up. He just wanted someone to talk to! And sure he teared up, but that's part of the mourning process. When you have lost someone—a spouse, a parent, or a child—you don't want their passing to be simply swept under the rug. You don't want that loved one to be forgotten.

Many times, simply because they don't want to be uncomfortable, be rejected, or look silly, people keep their distance from those who grieve. Or if they do spend time with that individual, they will steer clear of mentioning the one who died.

That's no comfort at all.

The grieving spouse or parent wants that loved one to be remembered. Sometimes you can simply say something like, "I miss John. I wish he was here with us right now. But thank God we will see him again in heaven."

You say, "Oh, I don't want to say that. They might cry."

Yes, they might. And a good cry might do them some good, too, as they are still dealing with the loss and mourning.

Many times we will say things that don't help at all, but actually deepen the sorrowing person's pain.

"I know how you feel...."

No you don't! So why say it?

"There's a reason for everything."

That may be true, but neither of you have any idea what that might be.

"Well, no one ever said life was fair."

What a rotten thing to say to someone in crisis!

"What doesn't kill us makes us stronger."

No what idiot came up with that little gem?

"Well cheer up. There's always someone worse off."

Believe it or not, I've heard that one many times. It has zero—no, negative—comfort value, and sounds about as callous as you can get.

"When life gives you lemons make lemonade."

Say that and your friend will be seriously thinking about hurting you.

"Don't worry. Be happy."

Now they are thinking of killing you.

"Have a nice day."

Now they will kill you for sure.

We have to give people—even fellow believers—time and room to grieve their loss. We will say, "She's with the Lord now. She's happier than she's ever been. Don't cry."

What do you mean, "Don't cry"?

That's holding people to a higher standard than even the Lord does! The Bible says there is a time to laugh and a time to mourn. Even Jesus wept at the tomb of His dear friend, Lazarus. In the book of Acts, after Stephen was stoned to death by a violent mob, we read that devout men wept over him. It's okay to weep when you lose someone. But, as the book of 1 Thessalonians says, we do not "grieve like the rest of men, who have no hope."[22] We *do* have hope. We have strong, unquenchable hope that we will be with our saved loved ones in heaven, and we will share eternity together.

Job's comforters always get a bad rap, and deservedly so, but just remember something: *At least they got it right in the beginning.* They wept with their friend, kept their mouths closed, and sat with him on the ground for *seven days* before they said anything. We think we're being a martyr if we sit with someone for seven minutes. At least initially, Job's friends did the right thing. Scripture says to "Rejoice with those who rejoice, and weep with those who weep."[23]

THREE SORRY COUNSELORS

If Hollywood had written the book of Job, it would focus in on the supernatural connection, zero in on gory scenes of lightning strikes, terrorist raids, and natural disasters, then skip to the last chapter of the book. Anyone watching the movie would say, "What a great story. A man suffers huge losses, God blesses him, and restores much of what he lost in the end."

The moviemakers would definitely skip all those long chapters filled with lame counsel from three loser friends. Yes, they had been mercifully silent for awhile, but then they more than for made up for it later. And the conversation went on and on.

Let's focus in for a moment on the bill of goods each of these men tried to sell their grieving friend, Job.

Eliphaz

First there was Eliphaz, who saw God as inflexible and hard, always giving us just what we deserve.

> "Stop and think! Does the innocent person perish? When has the upright person been destroyed? My experience shows that those who plant trouble and cultivate evil will harvest the same. They perish by a breath from God. They vanish in a blast of his anger." (Job 4:7-8, NLT)

Basically he is saying, "Job, I think you're just reaping what you've sown. You must have done some really bad things, and that's why this calamity has come upon you."

Now of course there is truth to the principle of reaping and sowing. There *is* cause and effect, and we've all seen the results of it. We see people who commit their lives to the Lord, begin to make wise decisions, and their lives begin to turn for the better. And we also see those who make sinful, destructive choices, and observe with sorrow how they reap the bitter consequences of those sins.

But it doesn't always work that way.

There are those inexplicable situations that will go against all conventional wisdom when the godly person—the man or woman who has mostly made right choices throughout life—has to undergo terrible suffering.

That's was Job's case.

Bildad

Bildad basically said "ditto" to Eliphaz's stern lecture. He too thought that bad things only happen to bad people, and that Job's sorrows were the result of his own misdeeds.

"But look!" he said to Job. "God will not reject a person of integrity, nor will he make evildoers prosper."[24]

In other words, "Job, if you were truly a man of integrity this would not have happened." The irony of this is that God Himself had declared Job a man of integrity. We need to be very, very careful about passing judgment on a person who is loved and treasured by God.

Zophar

Zophar was a real piece of work, even more blunt and critical than his two buddies. He coldheartedly suggested to Job that he was probably so sinful he deserved even *worse* from the hand of the Lord!

Here is Job, mourning the loss of all he has, covered from head to toe with loathsome boils, and Zophar declares, "Listen! God is doubtless punishing you far less than you deserve!"[25]

And then to add insult to injury, Zophar comes up with this little gem of consolation:

"Though the godless man's pride [speaking of Job] reaches to the heavens and though his head touches the clouds, yet he will perish forever, thrown away like his own dung. Those who knew him will ask, 'Where is he?' He will fade like a dream and not be found."

Wow. Thanks a lot, Zo. That's comforting.

Can you imagine Hallmark hiring these guys—Eliphaz, Bildad, and Zophar—to write sympathy cards?

Here is what Eliphaz's card would look like. On the cover it would say, "Sorry you are sick." Then you would open it up and it would read, "*You got what you deserved.*"

Bildad's card would say on the outside, "Hoping you get well soon." Then you would open up the card and it say, "*But if you were really godly this would have never happened.*"

But I think Zophar's card would have been the most brutal. I think on the cover it would have said, "I hope you get worse." Then you would open it up and read, "*You will die, no one will remember you, and you will be thrown away like garbage.*"

If Job's wife sent hubby a card, the cover would read: "Why do you still trust God?" Then you open it up and it says, "*Why don't you curse Him and die?*" And it's signed, "Love, your wife."

Not much comfort there.

THE QUESTION "WHY?"

Much of the book of Job is dedicated to asking the question, "Why?"

Toward the end of the book, beginning in chapter 38, God finally responds to His suffering servant. It's evident the Lord was getting tired of all the lame explanations offered by Job's unhelpful friends—and of Job's own complaints and questions.

"Who is this that questions my wisdom with such ignorant words? Brace yourself, because I have some questions for you, and you must answer them." (Job 38:2-3, NLT)

As God goes on speaking, He says in effect, "Excuse Me, but I guess I missed you when I was busy creating the universe. Were you there? I didn't notice you there." In this ironic sort of way, the Lord puts Job in his place and declares His own glory. At the bottom line, I think the book ends up by saying that Job really didn't need an explanation of life and all its perplexities.

What he needed was an encounter with God.

What he needed was a fresh revelation of the Lord.

Why? *Because when we see God for who He is, we will see our problems for what they are.* If we have a small God, we have big problems. But if we have a big God we have small problems (no matter how huge and overwhelming they may seem to us).

All of this being said, you and I still see fellow Christians suffering—or maybe we're going through a deep valley of our own—and we can't help wondering why God allows this kind of pain and heartache in the life of a believer.

Why God Allows Christians To Suffer

Never, never forget that God is in control of all the circumstances that surround a believer's life.

God is in control of your life, and involved in all the details.

Your suffering has not escaped His notice. Your situation has not somehow been buried in His in-box. He is intimately aware of everything going on in your world, and no detail is too small to escape His attention. The word "oops" is not in God's vocabulary. And as we can so clearly see from this book of Job, the devil can do nothing in the life of the believer without the express permission of God.

Okay, you say, but if He's in control, why does He allow these hurtful things to happen to me and to people I love?

Here are some of the reasons why.

#1: Suffering Makes Us Strong

The apostle James tells us,

When all kinds of trials and temptations crowd into your lives my brothers, don't resent them as intruders, but welcome them as friends! Realize that they come to test your faith and to produce in you the quality of endurance. But let the process go on until that endurance is fully developed, and you will find you have become men of mature character with the right sort of independence. (James 1:2-4, PHILLIPS)

God allows hardship in our life so that our beliefs—those handholds of faith in a troubled world—will became more and more real to us, and less and less theory. We can start living out our faith-life in the real world.

I'm reminded of all the people you see on the road these days driving those gleaming new SUVs. (We have one, too, by the way.) Most of these fancy rigs have 4x4 capabilities. In other words, you could drive them through the mud or power up some rocky track on a mountainside.

But how many people really do that? I've certainly never taken my SUV out "four-wheeling."

Some guys, of course, take it a notch above that, putting lifts in their rigs and buying those big gnarly tires, with huge lights mounted on the top. And what do they do with these powerful vehicles? They brag to their buddies, and say, "Yeah, just look at this thing. Look at what it can do. I could drive this baby up the side of a building."

"Well," someone might ask, "do you want to go out in the dirt?"

"Are you kidding? Do you know how much I paid for this thing? There is no way! In fact, I was just on the way to the car wash."

So they never want to actually use that vehicle for its intended purpose— what it was actually designed to do.

We can be that way with our beliefs. We talk about believing this and be- lieving that, and the truths we hold dear. But I can hear God saying to us, "You know, you have a lot of really great beliefs. You talk about them all the time. I think it's time you started putting some of them into practice. You talk about how you trust Me. You talk about how you believe I can provide for your every need. Okay. Let Me put you in a situation where you have no other resources and really have to trust Me for that provision."

You see, God can allow these hardships and trials and shortfalls in our lives so that we will exercise our sometimes-flabby faith muscles, and step out on trust alone. We need to transfer our faith from the realm of theory to in-the-trenches reality.

#2: Suffering Can Bring GOD Glory

Any fool can be happy and peaceful when the sun shines down from a blue and cloudless sky. But when those qualities shine out from the midst of a dark and destructive storm, that's another matter entirely.

That, in essence, was the challenge Satan laid before God. "Job follows You because You have blessed him in every way, but if those things were taken away, it would be a different story. He would curse You."

In order to show the falsehood of Satan's argument—and to strengthen Job's faith at the same time—God allowed these multiple tragedies to crash into Job's life.

The result? Job not only refused to curse God, he actually blessed Him.

What a rebuke to the enemy! What a witness to the world.

It is a powerful testimony when a believer can praise God while suffering. Remember the story of Paul and Silas, arrested for preaching the gospel in the city of Philippi? The Bible tells us that the jailer had them stripped and flogged—a punishment so severe some people didn't even survive it. Then they were put in a dungeon, where their feet were fastened in stocks—which meant that their legs would have been as spread as far apart as humanly possible, causing excruciating pain.

So there they were in this hellhole, this dungeon...their backs ripped open, their feet in stocks. And they hadn't done a thing to merit such terrible punishment! How did they respond? Here's what the Bible says:

> But at midnight Paul and Silas were praying and singing hymns to God, and the prisoners were listening to them. (Acts 16:25)

That word "listened" could be translated *listened with great interest.* Why? Because they had never heard anybody sing praises to God in such a place. And that's about the time the Lord sent an earthquake, "At once the prison doors flew open, and everybody's chains came loose. The jailer woke up, and when he saw the prison doors open, he drew his sword and was about to kill himself because he thought the prisoners had escaped. But Paul shouted, 'Don't harm yourself! We are all here!'"[26]

The Philippian jailer responded by saying, "Sirs, what must I do to be saved?" In effect he was saying, "I've been watching you guys. I've seen how you have taken such terrible punishment without cursing. I've seen how you can worship in the worst circumstances, and how you could have escaped but didn't. All I can say is, whatever you have, I want it."

Your circumstances may not be as dire as those of Paul and Silas. But never doubt it, people are watching you. If you're in the midst of a hardship or a difficulty, they're watching to see how you hold up, if you will really practice what you preach, and if you will live out what you proclaim. The way you handle suffering in your life can bring great glory to God.

Paul the apostle also suffered from an unnamed "thorn in the flesh." No one really knows what it was, but he spoke of it in his letter to the Corinthian church, and said that he had asked the Lord on three separate occasions to remove it.

But God said no.

Even though God had done miracles through Paul bringing healing to others, He chose not to bring that healing in the life of loyal His servant in this particular situation.

When Paul in essence asked, "Lord, why?" God gave him this answer: "My gracious favor is all you need. My power works best in your weakness."[27]

Was Paul discouraged by this answer, by God's refusal of his request? It sure doesn't sound like it! He goes on to say, "So now I am glad to boast about my weaknesses, so that the power of Christ may work through me. Since I know it is all for Christ's good, I am quite content with my weaknesses and with insults, hardships, persecutions, and calamities. For when I am weak, then I am strong."[28]

So God can be glorified through your weakness. His light and power can shine through the chips, cracks, and cracks in your life, drawing others to Himself.

WHEN GOD REMOVES SUFFERING

There is one more way God can be glorified through our suffering and hardships.

He can remove them. And sometimes, that's just what He does. He doesn't always say "no," and He doesn't always say "wait." Sometimes, He steps in immediately, bringing help, wisdom, comfort, and provision. I've seen that happen many, many times in my life and ministry.

On the other hand, He allowed His friend Lazarus to sicken and die. But then the Lord raised him from the dead—so he could eventually die again!

Poor guy. He had to die twice. How bad is that? Once is bad enough.

But the point is, the Lord sometimes will allow calamity into the life of His child, and then bring glory to Himself by removing it.

The gospel of John tells the story of Jesus and His disciples encountering a man who had been blind from birth. The disciples asked their Master, "Why was this man born blind? Was it a result of his own sins or those of his parents?"[29]

It sounds a little like a rehash of the accusations Job's counselors tossed out at him, doesn't it? "*Whose fault was this? Why is he sick? Who committed this sin?*" This is the same warped "word of faith" theology that says if you are sick, it's the result of your personal sin, because (they allege) God never wants you sick. And if you'll just 'confess it,' you will be healed. If you're not, it's because of your lack of faith.

It is Job's counselors revisited, and it is wrong counsel—because godly people can suffer, too, and still be right in the middle of God's good plans and purposes.

Jesus had a strong answer for the disciples when they asked, "Who sinned, this man or his parents, that he was born blind?"

"'It was not because of his sins or his parents' sins,' Jesus answered. 'He was born blind so the power of God could be seen in him.'"[30]

God wanted to display His power by healing this man—as He did when He raised Lazarus from the dead. But we must also recognize that there are times when God will not heal the blind. He will not raise the dead. He will not do what we ask.

And it is then that we trust Him.

It is then that we do what Job did when his whole world fell apart. He said, "Praise the name of the Lord." He didn't say, "I understand this, I understand

You." He simply said, "Lord, I trust You."

Job lived a real life in real time, and in the midst of his suffering, he couldn't read the end of his own story to see how things turned out. Yet he said, "Praise the name of the Lord."

We can ask God the "why" question anytime we want to. But I don't know if we're really going to be satisfied with His answers. If God came down to you on a shining cloud and explained His purposes to you, would it really make it any better? I don't know that it would. As far as we know, Job was never given the "why" of all the tragedies that befell him. But He was given an incredible revelation of God's wisdom and power.

There was a time when Jesus asked, "God, why?" It was when He was in great agony, dying on the cross for your sins and my sins, and He cried out, "My God, My God, why have You forsaken Me?"

He did ask why. But notice that He prefaced it with, "My God, My God." It wasn't an accusation against the Father. Jesus was merely stating the reality of what was taking place in those awful hours, as all of the sin of the world was being placed upon Him who had known no sin. And as the Father turned His holy face away, the Son cried out, "Why have You forsaken Me?"

The fact is, Jesus was forsaken that I might be forgiven. But even in His great cry of grief and loneliness over His separation from the Father, as He bore the sins of the world for all time, Jesus still said, "*My* God, *My* God." There was complete trust in the Lord.

At this point you might be saying, "Well, I have a lot of questions for God. When I get to heaven I'm going to ask Him some things. In fact, I've got a list."

You just keep that list with you. Take it with you everywhere you go, and then if you die unexpectedly, you'll have it handy to pull out and ask God when you stand before Him.

I can just see you now. . . .

"*Lord, it's good to be here. Wow, look at that sea of glass and the sapphire throne. Look at all those angels. Very impressive. But listen. . .I've got this little list of questions I've been carrying around. It's here somewhere. Where did I put that—in my pocket? Where did my pockets go?*"

Somehow, I don't think that's the way it will be. I suggest to you that when you arrive in heaven, when you see your Creator, your God, your Savior in all His blazing glory, you'll forget all about your little list of questions. One commentator wrote, "I had a million questions to ask God, but when I met Him, they all fled my mind and it didn't seem to matter."

Our perplexities, distressing as they may be, will one day be swept away.

Now we see things imperfectly as in a poor mirror, but then we will see everything with perfect clarity. All that I know now is partial and incomplete, but then I will know everything completely, just as God knows me now. (1 Corinthians 13:12, NLT)

Our sorrows and heartaches, heavy as they weigh on our souls, will one day be forgotten like a bad dream.

For the Lamb who stands in front of the throne will be their Shepherd. He will lead them to the springs of life-giving water. And God will wipe away all their tears. (Revelation 7:17, NLT)

SUFFERING AS PREPARATION

Suffering can also be used by God to prepare us for a special task out ahead of us. The Bible doesn't tell us what Job's task might have been after God completely restored him, but it certainly tells us what happened with Joseph, in the book of Genesis.

Through unbelievable adversity as a young man, God prepared him for a task beyond his imagination. You remember his story. Abandoned and betrayed by his brothers, and sold into slavery, he was eventually elevated to a position of great power. As the Prime Minister of Egypt, the second most influential man in the world, he was given charge of Egypt's food stores during a worldwide famine.

Then the day came when ten of his brothers, who thought Joseph was long dead, came down to Egypt from Canaan to get food for their starving families. The moment Joseph saw and recognized them, he could have had them summarily executed on the spot.

Instead, he forgave them, and made this amazing statement:

But as for you, you meant evil against me; but God meant it for good, in order to bring it about as it is this day, to save many people alive. (Genesis 50:20)

Earlier, he had told them: "But don't be angry with yourselves that you did this to me, for God did it. He sent me here ahead of you to preserve your lives."[31]

Did you catch that? Joseph didn't just say "God allowed it," though you could describe it that way, too. But he actually said, "God *did* it." Why? Joseph said, "To save many people alive."

God delivered Joseph from his brothers' jealousy, from a false accusation by his master's wife, and then from the dungeon, so he could interpret the dream of the Pharaoh and make provision for the future. And many, many people—across that ancient world—lived as a result. The suffering he went through prepared him for the job that God had for him to do.

Maybe the Lord is allowing you to go through some difficult circumstances right now to prepare you for something He wants you to do tomorrow. I realize that thought might not comfort you all that much in your present distress. You may be thinking, *"No, this suffering doesn't make any sense at all. It's meaningless. There's no point to it."*

Joseph might have thought that same thing at several points in his life journey. It's certain that Job did! But the truth is, God might very well be preparing you to touch someone else's life in a way no one else could. If someone just found out they have cancer and you are a cancer survivor, you have no idea how much encouragement and perspective you can bring to such a person, who feels as though he or she has been handed a death sentence.

Or maybe a couple you know lost a child through illness or some terrible accident, and they are walking on the ragged edge of sanity, feeling like they can't go on another minute, much less another day. If you have lost a child in the past, and God has brought you healing, you can come along and say, "We lost a child, too, and it was the hardest thing that ever happened to us. Though we still mourn that child, and though we're still dealing with it, and we miss them every single day, we want you to know that God can help you each step of the way. His grace really will be sufficient for you."

You have no idea how much comfort that can bring. *And it would be something that only you could say.* No one else could say those words with the same kind of credibility.

Recently we had a man named Brian Birdwell give his testimony at our church. Brian was in the Pentagon on September 11, 2001, when those planes crashed into the World Trade Center and the Pentagon. Many of Brian's friends were killed that day. He survived, though he was burned over much of his body and had to go through multiple, excruciating skin graft operations.

Afterwards I had lunch with Brian and, believe it or not, we had a lot of fun together. He is very witty and a great pleasure to be with. In my opinion, he is also a genuine American hero.

Before we finished our meal, I asked him if he wanted to do something with me that afternoon.

He thanked me, but then said, "Greg, I'd love to, but I can't. I have to go to a hospital."

"What's going on?" I asked him.

"Well," he said, "whenever I go speak in some location, I always find out where the local burn ward is, and I go and visit the patients."

I remember thinking how wonderful that was. Who could have a more effective ministry to burn victims than someone who had been through the agony of skin grafts and burn treatments as Brian had? Imagine being an individual burned over most of your body, and you think, "My life is over." But then a survivor comes along and says, "Look. I know how hard it is. I have been there. But I got through it! And here is what God has been doing in and through my life since I got out of the hospital. He can do the same for you!"

Paul, who had his own serious issues with suffering, as we have said, wrote: "He is the source of every mercy and the God who comforts us. He comforts us in all our troubles so that we can comfort others. When others are troubled, we will be able to give them the same comfort God has given us. You can be sure that the more we suffer for Christ, the more God will shower us with his comfort through Christ."[32]

God will give you that comfort—over and beyond what you can personally contain—so that you can share it with others.

THE REST OF THE STORY

In the final chapter of the book of Job, God restored to His righteous servant everything double. He had passed the test, leaving an unforgettable example for us in the pages of Scripture. Though he could never replace the children he had lost, God gave him more, allowing him to enjoy his children and his grandchildren.

Could it be that the hardships you find yourself facing today are preparing you for something just over the horizon—a ministry and a life beyond your imagination right now? I'll tell you this: God doesn't waste anything. Not one sorrow. Not one sigh. Not one tear.

Dr. Warren Wiersbe quotes a professor of history who said, "If Columbus had turned back no one would have blamed him. But no one would have remembered him either."

And Wiersbe concludes, "If you want to be memorable sometimes you have to be miserable."

You might say, "Honestly, I don't see how I could handle one tenth of all the things Job faced. In fact, I can't handle suffering at all."

Don't worry. God knows what you can manage. He knows what you can take. And He will parcel it out accordingly. You just need to trust Him.

God will give you what you need when you need it.

Not before, never after, but just when it is needed.

Until then, we must simply trust Him.

Corrie ten Boom, well-known author of *The Hiding Place*, was placed in a Nazi concentration camp along with her sister and her father. They were committed Christians and their "crime" had been hiding Jewish people in their home, trying to protect them from Nazi genocide against all Jews in Hitler's Reich.

Both Corrie's father and sister died, and Corrie herself went through deep suffering during that time. But she survived, and spent the rest of her life traveling around the world as a self-described "tramp for the Lord," declaring that there is no pit so deep that God is not deeper still.

When Corrie was a little girl, she was reading a story about martyrs for the Christian faith, and was trying to process what these saints of God had endured for the sake of Christ.

She said to her father, "Daddy, I am afraid that I will never be strong enough to be a martyr for Jesus Christ."

"Tell me," said that wise father, "when you take train trip to Amsterdam, when do I give you the money for the ticket? Three weeks before?"

"No Daddy," she replied. "You give me the money for the ticket just before we get on the train."

"That's right," he replied. "And so it is with God's strength. Our Father in heaven knows when you will need the strength to be a martyr for Jesus Christ. He will supply all you need just in time."

As it turned out, God never required Corrie to die as a martyr, as her father and sister did. Even so, Corrie had suffered much in her life, and God always gave her the strength she needed...just as her father had told her.

HOLD LIFE LOOSELY

Here's something that hit me pretty hard as I studied Job's life. We need to hold everything God has given us loosely. We like to say, "*My* life, *my* marriage, *my* kids, *my* career, *my* 401k"...and on it goes.

But wait.

Everything you have has come to you as a gift from God.

Job found that out, and had to declare before God and man, "The Lord gives and the Lord takes away. Blessed be the name of the Lord."

Maybe you drive your new SUV through the carwash and admire the way it sparkles and gleams after you wipe it down. Don't forget...that was given to you—it's a good gift from the Father.

Or you drive up into the driveway of your home. Don't take it for granted! God has graced you and privileged you to live there.

You get up in the morning and feel like a million bucks, or finish a game of tennis and grab a nice long shower...don't forget. Your health and strength are a gift from God.

"Oh," you say, but I'm very careful to eat only organic stuff and I have a regular exercise routine." Good for you. But remember, *God* gave you your health. God has given you your life. God has given you your wife. He has given you your husband. He had blessed you with children. He has given you everything. Hold it loosely. He may leave it in your hands for years; then again, he might take it tomorrow. That's up to Him to decide. But it all belongs to Him, and we praise Him every day for what He has given us.

The truth is, everybody suffers. Calamity comes into every life—the righteous and the unrighteous, the godly and the ungodly. The good news is that the Lord can use suffering in the lives of His sons and daughters...to strengthen us spiritually...to make us more Christ-like...to use us to minister to and comfort others...and to prepare us for future tasks that are completely off our personal charts.

But what about the unbeliever? What's his consolation? Where do the atheist and the agnostic go for comfort? What do they have to show for their pain, their tears, their bruises, and their calamities?

Not much.

It's just "hard luck"....and then you die.

But what comfort we have in Christ! What an indescribable hope! He is worthy of our complete trust and confidence, no matter what we might be enduring at the moment.

Sometimes God can use sickness, tragedy, hardship, or difficulty to get our attention. The psalmist said, "Before I was afflicted I went astray, but now I obey your word....It was good for me to be afflicted so that I might learn your decrees."[33]

Are you in a "hot place" right now? Do you find yourself in the fires of difficulty or crisis? You got bad news from the doctor. You were let go from your job. Your "significant other" dumped you. Maybe something else has happened that has rocked your world, and you don't know what to do.

You need to say, "God, help!"

He has thousands of years of experience helping, comforting, and saving those who reach up to Him in faith.

Chapter Three

SAUL: A STORY OF WASTED POTENTIAL

L ife is filled with choices—dozens, hundreds, even thousands of choices each and every day.

That's why I like my favorite burger place. It's just so simple. You can get a burger, you can get a double burger, or you can get either one with cheese. Add a soft drink and maybe some fries, and that's it. Period. End of menu. Your decision's made, and you haven't wasted a lot of time or emotional energy trying to make up your mind.

But there are other restaurants here in Southern California that make decision-making a lot more complicated. You encounter menus the size of family Bible. And then, even if you make the big decision to have chicken, you're really only getting started, because there are 25 different options for chicken alone.

Life is filled with choices, too, and mixed among many trivial decisions about burgers or chicken or which shoes you're going to wear today, there are some terribly important choices we're all going to make. These latter choices are the ones with consequences—with consequences that may stay with us the rest of our lives. Or even follow us into eternity.

The life of the man we'll be looking at in this "Greatest Story" revolved around just a few very key choices. After some initial success, he came to several major intersections in his life and—tragically took the wrong turn every time. Although he had everything it took to succeed, he squandered his resources.

His name is Saul. And this is his story.

A STUDY IN CONTRASTS

The life of Saul, the first king of Israel, is a study in contrasts. In some ways he was big, and in other ways he was very small. In some ways he was strikingly handsome, and in other ways decidedly ugly. He was both a hero and a renegade. He started his reign in victory and ended it in humiliating defeat. And somewhere along the way, he lost his character, his prestige, his power, and in the end, his very life.

His life stands as a warning to all of us that you can't play fast and loose with the commands of God and get away with it. It *will* catch up with you. Maybe not today. Maybe not even tomorrow. But sooner or later, the Scripture says your sin will find you out, unless you repent.[34]

In his book *Fascinating Stories of Forgotten Lives*, Chuck Swindoll makes this observation: "Saul's story reminds us that the impact of any one life, whether positive or negative, large or small, cannot be measured with accuracy until it has run its full course. Beware the temptation to form early opinions about certain individuals, especially those greatly gifted. Assume the best and be willing to give every benefit of the doubt. But remember that the end of life reveals more than the beginning."[35]

Saul started well, but he finished badly. In effect, he wrote his own epitaph when he said, "I have played the fool and erred exceedingly."[36]

We too are walking a path through life. And perhaps right now you find yourself at a place where the trail divides, and you have the choice of taking what you know to be the right fork, or taking a very tempting shortcut that leads away from God's desire and design for your life. Perhaps you're on the verge of entering a relationship that could either be productive and wonderful for you, or spiritually devastating. Or you're about to make a career choice that could prove to be a wise direction for years to come, or one that could prove to be your undoing.

Lean on God's wisdom—the wisdom He has promised for all who ask— and make the right choice.[37] Because if the story of Saul tells us nothing else, it tells us this: choices produce consequences and actions produce reactions.

Saul's story really begins with a fork in the road for the whole nation Israel. Up to this point in their history, Israel had been ruled by various judges. But they got tired of that, because what they wanted was a king. Why? Because the other nations had kings. So they effectively said to Samuel, "Why can't we have a king? Everybody else has a king but us."

It reminds me of spoiled little children. "Well, why can't I have it? Everybody else has it."

"We want a king," the Israelites insisted, "like everybody else. Moab has a king. Edom has a king. Ammon has a king. Why should we be any different?"

God said, "Are you very, very sure this is what you want?"

"*Yes!*"

And so He gave them what they asked for. Which reminds us, be careful of what you ask for, because you might really get it. And then you might not like what you have!

That is why I think the so-called "word of faith" teaching you encounter on Christian TV is so absurd. People are taught to go to God and demand what they want because "our words have power," and we essentially speak something into existence by claiming what we want in Jesus' name.

What absurdity that teaching is. And how terrible if it were true! If I have learned nothing else about myself, it's that I don't know what I'm doing half the time. Finite and failing man that I am, I really have no concept of the *implications* of what I'm asking for.

That's why I am so glad I can go to God and simply say, "Lord, this is what seems best to me at this point, and this is what I'm praying for...but let *Your* will be done in this, let *Your* kingdom come." In other words, "Lord, if what I'm praying is somehow outside of Your will, please overrule it, because You know best."

So Israel demanded a king "like all the other nations," and God gave them what they asked for. If King David would one day be identified as "the man after God's own heart," then Saul was the man after *man's* own heart.

Have you ever heard of the People's Choice Awards? Saul was the people's choice. Right at the first, Scripture highlights many fine qualities in Saul—things our culture values highly and were valued in his era as well. Saul was a strikingly handsome guy, literally the best looking man in all of Israel. A rock star, if you will. If *People Magazine* had been around back then, he would have been featured in a photo spread as "The Sexiest Man Alive."

Tall, charismatic, and blessed with many natural gifts, he seemed like a born leader. But as someone has said, handsome is as handsome does. Very early in his career, Saul squandered his resources and opportunities, and played the fool. And because of this, he was disqualified.

We are introduced to him in 1 Samuel chapter 9.

Kish was a rich, influential man from the tribe of Benjamin. He was the son of Abiel and grandson of Zeror, from the family of Becorath and the clan of Aphiah. His son Saul was the most handsome man in Israel—head and shoulders taller than anyone else in the land.

One day Kish's donkeys strayed away, and he told Saul, "Take a servant with you, and go look for them." So Saul took one of his servants and traveled all through the hill country of Ephraim, the land of Shalishah, the Shaalim area, and the entire land of Benjamin, but they couldn't find the donkeys anywhere. Finally, they entered the region of Zuph, and Saul said to his servant, "Let's go home. By now my father will be more worried about us than about the donkeys!" (1 Samuel 9:1-5, NLT)

Right off the bat, we learn a few of Saul's qualities.

SAUL'S QUALIFICATIONS
#1: He Had A Good Family

This was a young man who came from good stock. His father Kish was well known, wealthy, and influential. And Saul seemed to truly care about his dad.

After they'd been out for several days hunting for the donkeys, Saul said to his servant, "Man, let's get home, or Dad's going to really start worrying." From what we can see in Scripture, it would seem like Kish's household was a secure, nurturing place to grow up.

What an awesome legacy! Particularly in these troubled times.

If you have come from a Christian family where your mom and dad stayed together, that is a wonderful heritage you should thank the Lord for every day of your life.

#2: He Was Extremely Good Looking

The text tells us that Saul "was the most handsome man in Israel."[38] That's so important to people. I've never heard of *People Magazine* dedicating an issue to the most ordinary people in America. Who would buy it? Nor have I seen an issue highlighting "The World's Ugliest People." (Come to think of it, that might be an interesting article. I'd probably buy it and look through it…just to make sure I wasn't in there.)

There's no denying it, our culture puts a very high premium on physical beauty. The ABC news program 20/20 talked about this very thing. Host John Stossel noted that it's almost a given that attractive people are favored and chosen over those who are less attractive. Apparently, a certain music college auditioning hopeful musicians for possible scholarships had the artists perform from behind a curtain, so the judges wouldn't be influenced by the physical attractiveness (or lack thereof) of the candidates.

There's really no denying it, we are influenced by an individual's physical appearance—and it was no different in Saul's day. When the people saw Saul, they said, "Wow, what a physical specimen. What a great looking guy."

If you happened to be on the planet during the John Kennedy-Richard Nixon debates of the 1960 presidential race, you might remember the contrast between the two candidates. Kennedy was regarded as a handsome man, and those who watched the debates on television thought he had won the contest. But those who heard the debates on radio, responding only to the voices and to the content of their words, gave the nod to Nixon.

That may be the way our world rates people, but it's not the way God rates people. Isn't that good news?

Later on in the story, when God sent Samuel out to find a replacement king for Saul, who had become unfaithful, He actually had to remind His prophet not to be swayed by physical appearance:

> When they arrived, Samuel took one look at Eliab and thought, "Surely this is the LORD's anointed!" But the LORD said to Samuel, "Don't judge by his appearance or height, for I have rejected him. The LORD doesn't make decisions the way you do! People judge by outward appearance, but the LORD looks at a person's thoughts and intentions." (1 Samuel 16:6-7, NLT)

Or as another translation puts it: "Man looks at the outward appearance, but the LORD looks at the heart."[39]

#3: He Set Out To Seek GOD's Help

Still looking up and down the country for missing donkeys, Saul became concerned that he and the family servant had been gone so long that Kish would begin to worry. And that's when this sensible family servant had an inspiration.

But the servant said, "I've just thought of something! There is a man of God who lives here in this town. He is held in high honor by all the people because everything he says comes true. Let's go find him. Perhaps he can tell us which way to go."

…"All right," Saul agreed, "let's try it!" So they started into the town where [Samuel] the man of God was. (1 Samuel 9:6, 10, NLT)

It was a wise thing to do. Our natural tendency when we get lost or confused is to panic, run faster, or start moving in circles. But the servant in this story had his head screwed on right. He said, "Let's go get some counsel from the man of God. God knows which way we should turn, even if we don't." And Saul had enough humility and presence of mind to say, "You're right. Let's do that. Let's go." (Think of it. A man willing to stop and ask directions!)

When Saul approached Samuel, the prophet had already had advance word from God of the young man's doings. And the Lord specifically told Samuel: "About this time tomorrow I will send you a man from the land of Benjamin. Anoint him to be the leader of my people, Israel."[40]

Then, when Samuel caught sight of him, the Lord said, "That's the man I told you about! He will rule my people."[41]

So Samuel said, if I may paraphrase, "You boys need to spend a little time with me. Let's talk. And oh, by the way, you can stop worrying about your donkeys, because they've been found. We have bigger fish to fry." And then he anointed the tall young man from the tribe of Benjamin king over Israel.

Not surprisingly, Saul didn't feel adequate for the task. He protested: "But I'm only from Benjamin, the smallest tribe in Israel, and my family is the least important of all the families of that tribe! Why are you talking like this to me?"[42]

Nevertheless, the Bible tells us that "God changed Saul's heart" and that "the Spirit of God came upon him in power."[43]

Everything was going Saul's way. So far so good.

But none of us escape the inevitable tests of life…and Saul was no exception.

THE FIRST TEST

The first test for the freshly anointed king came before he'd even had time to print up new business cards.

Right at the beginning, just after the anointing, it wasn't at all obvious to Saul what he was supposed to do next.

What do *you* do when you don't know what to do next?

Most of us just keep doing what we were doing before, and that's what Saul did. He went back home, took the plow out of the shed, yoked up the family oxen, and began plowing his father's field. What was coming next? He had no idea. This was a time to just keep on keeping on and wait on the Lord for the next thing.

When you don't know the will of God for your life, go back to the last thing the Lord showed you, and stay faithful to that task. Be faithful in the little things, and the Lord will provide those new opportunities for you when the time is right.

As I look back on my life, it's interesting to me that most of the major opportunities that have come my way in serving the Lord have never been a result of my own attempts or efforts at self-marketing. Instead, they have virtually been dropped in my lap, and I simply sought to respond to them as best I knew how.

That's what Saul was doing. Just waiting. You can almost hear him thinking, "Okay, so I'm king now. Sounds like a big deal, but what does it really mean? What am I supposed to do? I have no idea. But in the meantime, here's a field that needs plowing."

But even as Saul walked behind those oxen in the newly turned soil, a drama was already unfolding in his country that would soon sweep him up into his destiny—and launch his reign as king.

> About a month later, King Nahash of Ammon led his army against the Israelite city of Jabesh-gilead. But the citizens of Jabesh asked for peace. "Make a treaty with us, and we will be your servants," they pleaded.
>
> "All right," Nahash said, "but only on one condition. I will gouge out the right eye of every one of you as a disgrace to all Israel!"
>
> "Give us seven days to send messengers throughout Israel!" replied the leaders of Jabesh. "If none of our relatives will come to save us, we will agree to your terms."
>
> When the messengers came to Gibeah, Saul's hometown, and told the people about their plight, everyone broke into tears.
> (1 Samuel 11:1-4, NLT)

When Saul got the news out in the field, the Bible once again tells us that "the Spirit of God came on him in power,"[44] and he knew what he had to do.

I like this part of the story. Saul had been anointed king, but it hadn't gone to his head (yet). Instead, he was just going on with life until God showed him clearly what was supposed to happen next. And when God did just that, Saul dropped everything and was ready to move.

What a great recipe for life: keep your integrity in the small things, wait on the Lord, and be ready to move or to act when the Holy Spirit gives you a clear green light.

In short order, Saul raised a national army, utterly smashed Nahash and the Ammonites, and set the besieged Israelite town free. And in the process, he established himself as legitimate king over the nation.

When events finally began to move, they moved *fast*.

He had passed the first test, and he had done it by simply waiting on the

Lord, and by being obedient to the Lord's call. After this great victory, the prophet Samuel reaffirmed Saul as king of Israel in front of all the people.

> "Now here is the king you have chosen, the one you asked for; see, the LORD has set a king over you. If you fear the LORD and serve and obey him and do not rebel against his commands, and if both you and the king who reigns over you follow the LORD your God—good! But if you do not obey the LORD, and if you rebel against his commands, his hand will be against you, as it was against your fathers." (1 Samuel 12:13-15, NIV)

It's as clear as clear.

God says, "I've told you over and over: Live by My Word, do what I say and your life will be blessed. Live apart from My Word, disregard or disobey it, and you will face the consequences."

There's really nothing complicated about walking with God and finding success and joy in the Christian life. Obedience—even when it seems difficult—brings blessing. Disobedience—even when it seems "easy and natural"—quickly dissolves God's blessing, and brings trouble and heartache in its wake.

As a pastor, I see so many people whose marriages are in trouble—teetering on the brink of disaster. When people come to counsel with me, it's usually a last resort, with their marriage already in meltdown.

I will usually begin a marriage counseling appointment with a few basic questions. I will say, "Now, are both of you Christians?"

"Oh yes, we love the Lord. We're both Christians."

"So you're telling me that Jesus Christ is your Savior and Lord?"

"Oh yes. Absolutely."

"And you both believe that the Bible is the Word of God?"

"Yes, yes. We believe the Bible. The Bible is the Word of God."

"And you're willing to submit to what the Bible says, even if you don't like what it says?"

That usually elicits a pause. They're not sure what I'm up to at that point. "Well..." they will say, "what do you *mean* by that?"

"I mean just what I said. Are you going to do what the Bible says even if it's difficult?"

"Well...uh...oh...yeah."

They hesitate because they know I'm about to talk to them about what the Bible really says about marriage. In the process, I'll probably find out whether or not the husband is loving his wife as Christ loves the church...and I will learn whether or not the wife is submitting to her husband, as unto the Lord. And I will ask them point blank if they are submitting to one another, in the fear of God. All of these concepts come straight out of Ephesians 5, and get right down to the nitty-gritty of the marriage relationship.

Do you know what happens? Far too often in these counseling sessions the couple will say, "Yes, we understand what you're saying. But we're the exception to that."

No. You aren't.

God has said, "If you will live in this way, and follow the pattern and template for success that I have placed before you in My Word, I will be with you in your marriage, and bring you great joy. But if you don't follow My path and My direction, your marriage will be damaged and broken, and you'll never know the happiness you might have experienced."

Do it God's way!

That's what Samuel is saying. "Here it is, guys. If you will fear and follow the Lord, if your king will fear and follow the Lord, everything will turn out great."

But that's not what happened. One act of blatant disobedience set the new king off on a wrong track…taking the nation with him.

THE SECOND TEST

Sadly, it didn't take Saul very long to self-destruct. And over a period of years, the young man who started out with sky's-the-limit potential would waste it all, becoming a paranoid tyrant and ultimately committing suicide on the battlefield.

It all began, interestingly enough, with a tendency we all wrestle with every day: impatience.

The Philistines, perennial enemies of Israel, had mounted an attack to crush the Israelites before they could ever get established as a kingdom. It was a moment of intense pressure and anxiety for the new king, as you might imagine. And in that moment of national and personal crisis, he faced his second great test.

The word of the Lord through Samuel couldn't have been more clear:

> "You shall go down before me to Gilgal; and surely I will come down to you to offer burnt offerings and make sacrifices of peace offerings. *Seven days you shall wait, till I come to you and show you what you should do.*" (1 Samuel 10:8)

The instructions were straightforward, leaving no room for misinterpretation. One, go to Gilgal. Two, wait for me seven days.

In the meantime, however…the Philistines massed for an attack and Saul's army melted away in fear. The new king was in a fever of anxiety. Where was Samuel? Why didn't he come? And anyway, why did he have to wait?

If Saul had only known it, his kingdom and destiny hinged on that brief moment at Gilgal. What great doors turn on such small hinges! If only Saul had held strong, waited on the Lord, and kept his head—even though everything seemed to be falling apart—who knows how the history of Israel might have read? On the other hand, if he caved to anxiety, fear, and impatience, he would lose God's blessing and God's best for the rest of his life.

After waiting for seven days with still no sign of Samuel on the horizon, Saul began talking to himself, thinking, "What do I need a prophet for? Aren't I the king? I can do this. I've watched these guys do these offerings. What's so hard about it? I'll just do it myself."

And right after he finished taking matters into his own hands, and offering that sacrifice, Samuel walked up and said, "*What are you doing?*"

If Saul would have waited one more hour...maybe even ten more minutes... everything would have been different.

> Saul answered, "When I saw I was losing my army from under me, and that you hadn't come when you said you would, and that the Philistines were poised at Micmash, I said, 'The Philistines are about to come down on me in Gilgal, and I haven't yet come before God asking for his help.' So I took things into my own hands, and sacrificed the burnt offering."

> "That was a fool thing to do," Samuel said to Saul. "If you had kept the appointment that your God commanded, by now God would have set a firm and lasting foundation under your kingly rule over Israel. As it is, your kingly rule is already falling to pieces. God is out looking for your replacement right now. This time he'll do the choosing. When he finds him, he'll appoint him leader of his people. And all because you didn't keep your appointment with God!" (1 Samuel 13:11-14, THE MESSAGE)

At first blush, this judgment seems a bit extreme on God's part. But we have to remember that while we look on actions, God looks on the heart *and* actions. God could see that Saul's heart had already turned away (as evidenced by what followed in the days to come). Saul's sin may seem relatively insignificant to us, but who are we to say something is small if it's a big deal to God?

Little things have a way of becoming big things. Furry little puppies become big hungry dogs. Cute little kittens turn into big ugly cats! And little sins that we somehow rationalize or justify may come back to wreak havoc in our lives later on.

It's not for you or me to say, "Well, I'll obey God in the big things, but I can keep these little sins around, because they really don't hurt anybody and it's not a big deal."

That's not true. In matters large or small, disobedience is *always* a big deal.

Jesus said, "You are My friends if you do whatever I command you."[45] He did *not* say, "You are my friends if you do whatever you personally agree with." Or, "You are My friends if you do whatever you find convenient."

No, the word "friend" is inseparably linked to the word "commands." So if

God says, "Don't do it," He means, *"Don't do it."* And He lays down such commands for very good reasons.

Saul blatantly disobeyed the Lord in this incident, revealing a pattern that was already developing as his heart was turning against God.

Recently I read about a man who wants to hold the world record of kissing venomous snakes. The present world record is apparently held by an American who kissed a poisonous snake 30 times. (I would be surprised if he was still with us.) So a man from Malaysia wants to break that record, kissing a venomous snake most often in a set amount of time.

They should call this the moron award! What could be more ridiculous than that? Talk about the kiss of death!

But that's a pretty good picture of how people deal with sin in their lives. They don't really think it will hurt them, or that it's a "big deal." They will say, "I'll just give it a little peck on the cheek. Just a little good night kiss. I can handle this." But the next thing you know, that harmless little thing bites back. And it is a lethal bite.

Predictably, life went from bad to worse for the unhappy King Saul.

The Third Test

In 1 Samuel 15, Saul had another chance to obey the Lord as king over Israel. Disobedience in the second test would irreparably damage his reign as king; disobedience in this third test would destroy his reign completely.

> One day Samuel said to Saul, "I anointed you king of Israel because the LORD told me to. Now listen to this message from the LORD! This is what the LORD Almighty says: 'I have decided to settle accounts with the nation of Amalek for opposing Israel when they came from Egypt. Now go and completely destroy the entire Amalekite nation—men, women, children, babies, cattle, sheep, camels, and donkeys.'"
>
> So Saul mobilized his army at Telaim. There were 200,000 troops in addition to 10,000 men from Judah. Then Saul went to the city of Amalek and lay in wait in the valley. Saul sent this message to the Kenites: "Move away from where the Amalekites live or else you will die with them. For you were kind to the people of Israel when they came up from Egypt." So the Kenites packed up and left.
>
> Then Saul slaughtered the Amalekites from Havilah all the way to Shur, east of Egypt. He captured Agag, the Amalekite king, but completely destroyed everyone else. Saul and his men spared Agag's life and kept the best of the sheep and cattle, the fat calves and lambs—everything, in fact, that appealed to them. They destroyed only what was worthless or of poor quality. (1 Samuel 15:1-9, NLT)

I can imagine Samuel saying to Saul afterwards, "What part of the word 'destroy' don't you understand?"

Instead of obeying the Lord's full instructions, Saul and the army partially obeyed the Lord, defeating the Amalekites in battle, but capturing the enemy king alive and keeping the best of the spoils for themselves. Even when Samuel showed up and confronted him with the disobedience, Saul wouldn't come clean. He lied to Samuel, saying, "Oh, I actually *planned* on giving it all back to God. I'm going to use these animals for burnt offerings to the LORD!"

Samuel's words to Saul, filled with anger and grief, are classic:

> But Samuel replied, "What is more pleasing to the LORD: your burnt offerings and sacrifices or your obedience to his voice? Obedience is far better than sacrifice. Listening to him is much better than offering the fat of rams. Rebellion is as bad as the sin of witchcraft, and stubbornness is as bad as worshiping idols. So because you have rejected the word of the LORD, he has rejected you from being king." (1 Samuel 15:22-23, NLT)

Did you know that God is more interested in our actions than our words? It's not rocket science! What God desires from us is *obedience*. He just wants us to do what He tells us to do.

Sometimes we find ourselves living outside of His will, doing some things that we know aren't pleasing to Him. But we'll reason with ourselves and say, "I'll put a little more in the offering this week." Or, "I'll attend that mid-week study." Or, "I'm going to sing a little louder during worship."

God would say to us, "I really don't want to hear your songs right now. I'm really not concerned about extra money in the offering plate. What I want from you right now is your obedience, because to obey is better than sacrifice."

In the Old Testament book of Amos, God says these words:

> "I hate all your show and pretense—the hypocrisy of your religious festivals and solemn assemblies. I will not accept your burnt offerings and grain offerings. I won't even notice all your choice peace offerings. Away with your hymns of praise! They are only noise to my ears. I will not listen to your music, no matter how lovely it is. Instead, I want to see a mighty flood of justice, a river of righteous living that will never run dry." (Amos 5:21-24, NLT)

Strong words! And what's the bottom line? God wants our walk to match our talk.

David came on the scene soon after this, "the man after God's own heart." After first welcoming this eager, godly young warrior, Saul's admiration quickly degenerated into paranoia and jealousy. He attempted to murder David on more than one occasion, and wasted countless man hours by leading Israel's army in a fruitless attempt to track the young man down and destroy him.

After the prophet Samuel's death, Saul became so desperate that he even consulted a witch. Despondent, desperate, and deceived, the once-promising king died a pathetic death on the battlefield, as he took his own life.

As I mentioned earlier, if Saul were to write his own epitaph, it would have been, "I have played the fool and erred exceedingly."[46]

What would you have written on your tombstone if you had a say so? On Boot Hill in Tombstone, Arizona, the words on one old gravestone read:

> Here lies Lester Moore
> Four slugs
> From a forty-four.
> No Les
> No More

In the cemetery in Silver Lake, Wisconsin, you encounter this epitaph for John Starkweather. Written on his tombstone are these words. "Here is where friend Starkweather lies. Nobody laughs. Nobody cries. Where he goes, how he fares, nobody knows. Nobody cares."

That's pretty sad.

On the tombstone of Henry Edsel Smith it says, "Born 1913. Died 1942. Looked up the elevator shaft to see if the car was on the way down. It was."

In a Georgia cemetery, someone noted these words on a tombstone: "I told you I was sick."

What will your epitaph be? What will you be remembered for? God keep us from playing the fool! How do you play the fool?

YOU PLAY THE FOOL...

#1: ...When You Disobey GOD Even In The Smallest Matters

Spiritual decline is gradual. Saul may have experienced total failure, but it wasn't immediate. Though he began his reign over Israel with humility, he allowed pride to gain a foothold in his heart, and with that pride came envy. Taking things into his own hands, he rationalized disobeying the Lord's clear commands, "adapting" them to suit his own convenience and desires.

The fact is, it's not for us to pick and choose what we like or don't like about God's will for our lives. It is for us to do what the Bible teaches.

You play the fool...

#2: ...When You Attempt To Justify The Wrong You Have Done

More than once Saul blamed others for what he himself had done, refusing to own up to his own sin. Like so many modern politicians, he was more concerned about public opinion than he was about the opinion of God.

You play the fool...

#3: ...When You Forget That How You Finish Is More Important Than How You Start

I've never heard a prospective bride or groom announce, "By the way, everyone, this marriage isn't going to last, so save your money and don't buy us a present." Every sane person gets married with a hope for success...a longing for happiness. When you stand before the couples at wedding after wedding as I have, you can see that hope and longing written on their faces. They want to begin well. But what really counts is *finishing* well—and making sure that you live every day with that goal in mind.

Saul forgot that, to his own regret.

In the 2006 Chicago Marathon, a runner from Kenya named Robert Cheruiyot just barely won that grueling contest. He ran a race that lasted 2 hours 7 minutes and 35 seconds and a few feet before the finish line, with his hands lifted in victory, Robert slipped and fell. Fortunately for the Kenyan, however, he slipped *forward* instead of backwards, and won the race.

Race referee Pat Savage said, "Luckily for him he slipped forward."

The fact is, we're all going to slip in life. The apostle James says, "For we all stumble in many things."[47] It's true! We all make mistakes, and we all sin. The Bible says, "If we say that we have no sin, we deceive ourselves, and the truth is not in us."[48]

But here's the question. Can you slip forward? Can you fail forward?

What does that mean? It means, can you learn from your mistakes? After a humiliating lapse or defeat, you say, "That was such a bitter experience, such a hard pill to swallow, I pray I *never* do that again." When you say things like that, you've learned something. Something good has emerged from the bad. You have fallen *forwards*. But if you go back and do the same foolish, self-destructive things again and again, then you are falling backwards, and you will ultimately play the fool.

One last thing. You play the fool...

#4: ...When You Allow Resentment And Hatred To Control Your Life Instead Of Love

It was Saul's insane jealousy that ultimately destroyed him. Instead of celebrating the gifted, talented people in his own kingdom (like David) he convinced himself that everyone was out to get him.

Maybe you're feeling a little of that right now—that "life isn't fair." It could be that someone you know passed you by in business, receiving the promotion that "by all rights" should have belonged to you. Or maybe you have a friend who has been blessed by God in a way that leaves you feeling empty, inferior, or deprived. *Why should he get all the breaks? Why should she have a happy family life and perfect kids? Why do they have all the nice vacations and I don't get to go anywhere?*

My friend, don't allow jealousy or resentment to destroy your relationships and begin to eat at you from the inside out. The best way to combat resentment or envy is with a blessing! Bless that individual out loud every chance you get. Compliment them before others. Draw attention to their positive qualities. And when you're with that individual, say, "I am just so glad God is using you, and blessing you. And I'm so glad He has blessed me, too."

Just be faithful with what God has given you and what He has set before you, and allow no room for envy over what He has given to someone else. Don't play the fool!

Life is way too short to spend your time kissing venomous snakes.

Chapter Four

JONAH: A SECOND CHANCE AT LIFE

Roy Riegels was an All-American center for the University of California Golden Bears, playing in the Rose Bowl of 1929 against Georgia Tech, then known as "the Golden Tornado."

Here's an account from the *New York Times* article of January 1, 1929:

> The game was marked by an unusual play, which, it ultimately developed, was of great importance in the final score. It led to Georgia Tech's safety. Captain-elect Roy Riegels of the Golden Bears, playing center, snatched up a Tech fumble in the second quarter and started toward the Georgia Tech goal. Tech men sprang up in front of him and in eluding them Riegels cut back across the field. He turned again to escape and in so doing apparently became confused and started toward his own goal, sixty yards away. As he pounded down the sideline both California and Tech players stood amazed in their tracks.
>
> Benny Lom, halfback for the Golden Bears, sensed the situation almost immediately and sprang into action. Down the field he went after the flying Riegels, who only put on more speed as he heard feet pounding in the turf behind him. Finally Lom grabbed hold of his mate at the California 3-yard line and turned him around. Making interference for Riegels, Lom started back up the field, but a wave of Tech tacklers hit Riegels before he could more than turn around, hurtling him back to the 1-yard line.

Normally, scooping up a fumble and running for the goal line would be a very positive thing for a football player to do. But in this case, there was one small problem. Riegels got turned around and ran toward the wrong goal. Watching all this with unbelieving eyes, Tech Coach Bill Alexander exclaimed, "*He's running the wrong way! Let's see how far he'll actually go.*"

Fortunately for Cal, Roy's own teammate tackled him before he could mistakenly score for the wrong team.

At halftime, as the two teams headed for the locker rooms, Roy Riegels was humiliated beyond words. Sitting on a bench in the corner, he thought he was not only through for the game, but with the game of football itself. How could he ever show his face on the field again? The room was very quiet, and all you could hear was the sobbing of Roy Riegels over in the corner.

Calling the team together, the coach said, "Okay, we're going now into the second half, and I want the same team in the second half that were there in the first half."

Riegels was shocked by this, because of the horrible mistake he had made in front of the capacity crowd. "Coach," he said, "I can't do it! I have ruined you. I have ruined the University of California. I have ruined myself. I couldn't face that crowd to save my life."

The coach looked Riegels right in the eyes and said, "Roy, get up and go on back. *The game is only half over.*"

Riegels did go back into the game, and went on to give one of the most inspiring individual efforts in Rose Bowl history.

Now it may be that you feel like old wrong-way-Roy right now. Maybe there was a time when you were walking right in the middle of God's will for your life, but something got you disoriented and turned around. And like the Georgia Tech coach in that long-ago Rose Bowl game, Satan is saying, "He's running the wrong way! Let's see how far he'll go."

But like the coach of Roy's team, the Lord essentially says, "Get up and go on back. The game isn't over yet!"

Millennia before Roy Riegels ever made his appearance on the planet, there was a prophet of the Lord who might well have been nicknamed "Wrong-Way Jonah." The Lord gave him a very specific job to do, and in response, he ran as fast and as far as he could go in the opposite direction.

But Jonah got "tackled" before he crossed the wrong goal line, finding out that it's not only impossible to run from God, but also that He is the God of second chances.

And the Lord accomplished all of this through a storm and one *very* large fish.

ANIMAL LAND

I've been fascinated by animals for as long as I can remember. Throughout my childhood and up until the present time I've possessed just about every kind of animal imaginable.

When I was little, I went through my reptile phase, collecting turtles, snakes, and lizards in every shape and size. And then of course I had mice, guinea pigs, hamsters, rabbits and all that. And birds? I was really into birds, keeping finches, parakeets, cockatiels, cockatoos, lovebirds, and parrots.

Dogs? I've always had dogs around the house—including three German shepherds, a couple of collies, two poodles, and a few mutts mixed in for good measure (but not all at the same time!)

Then I went through a huge fish phase, where I had every kind of fish you can imagine. In fact, I actually imagined myself becoming an ichthyologist, or a student of fish, at some point.

Cats? Well, no, I've never had a single cat. (I just never saw the reason why.)

Our God, of course, is the Creator of all these marvelous animals in His wildly diverse animal kingdom, and He cares about them. Jesus noted that God takes notice of every little sparrow that falls to the ground.

On rare occasions, when necessary, God uses animals to accomplish His purposes. You'll remember that there was a particular, pre-selected donkey that had the privilege of carrying Jesus Christ into Jerusalem. And speaking of donkeys, there was another one in the pages of the Old Testament that actually spoke with a human voice, rebuking the reckless prophet Balaam for his foolishness.

In the story of Elijah, we learn that God personally directed ravens to bring the prophet food during the time of his exile. Then there's the frightening story of the teenage boys who mocked the prophet Elisha—after which bears came out racing out of the forest and mauled them. (I particularly remember that one, because the boys were mocking the prophet's bald head... something some of us identify with!)

Whatever member of God's wildlife menagerie we may be talking about, I'm always interested in stories about animals. In the book of Jonah, one of the principal players in the story is a whale, or "a great fish," as Scripture puts it. (Even so, it *could* have been a whale. More about that later.)

In response to Jonah's rebellion against His will, God directed this beast of the sea to swallow the prophet—who remained swallowed-but-undigested for what must have been three very long and trying days.

Have I ever questioned the literal truth of this story? Not at all. I've never had trouble believing it to be authentic. The fact is, if you can believe Genesis 1:1, the rest of the Bible will be a snap for you! If you can accept the premise that, "In the beginning, God created the heavens and the earth," then there shouldn't be a miracle in the entire Bible that would trouble you.

I could go on and on with various proofs as to why I believe this story, but the greatest validation was that of Christ Himself when He said in Matthew 12:39, "A wicked and adulterous generation asks for a miraculous sign! But none will be given it except the sign of the prophet Jonah. For as Jonah was three days and three nights in the belly of a huge fish, so the Son of Man will be three days and three nights in the heart of the earth."[49]

So not only did Jesus validate the story of Jonah, but He used it as a metaphor for His own death and resurrection from the dead.

The account is true. Jesus said so.

The Old Testament book of Jonah is just a few pages long, but what a story! And what a prophet! The place from which he prophesied was the bottom of the sea. The pulpit from which he preached was the stomach of a fish. This is a real-life account of a man who refused a divine commission. But it's also a story of the grace and longsuffering of God.

RUNNING FROM GOD

Now the word of the LORD came to Jonah the son of Amittai, saying, "Arise, go to Nineveh, that great city, and cry out against it; for their wickedness has come up before Me." But Jonah arose to flee to Tarshish from the presence of the LORD. He went down to Joppa, and found a ship going to Tarshish; so he paid the fare, and went down into it, to go with them to Tarshish from the presence of the LORD. (Jonah 1:1-3)

Have you ever tried to run from God and His will for your life, or found yourself imagining you had a better plan for your life than He did?

Perhaps it was certain Biblical truths that you simply didn't want to accept. Then again, it may have been the calling of God on your life to do something specific; perhaps a ministry opportunity opened up before you, but you found yourself afraid to commit your life completely to God, and you drug your feet, or flat-out refused.

Yes, you want salvation in Jesus Christ, and all the benefits that go with it—assurance of heaven, forgiveness of sins, and the peace that passes all understanding. But as far as walking in the plan that God has for you, waiting for the man or woman God has for you, or pursuing the vocation God has for you... well, you're a little apprehensive.

Why? It may be because of a basic misunderstanding of the nature of God. You may even think, "Whatever God wants me to do will be difficult or boring or involve trials and suffering, and it's not going to be as good as what I would have chosen for myself."

I may have missed some of God's choice lessons for my life through the years, but here's one that I hold onto: *God's plans are better than mine.* Does it always seem that way in the moment?

Frankly, no, it doesn't.

I will admit there have been times when the Lord has directed me to do certain things and I've thought, *I don't really want to do this, but I will because I know it's right.* Then later, in retrospect, with 20/20 hindsight, I'm able to look back and say, "Ah Lord, You knew exactly what You were doing."

We need to remember just a couple of things about God and His leadership in our lives. First of all, *He is good.* The Bible affirms this truth over and over again.

Oh, give thanks to the LORD, for He is good!
For His mercy endures forever.
(Psalm 106:1)

Oh, taste and see that the LORD is good;
Blessed is the man who trusts in Him!
(Psalm 34:8)

Good and upright is the LORD;
Therefore He teaches sinners in the way.
(Psalm 25:8)

For the LORD is good;
His mercy is everlasting,
(Psalm 100:5)

You are good, and do good.
(Psalm 119:68)

Maybe in days gone by you had a bad experience in church. Perhaps you were mistreated by your parents, or you didn't have a father or a mother growing up and you've transferred that hurt and resentment over to God. Don't let that happen! It's a dead-end road, and beyond that, it simply isn't true. God is good.

A second thing to remember is that *God is love.*

The Bible doesn't just tell us that God *has* love but actually says God *is* love. Bear in mind that we're not talking about the Hollywood version of love here. Many depictions of "love" on the big screen are really all about lust, and having nothing to do with the genuine article. God's love is consistent, unchanging, inexhaustible. The Scripture says, "But God demonstrates His own love toward us, in that while we were still sinners, Christ died for us."[50]

And much to the shock and consternation of the prophet Jonah, God loved the people of Nineveh. Because they were lovable? Because they were worthy? Far from it! There's no doubt these Ninevites were a wicked people. In Jonah 1:2, the Lord says, "Their wickedness has come up before Me." Or literally, "Their wickedness has reached a high degree or its highest pitch." Another translation says, "It was full to the brim."

I hate to use this analogy, but it was like an overflowing septic tank. To get a grip on this verse, you have to think of something that is foul, offensive, and sickening. That is how Nineveh appeared to God—just overflowing with iniquity. And the Lord was saying, "Jonah, that place *stinks.* I can't take it anymore."

So what would you imagine His very next words might be? "...So I'm going to send fire down on Nineveh and destroy them all!"

No, God says, "Jonah, I want you to go and preach to them."

Nineveh was a city of the mighty Assyrian Empire, a people legendary for their cruelty. Graphic accounts of their sadistic treatment of captives have been found in the ancient records. Known across the world of that day for their savagery, the Ninevites would burn captive boys and girls alive and torture people in sick and fiendish ways—literally tearing the skin from their bodies and leaving them to die in the scorching sun.

Yet in spite of all this, God says to Jonah, "I want you to go there and preach to these people."

A good Jew, an Israelite patriot, preaching about God to the Assyrians, their arch-enemies? What a nightmare idea that was to Jonah! That would be like saying to an American evangelist, "Go to Pakistan or Somalia and preach to Al-Quaida."

Jonah was reluctant. Why? It wasn't because he didn't know the nature and character of God, but rather because he *did*. He knew very well that although God was holy and righteous, He was also gracious and merciful. That's the part that frightened Jonah. He reasoned that if someone preached to the Ninevites, there was at least an off-chance they might actually believe, repent, and God would spare them! And he *did not* want that to happen.

The fact is, God did care about the people of Nineveh, as He would later tell His prophet: "Nineveh has more than 120,000 people living in spiritual darkness, not to mention all the animals. Shouldn't I feel sorry for such a great city?"[51]

It wasn't fear that kept Jonah from obeying God and booking a ticket to Nineveh. It doesn't appear to me that he had any anxiety about his personal welfare in bringing God's message of warning to this enemy stronghold. No, it was Jonah's personal prejudice that kept him from obeying the Lord and warning these people. Nevertheless, the Lord Himself loved them and wanted to reach them.

Let's be honest, sometimes we just don't care very much about lost people. Worse yet, sometimes we actually have hatred for certain people outside of Christ. The Bible tells us that we are to love our enemies and pray for those that persecute us. But many of us don't do that; we actually hate the people who oppose us—or we simply don't care about them at all.

We basically figure, "Look I've already got my personal salvation, and I'm going to heaven. If someone else doesn't have it, that's their problem. They need to go find it."

The fact is, many of us give little thought to those who don't know the Lord. When push comes to shove, we really don't care that much about them. Jonah didn't care, either. And God wanted that to change. So the Lord said, "Get up and go, Jonah. Cry out to them and warn them for Me."

And Jonah got up and went.

In the opposite direction.

Verse 3 tells us that "he arose to flee to Tarshish from the presence of the LORD."

Escape from the presence of the Lord? What a joke! It's laughable. You'll remember that Adam and Eve thought they could do that. After they disobeyed the Lord and ate of the forbidden fruit, they hid in the bushes from Him when He came walking through the Garden on His daily visit. It's so absurd to think that someone can hide from God. It's like playing peek-a-boo with a toddler. You put a blanket over that little head, and say, "Oh...where did he go? Oh...there he is!"

Of course you know where that little one is all along. You're just humoring him, playing with him. It's a game.

And that's what it's like when we think, "Oh...I am hiding from God. He will never see me here. The Lord will never discover this little plan I've devised. He'll never figure this out."

Are you serious? Scripture says, "Nothing in all creation is hidden from God's sight. Everything is uncovered and laid bare before the eyes of him to whom we must give account."[52]

In Psalm 139, David declared:

> I can never escape from your spirit!
> I can never get away from your presence!
> If I go up to heaven, you are there;
> if I go down to the place of the dead, you are there.
> If I ride the wings of the morning,
> if I dwell by the farthest oceans,
> even there your hand will guide me,
> and your strength will support me.
> (vv. 7-10, NLT)

Thankfully we cannot escape from the presence of the Lord.

But Jonah tried anyway.

Down, Down, Down

"Jonah found a ship." (1:3)

Satan will always open the doors for disobedience. Sometimes when we're about to do the wrong thing, all the doors start opening up for us, and we can almost rationalize our behavior and say, "Hey, this is going so smoothly. Maybe God is in this after all. Maybe it's okay."

No. God is not in it, and it's not okay. But the devil will make it easy for you to sin. After that, it's one step down after another on the path of least resistance. It's interesting to me how that word "down" keeps popping up as Jonah turns his back on God's will.

- *He went down* to Joppa, and found a ship.... (v. 3)
- He paid the fare and *went down* into it.... (v. 3).
- But Jonah had *gone down* into the lowest parts of the ship...(v. 5)
- ...and *laid down*, and was fast asleep. (v. 5)

Any step away from God is always a step down.

Scripture also says, "He paid the fare." That's a reminder that sin will always cost you. Sin is very, very expensive. Adam's sin cost him paradise. David's sin cost him his family and his reputation. Samson's sin ultimately cost him his life. What is your sin costing you?

I look back on my own life and think about the kids I grew up with and went to high school with, and how we all partied together. Then I found the Lord at age 17, and I walked away from that lifestyle. But every now and then I will run into some of that old gang, and it's almost shocking to see how sin has chewed them up and spit them out—spiritually, physically, mentally. Many of them are into their second, third, and fourth marriages, and often estranged from their children.

Jonah might have thought, *I'll go ahead and do this, and there won't be any price to pay.* But no, there was a price to pay beyond the fare he paid for his passage to Tarshish.

But the Lord sent out a great wind on the sea, and there was a mighty tempest on the sea, so that the ship was about to be broken up.

Then the mariners were afraid; and every man cried out to his god, and threw the cargo that was in the ship into the sea, to lighten the load. But Jonah had gone down into the lowest parts of the ship, had lain down, and was fast asleep.[53]

Look at those first eight words of this passage: "But the LORD sent out a great wind...."

Know this. *God will always have the last word.* No matter what you do, no matter what anybody else does, it's always going to be, "But the Lord..." The Lord will always say what He wants to say and do what He wants to do.

Nahum, another Old Testament prophet who had a message for Nineveh, wrote: "The LORD has His way in the whirlwind and the storm...."[54]

Jonah was about to discover that first-hand.

STORMS

God didn't send this storm to destroy Jonah, but to get his attention—and to turn him in the right direction. The Bible tells us that "whom the Lord loves He chastens."[55] Another translations says, "It's the child he loves that he disciplines; the child he embraces, he also corrects."[56]

So maybe you're in a storm right now as a direct result of something you have done wrong, and your life is in turmoil. How do you stop the storm? You get on your knees and say, "Lord, You have my attention. I'm all ears. I want You to know that I'm sorry for turning away from You and going my own direction. I repent. I want to correct this."

The text says, "The mariners were afraid; and every man cried out to his god." That's pretty typical, isn't it? People cry out to God in a crisis. They'll ignore Him in all of their choices and do their best to shut Him out of their thoughts and out of their lives. But then, when the chips are down or a crisis hits, what's the first thing out of their mouths? "Oh my God!"

Somehow, these sailors figured out that their mysterious passenger, Jonah, was the real culprit. Finding him sound asleep deep within the ship's hold, they said to him, "Please tell us! For whose cause is this trouble upon us? What is your occupation? And where do you come from? What is your country? And of what people are you?"[57]

In other words, "Who in the world are you, and what kind of a God do you serve who is powerful enough to send such a storm?"

These men, even though pagans with no relationship to the living God, recognized that sin results in judgment—and that one man or woman's personal sin will have an impact on others.

Jonah's reply doesn't give them any comfort at all.

"I am a Hebrew, and I worship the LORD, the God of heaven, who made the sea and the land." Then he told them that he was running away from the LORD.

The sailors were terrified when they heard this. "Oh, why did you do it?" they groaned. (1:9-10, NLT)

Jonah went on to tell them that if they would just toss him overboard, the storm would stop.

At first they said, "No, no," but as the storm got worse, they finally said, "Yes, yes," and over the side he went. Then, just as Jonah had predicted, the storm suddenly ceased.

Jonah 1:17 says: "And the LORD had prepared a great fish to swallow Jonah. And Jonah was in the belly of the fish three days and three nights."

The word prepared means "ordained."

The focus of this story is not the big fish. That's just part of it. The focus of the story is a man who ran from God, found out you can't do that, and went back and preached...resulting in perhaps the greatest revival in human history. That is the message of Jonah.

But the fish aspect of the story is an interesting sidelight, because there's nothing else in the Bible quite like it.

When Scripture tells us that God prepared a great fish, it could also be translated "called" or "ordained." In fact, it's entirely possible God created a unique creature to accommodate Jonah on this particular occasion that was never to be seen again.

Then again, God could have chosen from any number of fish or whales who could have performed such a taxi service for the runaway prophet. Take the blue whale, for example, that can grow to a length of 110 feet long, weighing up to 150 tons. For that matter, it could have been an actual fish. The largest fish in the ocean right now is the whale shark, at 41-and-a-half feet long. Some speculate it may have even been a sperm whale, which can grow to lengths of 50 feet.

By the way, most of the items recovered from sperm whales' stomachs are not chewed, but swallowed whole. They just open their mouth and everything gets sucked in. Not long ago, they opened up a sperm whale and found an intact 40 foot long giant squid, weighing 440 pounds. So if a sperm whale can accommodate a full-grown squid, certainly it could certainly ingest one measly little Hebrew prophet. Jonah would have hardly been more than an appetizer.

Whales are magnificent creatures. A number of years ago we were over in Maui with some friends, and one of them said, "Let's go out whale watching." So we went out in one of those little boats they call "Zodiacs."

At that time of year in Maui, the humpbacks were in season, and when you see one come up out of the water, that's called a "breach." When it happens—and if you happen to be near—it's an awe-inspiring sight. And also just a little bit scary.

So we were watching where the whales breached, and wanted to get closer. One of my friends told me his wife had not only been close to such a breach, she had actually gone in the water and *touched* the whale as it went by.

Well, that did it. I wanted to touch a whale, too.

The next moment—wow, watch out what you wish for!—a baby whale cruised right underneath us. I say a "baby" whale, but it was huge. Like a small boat. And it was close enough to us that we could see the little barnacles on it.

But then came Mama, right behind.

The mother ship! If the baby was like a small boat, its mother was like a submarine, covered with barnacles. As quickly as I could, I slipped on my mask and jumped into the water to see if I could touch her. But no, she was too fast. It was just *whoosh*, and she was gone, chasing her baby.

As I thought about it later, it made me a little weak in the knees. I'm glad that mother whale wasn't interested in having preacher for breakfast.

So Jonah the prophet, rather than drowning in the angry sea as he surely thought he would, was swallowed whole by a specially-prepared and divinely-appointed fish. That would be an interesting place for the story to end, if the moral was: Don't run from God or things like this might happen to you. But there was more to the story. Much more.

And what no doubt seemed like "the end" to Jonah, was actually only the beginning of a second chance.

A SECOND CHANCE

Then Jonah prayed to the LORD his God from the fish's belly. And he said:

"I cried out to the LORD because of my affliction,
And He answered me.

"Out of the belly of Sheol I cried,
And You heard my voice.
For You cast me into the deep,
Into the heart of the seas,

And the floods surrounded me;
All Your billows and Your waves passed over me.
(Jonah 2:1-3)

So the LORD spoke to the fish, and it vomited Jonah onto dry land.
(Jonah 2:10)

So *when* did Jonah pray? *After three days and three nights.*
Talk about stubborn! Three days and three nights wrapped in seaweed. Fish smacking him in the face. Terrible stench. Temperatures probably exceeding 105 degrees. And after 72 hours of this, he finally says, "Okay, okay, I give up! Lord, I surrender. You're in charge." And he cried out to God.
Then, after that long, amazing ordeal, we read these words:

Now the word of the LORD came to Jonah the second time, saying, "Arise, go to Nineveh, that great city, and preach to it the message that I tell you." (Jonah 3:1-2)

Isn't that good? There's no scolding or finger pointing. God simply repeats His original commission to Jonah, and gives him another chance.
The Bible doesn't tell us the location of the dry land where the fish deposited the prophet. Some scholars say it was somewhere on Israel's northern coast. But one thing is very clear: There were no delays, no foot-dragging in response to this second commission. The Bible says, "So Jonah arose and went to Nineveh, according to the word of the LORD."[58]
You know, I imagine that however far Jonah had to walk to get to Nineveh, that was a peaceful journey. The prophet knew where God wanted him, knew he was (now) in the center of God's will, and knew that he was acting "according to the word of the LORD." No robbers or assassins would waylay him or block his progress; he was on the Lord's business. That's a great place to be.

So Jonah arose and went to Nineveh, according to the word of the Lord. Nineveh was an exceedingly great city, a three-day journey in extent. And Jonah began to enter the city on the first day's walk. And he cried out and said, "Forty days, and Nineveh will be overthrown!"

So the people of Nineveh believed God, proclaimed a fast, put on sackcloth, from the greatest to the least of them. (Jonah 3:3-5)

When God tells you to do something, He wants you to do it. Now for Jonah, it was to go to a people he didn't want to go to. Maybe there's a call on your life to do a certain thing, but you don't want to do it. Maybe He has placed a particular neighbor, co-worker, or friend at school on your heart, and He wants you to go to that person and share the gospel. But you don't want to do it.
Perhaps this individual is quite "different" from you. Sometimes we only

like to hang around with people who look like us, dress like us, think like us, and talk like us. But God wants us to leave our comfort zone and go to people that are a different age than us, a different race than us, a different socioeconomic group than us—or even people who are in a different nation from us. God has people on His heart who need to hear about new life in His Son, and we're His messengers, His ambassadors.

Jonah didn't want to obey that call. But reluctantly, he did.

Notice his message: "Forty days and Nineveh will be overthrown!" Jonah knew very well about the mercy and grace of God, and he could have said, "This city is under judgment, but God is merciful and gracious!" He chose not to add that last part, *because he didn't want them to repent*. He still wanted the judgment of God to fall on them. So basically his message was, "Forty days and you're all gonna die!" And he might just as well have added, "To be quite honest, I'm not really that broken up about it. You guys deserve this. So prepare to die!"

That was his compassionate evangelistic message.

But in spite of this harsh, abbreviated sermon, God intervened and His Holy Spirit brought about a sense of conviction in that city, and the people repented and turned *en masse* to the Lord.

Unexpectedly, inexplicably, they believed, knew this message was true, and threw themselves on the mercy of God. This is probably the greatest revival in human history, because the population of Nineveh was something like 600,000 people at the time.

Jonah, however, was the right man at the right place at the right time... whether he was excited about it or wanted to be there or not.

I wonder if any of us are missing God's best for our lives at this point. Don't be afraid to yield yourself to the Lord. My life aspirations early on were to be a cartoonist or a pet store owner. But the Lord had a different plan in mind for me, and I've never regretted it. I can look back on things that I wanted to do, and realize that God always had something better in store for me.

Here's the best advice I can give you, no matter what your age, no matter what your circumstances. *Never be afraid to commit an unknown future to a known God.* If you're young, if you're middle-aged, of if you're 99 years old, just say, "Lord, I commit my life to You." Don't say, "Lord, please reveal Your plan to me and then I'll tell you whether I want to do it or not." No, how much better to say, "Lord, here's my life. I'm placing it in Your hands. I don't even to know what Your plan for me might be, but I trust You. Use me, Lord!"

Pray a prayer like that...and just watch what God will do.

Jonah didn't give the Ninevites any good news in his message of doom, but God used it anyway. God touched their hearts in spite of the messenger, and they turned to faith in God and believed.

Why do I like Jonah so much? I think it's because he's so flawed—prejudiced, opinionated, and sometimes a little grumpy. I can relate to him! This is an authentic, flesh-and-blood guy. And even though he really didn't do what

God had wanted him to do, in the end, he went ahead and obeyed. And God graciously used him anyway.

There are some men and women of God we may have a little difficulty relating to. But not old Jonah. He didn't really do anything great. He is more of a companion in our ineptness. Yet God worked through him, despite his short-comings. God used him, even though he was a reluctant servant at times.

In the end, he obeyed God.

And God used Him to change his world.

Chapter Five

NAAMAN: THE MAN BEHIND THE ARMOR

Arecent *USA Today* article asked today's young people the question: "What do you want more than anything else?"

They were polling the so-called "millennial generation," also known as Generation Y—those born since the early 1980s.

So what does this generation desire beyond all else? Before I give you that answer, let me contrast it to a poll of Baby Boomers back in 1967, when asked a similar question.

When queried, "What do you want more than anything else?" the Boomers answered: "A meaningful philosophy of life."

And Generation Y? Their answer was, *"I want to be rich and famous."*

The "greatest story" we'll be looking at in this chapter features a powerful man who was both rich and famous. But all his fame and wealth couldn't help him in the most devastating crisis of his life.

Naaman, the Syrian general, had a problem that was eating him alive.

GENERAL NAAMAN'S SECRET GRIEF

The king of Aram had high admiration for Naaman, the commander of his army, because through him the LORD had given Aram great victories. But though Naaman was a mighty warrior, he suffered from leprosy.

Now groups of Aramean raiders had invaded the land of Israel, and among their captives was a young girl who had been given to Naaman's wife as a maid. One day the girl said to her mistress, "I wish my master would go to see the prophet in Samaria. He would heal him of his leprosy."

...So Naaman went with his horses and chariots and waited at the door of Elisha's house. But Elisha sent a messenger out to him with this message: "Go and wash yourself seven times in the Jordan River. Then your skin will be restored, and you will be healed of leprosy."

But Naaman became angry and stalked away. "I thought he would surely come out to meet me!" he said. "I expected him to wave his hand over the leprosy and call on the name of the LORD his God and heal me! Aren't the Abana River and Pharpar River of Damascus better than all the rivers of Israel put together? Why shouldn't I wash in them and be healed?" So Naaman turned and went away in a rage.

But his officers tried to reason with him and said, "Sir, if the prophet had told you to do some great thing, wouldn't you have done it? So you should certainly obey him when he says simply to go and wash and be cured!" So Naaman went down to the Jordan River and dipped himself seven times, as the man of God had instructed him. And his flesh became as healthy as a young child's, and he was healed! (2 Kings 5:1-3, 9-14, NLT)

Naaman of Aram, or Syria, was a nationally-celebrated war hero, famous, well-respected, and in good favor with his king.

You might say he had it all. He had great power because of his high military rank, most likely second only to the king himself. He had great celebrity, and was really something of a legend in his own time.

And here's something remarkable. The Bible tells us that through Naaman, God Himself had given the king of Aram great victories. This tells us that even though Naaman was not yet a believer in the God of Israel, that God was already involved in his life in a positive way.

But there was a problem in this man's life, and it was a big one. He found out he had leprosy.

How did he discover the disease? The Bible doesn't tell us. Maybe one day he was getting ready for work, admiring his well-chiseled, soldier's body, as he prepared to slip on his rich garments and shining armor. We can imagine him suddenly noticing a bright red spot on his arm.

Hmmm, he thinks to himself. *Never saw that before. Where did that come from? Probably nothing to worry about.* So he ignored it.

The next day he notices another spot—this time on his thigh. The day after that there are several more—two on his chest and another on his face. As you might imagine, the general would have been very concerned. So he goes to his doctor and asks, "What's up with these spots?"

And the doctor replies, "General Naaman, sir, I wish I could give you better news. But this is leprosy."

Leprosy.

Just that quickly, the bottom falls out of this man's life. Suddenly, he has a new, horrible identity. He's a leper! He has become one of the walking dead. I can imagine him getting that news, and then walking out on the balcony of his beautiful home, and looking out over Damascus, Syria's ancient capitol. Maybe he thinks through all of his accomplishments, all of the battles he has won, all of his fame...but how does all that help him now? There's no cure for leprosy! He's doomed to die a slow, disfiguring death.

But what he didn't realize in that moment was that God, the true and living God, was tapping the general on the shoulder.

Maybe God has tapped you on the shoulder recently. Possibly something has happened in your life to wake you up and capture your attention. After your normal yearly check up, the clinic called back, saying, "One of the tests has come back, and it concerns us. You need to come back in and see the doctor." Or maybe you were in an unexpected accident recently, or some kind of tragedy has befallen you, or something else is going on. And it's as though the Lord is trying to get your attention.

Should you respond to Him?

Yes.

How should you respond?

"Lord, I'm all ears. I'm listening. What do You want to say to me?"

Now if Naaman had been a Hebrew, he would have been completely ostracized. In the Jewish culture, lepers were allowed no contact at all with uninfected people. That was because leprosy was highly contagious—and ultimately fatal. In fact, if you were a leper in Israel and you were walking down the street and saw someone coming toward you, you would have to cry out, "Unclean, unclean," so the person would have time to cross over to the other side of the street and avoid any kind of contact with you whatsoever.

But apparently in the Syrian culture Naaman could still (at least for at time) maintain his position of influence. Nevertheless, this disease was slowly but surely eating its way through his body.

This disease is still alive today, renamed Hansen's Disease. It was formerly thought when you had Hansen's Disease, or leprosy, that your limbs would basically just rot and fall off. But in recent years, through the research of Dr. Paul Brand and others, it has been proven that the disfigurement associated with Hansen's Disease usually comes because the body's warning system of pain has been destroyed. In other words, you could cut your finger or be washing your hands in scalding hot water and not know it because you have lost your sense of touch.

I imagine Naaman hid most of the evidence of his disease beneath his beautiful clothing and gleaming armor. Though the king knew about it, I doubt most people were even aware of the fact that Naaman was a leper.

The Thing About "Beautiful People"

You and will sometimes look at some of the "beautiful people" portrayed in our media—pretty, handsome, wealthy, or multi-talented—and we'll think to ourselves, "Man, wouldn't it be great to be like her!" Or, "Wouldn't it be fantastic to be in his shoes?"

That's the way it is with human nature. If you don't have much, you want to have more. If you already have an abundance, there's always someone who has more than you. And even if you manage to amass more than anybody else, you find yourself worrying about maintaining and keeping it.

I guess it's all relative. Someone once observed: "If you have money in the bank, in your wallet, and spare change in a dish somewhere, you are among the top eight percent of the world's wealthy." So that would mean that even an American on the lowest rung of our economic ladder would be wealthy compared to the standards of the rest of the world.

Even so, we tend to look at wealthy people or celebrities and just assume they have life by the tail. In reality, they're just like you and me, with all the problems, worries, and heartaches we have—and more besides!

That's one dynamic that keeps the supermarket tabloids alive. I saw one recently with the headline: "Cellulite of the movie stars." It featured really tight shots of famous people at the beach who were, well…not looking their best, if you know what I mean. Somehow, it makes us feel better when we see someone we assumed to be beautiful or handsome looking maybe a little worse than we do in a bathing suit.

(For the record, I didn't touch the tabloid!)

Even these famous, successful, fabulously wealthy men and women have many of the same problems and worries that you do…with the additional burden of never having a moment's privacy.

There's an old legend about a group people living in a certain village who were constantly complaining about their troubles. So one day every one of them was invited to bring all of his or her burdens and problems and cast them into a big heap in the middle of town. Then, according to this story, each was given the privilege of choosing another's trouble—someone else's heartache or worry—to replace his or her own. After careful deliberation and consideration, each person selected the same problem they had originally cast aside, feeling that his or her own problem was less difficult than the others.

Here's something we need to know: below the surface, most people are essentially the same. Years ago, Billy Graham addressed a large group of itinerant evangelists in Amsterdam. And in that address he said, "When I go to proclaim to the gospel—whether it's a street corner in Nairobi or a meeting in Seoul, Korea—there are certain things that are true in the hearts and minds of all people."

First, he said, there is an emptiness in every life without Christ.

Pascal put it right when he described a God-shaped vacuum in every life that only God can fill. The Scripture tells us in Romans 8:20, "For the creation was subjected to futility, not willingly, but because of Him who subjected it in hope." It doesn't matter where you go in the world, every person alive has an empty place in his or her heart that only Jesus can fill.

Second, Dr. Graham noted that every individual, no matter how rich or beautiful or powerful or famous, is lonely.

Even though we may not acknowledge it or even put words to it, we're lonely for God! It's in our spiritual DNA. That's why people go from one one-night-stand to another, from one marriage to another, from one relationship to another, desperately trying to find a person to fill a void that only God Himself can occupy.

Third, every person has a sense of guilt.

The head of a mental institution in London once said, "I could release half of my patients if I could find a way to relieve them of their guilt." And why do we feel such guilt, deep within us? It's because we're guilty! Every one of us. Romans 3:22-23 (NIV) declares: "There is no difference, for all have sinned and fall sort of the glory of God."

Finally, there is a universal fear of death.

Now I know that some people will act really tough and say, "Not me. I'm not afraid to die. I don't care about death." Woody Allen said, "I'm not afraid to die. I just don't want to be there when it happens!" I think that's how some of us feel. But really, deep down inside we are afraid to die. Hebrews 2:15 speaks of those who "all their lives were held in slavery by their fear of death."[59]

Now as believers who have put our faith in Christ, we no longer have to fear death, because Christ has conquered the grave and promised us a place in His Father's house, after we depart this earth. But even so, death is still our "last enemy," and something each one of us must face, if the Rapture doesn't happen first.

In summary, then, even famous, successful, so-called "beautiful people" have certain things in common: Apart from a relationship with Jesus Christ, they are empty, lonely, guilty, and afraid to die.

So it was for the mighty Naaman.

Who, then, do you suppose God used to touch the heart of this military legend and mighty man of renown?

An angel? A statesman? A king? A priest? A powerful warrior?

Would you believe a little slave girl?

A FAITHFUL WITNESS

One day the girl said to her mistress, "I wish my master would go to see the prophet in Samaria. He would heal him of his leprosy." (2 Kings 5:3)

Who was this girl? She was a young Jewish girl who had been taken captive by the Syrians—kidnapped and snatched away from her friends, family, and people of her own faith, and taken to a foreign land.

How easily she could have been angry at God and said, "Lord why did You let this happen to me? Why did You put me in the house of this man Naaman?" How easily she could have thought of Naaman as her enemy, and even said, "I'm glad he's a leper. I'm happy he's dying a slow death. I hope he suffers a lot because of all the suffering he has brought to me."

But that's not how this Israelite girl responded. Instead, she saw an opportunity to bring the Word of the Lord to her Syrian master.

Maybe you, too, find yourself in a strange or uncomfortable place in life right now, and can't understand how or why you've ended up there. In your prayers, you say, "Lord, why did You put me in this family?" Or, "Why am I in this neighborhood?" Or, "Why am I in this office or on this work site?" Or, "Lord, why do I have to sit next to that person or be in this classroom with this other person? Why am I here?"

Did you ever stop and think that God may have put you where are for "such a time as this"?[60] It's obvious that this girl in Naaman's household—slave though she may have been—had earned the right to speak. We can deduce this because Naaman took her at her word, and went to see the Syrian king. Then, a few verses later, we find him down in Israel, knocking on Elisha's door. So this slave girl's words apparently carried a lot of weight. We can conclude that she was a godly girl who had earned the respect of her boss. Otherwise, why would he have heeded her words at all?

It's a wonderful thing when we live such a godly, joyful, consistent life that we earn the right to speak to people in times of crisis. Augustine once said, "Preach the gospel, and when necessary use words." To say it another way, unless our witness for Christ is backed up by the way we truly live, our words simply won't ring true. In fact, they will be empty.

It might surprise you to hear me say this, but I would suggest to you that if you don't intend to live a godly life, then do us all a favor and don't talk about Jesus.

Am I saying you need to be perfect? No, because if that were the case, then none of us would ever speak up again. We're all flawed. We all fail. We all have our shortcomings. We all sin. But having said that, our witness for Christ has to be grounded in the reality of His work in our lives. If it isn't, the message won't have credibility.

After this girl gets her master pointed toward the God of Israel, she just disappears from the biblical record. We never hear of her again. But she had a part to play in God's great scheme of things, and God used her life to great effect. Think of it: Here we are reading about her thousands of years later!

That's the way it sometimes works, doesn't it? God will reach down and use some unknown person in His kingdom to impact the life of an individual who will become very well-known in that kingdom.

A pastor friend of mine tells the fascinating story about how he came to Christ. Raised in the streets of Philadelphia, he started experimenting with drugs at age 11, and went on to use every drug he could find for the next ten years of his life.

Then he joined the Marines, and was stationed for awhile at Camp Pendleton. One day as he was walking to the PX he encountered a street preacher, who was talking about Jesus Christ. Curious, Rodney began to edge closer to listen to him.

When the preacher noticed Rodney listening, he said, "Hey, why don't you come to church with me tonight?"

"Okay," Rodney said. "I'll come." But he didn't.

The next day the preacher saw him again and said, "You weren't at church last night."

"Yeah," Rodney replied. "I guess I didn't show up."

The preacher said, "Tell you what. I'm just going to hang out with you for the rest of the day."

Rodney said, "No, please don't." But the preacher insisted. Rodney later reflected, "I was even doing drugs and getting high in front of this preacher, and he was saying to me, 'You don't need that any more. God is going to deliver you from that.'"

Rodney went that night to hear his new friend preach, and gave his life to the Lord. At the same meeting, he also met his future wife, and his life was transformed.

I asked him, "Do you know the name of that preacher, Rodney?"

He shook his head. "No, I don't. I never learned his name."

But God had raised that man up to reach Rodney, who in turn is reaching *thousands* of people.

My point is, God will sometimes take a person we have never heard of, and use him or her to touch a Naaman or a Rodney or whomever. Are you willing to be that person, to be used of God in that way? You see, you're never too small for God to use. Only too big. But if you will say, "Here am I, Lord, send me," you will be truly amazed at what the Lord will do through you.

Beneath The Armor

It must have been a sight to behold when the great Syrian general came rumbling into Elisha's town on his chariot. You've got to believe it was an awesome chariot—gilded with gold and silver, drawn by fine Arabian stallions, and surrounded by his personal guard, all in matching uniforms and looking fierce.

Anybody would have expected the Hebrew prophet to come out of his house and say, "Oh, welcome, Naaman. I'm so honored by your visit. I've prepared a meal for you—and a fine little speech for the occasion."

But if Naaman was waiting for Elisha to come out and greet him, he waited in vain. The prophet's house was probably a funky little place with a broken down front door. Knowing that the nobleman was waiting out in front, Elisha sent his servant Gehazi out with a message: "Tell him to immerse himself in the Jordan River seven times, and he will be healed."

So the little door pops open, and Gehazi walks out and delivers his one liner: "The prophet Elisha says, 'Go dunk yourself in the Jordan River seven times and you'll be healed.' Have a nice day." And then he goes back inside and closes the door.

Naaman can't believe his eyes. "WHAT? Do these guys have any concept who they're talking to? Nobody disrespects the great General Naaman!"

Bitterly disappointed and angry, Naaman protested to his companions, "Look...I thought at least he would come out and talk to me! I expected him to wave his hand over the leprosy and call upon the name of the Lord his God and heal me! Aren't the Abana River and Pharpar River of Damascus better than all the rivers of Israel put together? If it's rivers I need, I'll wash at home and get rid of my leprosy."[61] And he went away in a rage.

It's almost as though this remedy given by the prophet was designed to humble Naaman. And in a way, it was. I think one reason the Lord gave this command was because He wanted Naaman to come clean. It may be that one of the reasons Naaman was so resistant to stripping and dipping in the Jordan was simply because he didn't want everyone to know he was a leper. I think it had been a well-kept secret. And he knew that if he went down to the Jordan River, he would have to peel off his armor and expose himself for what he really was.

The truth is, we all have our protective armor. And most of us have it for good reason—to hide behind and protect ourselves! When I was growing up as a boy, I developed an elaborate suit of armor for that very purpose. My mom was an alcoholic, married and divorced seven times, and the chaos of her life made a chaos out of mine. Sometimes I lived with her, sometimes I lived with my aunts, sometimes I lived with my grandparents, sometimes I lived in a military school. I was here, there, and everywhere.

For the most part, the adults in my life were disappointments to me. I put on armor for protection, telling myself, "Don't set yourself up for disappointment. Don't love and don't allow yourself to be loved. Don't be vulnerable. Be tough and hard and self-sufficient." I learned to do those things to survive, and to get through life.

When I heard the gospel for the first time, and was told to "surrender to the Lord," that was hard for me. And then when I met Christians for the first time and they started calling me "brother," I didn't know how to deal with that. When total strangers would come up and say, "I love you, bro," my response would be something like this: "I don't even *know* you. What do you mean you love me? And no thanks, I really don't want to hug you, either."

That was my suit of armor, and it's one of the issues I have to deal with personally to this day. Most likely, you have your own suit of armor, your own protective devices that you hide behind for protection. But if you really want to know God, you have to peel that armor away, becoming totally vulnerable to the One who loves you and died for you.

That's what Naaman had to do. He had humble himself, strip off his armor, and make himself vulnerable. I think some of his men must have been shocked to see the condition of his skin beneath that rich clothing and the gleaming armor. Some may have not known he was a leper at all. And those who did know might not have realized how badly the disease had progressed, how it had ravaged and disfigured his body.

So there was General Naaman, humiliated, exposed for all to see, standing there in the Jordan River. And following the prophet's instructions, he dips himself in the water, with everyone watching. He does it again. Again. Again.

Again. Again. Still a leper. Approaching the sixth time, he might have been thinking, *"I hope that prophet wasn't playing a practical joke on me, because I'm not going to be a happy camper if he was. But oh! Could it be that God would really heal me?"* He dips himself the seventh time, and you have to wonder if he stayed in the water just a little bit longer, perhaps offering a prayer to heaven: *"Lord, please, if You are out there, heal me now. I will serve You. I will follow You."*

Then he comes up for the seventh time, and may have kept his eyes closed for a minute, not wanting to see, not wanting to be disappointed. Finally, he opens his eyes and looks. And what he sees is not the mottled, disfigured skin of a leper, but the smooth, healthy skin of a young child. He has been transformed.

No doubt you've seen and touched the skin of a baby. It's like velvet. It's perfect—fresh and clean and new.

Can you see him standing there in the water, his hair and beard streaming water, staring at his hands and legs and stomach? What a moment that must have been. His men probably broke out in cheers, because they loved and admired him.

WE HAVE A ROLE TO PLAY

Can you imagine how that little Israelite maid felt, when news got back home that Naaman had been completely healed? Her heart must have leapt to think that God—*her* God—would allow her to play a role in the healing of someone like this.

It's every bit as exciting to think that God would allow us to play a role in the eternal salvation of another man or woman. Yes, I know, conversion is ultimately of God. The Scripture affirms that the Lord is the One who brings about salvation. But then the Bible also says, "The Lord has assigned to each his task. I planted the seed, Apollos watered it, but God made it grow."[62] There is a place for sowing, a place for watering, and a place for reaping.

God could have chosen to reach humanity by simply speaking directly to each of us, and in a sense He does. But His plan from the beginning has been to reach people through people. In the book of Romans Paul asks a series of penetrating questions: "How then shall they call on Him in whom they have not believed? And how shall they believe in Him of whom they have not heard? And how shall they hear without a preacher? And how shall they preach unless they are sent? As it is written: 'How beautiful are the feet of those who preach the gospel of peace, who bring glad tidings of good things!'"[63]

God wants to use you to reach another person. It doesn't mean you'll necessarily be the one to explain the whole gospel message to someone, and pray with them to receive Christ (which would be wonderful). Sometimes, your role may be like that of Namaan's servant girl: Simply pointing someone in the right direction, and telling them where they can find healing and life.

Maybe it's just a matter of living the Christian life in such a dynamic, beautiful way that someone observes and becomes intrigued. That's what Peter implies in 1 Peter 3:15: "But in your hearts set apart Christ as Lord. Always be prepared to give an answer to everyone who asks you to give the reason for the hope that you have."[64]

It might be the kind, loving way you treat your husband or your wife, your kids or your employees. It might be the way you deal with a disappointment or a tragedy in your life, where unbeknownst to you, someone is watching the way you respond, and saying to himself, "Man, I want what he's got. I want what she's got."

God wants to use you in this way, just as He was pleased to use this young girl in the household of her Syrian master.

So how did Naaman react after he was healed?

He believed in the Lord.

> Then Naaman and his entire party went back to find the man of God. They stood before him, and Naaman said, "I know at last that there is no God in all the world except in Israel.... Please allow me to load two of my mules with earth from this place, and I will take it back home with me. From now on I will never again offer any burnt offerings or sacrifices to any other god except the Lord. However, may the Lord pardon me in this one thing. When my master the king goes into the temple of the god Rimmon to worship there and leans on my arm, may the Lord pardon me when I bow, too."

> "Go in peace," Elisha said. So Naaman started home again.
> (2 Kings 5:15, 17-19, NLT)

Admitting Our Need

This is the classic story of a proud man without God who comes to the end of himself, and in humility reaches for God's salvation. And it wasn't easy! Naaman hated the idea of humbling himself. He despised the idea of admitting his need, and that he couldn't save himself.

But when he did, his life changed forever.

The idea of dipping himself in the Jordan River had seemed absurd to him, and demeaning. He didn't want to do it. It's the same for many people when they learn that finding salvation means admitting they're lost sinners, bound for hell, and that they must reach out and receive Jesus Christ as Savior and Lord.

It would be easier for some if you said, "Okay, the way for you to be forgiven of your sin is to first shave your head. Then you have to wear a lime green robe and sell watermelons at LAX. And if you do this for three months you'll be saved."

Or maybe, "If you want to find eternal life, you need to soak in prune juice for three years, then put on a pair of flippers and climb to the summit of the highest mountain of Tibet. Then cluck like a chicken for three more years, and you'll be forgiven." People would do it! People naturally love to have a hand in their own salvation.

But if you say, "You simply need to admit that you are a sinner, turn from your sin, and put your faith in Jesus Christ as Savior and Lord and follow Him," they will say, "What? No way! I could *never* do that."

You would think that this message of salvation and eternal life in Jesus Christ would be the easiest message to give away, wouldn't you? And yet many people will bitterly resist it.

A number of years ago my wife and I had been given four tickets to Disneyland, but the couple we were supposed to meet there didn't show up. After waiting for awhile, we went on into the park and started to walk around. Now even though this is supposed to be the "happiest place on earth," I started to feel guilty about it. I had two admission tickets in my back pocket that were being completely wasted.

So I said to my wife, "You know, I feel bad about hanging on to these tickets. I need to go give them away."

She said, "Greg, no one will take them."

"Are you kidding?" I said. "Free tickets to Disneyland? I'll get rid of these things in a heartbeat!"

So I run out the gate and offered them to some people standing in line to get in.

But they turned me down cold!

So I went to someone else, and he said, "How much you want for them?"

"Nothing! I'm giving them to you. Free."

But he wouldn't take them.

Giving away those free tickets ended up taking a lot longer than the "heartbeat" I'd promised Cathe. Everybody wanted to know what my angle was. It was hard for them to believe they could get something for nothing.

Why is it so difficult to give away something so wonderful...like salvation, God's most precious gift? I don't know. But there is something in human nature that says, "No, I want to buy it. I want to earn it. I want to merit it. I want to get it with my own ability." This is instead of simply saying, "I am a sinner. I am hopeless. There's no way I can help myself or save myself. Jesus, I need You! Come into my life!"

Naaman could have never earned his miracle cleansing in a million years. But he obtained it through two to three minutes of humility and surrender.

Chapter Six

GEHAZI: THE POSER

I read about two university students taking an organic chemistry class. Apparently, they'd done so well on their mid-terms that they didn't feel the need to study or prep for their final...so they partied the night before the big exam. Unfortunately, they ended up sleeping in the next day, missing the test altogether.

Putting their heads together, the two students concocted a story to present to their professor. They told him they'd been visiting a sick friend out of town, and on their way home (wouldn't you know it?) they got a flat tire, and hadn't been able to get back on time.

"I see," said the professor. "Well, that's fine. I accept that. You can retake the test."

He had them go into separate rooms and, to their great surprise, the make-up exam he had given them only contained two questions. Nevertheless, the professor had assured them that if they could answer those two questions correctly, they would ace the test and get an A.

Question number one they answered easily, and that was worth five points. Question number two, however, was worth 95 points, and it was this:

"Which tire?"

They both got busted.

Have you ever tried to cover up something you'd done that you knew was wrong? Here before us in the book of 2 Kings chapter 5 is the story of a man who sinned, was given an opportunity to confess his transgression and come clean, but couldn't bring himself to do so.

As a result, he paid a very heavy price.

NAAMAN'S BIG DAY

The story of Gehazi is really a continuation of what we read in the last chapter— the account of Elisha the prophet and the powerful Syrian general, Naaman.

After Naaman had been gloriously healed of his leprosy, he returned to the prophet's little house, overcome with humility and joy.

> Then Naaman and his entire party went back to find the man of God. They stood before him, and Naaman said, "I know at last that there is no God in all the world except in Israel. Now please accept my gifts."

But Elisha replied, "As surely as the LORD lives, whom I serve, I will not accept any gifts." And though Naaman urged him to take the gifts, Elisha refused.

Then Naaman said, "All right, but please allow me to load two of my mules with earth from this place, and I will take it back home with me. From now on I will never again offer any burnt offerings or sacrifices to any other god except the LORD. However, may the LORD pardon me in this one thing. When my master the king goes into the temple of the god Rimmon to worship there and leans on my arm, may the LORD pardon me when I bow, too."

"Go in peace," Elisha said. So Naaman started home again.
(2 Kings 5:15-19, NLT)

Can you begin to imagine this man's soaring joy? His leprosy was GONE—without a scar, without a trace. The text describes his skin like that of a new-born baby. What did that mean to Naaman? It meant his shame was a thing of the past. It meant he could be with his family and friends again—kiss his wife, hold his children. It meant his death sentence was lifted. It meant the great-est worry and fear in his heart—that awful sense of dread and heaviness that weighed on him every morning as he opened his eyes—was completely wiped away in an instant.

But more than that, he'd found God!

He told Elisha, "*I know AT LAST that there is no God in all the world except in Israel.*" Another translation puts it like this: "I now know beyond a shadow of a doubt that there is no God anywhere on earth other than the God of Israel."[65]

Naaman was excited about that. Perhaps all his life he had been expected to worship this false Syrian god, Rimmon, and felt the emptiness of it. But now he knew—and *knew* that he knew—that God actually existed, and that He was not only powerful, but merciful as well. The once-proud general's heart over-flowed with gladness as he thought about that.

Not surprisingly, the grateful Syrian's first desire was to give Elisha a gift—and he'd brought plenty of good stuff along with him for that very purpose.

We read earlier in the chapter: "So Naaman started out, taking as gifts 750 pounds of silver, 150 pounds of gold, and ten sets of clothing."[66]

In other words, he was prepared to pay!

But Elisha refused. It wasn't the time to line his own pockets. As one com-mentary puts it: "It was important that Naaman should not suppose that the prophets of the true God acted from motives of self-interest, much less imag-ine that 'the gift of God might be purchased with money.'"[67]

A happy ending, right?

Well, yes…and no.

Gehazi's Greed

This is where the story takes a very sad turn.

> But Gehazi, Elisha's servant, said to himself, "My master should not have let this Aramean get away without accepting his gifts. As surely as the LORD lives, I will chase after him and get something from him." So Gehazi set off after him.
>
> When Naaman saw him running after him, he climbed down from his chariot and went to meet him. "Is everything all right?" Naaman asked.
>
> "Yes," Gehazi said, "but my master has sent me to tell you that two young prophets from the hill country of Ephraim have just arrived. He would like 75 pounds of silver and two sets of clothing to give to them."
>
> "By all means, take 150 pounds of silver," Naaman insisted. He gave him two sets of clothing, tied up the money in two bags, and sent two of his servants to carry the gifts for Gehazi. But when they arrived at the hill, Gehazi took the gifts from the servants and sent the men back. Then he hid the gifts inside the house.
>
> When he went in to his master, Elisha asked him, "Where have you been, Gehazi?"
>
> "I haven't been anywhere," he replied.
>
> But Elisha asked him, "Don't you realize that I was there in spirit when Naaman stepped down from his chariot to meet you? Is this the time to receive money and clothing and olive groves and vineyards and sheep and oxen and servants? Because you have done this, you and your children and your children's children will suffer from Naaman's leprosy forever." When Gehazi left the room, he was leprous; his skin was as white as snow. (2 Kings 5:20-27, NLT)

What lessons can we learn from the life of this privileged, yet fatally flawed, servant of Elisha the prophet? Three truths come immediately to mind.

#1: Covetousness And Greed Can Destroy You

Gehazi greedily coveted that which was not his to take.

It was Donald Trump who once said, "The point is, you can't be too greedy."

Really! Sorry, Donald, but I think Jesus would disagree with you on that one. In fact, the Bible classifies greed and covetousness right up there with the sins of theft, adultery, and even murder.

The Bible warns us time and again to beware of greed and coveting. Coveting is such a serious sin it made God's top ten.

"You shall not covet your neighbor's house; you shall not covet your neighbor's wife, nor his male servant, nor his female servant, nor his ox, nor his donkey, nor anything that is your neighbor's." (Exodus 20:17)

While He walked on earth, Jesus gave a stern warning about coveting, saying, "Watch out! Be on your guard against all kinds of greed; a man's life does not consist in the abundance of his possessions."[68]

Yet in spite of God's stern warnings, we live today in a culture where we're essentially taught from our very earliest years to covet. Television advertising tells our little children that if you don't get this toy, this video game—or even this breakfast cereal—then you're not going to be happy.

Sophisticated marketers, investing billions in their craft, aren't so much selling a car or a perfume or a pair of jeans, they're selling a *lifestyle*. If you use this perfume, if you drive this car, if you buy this iPod, here's what your life will be like. If you don't, then…well, life may not be worth living!

In music videos, many contemporary performing artists (if you want to call them that) continually flaunt all the stuff they have. *"Hey, look at my car. Look at my bling. Look at my crib (house). Look at my body. Go ahead and covet what I have! You know you want it!"*

It is all about reaching and reaching for something that you don't currently possess.

In the last chapter, I referenced a *USA Today* article where they polled 18-to-25-year-olds, asking them about their top priorities in life. And the poll revealed that more than anything else, Generation Y wants to be "rich and famous."

Coveting isn't just harmless daydreaming, or wishing upon a star, it is *sin*—an open door for Satan to gain a foothold in your life and eventually destroy you, as it destroyed Gehazi.

Coveting isn't about wanting money; we all need money to live in this world. It's about wanting *more* money. It's not about wanting to be known, it's about wanting to *more* well-known. It's not about wanting to be influential; it's about wanting more and more and more influence and power.

In Proverbs 27:20 (NIV), Solomon (who ought to know), wrote: "Death and Destruction are never satisfied, and neither are the eyes of man." Another translation renders the verse like this: "Death and the grave are never satisfied, and neither are we."[69]

We will say, "Once I have *this*, I'll be happy." So you manage to obtain that object of your desire, and it's not nearly as satisfying as you imagined it would be. So you find yourself wanting something else…and something else beyond that. Isn't that the way of it? We keep reaching for something that's always just beyond our grasp.

That is coveting. And if it gets a grip on your heart, it will devastate you and those you love.

Of course it's not a sin to want to be married and have a family, or to be successful in business or make a good living. But if you become obsessed with those things, and you're willing to do whatever it takes to get there—including stepping on others or compromising your principles—then you have crossed the line.

Actually, there's another biblical word for it that's just a little more direct. It's *idolatry*. Because the Bible actually tells us in Colossians 3:4, "Covetousness is idolatry."

A number of people come to mind who allowed greed and covetousness to destroy them. Way back in the Garden of Eden, we read what happened in Eve's heart as she fixated on that forbidden fruit.

> So when the woman saw that the tree was good for food, that it was pleasant to the eyes, and a tree desirable to make one wise, she took of its fruit and ate. (Genesis 3:6)

She coveted, and then she ate. And the results were sin and death entering the human race.

In the book of Joshua, a man named Achan coveted some of the loot from the conquered city of Jericho and, directly disobeying God's command, took some clothing and gold and hid them under his tent. That particular sin brought a humiliating military defeat to the whole nation—and death to himself and his family.

King David, who already had multiple wives, coveted Bathsheba, the wife of another. As a result he brought the sword on his own household for generations.

In the New Testament, Ananias and Sapphira lied to the Holy Spirit and the church in Jerusalem because they coveted both the admiration of their fellow believers and the money they wanted to hang onto.

That's why we're told in 1 Timothy 6:10, "For the love of money is the root of all kinds of evil: which while some have coveted after, they have erred from the faith, and pierced themselves through with many sorrows." Or as another translation puts it, "For the love of money is a root of all kinds of evil. Some people, eager for money, have wandered from the faith and pierced themselves with many griefs."[70]

Bending every effort to grasp. If that's what you're living for, your life will end in ruin.

American psychologist Eric Fromme said, "Greed is a bottomless pit which exhausts the person in an endless effort to satisfy the need without ever reaching satisfaction."

If covetousness is the disease, then, what is the antidote?

The antidote to covetousness is contentment.

Hear the apostle Paul:

Not that I was ever in need, for I have learned how to get along happily whether I have much or little. I know how to live on almost nothing or with everything. I have learned the secret of contentment in every situation, whether it be a full stomach or hunger, plenty or want; for I can do everything God asks me to with the help of Christ who gives me the strength and power. (Philippians 4:11-13, TLB)

Paul was saying, "I know what it's like to live with a lot, and I know what it's like to live with very little. But it doesn't really matter, because I've learned to be content with whatever God gives me."

How could he say that? Because Paul understood that contentment doesn't come from what you have, it comes from whom you know. The book of Hebrews backs up those words:

Keep your lives free from the love of money and be content with what you have, because God has said, "Never will I leave you; never will I forsake you." So we say with confidence, "The Lord is my helper; I will not be afraid. What can man do to me?" (Hebrews 13:5-6, NIV)

No matter what happens to you in life, the Lord is there with you, and He will stand by your side.

But greed and covetousness can destroy a life.

#2: Spiritual Privilege Brings Great Responsibility

If Gehazi had been the average Israelite man on the street, his story wouldn't have been so amazing—or so tragic. But when you put his life into context, considering what he had seen and what he had experienced, you have to shake your head and wonder, "What was he thinking about?"

Understand what Gehazi's position was. We might well describe him as an executive assistant to the prophet Elisha. He wasn't just Elisha's "gopher," running out in the morning to get the prophet a latte and a bran muffin. He was also one that would give counsel and even advice to Elisha. The mighty prophet actually included Gehazi in his decision making.

For instance, when Elisha was staying in the home of the lady known as the Shunammite (she was from the town of Shunem), the prophet wanted to repay her in some way for her kindness.

Later Elisha asked Gehazi, "What do you think we can do for her?"

He suggested, "She doesn't have a son, and her husband is an old man."

"Call her back again," Elisha told him. When the woman returned, Elisha said to her as she stood in the doorway, "Next year at about this time you will be holding a son in your arms!" (2 Kings 4:14-16, NLT)

He included Gehazi in that decision. And later on, when that child died, Elisha dispatched Gehazi with his staff to hold it over the son, and hopefully raise the boy from the dead. Gehazi did this, but with no success. Ultimately Elisha himself had to return to the Shunammite's home to raise up the boy himself.

This last incident reveals something about Gehazi. Though he was included in these decisions and in the prophet's activities, he didn't seem to have his own relationship with God. It seemed like the glory that Gehazi experienced was but a reflection of another's. He needed someone else to prop him up spiritually.

There are people like that in our churches today. (I hope you're not one of them.) Lacking their own vital relationship with God, they depend on others to hold them up and hand-feed them. That's fine, of course, if you happen to be a brand new Christian. But there comes a point where you need to grow up spiritually.

When our granddaughter Stella was a baby just learning how to eat a little solid food, it was fun trying to get her to open up her mouth to slip in the spoonful of the strained peas, or whatever. She was so cute, and it was our joy to feed her.

But it wouldn't be so cute if we were still feeding her strained peas at 16. It would be tragic.

In the same way, there are people who have known the Lord for years, but they're like spiritual babies or toddlers. Someone always has to be holding them by the hand or spooning spiritual food into their mouths. The author of Hebrews dealt with this when he said, "You have been Christians a long time now, and you ought to be teaching others. Instead, you need someone to teach you again the basic things a beginner must learn about the Scriptures. You are like babies who drink only milk and cannot eat solid food. And a person who is living on milk isn't very far along in the Christian life and doesn't know much about doing what is right. Solid food is for those who are mature, who have trained themselves to recognize the difference between right and wrong and then do what is right."[71]

It's apparent that, for all the wondrous things he observed, Gehazi never developed his own relationship with God. He remained dependent upon Elisha. We see this clearly demonstrated in his disastrous decision to lie to Naaman and Elisha, in order to line his own pockets.

Are you dependent upon someone else for your spiritual life? A wife or husband? A friend or pastor? An author or a TV personality? Please understand what I'm saying here. We should all have godly men and women in our lives whom we look up to—and even imitate. There's nothing wrong with saying, "I want to follow the Lord just like he does," or, "I want to know my Bible the way she knows her Bible." There are people in the ministry and out of the ministry that I admire very much, and I love spending as much time with them as I can.

We *need* the positive influence of godly men and women around us. And more than that, we also need to *be* such an individual for those who are younger in the faith than we are.

But at the same time, we must never allow ourselves to become totally dependent upon anyone else to lead and inspire us in the Christian life. And I mean *anyone*.

Why? Because first of all, we don't *need* to. We have the Word of God that we can read for ourselves, and we have the indwelling Holy Spirit who is ready to apply those truths to our lives. Besides that, people will let you down! Even mature, godly people who have walked with the Lord for years. Even confident, attractive, well-spoken people who know their Bibles inside out.

Christian leaders have feet of clay. They have shortcomings. They will disappoint you, and ultimately, won't measure up to your expectations. And that's why you need your own relationship and walk with God.

You and I have both known people who will keep going spiritually as long as there is someone to prod them along. If someone says to them, "Let's pray," then they'll pray. If someone says, "Let's do a Bible study," or "Let's go to church," then that's what they'll do.

But what happens if no one is around to prompt? Will his or her spiritual life begin to unravel? The fact is, all of us need our own relationship with God. We need to stand on our own feet, spiritually, and we need to be able to feed ourselves!

Gehazi may have fooled himself in this regard, but his actions reveal that he didn't have his own relationship with the Lord. He was simply leaning on the spiritual life and dynamic of the prophet Elisha.

Amazingly, he even rationalized his deception as the will of God.

> But Gehazi, the servant of Elisha the man of God, said, "Look, my master has spared Naaman this Syrian, while not receiving from his hands what he brought; but as the LORD lives, I will run after him and take something from him." (2 Kings 5:20)

Notice the phrase, "as the LORD lives." In other words, Gehazi was saying, "Hey, all Naaman wanted to do was express a little gratitude. All he wanted to do was say thanks, and my master blew him off. Didn't even give him the time of day! I would be doing a good turn by accepting those gifts. It would be the gracious thing to do, after all. I think that would be the Lord's will!"

To tell the truth, a decision like that was way beyond Gehazi's pay grade! What did the Lord have to do with it? Nothing at all. Saying "as the LORD lives" was just a way to put a spiritual spin on the man's sheer greed. If what he was doing was such a good thing, why did he have to hide it and lie about it?

It's truly astonishing how our old, sinful nature can rationalize the most aberrant and bizarre behavior. That's one of the reasons we need the church.

That's one of the reasons why we need fellow believers to knock some sense into our heads now and then.

David wrote: "Let a righteous man strike me—it is a kindness; let him rebuke me—it is oil on my head. My head will not refuse it."[72] (It's just too bad that David didn't have a godly friend around to whack him on the head on the night he went after Uriah's wife, Bathsheba! That was the moment when he needed a little tough love.)

We all need to be confronted and challenged by mature saints at different times in our lives. When you're a new believer, you are filled with excitement and zeal. But sometimes, not knowing the Word of God or the ways of God, you can come up with some pretty strange ideas. You need an older believer who knows his way around the Word to say, "You know what? I think you're on the wrong track with that idea, because the Bible says thus and so." We need to learn to measure what we do by what the Word of God says, not by what our feelings tell us.

Gehazi, who had great spiritual privilege, took that privilege for granted. He wasn't the only one who did that. In the New Testament we read the story of a man named Demas.

And who was *his* friend?

Would you believe…the apostle Paul?

Talk about having a great friend. Can you imagine hanging out with the apostle—maybe getting a cup of coffee?

"Hey Paul, what are your thoughts on justification?"

"Funny you should ask…."

Paul was a scholar, an apostle of God, and a man blessed by the Lord to write more of the Bible than any other single individual. And Demas? He had the privilege of traveling with the apostle, ministering with him, and spending all kinds of quality time with him. (Can you imagine doing morning devotions with the apostle Paul? Think he might have a few spiritual insights?)

Here is some biblical evidence of this relationship:

Our dear friend Luke, the doctor, and Demas send greetings….

Epaphras, my fellow prisoner in Christ Jesus, sends you greetings. And so do Mark, Aristarchus, Demas and Luke, my fellow workers. (Colossians 4:14; Philemon 23-24, NIV)

But in the end, he threw it all over, caving in to the allure of the world. Paul's last words about Demas, coming soon before the apostle's martyrdom, are not words any believer would like on his or her gravestone.

Be diligent to come to me quickly; for Demas has forsaken me, having loved this present world, and has departed for Thessalonica….
(2 Timothy 4:9-10)

Imagine having Paul as your friend…and yet forsaking the Lord.

But there's one more example even more bizarre than Gehazi or Demas. How about Judas Iscariot? If Gehazi has a counterpart in the New Testament, I suppose it would be Judas, who sold out the Lord for 30 pieces of silver.

Though he was certainly a good and godly man, the apostle Paul was still human, and made mistakes. But Jesus never made a mistake. Was never hypocritical. Never selfish. In fact, He lived a flawless life. Judas had been present with Jesus, day and night, for up to three years, hearing the greatest teachings ever uttered in human history, and observing first-hand miracles like the world had never seen.

Yet for all that, Judas' heart only grew harder and harder, and in the end, he stabbed His Lord and Friend in the back.

For me, this is a startling reminder that *exposure to spiritual truth can be very damaging*. Conventional wisdom says, study more and listen more, and you'll just keep growing. And that's true…*if* you have a desire to know God. *If* you are in relationship with Him. On the other hand, if you are continually exposed to spiritual truth and yet have no real inclination or intention of responding appropriately to it, your heart can become very hard. As the old saying goes, the same sun that softens the wax hardens the clay. The same sun that makes the living tree grow dries up the dead tree. And the same gospel message that transforms one can drive another deeper into sin. It's not the fault of the message. It's the fault of the listener.

Some people hear a Bible message and spend the whole time rating the preacher and the sermon, with no real thought that the message might be *for them*, from the Lord. You can become so busy critiquing the sermon or giving the pastor style points or demerits for this or that, that you won't even hear the message God has for your heart. So you become more and more hardened to spiritual things…without even realizing it.

That happened to Gehazi. It happened to Demas. It happened to Judas. And make no mistake about it, it can happen to you. So have an open, receptive, tender heart toward the things of God, realizing that He has a plan for *your* life and wants to communicate important truths to *your* heart.

And here's one final thing we can learn from the life of Gehazi.

#3: You Can't Hide Your Sin From GOD

Although he may not have admitted it to himself, Gehazi knew very well that what he was doing was wrong, because he hid it from Elisha.

That's a pretty good method to determine if what you're doing is right or wrong. Are you hiding it from others? Let's say that you're looking at a particular website on your computer. Then, when someone walks into the room, you click it off really fast.

Why do you do that?

"Well...um, he probably wouldn't understand it."

Really?

"I'm...a...doing a research paper on lust, and I'm just checking out a few contemporary examples."

The truth is, you are doing something you have rationalized in your mind, but then when someone else comes along, you suddenly feel uncomfortable with it. And what do you do? You hide it.

Be very careful about what you hide! Jesus said, "There is nothing concealed that will not be disclosed, or hidden that will not be made known."[73]

Nevertheless, that's what Gehazi did. He was first of all trying to hide from his master and friend, the prophet. But he was also trying to hide from God— the one thing that he could never get away with.

That's one of the reasons God gave us the ordinance of the Lord's Supper, or the communion table. In his letter to the Corinthians, Paul wrote:

> So if anyone eats this bread or drinks this cup of the Lord unworthily, that person is guilty of sinning against the body and the blood of the Lord. That is why you should examine yourself before eating the bread and drinking from the cup. For if you eat the bread or drink the cup unworthily, not honoring the body of Christ, you are eating and drinking God's judgment upon yourself. That is why many of you are weak and sick and some have even died.

> But if we examine ourselves, we will not be examined by God and judged in this way. (1 Corinthians 11:27-31, NLT)

Before we take the bread and the cup of communion, remembering our Lord's broken body and His blood poured out for us, God gives us the opportunity to search our own hearts. Is there something we've been foolishly trying to hide? To hide from our spouse? To hide from our Christian friends? To hide from the Lord? (As if we could.)

King David, recognizing how we easily we can deceive even ourselves, invited the Lord to examine him—to give his heart the white glove test. He prayed: "Search me, O God, and know my heart; test my thoughts. Point out anything you find in me that makes you sad, and lead me along the path of everlasting life."[74]

God has also given us His Word as a tool to cut through self-deception. He tells us in Hebrews 4:12-13, "For the word of God is full of living power. It is sharper than the sharpest knife, cutting deep into our innermost thoughts and desires. It exposes us for what we really are. Nothing in all creation can hide from him. Everything is naked and exposed before his eyes. This is the God to whom we must explain all that we have done."[75]

Before we read the Word, we need to ask God's Holy Spirit to reveal truth to us—to open our hearts to things we might not have seen before.

In a highly significant moment, Elisha gave his servant the opportunity to confess his sin...but Gehazi missed it.

Now he went in and stood before his master. Elisha said to him, "Where did you go, Gehazi?"

And he said, "Your servant did not go anywhere."
(2 Kings 5:25)

Elisha gave Gehazi a chance to admit what he had done, but instead of coming clean, Gehazi chose to wade deeper into deception, using a lie to cover a lie. (It never works.) Why did Elisha ask him this question? Was it because he didn't know where Gehazi was? Of course not, because God had revealed it to him.

Then he said to him, "Did not my heart go with you when the man turned back from his chariot to meet you?" (2 Kings 5:26)

What should Gehazi have said? I think the appropriate response would have been, "Okay, Elisha. It's stupid to think I could have ever pulled this off. I've been out telling lies and taking things that don't belong to me. I've been hiding stuff from you and the Lord, and now I feel a great sense of guilt and conviction over what I've done. Will you forgive me?"

I personally believe that if Gehazi had said those words from his heart, Elisha would have replied, "All right, Gehazi. You go on back to Naaman and return those things, telling him the truth. And then get on your knees before the Lord and repent with all your heart, and you'll be forgiven and restored."

What a marvelous door of grace opened in that moment! But an open door does no good at all if you don't step through it. Tragically, Gehazi didn't. He foolishly replied to Elisha, "I haven't been anywhere. Haven't been doing anything." And he missed the opportunity that Elisha—and the Lord—had extended to him.

Have you ever heard God ask you the question, "What are you doing? Why are you here?" It's a question as old as time. When Adam was in Eden, after he had sinned and heard the sound of the Lord God walking in the garden in the cool in the day, he heard God's voice calling: "Adam...where are you?"

Was it because God couldn't see Adam hiding in the bushes? Of course not. But He wanted Adam to confess, and get his heart made right. God wasn't looking for information, He was looking for confession. He wanted Adam and Eve to confront what they had done so they could set it right and be restored to fellowship with Himself.

So how do we respond when the Lord asks us, "What are you doing? Where are you at? Where have you been?"

If we have been running from him or trying to hide something from Him, we need to respond, "Lord, You know. I'm not really where I ought to be." The

Bible tells us in 1 John 1:9-10 (NIV) that, "If we confess our sins, he is faithful and just and will forgive us our sins and purify us from all unrighteousness. If we claim we have not sinned, we make him out to be a liar and his word has no place in our lives."

But Gehazi covered it up. And judgment came upon him as a result. Proverbs 28:13 says, "He who covers his sins will not prosper, but whoever confesses and forsakes them will have mercy."

Examine yourself and ask yourself the question: *Am I really a true follower of the Lord? Does my walk really match my talk?* In the story we just looked at, Elisha was a believer, and Naaman became a believer. But Gehazi was a *poser*—someone who pretends to be something they're really not.

I'm something of a poser when I ride my Harley. My bike is big and black with high handlebars, and looks like a chopper. I wear a helmet and a black leather jacket, and when I get out there on the freeway with my some of my other pastor friends—with our loud pipes blaring—we look like tough, outlaw bikers. People kind of pull away from us when they see us coming. But little do they realize that underneath that gnarly exterior is a loving, warm-hearted pastor just looking for someone to pray for!

Now that's a situation with some humorous aspects to it, but posing as a follower of the Lord isn't funny at all.

Some people in the church will put on an act like Gehazi. They'll say that the Lord spoke to them and told them to do this or that, when He hasn't said anything to them at all. They'll hang around with Christians, get involved in Christian work, and even participate in a Bible study...when all along the truth has never penetrated their hearts, and their lives are not right with God.

Gehazi actually thought he could play the game and stay a step ahead of Elisha and the Lord. He thought he could play his part, but keep his secrets, too.

He should have dropped the pretense and made things right when God gave him the chance. Apparently, however, he'd worn the mask for so long he forgot how to take it off.

Chapter Seven

BELSHAZZAR: WHEN YOUR NUMBER IS UP

W hy are you here on earth? Why did you open your eyes this morning to a new day of life...and what does it all mean? What is the purpose of our existence?

A recent poll of Americans revealed that 61 percent of us said the main purpose of life is *enjoyment and personal fulfillment*. And 50 percent of those who responded in that way identified themselves as born again Christians.

Could that be true? Our reason for being is to simply please ourselves? Is that truly the purpose of life? We will see an answer to that question in the lives of two men that Scripture places side by side to teach us a very important lesson. Their names are Nebuchadnezzar and Belshazzar. Both were kings over Babylon, and they were related. Belshazzar was the grandson of Nebuchadnezzar.

Grandpa Nebuchadnezzar wasted most of his life, but in the end made a wise decision. Grandson Belshazzar wasted *all* of his life, and in the end made the wrong decision.

A HARD MAN TO REACH?

In Daniel chapter 4, we read about the mighty King Nebuchadnezzar, a man with everything this world could offer a person, including unparalleled wealth, seemingly limitless power, worldwide fame, and the ability to fulfill his every desire.

He was also a man who had been exposed to spiritual truth—truth about the true and living God—but had pretty much blown it off. Four godly Hebrew young men, Shadrach, Meshach, Abednego, and Daniel had been captured in Jerusalem, and brought into his palace, where he was schooling them in the ways of Babylon. Scripture tells us that these young Jews—who loved and served the Lord—had ten times more wisdom than all of the other counselors to the king.

Then the king had a dream, which Daniel interpreted for him when no one else could. Later on, when the king foolishly set up a golden image of himself and commanded everyone to worship it, he saw with his own eyes how the Lord preserved Shadrach, Meshach, and Abednego in the fiery furnace. And the king himself, to his wonder and awe, described a Fourth Man walking with them through the flames.

> "Look! ...I see four men loose, walking in the midst of the fire; and they are not hurt, and the form of the fourth is like the Son of God" (Daniel 3:25).

This was a man who was exposed to spiritual truth time and again. Yet for the most part, he rejected it, not allowing the implications of what he had personally seen and experienced to penetrate his personal world.

But God wasn't finished with this proud king. The Lord sent Nebuchadnezzar a frightening vision in the night, that had him running to track down Daniel, a man he knew walked with God.

"I, Nebuchadnezzar, was living in my palace in comfort and prosperity. But one night I had a dream that greatly frightened me; I saw visions that terrified me as I lay in my bed. So I issued an order calling in all the wise men of Babylon, so they could tell me what my dream meant. When all the magicians, enchanters, astrologers, and fortune-tellers came in, I told them the dream, but they could not tell me what it meant. At last Daniel came in before me, and I told him the dream. (He was named Belteshazzar after my god, and the spirit of the holy gods is in him.)

"I said to him, 'O Belteshazzar, master magician, I know that the spirit of the holy gods is in you and that no mystery is too great for you to solve. Now tell me what my dream means.'" (Daniel 4:4-9, NLT)

Here are some things we learn from this remarkable story—truly one of "the greatest stories ever told."

#1: No One Is Beyond The Reach Of GOD

How would you go about reaching a man as powerful as Nebuchadnezzar? In verse 1, the king says he was living in his palace in "comfort and prosperity." For some of us, that would mean a nice apartment or a house in the suburbs with a little money in the bank. For Nebuchadnezzar, however, it meant he was probably the wealthiest man on the whole planet.

Talk about having it made! With his armies he had effectively conquered the civilized world, and there was no longer any need for war. Instead, he concentrated his energies into building Babylon into the most magnificent city on the face of the earth.

Now if you've ever tried to add a room on to your home or do a little remodeling, you know all about the plans that have to be drawn up and the permits that have to be applied for and approved and on and on. Then you have to deal with contractors and unions and inspectors. Sometimes it seems like you'll never get to drive that first nail! But Nebuchadnezzar didn't have to worry about submitting plans to the city. He was the city. He was the nation. He was the world. His word wasn't as good as law, it *was* law.

Nebuchadnezzar didn't have to trouble himself about dealing with unions. Why should he? He had all the slave labor he could ask for, thousands of captives taken from defeated nations all over that part of the world.

So here was this incredible city that was built by these slaves.

The walls of Babylon alone were 350 feet high, and 87 feet wide—wide enough to ride six chariots abreast around the top! The city also had 250 watchtowers placed in strategic locations, and 100 gates, each made of burnished bronze. One palace alone in the great city covered 11 acres. One banquet hall alone would seat upwards of 10,000 people. The famous hanging gardens of Babylon were one of the wonders of the ancient world.

So this was a magnificent city, under the control of a man of great power.

How do you reach such a man for God? Can it really be done? How do you get through to a man like this? Who knows how?

God knows how. He has His own methods!

And it began with an unforgettable dream.

In verse 5, Nebuchadnezzar writes: "I had a dream that greatly frightened me; and I saw visions that terrified me as I lay in my bed." Here was the most powerful man on earth, in bed in his royal palace behind towering walls sealed by massive gates of bronze, and surrounded by a small army of armed guards.

And he was afraid?

Yes, he was frightened by a dream. A dream sent by God Himself.

This is yet another reminder that no one is beyond the reach of God. You and I look around the world today at those who would threaten our nation and the peace of our planet—dictators in Iran, China, North Korea, or Russia. Did the thought ever occur to you that you could actually pray for those individuals, that they might come to faith in Jesus Christ?

Listen, if Nebuchadnezzar could be converted, *anyone* can be converted. God can reach any person, no matter if they are dictators, famous rock idols, movie stars, hardened journalists, or even atheistic university professors. It may be hard for our natural minds to believe, but it could happen. No one is beyond the reach of God.

So we need to pray for people. Like…that unsaved boss who gives you all that trouble…that spouse who doesn't yet know the Lord, and has waited so long to believe…that child who won't even talk to you about the things of the Lord. They *can* be converted. No one is beyond the touch of an all-powerful God. He has plans and purposes beyond what you could ever dream. So don't give up hoping and don't give up praying.

I love what the gospel writer says in Luke 18:1 (NIV): "Then Jesus told his disciples a parable to show them that they should always pray and not give up."

In my own heart, I'm certain that Daniel—a great man of faith and prayer—prayed for Nebuchadnezzar, asking the Lord to touch this proud king's heart.

So Nebuchadnezzar had a dream, and as a result, rounded up the usual suspects—the magicians, enchanters, astrologers, and fortune tellers—and said, "Someone tell me what this means."

This is so typical of people today. When we have a crisis we will turn first to a psychiatrist or psychologist or even a psychic before we will turn to God and His Word.

As a last resort, probably figuring he'd better cover all of his bases, Nebuchadnezzar called for the prophet Daniel. Now Daniel had interpreted dreams for him before. He interpreted the dream of the great image that Nebuchadnezzar had seen.

As Daniel hears *this* dream, however, it must have truly frightened him.

Upon hearing this, Daniel (also known as Belteshazzar) was overcome for a time, aghast at the meaning of the dream. Finally, the king said to him, "Belteshazzar, don't be alarmed by the dream and what it means."

Belteshazzar replied, "Oh, how I wish the events foreshadowed in this dream would happen to your enemies, my lord, and not to you!" (Daniel 4:19, NLT)

Daniel knew very well what the dream meant; it was foretelling the ultimate destruction of Babylon and the radical humbling of King Nebuchadnezzar himself. If he told the king the truth, it could easily cost him his head.

It's hard to tell people the truth sometimes, isn't it? Someone may ask us a question, and we know if we tell them the truth, it may very well hurt their feelings. What if your wife gets a new outfit and says, "Honey, do I look fat in this?"

You don't want to lie, but you do want to be very, *very* diplomatic. For the sake of peace and harmony, you want to think of something creative and positive to say!

Imagine how difficult it is for a doctor sometimes. Someone's getting ready to go on their vacation, and they come in for their annual checkup before they leave town. After you've seen the test results, what you really want to do is call them up and say, "Hey, everything's good. Have a great vacation. No problems." But what if one of those tests has revealed cancer in this person's body?

You really don't have any choice. You have to call them in, sit them down, and break the news. It isn't easy, but if you're a good doctor, you have to tell them the truth. You have to give them the bad news, straight up, and allow them to deal with the issue. Of course, along with that, you give all the good news you can…ideas, treatment options, and every hopeful scenario you can think of.

But first you have to tell the truth.

As believers, you and I have been given the message of the gospel. And like Paul in Acts 20:27, we know that we need to declare "the whole counsel of God." But sometimes it's a temptation to edit the message, isn't it?

You might say to someone, "Jesus Christ has changed my life. He has filled the void inside of me, given me peace and purpose, and I know I'm going to go to heaven when I die. And I wish you would believe in Jesus, too."

The person replies, "You know what? I'm never going to believe in Jesus. But

I want to ask you a question point blank. If I *don't* believe in Jesus and I reject Him for my entire life, what will happen to me when I die?"

Now what are you going to say?

Suddenly, you're reluctant. You know the answer, but you don't want to use the "h" word. You don't want to say the word "hell."

Why? Well it might offend them. But if you don't say it, if you neglect to warn that person, you might offend God! In other words, if I don't tell a man the repercussions of not believing in Christ for salvation, then I am not declaring the whole counsel of God. I'm no better than a doctor who would say to a dying person, "You have a clean bill of health."

I have to tell them, "I'm sorry to tell you this, but there is a hell. There is judgment coming for those who have rejected God's Son. And the last thing God wants is for you to go there. But I have to tell you, because that's what the Bible clearly teaches."

You see, we can want to hold back on the truth because we're afraid it might offend someone.

Imagine how easy it would have been for Daniel to pull his punches. "Wow king…that's, um…quite a dream you had. But you know, I think everything's going to be okay."

Instead, Daniel says, "Oh man. This dream isn't good at all." He would have been tempted, of course, to not disclose the full meaning to the king, because people had lost their lives for far less. But Daniel told him the truth.

And then he added a little P.S. in verse 27:

"O King Nebuchadnezzar, please listen to me. Stop sinning and do what is right. Break from your wicked past by being merciful to the poor. Perhaps then you will continue to prosper."

To paraphrase, Daniel is saying, "Nebuchadnezzar, this dream is foretelling your destruction. But here's some good news. If you will repent, if you will stop sinning, God may spare you."

Following this incident, by the way, the Lord gave Nebuchadnezzar 12 long months to think about it all. But instead of changing his ways, the king shrugged off God's truth (again) and persisted in his path of pride…and pleasing himself.

And then the hammer dropped.

The Lord warns you and me and in the same way. In Galatians 6:7-8, we read: "Do not be deceived: God cannot be mocked. A man reaps what he sows. The one who sows to please his sinful nature, from that nature will reap destruction; the one who sows to please the Spirit, from the Spirit will reap eternal life."[76]

The Lord says, don't be fooled! You will reap what you sow. The crop may not come in this year or next year, but it will come in. God will keep His Word. The wheels of God's justice may grind slowly, but they grind surely.

Nebuchadnezzar was a flat-out wicked man. Earlier in the book of Daniel, we read how he had erected a golden image, commanding everyone to worship it, or be put to death. He was a powerful, ruthless, cruel dictator. And despite receiving warning after warning from God to repent, he wouldn't do it.

In interpreting the dream for the king, the prophet told him, "If you don't turn to God, you're going to lose your sanity—to the point that you'll be like a wild animal out in the field, eating grass like a cow. Your hair and beard will be long and matted, and your fingernails and toenails will grow out. This is what *will* happen to you if you don't repent."

Nebuchadnezzar thought to himself. "That's an interesting interpretation. But he can't mean it will happen *literally*. After all, I'm the great Nebuchadnezzar. How could that happen to me?"

But it did.

All these things did happen to King Nebuchadnezzar. Twelve months later, he was taking a walk on the flat roof of the royal palace in Babylon. As he looked out across the city, he said, "Just look at this great city of Babylon! I, by my own mighty power, have built this beautiful city as my royal residence and as an expression of my royal splendor."

While he was still speaking these words, a voice called down from heaven, "O King Nebuchadnezzar, this message is for you! You are no longer ruler of this kingdom...." (Daniel 4:28-31, NLT)

God says, "You can't take credit for what you have done. I have given it to you." It reminds us that even secular man, in all his arrogance and pride, can't take credit for his accomplishments.

Everything you and I have been given is from God. It's God Himself who gives us the ability to make wealth. So if you have been successful in business, don't be patting yourself on the back too much. Yes, you may be resourceful, bright, and hard-working. But your very ability to think, to plan, to work, *and to breathe* has been given to you as a gift from God. Don't forget that for even a moment. Don't look at your accomplishments and say, "Look at what I've accomplished! Look at this great family that I've had. Look at my awesome ministry."

Don't do it! Receiving great gifts from God is an occasion for great humility. *"Lord, all this has come from You, and You alone, and I thank You for it."*

Nebuchadnezzar was just one of many world leaders that dared to defy God, and found out that God will not be mocked.

The mighty empire of Rome tried to crush the Christian faith. There were ten waves of persecution against the church, beginning with the wicked Caesar Nero and culminating with Diocletian. Christian believers were fed to animals in the Coliseum for blood sport to entertain the Roman citizens. Followers of Jesus were covered with pitch and lit on fire to light the gardens of Caesar Nero.

Christians were tortured, beheaded, crucified, and treated in all manner of horrible ways to eradicate them and their beliefs from the face of the earth. So confident was Diocletian in his success that he had a coin struck in Rome, with this statement on it: "The Christian religion is destroyed, and the worship of the Roman gods are restored."

As to that, I've had the privilege of being in Rome recently. There are some beautiful ruins in the city, and some really great pasta. But the mighty Roman Empire? It's been gone for centuries. Meanwhile, Christianity is alive and well. So much for the plans of the Caesars to destroy the faith utterly. And so will go the plans of every person who opposes God.

Nebuchadnezzar defied God and paid the price for it. But God graciously restored his sanity to him after seven long years of insanity and living in the wilds like a beast.

> "After this time had passed, I, Nebuchadnezzar, looked up to heaven. My sanity returned, and I praised and worshiped the Most High and honored the one who lives forever." (v. 34)

The king was restored to his former position, and he was so moved by the memory of God's discipline and grace that he composed a little psalm:

> "His rule is everlasting,
> and his kingdom is eternal.
> All the people of the earth
> are nothing compared to him.
> He has the power to do as he pleases
> among the angels of heaven
> and with those who live on earth.
> No one can stop him or challenge him,
> saying, 'What do you mean by doing these things?'"
> (vv. 34-35)

So Nebuchadnezzar (finally) came to his senses and believed. The most powerful man on the face of the earth put his faith in the true God of Israel. It shows that a person even at the end of his or her life can still come around. In fact, the king had only one year of life left after his bout of insanity, and then he died.

I believe that he will be in heaven, and that we'll have opportunity to meet him, and hear his amazing story first hand.

#2: Having Received The Truth, We Need To Pass It On

In the short time that he had left after his return to sanity, Nebuchadnezzar may have tried to pass his hard-won truths about the true and living God on to his successors. We can only assume he was unsuccessful, as we will see in the story of his grandson, Belshazzar.

Even so, it's easy to imagine Grandpa Nebuchadnezzar trying to communicate what had happened in his life, perhaps even repeating the hymn he wrote about the power and greatness of God.

The Bible puts a huge emphasis on passing on truth to your friends and neighbors, and to the next generations—your sons and daughters, nieces and nephews, grandchildren and great-grandchildren. Does your family know where you stand with Jesus Christ? Do your co-workers know of your faith? Do your friends know you have placed your trust in Jesus as Savior and Lord?

Or…would you describe yourself as more of a silent witness?

That's an oxymoron if I have ever heard one! A silent witness? That's one of those terms that don't make sense, like "fresh frozen," "jumbo shrimp," or "freezer burn."

A witness is one who *speaks*, telling what he has seen, heard, and experienced.

Belshazzar's story begins in Daniel 5.

A number of years later, King Belshazzar gave a great feast for a thousand of his nobles and drank wine with them. While Belshazzar was drinking, he gave orders to bring in the gold and silver cups that his predecessor, Nebuchadnezzar, had taken from the Temple in Jerusalem, so that he and his nobles, his wives, and his concubines might drink from them. So they brought these gold cups taken from the Temple of God in Jerusalem, and the king and his nobles, his wives, and his concubines drank from them. They drank toasts from them to honor their idols made of gold, silver, bronze, iron, wood, and stone.

At that very moment they saw the fingers of a human hand writing on the plaster wall of the king's palace, near the lampstand. The king himself saw the hand as it wrote, and his face turned pale with fear. Such terror gripped him that his knees knocked together and his legs gave way beneath him.
(Daniel 5:1-6, NLT)

Here is yet another example of an age-old truth: Drinking makes you do stupid stuff.

But in this situation it isn't just the alcohol. It's pride, too.

Surely King Belshazzar had heard the stories about his predecessor, how he had lost his sanity and then was restored when he gave glory to the true and living God. But it seemed to have no effect on the young king whatsoever. In fact, he went out of his way to taunt and insult the God of Israel.

No doubt the king had seen many strange things when he was drunk. But odds are he had never seen a detached human hand writing a message on the wall before! His knees *literally* knocked together. He was absolutely terrified!

God had certainly given this king warning. Through the prophet Jeremiah, God had already foretold the destruction of Babylon, declaring that the Babylonian empire would end with the reign of the grandson of Nebuchadnezzar.

> All nations will serve him [Nebuchadnezzar] and his son and his grandson [Belshazzar] until the time for his land comes; then many nations and great kings will subjugate him. (Jeremiah 27:7, NIV)

Certainly that information would have been out there, if Belshazzar had been the slightest bit interested. He would have known, "The prophet says this thing is going to end with me. Hmmm. Maybe I'd better exercise a little caution here. Maybe I'd better watch my step."

The prophecy in Jeremiah foretold the fact that Babylon's grip on the world would end with Belshazzar; in Isaiah's prophecy, the Lord actually named the man who would lead the forces that would overtake and conquer mighty Babylon!

> This is what the LORD says to Cyrus, his anointed one, whose right hand he will empower. Before him, mighty kings will be paralyzed with fear. Their fortress gates will be opened, never again to shut against him. This is what the LORD says: "I will go before you, Cyrus, and level the mountains. I will smash down gates of bronze and cut through bars of iron." (Isaiah 45:1-3)

A mighty king paralyzed with fear? Fortress gates opening? Smashing through gates of bronze? Whether that scripture was specifically referring to the fall of Babylon or not, it certainly paints a picture of what happened on that fateful day. And that prophecy was given 175 years before Cyrus was born, which shows the incredible accuracy of Bible prophecy.

At the very moment that Belshazzar was having his drunken feast, and drinking wine from the sacred vessels, Cyrus and the Medo-Persian forces were outside the walls of Babylon looking for a way in.

And they found one.

To me, Belshazzar's drunken party is a picture of how people ignore God's plain warnings and go on doing whatever they want to do.

"It's okay to have sex anytime. It doesn't matter. As long as it's between two consenting adults, right?"

"Sure, I'm going to party and drink. But I'll still drive home. I can make it okay. Everything will be fine."

"I've found a way to cheat on this exam, and that's what I'm going to do. No one will ever find out about it."

"So what's the harm of a little stealing, a little five-finger discount? Everybody does it. The store expects it to happen, and writes it off on their taxes every year."

"Okay, so I lied. I thought it would keep me out of trouble. Is that such a big deal?"

But the Bible assures us that there *will* be a reckoning. A person's sins *will* catch up to them and overtake them. It's only a matter of time.

What was this writing on the wall?

It was a warning. It was a clanging alarm bell. It was the stroke of doom. Naturally, when they wanted to solve the mystery of the hand and the writing, they found good old Daniel. Official Babylon would ignore this man of God until there was a crisis, and then everybody would be looking for his cell number.

Before Daniel revealed the meaning of the words on the wall, however, he gave a little lesson on the meaning of life. First of all, he reminded this grandson of Nebuchadnezzar what had happened to his grandfather, and the hard lesson that had been learned. Then, looking the foolish, powerful king right in the eyes, he said:

> "But you his son, Belshazzar, have not humbled your heart, although you knew all this. And you have lifted yourself up against the Lord of heaven. They have brought the vessels of His house before you, and you and your lords, your wives and your concubines, have drunk wine from them. And you have praised the gods of silver and gold, bronze and iron, wood and stone, which do not see or hear or know; and the God who holds your breath in His hand and owns all your ways, you have not glorified. Then the fingers of the hand were sent from Him...." (Daniel 5:22-24).

Daniel says, "You *knew* what was right, but you have been proud and arrogant, and you have refused to glorify the God who gives you breath and controls your destiny! You knew about your grandfather and his wickedness—how he was stricken with a form of mental illness. You knew how he was restored, and how he believed in the Lord God. But you blew this off, didn't you? And Belshazzar, you knew that I was here in this city—a prophet of the true and living God, ready and available to help and counsel you. But you never called for me. Now you've gone out of your way to mock God, and the time has come to face the consequences of what you've done. You've brought this on yourself. You have not fulfilled the purpose for which you were created, to glorify your God and Creator."

And that brings me to my third point.

#3: I Am Put Here On This Earth To Glorify GOD

Why am I here? No matter what popular opinion may say, it is *not* to seek after personal fulfillment and enjoyment. God has placed me here on this planet to know Him, honor Him, and to bring glory to His name. That is why we exist. Any other "purpose" for living is a sham and an illusion.

In Isaiah 43:7 God speaks of "Everyone who is called by My name, whom I have created for My glory; I have formed him, yes, I have made him." The psalmist cries out, "Give unto the LORD the glory due to His name; Worship the LORD in the beauty of holiness."[77]

The truth is, you and I were hard-wired to worship. The Bible says of God that "He has also set eternity in the hearts of men; yet they cannot fathom what God has done from beginning to end."[78] When I worship God, I am ful-filling the purpose for which I was made.

You and I were made to glorify Him.

Belshazzar, however, failed to do this, though he knew better. So now Dan-iel says, "This is the message that was written: MENE, MENE, TEKEL, PARSIN. This is what these words mean: Mene means 'numbered'—God has numbered the days of your reign and has brought it to an end. Tekel means 'weighed'—you have been weighed on the balances and have failed the test. Parsin means 'divided'—your kingdom has been divided and given to the Medes and Persians."[79]

Loose paraphrase: Your number is up. The party's over. This is it.

That was the night Belshazzar's number was up. But the truth is, each of our numbers will be up as well, and we don't know when that day will be. The Bible tells us that some may live to be seventy, and some may even reach 80. There are exceptions to that, of course, with people living into their 90s and 100s. Others will die suddenly because of an accident or violence, and will never get a chance to live out their expected years.

The truth is, you can employ all the fads and health remedies you want, and eat all the wheat germ, tofu, and organic sprouts that you like, but you will not extend your life one minute beyond the time that God has set for you. All the lotions and potions in the world won't turn the clock back. I read recently that 13 billion dollars worth of anti-aging cosmetics are sold annually in the United States. Yet Jesus asked in Matthew 6:27, "Who of you by worrying can add a single hour to his life?"[80] The answer? Of course not.

God told Belshazzar that he had been weighed in the balances or scales and found lacking.

Usually when you get on a scale, you want to weigh less, right? Not more! Most of us aren't too happy with the idea of putting on weight.

But God's scales are different. God wants you to have weight. He doesn't want you to be a lightweight or a bantamweight; He wants you to be a heavy-weight. In other words, He wants your life to have a substance, depth, and a spiritual weight to it.

Belshazzar was a spiritual lightweight. His life was meaningless. He had spent his days chasing after whatever entertained him. Which brings us to our final point in this greatest story...

#4: One Day We Will All Be Weighed In GOD's Divine Scales

What kind of spiritual weight does your life have?

As we have seen, God doesn't see or weigh things as we do. He looks at the heart—the motive for why we do what we do and say what we say. Proverbs 16:2

says, "All a man's ways seem innocent to him, but motives are weighed by the Lord."

In the book of Daniel, we go on to read, "That very night Belshazzar, king of the Babylonians, was slain."[81] And he had been warned.

For every person, including you and me, there will be a last night, a last meal, a last statement, and a last breath. Then we will stand before God. The Christian will stand before God in heaven, and will be rewarded for the kind of life he or she lived. How sad it would be to get up to heaven and say, "Well Lord, first all I want to say thank You for getting me up here. And now that I'm here, well, I'm wishing I hadn't been so self-absorbed in the life You gave me. It occurs to me now that I pretty much lived for myself. I certainly didn't glorify You with my life, and well, Lord, I don't have much to offer You. But thanks for sending Your Son to suffer and die on the cross of Calvary, so I could enter Your house."

How pathetic that would be!

How much better to say to Him, "Lord, I know I missed some opportunities. I've made some mistakes—some real doozies—and have fallen short of Your glory again and again. But Lord, I made an attempt to honor You with my life. Not to earn Your approval, or pay the debt that only you could pay, and not to merit heaven. But Lord, I just offer my life as a sacrifice to You. Here it is." And then, to hear the best words we will ever hear: "Well done, good and faithful servant."

For the Christian, heaven has already been purchased for us. But we will be given rewards according to the faithful service we have rendered to the Lord through our days of life.

The nonbeliever, too, will stand before God at what the Bible describes as the Great White Throne judgment. Now this particular judgment isn't about getting into heaven, because if you find yourself at this judgment, you're not getting in. The Bible says that the Lord will look in His book of life, and whoever is not found in that book, will be cast into the lake of fire.

Nebuchadnezzar had ample warning—twelve months, in fact, to think about what the prophet said before judgment fell. Belshazzar was warned, too, but didn't heed it. More quickly than he would have ever imagined it, his number was up, and the handwriting was on the wall.

A story like that makes me want make sure I've found God's purpose and plan for me...and then live life to the hilt.

Chapter Eight

ESTHER: "FOR SUCH A TIME AS THIS"
PART 1

The book of Esther is a classic story of an unknown Hebrew girl who becomes the queen of Persia...and ends up saving the Jewish people.

What is it about girls wanting to become a princess or a queen? My wife and I were in a children's clothing store the other day, looking at outfits for our granddaughters. You should have seen all the princess outfits! Evidently that whole "beautiful princess" dream is something that's especially fun for little girls.

Maybe that's why so many people all over the world tuned in to the story of Prince Charles and Princess Diana, and their lavish summer wedding in 1981. Diana had been a school teacher. Then she met the prince, and eventually they were married in front of a global television audience. Remember her ride through London in the ornate horse-drawn carriage? It was like something right out of a storybook, and everyone hoped it would all end happily ever after.

It didn't, of course. It didn't end happily at all. But for that brief moment in time, the world was caught up in what seemed like a fairy tale romance.

Cynics might say, "Well, there really is no such thing as a story that ends happily ever after."

Really? I beg to differ. The story of Esther is a princess dream come true—only Esther became much more than a princess, she rose to be queen of the greatest superpower in the world.

Oh sure, there are many twists and turns before you arrive at the satisfying conclusion, but it worked out so well for the Jewish people that a holiday has commemorated the crowning events for thousands of years.[82] It truly it is one of the Greatest Stories Ever Told.

A unique, somewhat surprising feature of this small Old Testament book is that the name of God is never specifically mentioned. The Lord isn't referenced or overtly even prayed to. Yet having said that, God's footprints and fingerprints are all over this book from beginning to end. The Lord is so obviously present in every scene and behind the movement of every event, moving everything toward His intended purpose. At the end of the day, the story of Esther reminds us that history is truly His Story.

Frankly, I think many of us need a little reminding on that score.

Sometimes—especially when we find ourselves feeling that God isn't paying attention to the circumstances and details of our daily lives—we need to remember that He has promised to walk with us through the floods and through the fire. He has promised that He will never leave us or forsake us.[83]

In his commentary on the book of Esther, Chuck Swindoll wrote: "God's presence is not as intriguing as His absence. His voice is not as eloquent as His silence. Who of us would have not longed for a word from God, or searched for a glimpse of His power, or yearned for the reassurance of His presence, only to feel that He seems absent from the moment, distant, preoccupied. Yet later we realized how very present He was all along."[84]

The Lord is certainly present through the pages of this book, and if you belong to Jesus Christ, He is involved in all the details of your life as well.

A PARTY THAT CHANGED HISTORY

As the story begins, we are introduced to Xerxes, king of Medo-Persia, a vast empire ranging from India to Ethiopia. Raised as a royal, he was the son of Darius the Great, the grandson of Cyrus the Great, and the father of Artaxerxes, who gave the permission to Nehemiah and the Jews to return to their homeland and rebuild the walls of Jerusalem.

History depicts Xerxes as a towering figure, a large man who stood taller than his contemporaries. He is also depicted as a man who was intolerant and insensitive. You might say he was lacking in people skills! While he excelled at killing people and subduing kingdoms, he apparently wasn't the most personable guy you'd ever hope to meet.

So maybe that's why Xerxes decided to throw a lavish feast for his entire kingdom. Everyone was invited onto the palace grounds to eat the finest foods of the day and to drink as much as you wanted to drink. The drinks were on the house, courtesy of the king (who could afford it).

Everybody was getting drunk and enjoying this mammoth feast that the king was throwing. After he'd had a few drinks too many, the king had the not-so-bright idea to bring out Vashti, his beautiful queen, and parade her in front of his lords.

Oh, the strange ideas people come up with under the influence of alcohol! Scripture implies that the king would later regret what took place as a result of that rash decision, but after it was too late.

So Vashti received the royal summons and…refused it.

Why?

Some commentators believe the text implies that Xerxes wanted her to come wearing her crown—and *only* her crown.

If that's the case, you can understand Vashti's resistance to this idea. Or at the very least, he wanted to parade her about as a mere object, a possession. But Vashti said, "No, I won't do that." This was to her credit, yes, but this was not a man who was used to hearing the word "no."

The king's advisors said, "Oh, King, you can't allow this! If she gets away with rebelling against you, the other women in the kingdom will hear about it, and no woman will ever do what her husband says again. So you have got to get rid of Vashti. Reject her from being queen, and find a new one."

Then someone came up with the idea of having a beauty contest throughout the kingdom and the most beautiful woman who won would become the next queen of Persia, taking the place of Vashti. Exit queen Vashti. Enter Hadassah or Esther.

And that brings us to Esther chapter 2 verse 5.

> Now at the fortress of Susa there was a certain Jew named Mordecai son of Jair. He was from the tribe of Benjamin and was a descendant of Kish and Shimei. His family had been exiled from Jerusalem to Babylon by King Nebuchadnezzar, along with King Jehoiachin of Judah and many others. This man had a beautiful and lovely young cousin, Hadassah, who was also called Esther. When her father and mother had died, Mordecai adopted her into his family and raised her as his own daughter. As a result of the king's decree, Esther, along with many other young women, was brought to the king's harem at the fortress of Susa and placed in Hegai's care. Hegai was very impressed with Esther and treated her kindly. He quickly ordered a special menu for her and provided her with beauty treatments. He also assigned her seven maids specially chosen from the king's palace, and he moved her and her maids into the best place in the harem. (Esther 2:5-9, NLT)

So the king's servants combed the kingdom for the most beautiful women. It was a huge Miss Persia Beauty Pageant. To most of the young girls, this would no doubt have been exciting. Here was a chance to become the next queen, living in the lap of luxury with unparalleled wealth and influence.

I don't think Esther would have been one of those girls. I think she was probably content living among her people—and probably had some handsome Jewish boy she had her eye on that she hoped to marry one day. No question about it, however, she was stunningly beautiful. And because of her beauty, she was immediately identified and chosen to be one of the contestants in this kingdom-wide event.

The Jewish historian Josephus says there were as many as 400 young virgin women involved in this remarkable competition. After being selected for the program, the women were to undergo an extensive makeover for a full year, preparing them for that short time they would spend with the king, in hopes that he would pick them to be the next queen. The women would also learn to polish every seductive art to enhance their beauty by pampering their bodies.

So young Hadassah, Esther, was separated from her older cousin Mordecai (who was really more like a guardian uncle), pulled away from her people, and placed in the middle of a godless, secular court—where the competition among the women must have been fierce.

Who could have predicted any of this? What a turn of events!

Sometimes I think it's hard for us to grapple with the fact that God often works in unexpected places, in the lives of unexpected people, in unexpected ways, with unexpected results!

This is certainly one of those cases. And here is one point we learn from this story.

#1: We All Have God-Given Talents And Gifts

For Esther, it was extraordinary beauty.

Physical beauty, however, can be both an advantage and a disadvantage. When you're an especially attractive individual, you get used to people giving you special favors. You get used to people complimenting you, wanting to be with you, or letting you go to the front of the line. Sometimes those who are very attractive on the outside can become rather shallow on the inside.

Esther wasn't one of those people. Along with her outward beauty she had inward character and great courage, as we will discover in this chapter, one of the Greatest Stories Ever Told.

Maybe you have been blessed with beauty. Then again maybe you have been blessed with brains. Or maybe you have been given a musical talent, artistic talent, or a facility for math and crunching numbers. Maybe you're a natural at building things or expressing yourself through writing. Maybe you're a visionary, who was never very good at working out details. Then again, you may be a person who's sharp at details but doesn't have much vision. There is a place for everyone in the church of Jesus Christ. We need to discover our talents and gifts, cultivate them to their fullest, and use them for the glory of God.

First Timothy 4:14 tells us not to neglect the gift that has been given to us. Or as another translation puts it. "Keep [your gift] dusted off and in use."[85]

Walt Disney, a great visionary, liked to tell a story about a circus that came to town many years ago. As with most circuses in that day, it was preceded by a parade that wound its way through town. The trombone player in the band however, became sick the night before the parade, and the band master needed somebody to fill in. A young boy volunteered, and the bandmaster gratefully signed him up.

The band hadn't marched even a single block, however, when a horrible racket blared out of the boy's trombone—causing two old ladies to faint and a horse to bolt in terror.

Stopping the parade, the bandmaster turned to the little boy and said, "Why didn't tell me you couldn't play the trombone?"

"How did I know?" he replied. "I'd never tried before."

I would rather try and fail than never try at all. I can tell you I never planned on becoming a public speaker. I can still remember the high school speech class, where we were required to make an impromptu speech, and I found myself absolutely dumbstruck. Couldn't do it. I took an F in the class rather than standing before my classmates and making a fool of myself.

My real desire was to be a graphic designer. I had a sense of humor and loved to draw—a talent I'd developed as a survival skill living through my turbulent childhood with my seven-time divorced and alcoholic mother. When my mom was out partying, and I was sometimes in the bars waiting for her, I retreated into my personal world of art, complete with characters and happy endings. One of the things I liked best about design was that I could work behind the scenes, and not be in front of people.

Then one day, through some strange alignment of circumstances, I ended up speaking at a Bible study. It wasn't something I had planned on doing at all; it just happened. To my astonishment, I discovered God had given me an ability in that area, and I sensed it was something I needed to cultivate. (I *still* need to cultivate it!)

My point is simply this: take the gift God has given you, and use it. God used Esther's natural gifts—coupled with her integrity of heart—to save her people.

#2: There Is A Time To Speak, And A Time To Be Quiet

> Esther had not told anyone of her nationality and family background, for Mordecai had told her not to. (Esther 2:10)

We read in this verse that Esther had kept her Jewish identity under wraps. No one really knew that the new Miss Persia—and now queen of the realm—was a Hebrew. Had Mordecai given Esther good advice in this regard? Was it right or wrong for him to tell this to Esther to keep quiet about her ethnicity?

It could be argued either way. Some say Esther should have identified herself as a Jew right up-front to everyone, and especially to the king. By not doing so, they argue, she was compromising her faith.

There is merit to that argument, but perhaps some flaws as well.

Sometimes we may think we have to bombard everyone we meet with the whole gospel message. But you might be surprised to hear me, a preacher, say that everyone doesn't necessarily need to hear a sermon. Yes, there is a place for sermons and verbal communication, but there is also a place for *living* the sermon. There is a place for being an example, and, as we mentioned in the chapter on Naaman, earning the right to share those words with that person.

In other words…live the life, sow all the seeds you can, and pray for the leading of the Holy Spirit about when to speak up, and when to remain silent. Some people are quick to speak up, and then contradict it all by the way they live. Frankly, I wish those people would just shut up!

Other people live the Christian life in a beautiful way, but never speak up, missing what might be choice, God-given opportunities. This, I believe, is where "keeping in step with the Spirit" comes in, looking to Him for moment by moment guidance.[86] He will lead us to an appropriate balance.

Let's say you are married to a non-Christian man, and you're wondering how to reach him. Maybe you say to yourself, *I think the way to reach him is give him a sermon every single day.* So when he gets up for breakfast, before he gets that first cup of coffee, you begin pleading with him, "Honey, why aren't you saved? I'm just in pain and heartache because you don't know the Lord." You proceed to do that every day. In addition, you wrap gospel tracts with his sandwiches in his lunch. Superglue his car radio dial to Christian stations only, so he can't listen to anything else. And will that reach him?

No.

That will never reach him.

Here's what God says in His Word:

> Be good wives to your husbands, responsive to their needs. There are husbands who, indifferent as they are to any words about God, will be captivated by your life of holy beauty. What matters is not your outer appearance—the styling of your hair, the jewelry you wear, the cut of your clothes—but your inner disposition. Cultivate inner beauty, the gentle, gracious kind that God delights in. (1 Peter 3:1-4, THE MESSAGE)

In essence, that is what Esther was doing. She thought, "There is a time to be quiet, and there is a time to speak." She practiced what we might call "discretion"—a careful way of living and conducting herself that contributed to the attractiveness of her person. Yes, she had the physical attributes and the standout beauty, no question about it. But she also had the inner character to go along with it. And that is what attracted the king to her. Esther wasn't like those other sleazy Persian girls, trying all the tricks to make themselves look seductive. Esther was a virtuous young woman, unstained by her culture, who carried herself with dignity, grace, and strength.

How we need such models today, for young girls looking for someone to emulate!

Now if the book of Esther had been a fairy tale, the story would have ended right here. The last sentence would have read: "So Esther was chosen by the king, and they lived happily ever after."

But Esther is not a fairy story, it is a Bible story. And Bible stories tell us the truth. In fact, sinister forces were at work in the opening chapters of Esther. An assassination plot was afoot, uncovered and exposed by Mordecai, the cousin of Esther, who revealed it to the queen. She in turn told the king about it, and he stopped the plot, executing the would-be assassins. What's more, the incident was duly recorded in the history books of Persia—a fact that would later have major significance to the story.

In Esther 3, a villain emerges on the stage: His name is Haman, a wicked, ambitious man, filled with lust for power and control. In the first verse of the chapter, King Xerxes elevates Haman to the position of prime minister. In those days, apparently, prime ministers expected to be treated like junior kings: citizens were supposed to fall to their knees at their approach. Nevertheless, when Haman came by the king's gate, strutting like a peacock, Mordecai refused to play along. He would not bow down to Haman.

When the king's officials ratted on Mordecai and told Haman the story, he was enraged. What was this guy's name, and who did he think he was?

The officials happily supplied that information: "He is Mordecai, a Jew."

As Mordecai steadfastly refused to bow, Haman said, "I'll show you. It's not enough just to put you to death; I'm going to exterminate your entire race." And Haman actually hatched a plot to wipe out the Jewish race across the whole empire. Then he took the idea to the king.

Xerxes, who apparently wasn't overly troubled with the idea of genocide, went along with the plan with a shrug of the shoulders.

> Then Haman approached King Xerxes and said, "There is a certain race of people scattered through all the provinces of your empire. Their laws are different from those of any other nation, and they refuse to obey even the laws of the king. So it is not in the king's interest to let them live. If it please Your Majesty, issue a decree that they be destroyed, and I will give 375 tons of silver to the government administrators so they can put it into the royal treasury."

> The king agreed, confirming his decision by removing his signet ring from his finger and giving it to Haman son of Hammedatha the Agagite—the enemy of the Jews. "Keep the money," the king told Haman, "but go ahead and do as you like with these people." (Esther 3:8-10, NLT)

Then the king and Haman had a drink together as news of the upcoming genocide began to be published across the vast empire. The memorandum basically said that all Jewish people—every man, woman, and child—were to die on such and such a day, eleven months hence.

So not only did Haman want them dead, he wanted them to see death coming, and suffer mental anguish as well. What a wicked and deranged person he was! He reminds us of another wicked man to come later with a similar scheme—a nightmare plan he called "The Final Solution."

It was his desire to eradicate all the Jews in Europe, and he actually succeeded in killing six million of them. As you know, his name was Adolf Hitler.

Back to Haman and the king...

Little did the king realize, however, that by signing Haman's evil decree, he had essentially signed a death sentence for Esther, his beautiful young queen.

What a depraved plot! But as will see, God would even turn Haman's (and Satan's) most evil designs into a plan to protect and promote His people. And in the coming days, it would become increasingly clear just why Esther won the beauty contest. It wasn't so she could just live in the lap of luxury. No, it was so she could use her strategic position to influence the king.

As you might imagine, there was mourning in the streets of the capital city, and across the empire. The Jews wept over the death edict, and their power-lessness to stop it. Cousin Mordecai, too, in his usual place out in the street near the palace wept, walking about in sackcloth, and word of it reached the queen.

> The queen was stunned. She sent fresh clothes to Mordecai so he could take off his sackcloth but he wouldn't accept them. Esther called for Hathach, one of the royal eunuchs whom the king had assigned to wait on her, and told him to go to Mordecai and get the full story of what was happening. So Hathach went to Mordecai in the town square in front of the King's Gate. Mordecai told him everything that had happened to him. He also told him the exact amount of money that Haman had promised to deposit in the royal bank to finance the massacre of the Jews. Mordecai also gave him a copy of the bulletin that had been post-ed in Susa ordering the massacre so he could show it to Esther when he reported back with instructions to go to the king and intercede and plead with him for her people. (Esther 4:4-8, THE MESSAGE)

So Mordecai took a copy of the decree and sent it back for his adopted daughter to read. Esther reads it for the first time, and to her shock and dismay, finds out what's really going on, and why the people are weeping.

"Esther," Mordecai is saying, "you've been silent, just as I asked you to be. But now it's time to speak up. It's time to use your influence. Go in to the king and talk some sense into him. Don't let this happen to us."

But Esther wasn't quite prepared to act yet. She had been isolated and secure in the confines of the palace and the harem, and all of this news about genocide came as a shock to her.

The incident reminds me of some people in the church today. They do everything they can to isolate and insulate themselves from the world. They don't want to hear what's going on in that big, bad world out there, and they don't want to know about it so they won't have to care about it.

It's almost possible to live such an isolated life in an American Christian subculture. In the church today, we have a Christianized version of just about everything, don't we? We have Christian radio, Christian television, Christian books, Christian movies, Christian art, and Christian music. We can go to Christian doctors and Christian dentists, stay in Christian hotels, and pretty much a Christian version of everything in the culture. While I'm thankful for all the wonderful resources available to the believer today, I do think we need to try not to isolate from our culture so much as to infiltrate it.

We need to come outside of our Christian bubble and find out what's going on in the real world, and do something about it.

Esther had been too isolated, and had no real idea what was transpiring in the streets. When she heard her guardian Mordecai was walking around in sackcloth, distraught and in mourning, she thought, "Well, I'll send him some new clothes. That will solve the problem."

But Mordecai was telling her, "We don't need more clothes, Esther. We need help. We need deliverance. We need salvation. Is there anything you can do?"

Esther told Hathach to go back and say to Mordecai,

> "All the world knows that anyone, whether man or woman, who goes into the king's inner court without his summons is doomed to die unless the king holds out his gold scepter; and the king has not called for me to come to him in more than a month." (Esther 4:10-11, TLB)

In other words, "Mordecai, what you're asking me is terribly dangerous. I could die if I enter the king's presence unbidden! It would be a huge risk."

Reading Esther's note, Mordecai realizes he's going to have to speak to this girl in plain English (or Hebrew).

> Mordecai sent back this reply to Esther: "Don't think for a moment that you will escape there in the palace when all other Jews are killed. If you keep quiet at a time like this, deliverance for the Jews will arise from some other place, but you and your relatives will die. What's more, who can say but that you have been elevated to the palace for just such a time as this?" (Esther 4:13-14, NLT)

This brings me to my third point, which I pose to you as a question:

#3: Where Has GOD Placed You, "For Such A Time As This"?

You may have heard it before, but there is only one you. There is only one person like you walking this earth with your exact heritage, who has gone through the precise events and sufferings of life that have brought you to this hour.

If you have suffered in life, if you have been neglected, mistreated, abused, or abandoned, I'm sorry you've had to endure such things. But let me also say this: God can take all of the hurt and pain the world has dealt you and use it to make you into the man or woman He wants you to be...for such a time as this.

So many of us have allowed a difficult past to cripple us. *"Why did this happen to me? Why did I have such a horrible childhood? Why did my parents get divorced? Why did I end up divorced? Why are my kids turning out this way? Why do I have this health issue? Why did my loved one die? Why did I go through that experience? Why? Why? Why?"*

We can even get upset with God because of our situation in life. "Lord, why do I have a neighbor like this? Why do I have an extended family member like that? Why do I have to work with such a person day in and day out?"

Hold on for just a moment. Did you ever stop and think that all of those experiences you have gone through have brought you to where you are for such a time as this?

And God can even use our missteps and mistakes. We can bring the broken pieces of our lives before God's throne and in humility say, "Father, I know I have failed—big time! I have sinned and made some terrible decisions. But even now, would You help me?"

God says He can work all things together for good to those who love Him, and are the called according to His purpose.[87]

Sometimes when we've sinned and made a mess of things, we might find ourselves thinking, "Well, I've already messed up, so it doesn't much matter. I may as well just mess up some more."

No!

In such a time, we need to get down on our knees before the Lord and say, "Lord, I don't know what to do. I don't know how to sort this out. I don't know how to correct or fix this. Would You help me?" And then just watch what the Lord will do!

Although Esther hadn't realized it (yet), God had been working behind the scenes to position her in the right place at the right time. It may be the same for you at this very moment. God has been preparing and equipping you, allowing you to go all through all that you have endured in order to use you right where you are. But you need to keep your eyes open, and be aware of what is happening around you. And instead of isolating, you need to infiltrate and permeate your world.

And ask yourself questions like these:

How can I use my Christian influence here?

How could God be glorified in this situation?

What does God want me to say—or not to say—in this situation?

Yes, if Esther went ahead and obeyed Mordecai, she risked losing everything—even her very life. But at that particular moment in time, it was a risk that had to be taken.

Esther had been raised well, and no doubt taught the Scripture from her youth. She was not only beautiful on the outside; she had character on the inside. In spite of her lovely appearance, she was not a fragile queen...she was a Hebrew warrior.

And it was time to fight.

It was time to stand up and be counted, and put that legendary beauty and feminine influence to great use.

One commentator said this: "Whenever there is a people of God, there are enemies of God. A realization that there is in fact an enemy forces a reassessment of priorities. The moment that Haman surfaced, Esther began to move from being a beauty queen to becoming a Jewish saint. From living an indolent life in the harem to the high-risk venture of speaking for and identifying with God's people."

Maybe something like that has happened to you lately, where the Lord is saying, "I have been prepping you for this. Now you have got to step up to the plate. This is your moment. I've brought you to where you are for such a time as this."

I love her statement in response to Mordecai's plea.

> Then Esther sent this reply to Mordecai: "Go and gather together all the Jews of Susa and fast for me. Do not eat or drink for three days, night or day. My maids and I will do the same. And then, though it is against the law, I will go in to see the king. If I must die, I am willing to die." (Esther 4:15-17)

Esther says, "Okay, Uncle Mordecai, I'll put it on the line. I'll go for it." It's a reminder to all of us that our lives belong to God. He created us, called us, and gifted us. Now He wants to use us.

I think back to Psalm 31, where David wrote:

> But I trust in you, O Lord;
> I say, "You are my God."
> My times are in your hands.
> (vv. 14-15, NIV)

What a great place to be…in the hands of an all-wise, all-powerful God who loves us! There's no better place in the universe, no better place in time or eternity to be. When you belong to God you can take whatever you're going through in life, even the mistakes you've brought on yourself, and lay them at His feet, asking for His help. It doesn't mean you'll escape the consequences of your sin, but it does mean that God can wonderfully, gloriously, and I might add, very imaginatively, use it all for His glory.

When you're outside of Christ, however, you don't have that kind of hope. You won't be able to look at your hardships and say, "Well, all things work together for good"—because they probably won't! In fact, they may work together for bad, not good, because you have to reap the results of your sins without the help of God's intervening grace.

But if you will come to God and say, "Help me, Lord. I need Your forgiveness. I need Your pardon. I need Your intervention." Then life can take a turn for the better in ways you may have never anticipated or imagined.

That is the hope of every Christian: That God can intervene in a life that has even gone the wrong direction, turn it around, and create a new person in Christ.

Chapter Nine

ESTHER: "FOR SUCH A TIME AS THIS"
PART 2

My wife came home from the supermarket the other day with the SUV loaded up with groceries, and asked me to unload them. The back end of the SUV was stuffed to the rafters with grocery bags. All kinds of groceries! Bags filled up with cereal, vegetables, cans, cartons of milk, paper towels, and on and on.

In one of those bags was a carton of eggs.

As I opened up the hatch, one of the bags fell out. Take a guess...what do you think was in the bag that fell out?

Of course. The eggs! It couldn't have been the vegetables, or a can, or a package of napkins. It had to be the eggs. Why? Because there is a law of the universe we all know.

It is called Murphy's Law! Which basically says that if anything can go wrong, it will—and usually at the most inopportune moment.

Obviously, that law is merely a joke. It really only seems like the worst thing always happens; many times, the best things happen to us. But we don't keep track of those.

There are, however, very real natural laws at work in our world, and also spiritual laws. Think, for instance, of the biblical law of sowing and reaping, expressed so succinctly in the book of Galatians:

"Do not be deceived, God is not mocked; for whatever a man sows, that he will also reap. For he who sows to his flesh will of the flesh reap corruption, but he who sows to the Spirit will of the Spirit reap everlasting life."[88]

There's another way of saying those words: *What goes around comes around.*

That's what we see—illustrated so dramatically—in this second look at the story of Queen Esther.

ESTHER'S REQUEST

Responding to Mordecai's challenge to take action on behalf of her people, Esther took her life in her hands to make an entreaty to the king. As she did so, she knew she could very well be dead within the hour.

> Three days later, Esther put on her royal robes and entered the inner court of the palace, just across from the king's hall. The king was sitting

on his royal throne, facing the entrance. When he saw Queen Esther standing there in the inner court, he welcomed her, holding out the gold scepter to her. So Esther approached and touched its tip.

Then the king asked her, "What do you want, Queen Esther? What is your request? I will give it to you, even if it is half the kingdom!"

And Esther replied, "If it please Your Majesty, let the king and Haman come today to a banquet I have prepared for the king."

The king turned to his attendants and said, "Tell Haman to come quickly to a banquet, as Esther has requested." So the king and Haman went to Esther's banquet.

And while they were drinking wine, the king said to Esther, "Now tell me what you really want. What is your request? I will give it to you, even if it is half the kingdom!"

Esther replied, "This is my request and deepest wish. If Your Majesty is pleased with me and wants to grant my request, please come with Haman tomorrow to the banquet I will prepare for you. Then tomorrow I will explain what this is all about." (Esther 5:1-8, NLT)

Some might criticize the queen for not pleading her case right then and there, at her first opportunity. But Esther was wiser than that. In fact, a certain irony was about to unfold that could not take place if Esther played her hand prematurely.

Solomon told us that there is a time for every event under heaven. As we noted in the last chapter, there is a time to be silent and a time to speak. Esther recognized that this was not the time to speak. Not yet! But that time was coming, and she was waiting for the Lord to lead her.

So here now is Esther, not cringing or cowering in the place of danger, but dignified and beautiful, standing confident in the Lord.

Look again at verse 2: "...When he saw Queen Esther standing there in the inner court." Not the outer, but the inner court. That had huge implications. If Xerxes for whatever reason had decided not to hold his scepter for her to touch, she could have been put to death.

Although the text doesn't say so, we can imagine her shooting up a quick prayer (like Nehemiah did when he was in the presence of the king) saying, *"Lord, please help me right now! No matter what happens, help me to be strong."*

The king's response, however, could not have been more gracious.

He says, in essence, "Why Queen Esther! What is it that you want? I'm so pleased with you. What can I do for you?"

Again, she could have blurted out her whole complaint right then. But no, she sensed it still wasn't the right moment. So she used that occasion to invite the king—and Haman!—to a banquet set for the following day.

The king, who was no dummy, probably sensed that something was up at that point, and immediately agreed.

When Haman got the news, he was thrilled.

The New Living Translation renders Esther 5:9: "What a happy man Haman was as he left the banquet!" He was thinking, "Man, everything's going my way. I love it when a plan comes together! All of the manipulation, all of the scheming, all of the lying, all of the treachery. It's all working out beautifully. And now I'm going to go have a meal with the king and queen of Persia."

The word "happy" in verse 9 could be translated "pure joy." Yes, he was joyful...but there was nothing pure about it. The man's heart was laced with twisted, unadulterated evil. It didn't matter that he had forced through a death warrant on millions of innocent men, women, and children. No, this was all about his career—which seemed to be on the rise!

It's bizarre to see how some people can actually take delight in the suffering of others. And seeing their plans of treachery succeed brings a perverted pleasure to their wicked hearts.

As Haman left the palace, however, happy and whistling his favorite tune, he saw Mordecai again. And the mere sight of Mordecai made him burn with hatred. The Jew was as good as dead, of course, along with all the other Jews across the empire. It was only a matter of time until the deadly edict went into effect. But it was so galling to see Mordecai standing there, and Haman found himself thinking, *"I hate this guy. Why should I have to wait? Why shouldn't I kill him right now? But I guess I have to have the king's permission first."*

So he restrained himself, and went home to boast to his wife about how everything was going his way, and how successful he was. And now the best news of all. He had been summoned to be with King Xerxes and Queen Esther for a special banquet! If only he could get that guy Mordecai out of his sight. Mordecai was like a burr in his saddle, a pebble in his shoe. What should he do about it?

That's when his wife came up with the creative idea of building a gallows 75 feet high, and hanging Mordecai on the gallows.

"What a great idea," Haman exults. "I'll do it."

So at the prime minister's command, the work crews set about the task immediately, sawing and hammering into the night. It was all music to Haman's ears. It was the sound of death for Mordecai. The Jews were going to die—every last one of them. And Mordecai would die even sooner! Or so Haman thought.

But here's some good news. God wasn't on vacation while all this was happening. He wasn't taking a nap, or distracted by events in a different part of the universe. In fact, God was paying very close attention. Man will have his way and his day...for awhile...and then it's God's turn.

Esther, you'll remember, had gone to Mordecai and said, "Get everyone fasting and praying for me." And now those prayers would begin to be answered, as

God started pulling many loose strings together, as only He can do.

In our last chapter, we noted an averted assassination plot.

> One day as Mordecai was on duty at the palace, two of the king's eunuchs, Bigthana and Teresh—who were guards at the door of the king's private quarters—became angry at King Xerxes and plotted to assassinate him. But Mordecai heard about the plot and passed the information on to Queen Esther. She then told the king about it and gave Mordecai credit for the report. When an investigation was made and Mordecai's story was found to be true, the two men were hanged on a gallows. This was all duly recorded in *The Book of the History of King Xerxes' Reign*. (Esther 2:21-23, NLT)

Somehow, Mordecai was never acknowledged or rewarded for what he had done, and the incident was largely forgotten.

Do you think he might have wondered about that—"Lord, what's up with that? Why didn't I get acknowledged? Maybe a little parade or trophy or something. After all, I saved the king's life!"

As it happened, however, Mordecai never got so much as an "Atta boy!" And as time went by, it seemed pretty obvious that he never would.

But the Lord had been paying attention.

> That night the king had trouble sleeping, so he ordered an attendant to bring the historical records of his kingdom so they could be read to him. In those records he discovered an account of how Mordecai had exposed the plot of Bigthana and Teresh, two of the eunuchs who guarded the door to the king's private quarters. They had plotted to assassinate the king. "What reward or recognition did we ever give Mordecai for this?" the king asked.
>
> His attendants replied, "Nothing has been done."
>
> "Who is that in the outer court?" the king inquired. Now, as it happened, Haman had just arrived in the outer court of the palace to ask the king to hang Mordecai from the gallows he had prepared.
>
> So the attendants replied to the king, "Haman is out there."
>
> "Bring him in," the king ordered. (Esther 6:1-5, NLT)

This all took place on the night before Esther's fateful banquet. She had done all that she knew how to do, and now God was doing what only He could do—drawing together events and outcomes in such a way as to help His people.

That night, the king couldn't sleep, and none of the usual remedies seemed to help. It could be that he was bothered by the beautiful Esther's shocking breach of protocol, appearing in his outer court without permission.

Why would she risk her life like that? Why the banquet? What was she up to? What was really going on?

"Well," the king thought, "I may at least do something productive besides tossing and turning." And he began reviewing the recent records of his reign. That's how one of his aides happened to read to the king the account of how Mordecai had foiled the assassination plot.

Xerxes was stunned that this loyal subject of his had never been rewarded. How had that happened? Something had to be done!

For Mordecai's part, there's no record that he felt deflated over this lack of recognition. But he was human, and you have to think he wondered about it a little. Maybe you've wondered about some things, too. Maybe one of your ideas got borrowed, leading to someone else's promotion. Someone else got the credit for your initiative, your plan, your brainchild. They got the strokes, and maybe even the financial rewards, and you got nothing.

Every eye in the world might have missed what happened in that instance. But there were eyes outside this world that did not miss it. The Lord knows what you did, and He knows the outcome. Jesus said, "Your Father who sees in secret will Himself reward you openly."[89]

You will be rewarded for every act of kindness and word of testimony that you have engaged in for the glory of God. Your reward may come in this life, or it may come on the other side, but God will not forget! Hebrews 6:10 (NIV) says, "God is not unjust; he will not forget your work and the love you have shown him as you have helped his people and continue to help them."

As Esther, Mordecai, and the Jewish people were asleep that night, facing an uncertain future, *God was working on the king's heart.*

Psalm 30:5 says, "Weeping may last for the night, but joy comes in the morning." Isn't that great to know? Sometimes we take our worries to bed with us, and they prove to be uncomfortable sleeping partners. We keep turning something around and around in our minds, wondering, *"How in the world am I going to solve this?"* Do you really think worrying about your problems is going to help?

Here's what you need to do. Tell the Lord: "This is more than I can handle right now, and I'm tired. I'm going to go to bed now, and I'm just going to let You take care of this stuff. Here's the problem, Lord. Thanks for taking it on. Good night, talk to You in the morning."

So while many in the Persian Empire slept, God was awake and on task. And it was all beginning to come together.

HAMAN'S RUDE SURPRISE

The very first thing in the morning, Haman shows up at the king's court. The prime minister had his own reasons for being there; he wanted to get to the king to sign off on his plan to hang Mordecai from the 75-foot gallows he had just finished constructing.

So there was Haman, up early on his mission of hate and death, waiting for an audience with the king. But as it happened, the king didn't have hate and death on his mind...he had gratitude and honor.

Xerxes had just heard about Mordecai's act of courage and sacrifice on the king's behalf. But how should he reward Mordecai? He needed some advice.

Can't you just hear the exchange?

"Are any of my aides around this morning?"

"Yes, your majesty. Haman just happens to be here, waiting in the outer court."

"Perfect. Bring him in. Haman, how are you doing?"

"Oh, I'm really good King. I wanted to talk to you."

"Fine. But let me ask you something first."

"Of course."

"There's someone that I want to honor in my kingdom."

"Oh...really?"

"Absolutely. There's someone I want to honor and lift up. I want to do wonderful things for this man. What should I do?"

Now Haman, self-absorbed and stuck on himself as he was, thought the king was talking about honoring him. He wouldn't have guessed the king was talking about Mordecai in a hundred years.

"So what do you think should be done for a person like this?" the king asks.

"You know," Haman replies with a smile, "it's funny you should ask." And he comes up with this incredible plan of how to lavish the maximum amount of honor on this deserving person. Let's pick up the story now in the biblical text:

> Haman thought to himself, "He must be talking about honoring me— who else?" So he answered the king, "For the man the king delights to honor, do this: Bring a royal robe that the king has worn and a horse the king has ridden, one with a royal crown on its head. Then give the robe and the horse to one of the king's most noble princes. Have him robe the man whom the king especially wants to honor; have the prince lead him on horseback through the city square, proclaiming before him, 'This is what is done for the man whom the king especially wants to honor!'"

"Go and do it," the king said to Haman. "Don't waste another minute. Take the robe and horse and do what you have proposed to Mordecai the Jew who sits at the King's Gate. Don't leave out a single detail of your plan." (Esther 6:6-10, THE MESSAGE)

You have to love the irony! Haman, having driven the last nails in the 75-foot gallows built for Mordecai, enters the king's presence to ask permission to hang him. Instead, Haman is given the task of putting a royal robe on Mordecai's shoulders, placing him on the king's horse, and leading him through the city square, shouting, "This is what happens to those the king wishes to honor!"

Afterward Mordecai returned to the palace gate, but Haman hurried home, dejected and completely humiliated. And when Haman told his wife, Zeresh, and all his friends what had happened, they said, "If this Mordecai is in fact a Jew, your bad luck has only begun. You don't stand a chance against him—you're as good as ruined."[90]

What a family! On one hand his wife says, "Build a gallows 75 feet high and hang your enemy on it." Then when Haman comes home and gives her the latest developments, she says, "You're history!"

And Haman has to be thinking, "What happened? Everything was going so well! What do I do now?" In fact, Haman's hateful chickens were coming home to roost. He was about to reap what he had sown.

And it was happening fast! The Bible says that while Haman was still talking to his wife, the king's eunuchs arrived to escort him to the banquet with the king and Esther.

So the king and Haman went to Queen Esther's banquet. And while they were drinking wine that day, the king again asked her, "Tell me what you want, Queen Esther. What is your request? I will give it to you, even if it is half the kingdom!"

And so Queen Esther replied, "If Your Majesty is pleased with me and wants to grant my request, my petition is that my life and the lives of my people will be spared. For my people and I have been sold to those who would kill, slaughter, and annihilate us. If we had only been sold as slaves, I could remain quiet, for that would have been a matter too trivial to warrant disturbing the king."

"Who would do such a thing?" King Xerxes demanded. "Who would dare touch you?"

Esther replied, "This wicked Haman is our enemy." Haman grew pale with fright before the king and queen. Then the king jumped to his feet in a rage and went out into the palace garden. (Esther 7:1-7, NLT)

I'm sure all the blood rushed out of Haman's face. While the king walked through the palace gardens in a white-hot rage, Haman stayed behind to plead for his life with Queen Esther; for he knew he was doomed.

In despair he fell on the couch where Queen Esther was reclining—just as the king returned from the palace garden.

> "Will he even assault the queen right here in the palace, before my very eyes?" the king roared. And as soon as the king spoke, his attendants covered Haman's face, signaling his doom.

> Then Harbona, one of the king's eunuchs, said, "Haman has set up a gallows that stands seventy-five feet tall in his own courtyard. He intended to use it to hang Mordecai, the man who saved the king from assassination."

> "Then hang Haman on it!" the king ordered. So they hanged Haman on the gallows he had set up for Mordecai, and the king's anger was pacified.

> On that same day King Xerxes gave the estate of Haman, the enemy of the Jews, to Queen Esther. (Esther 7:7-10, 8:1)

Truly, this is one of the greatest stories ever told! And not only is it an exciting true story, it has rich life lessons for every one of us.

LIFE LESSONS FROM ESTHER

#1: GOD Is Always Present And At Work Whether We Sense His Presence Or Not

As I mentioned in the last chapter, even though the name of the Lord is never specifically mentioned in the book of Esther, it's obvious that He is in every scene, as events move toward fulfilling His intended purpose.

The same is true in your life, if you belong to Jesus Christ. Whether you know it, sense it, or can discern it or not, the Lord works continually through the most humdrum day-to-day circumstances of life. Yes, there are certainly those big, awe-inspiring, obviously-supernatural events that happen in our lives from time to time. And praise God for them! But far more often, God works through the small events and the little details, accomplishing His purposes and desires in your life.

Look at how it comes together in this story! Human events like a night of insomnia, the reading of a particular passage of a book, the anger of a man that rebounds back on his own head, the perfect timing of events… God is always present and at work whether we feel Him or not. He as at work in your life if you are a child of God.

#2: GOD Can Take Impossible Situations
And Turn Them Around For His Glory

Things looked bleak in the early chapters of Esther. An indifferent king. A wicked Haman. A paralyzed people. An evil man gaining in power. A good man headed to the gallows. And Esther and her people condemned to certain death by a decree of the king himself.

But the people prayed and God intervened.

And how does this story end? Mordecai ends up in Haman's position as prime minister, the Jews are saved, and Haman ends up hanging from his own rope, and his own gallows.

That is called "perfect justice."

So I encourage you to keep praying about the particular circumstances in which you find yourself right now. You say, "Well, I could manage except for this, and this is what's getting me down." Yes, but that may be the very thing God uses to turn your circumstances in a surprising way. The very bad thing may lead to a very good thing.

Chuck Swindoll tells a story about a man who was shipwrecked on an uninhabited island. Seeing that rescue might be a long time in coming, he painstakingly built a little hut to provide himself protection from the elements, and a place to store the few items he had managed to salvage from the wreck. And for weeks this man lived in this little hut with only the hot sun and the cold nights to keep him company. But each and every day he would prayerfully scan the horizon, hoping for the approach of a ship.

But there was nothing.

Then one evening after he had been out and about on the island searching for food, he came back to see that his little hut was in flames. He tried to put the fire out but it was too late. And everything he had in this world had gone up in smoke. He went to sleep that night listening to the pounding of the surf, stunned by his own misfortune.

The next morning he awoke to find a ship anchored off the island—the first ship he had seen since he had been marooned. And still trying to believe his eyes, he heard footsteps, and then a human voice, saying, "We saw your smoke signal and we came to rescue you."

That's how it happens sometimes. In sovereignty and grace, the worst case scenario somehow becomes the best case scenario.

Sometimes disasters can turn out to be great opportunities for God to work in your life. The Lord is always present with us, always intimately acquainted with our circumstances, and He can take impossible situations and turn them around.

#3: You Will Reap What You Sow

Everything we sow will eventually bear some kind of fruit. It is the law of sowing and reaping. Let's look at a passage we considered earlier, but in a different translation:

"Don't be under any illusion: you cannot make a fool of God! A man's harvest in life will depend entirely on what he sows. If he sows for his own lower nature his harvest will be the decay and death of his own nature. But if he sows for the Spirit he will reap the harvest of everlasting life by that Spirit."[91]

If what you are sowing is bad, then the harvest will be bad. But if you are following the lead of God's Spirit, speaking and acting at His direction, the harvest of good in your life will exceed your dreams.

Just remember, there are no secrets with God. Zero. I don't care how cleverly you have hidden it, how well you have disguised it; in the end, your sin will be exposed. The Bible says, "Your sin will find you out." It may not happen today, and it may not happen tomorrow. You may die and it will be revealed after you're gone. Or it may not even totally come out until you are in eternity.

But it will come out. You have God's word on it. And that's what Haman experienced. But here's the flip side of the coin. Proverbs 11:18 tells us, "Sow for yourselves righteousness, reap the fruit of unfailing love."

Haman sowed to the flesh, reaped the consequences of it, and ended up dying on the gallows he had built for another. Mordecai, who never sought glory, never sought fame, never sought adulation, ended up having it all. He ended up having what Haman had lived for, because he was faithful to God.

Every day of your life, you will make choices and decisions that are sowing to the flesh, or sowing to the Spirit. And those actions will have an effect on your character and destiny. Sow a thought, reap an act; sow an act, reap a habit; sow a habit, reap a character; sow a character, reap a destiny.

Maybe you find yourself reaping a crop right now—the consequences of foolish and sinful decisions you have made in days gone by. It's not pretty, and as you look at the mess in your life, you wonder what in the world you can do about it.

Here's the good news. While God may not reverse a bad harvest, *He can work in the middle of a bad harvest.* If you surrender your life to Him, He will begin to rearrange circumstances and events in ways that you never, never could—not in a million years. He can take the mess you've made of your life and sort things out in ways that will continually surprise you. As Galatians 5:17, says, He can make you a new person in Christ. Old things have passed away—all things become new.

There is no limit to what He can accomplish in your life…if you hand over the keys to Him.

ENDNOTES: VOLUME ONE

1   Psalm 84:11
2   See 1 Timothy 2:14
3   Betsy Hart, *It Takes a Parent*
4   See Genesis 1:18; Proverbs 12:4, 18:22; 1 Corinthians 7:9
5   See Psalm 46:10
6   Acts 8:5-8, 26-40
7   James 4:2
8   Matthew 7:7
9   Genesis 25:23
10 Romans 12:18
11 Genesis 18
12 Joshua 5:13-15
13 Genesis 18
14 Deuteronomy 9:25-26
15 1 Kings 18:42-44
16 Psalm 39:12
17 Matthew 10:39
18 John 3:20, NIV
19 Luke 2:19, NLT
20 Proverbs 22:29
21 Proverbs 16:18
22 Genesis 39:6, NLT
23 James 4:7, NIV
24 2 Samuel 12:14, NLT
25 Dr. Lana Stanel, *Marital Infidelity*
26 Psalm 97:10, NIV
27 Psalm 51:4, NLT
28 Judges 16:6, NLT
29 1 Corinthians 10:13
30 James 3:16, NLT
31 1 Corinthians 3:3, NLT
32 Psalm 119:91, NIV
33 Exodus 8:19
34 Ephesians 4:27, NIV
35 2 Corinthians 2:11, NIV
36 Ecclesiastes 12:13, NIV
37 *Why The Ten Commandments Matter*, D. James Kennedy, Warner Books, New York, New York.
38 Exodus 3:14
39 1 Timothy 2:5
40 John 4:24

41 1 Timothy 6:8-10, NIV

42 2 Timothy 3:1, 4

43 Ephesians 5:12

44 1 Timothy 5:6

45 Luke 14:26

46 Read the full story in Luke 15:11-32.

47 Exodus 20:7

48 Exodus 6:7

49 Revelation 3:8, NLT

50 Romans 12:9, NLT

51 See John 19:30

52 Psalm 46:10

53 Mark 3:21

54 1 John 3:15, NLT

55 Ephesians 4:31-32, NIV

56 James 2:10, NIV

57 "The Thrill of Theft," by Jerry Adler, *Newsweek*, February 25, 2002.

58 Luke 19:8, NIV

59 *The Day America Told the Truth*, James Patterson and Peter Kim, Prentice Hall Trade; 1st edition (May 1991)

60 Ibid.

61 Hebrews 6:18

62 Exodus 32:30

63 John 19:11

64 Luke 12:48, NIV

65 Exodus 32:5

66 2 Samuel 12:10

67 John 4:48

68 See Jonah 4:2, and Lamentations 3:33

69 2 Corinthians 12:4, NIV

70 Romans 8:34; Hebrews 4:14-16; 9:24-28

ENDNOTES: VOLUME TWO

1   John 1:18; 6:46, NIV
2   Genesis 1:27-28
3   Luke 12:32, KJV
4   John 10:7, 9, NLT
5   John 13:1
6   Isaiah 49:15-16, NLT
7   Jude 21
8   John 16:33
9   Romans 8:31-32
10 Ezekiel 43:2, NIV
11 2 Corinthians 12:9
12 Matthew 1:23
13 Read the story in Acts 16.
14 Philippians 1:21
15 See Exodus 2:14.
16 Psalm 106:15, THE MESSAGE
17 Proverbs 14:14
18 1 Timothy 4:12
19 Judges 7:3, NIV
20 Psalm 103:14, NASB
21 See 2 Kings 5:1-19.
22 1 Corinthians 6:19-20, NIV
23 See Colossians 3:5.
24 Jeremiah 23:24
25 Numbers 32:23
26 Romans 8:31, KJV
27 NLT
28 Luke 16:11, NLT
29 See John 19:38-39.
30 Genesis 50:20-21, NASB
31 Read Jeremiah 18 for the full word picture.
32 Judges 13:5, NIV
33 Judges 13:24-25, NIV
34 Judges 14:3, NASB
35 Galatians 6:7, THE MESSAGE
36 James 1:14-15
37 1 Corinthians 15:33, NIV
38 Judges 16:21, NLT
39 1 Corinthians 10:12
40 1 Samuel 10:10
41 Acts 8:8, NIV

42 Acts 8:26-27, NASB

43 1 Samuel 16:4, KJV

44 1 Samuel 16:11

45 Psalm 27:10, NIV

46 1 Corinthians 1:26-28, THE MESSAGE

47 1 Timothy 3:6

48 1 Corinthians 1:29, NASB

49 Philippians 3:13-14

50 Luke 10:41-42

51 Matthew 6:33, NIV

52 *David: A Man of Passion and Destiny*, by Charles R. Swindoll, Word Publishing, 1997.

53 See 1 Samuel 24:7-12.

54 Romans 5:8

55 Luke 14:23, NIV

56 Ecclesiastes 3:11, ESV

57 Romans 8:15

58 Deuteronomy 17:17

59 2 Samuel 11:3, NIV

60 Psalm 141:5, NIV

61 Romans 14:13, THE MESSAGE

62 Psalm 32:4, THE MESSAGE

63 Proverbs 28:13

64 See Matthew 7:3-5.

65 2 Samuel 12:13

66 1 Chronicles 28:9-10, NLT

67 Ruth 1:16

68 John 15:7

69 Matthew 6:33, NASB

70 See 1 Kings 10.

71 See 2 Corinthians 6:14-15.

72 1 Timothy 5:6; Proverbs 14:13, NIV

73 NLT

74 3 John 1:4

75 James 5:17, NLT

76 Job 19:25

77 Psalm 91:1

78 Proverbs 28:1

79 See Acts 20:27.

80 2 Timothy 3:12

81 Matthew 5:11-12, NLT

82 Proverbs 21:1

83 1 Kings 18:21

ENDNOTES: VOLUME THREE

1   Luke 18:19, NASB
2   Romans 3:4, NIV
3   NLT
4   Mark 4:18-19, NLT
5   Colossians 3:5, NIV
6   1 Thessalonians 5:17-18
7   1 Samuel 16:7
8   NLT
9   2 Corinthians 2:11
10 James 4:7
11 Revelation 12:10
12 NLT
13 Hebrews 4:16
14 Luke 22:32
15 James 5:11, NIV
16 Luke 22:53, NLT
17 Zechariah 12:10; Psalm 22
18 Isaiah 53:10, NIV
19 Zechariah 11:12-13
20 Job 2:11, NIV
21 See Matthew 26:36-44
22 1 Thessalonians 4:13, NIV
23 Romans 12:15
24 Job 8:20, NLT
25 Job 11:6, NLT
26 Acts 16:26-28, NIV
27 2 Corinthians 12:9, NLT
28 2 Corinthians 12:9-10, NLT
29 John 9:2, NLT
30 John 9:3, NLT
31 Genesis 45:5, NLT
32 2 Corinthians 1:3-5, NLT
33 Psalm 119:67, 71.
    See also Psalm 119:75
34 Numbers 32:23
35 Charles R. Swindoll, *Forgotten Stories of Fascinating Lives*, Word Books.
36 1 Samuel 26:21
37 See James 1:5-8
38 1 Samuel 9:2
39 NIV
40 1 Samuel 9:16

41   1 Samuel 9:17
42   1 Samuel 9:21, NLT
43   1 Samuel 10:9, 10, NIV
44   1 Samuel 11:6, NIV
45   John 15:14
46   1 Samuel 26:21
47   James 3:2
48   1 John 1:8
49   NIV
50   Romans 5:8
51   Jonah 4:10, NLT
52   Hebrews 4:13, NIV
53   Jonah 1:4-5
54   Nahum 1:3
55   Hebrews 12:6
56   Hebrews 12:6, THE MESSAGE
57   Jonah 1:8
58   Jonah 3:3
59   NIV
60   See Esther chapter 4!
61   2 Kings 5:11-12, TLB
62   1 Corinthians 3:6, NIV
63   Romans 10:14-15
64   NIV
65   THE MESSAGE
66   2 Kings 5:5, NLT
67   From *Barnes' Notes, Electronic Database*, copyright © 1997, 2003, by Biblesoft, Inc.
68   Luke 12:15, NIV
69   CONTEMPORARY ENGLISH VERSION
70   NIV
71   Hebrews 5:12-14, NLT
72   Psalm 141:5, NIV
73   Matthew 10:26, NIV
74   Psalm 139:23, TLB
75   NLT
76   NIV
77   Psalm 29:2
78   Ecclesiastes 3:11, NIV
79   Daniel 5:25-28, NLT
80   NIV
81   Daniel 5:30, NIV
82   Purim
83   Isaiah 43:2-3; Hebrews 13:5-6

84   Charles Swindoll, *Esther, A Woman of Strength and Dignity*, Nashville, Word Books, 1997.

85   THE MESSAGE

86   See Galatians 5:25, NIV

87   Romans 8:28

88   Galatians 6:7-8

89   Matthew 6:4

90   Esther 6:13, THE MESSAGE

91   Galatians 6:7-8, PHILLIPS

About The Author

Greg Laurie is the pastor of Harvest Christian Fellowship (one of America's largest churches) in Riverside, California. He is the author of over 30 books, including the Gold Medallion Award winner, *The Upside-Down Church*, as well as his devotional books *For Every Season* and his best-selling autobiography *Lost Boy*. You can find his study notes in the *New Believer's Bible* and *The Seeker's Bible*. Host of the *Harvest: Greg Laurie* television program and the nationally syndicated radio program *A New Beginning*, Greg Laurie is also the founder and featured speaker for Harvest Crusades—contemporary, large-scale evangelistic outreaches, which local churches organize nationally and internationally. He and his family live in Southern California.

OTHER ALLENDAVID BOOKS
PUBLISHED BY KERYGMA
PUBLISHING

Visit: www.kerygmapublishing.com
www.allendavidbooks.com
www.harvest.org